A STUDENT OF COLLEGES

Fundamentals of Independent Educational Consulting

STEVEN R. ANTONOFF, PhD

A Student of Colleges
Fundamentals of Independent Educational Consulting

Book Design by I/O Designs
Cover and chapter illustrations by Milan Glosic

For permission requests, write to the author at info@astudentofcolleges.com.

Ordering Information:
Special discounts are available on quantity purchases by universities, associations, and others. For details, contact the author at info@astudentofcolleges.com.

Address correspondence to:
info@EDUconsultingMedia
info@astudentofcolleges.com

ISBN 978-1-7335784-0-0

PRINTED IN THE UNITED STATES OF AMERICA

Visit astudentofcolleges.com for supplementary resources.

DEDICATION

To Mom, Dad, Sandy and Gary.
I wish you were here.

Praise for *A Student of Colleges*

"In *A Student of Colleges: Fundamentals of Independent Educational Consulting*, Dr. Antonoff provides a master class in the field of independent educational consulting. Drawing on years of experience counseling students and families and instructing new independent educational consultants, he weaves together personal insights, industry best practices, and compelling stories of life as an IEC. An acknowledged authority in the field, Antonoff is respected for his scholarship, teaching acumen, and willingness to mentor and guide young IECs entering this growing profession. Over decades, he has investigated the many aspects of what it means to operate as an independent consultant and how to serve families, balance competing interests, and maintain integrity, humanity, and ethical standards. His new book is well researched, accessible, deeply informed, and a must-read for aspiring IECs or anyone seeking to understand the fundamentals of this profession."
— Jed Applerouth, PhD; Founder, Applerouth Tutoring Services, Atlanta, GA

"Written by one of the most experienced and respected practitioners in the field, *A Student of Colleges: Fundamentals of Independent Educational Consulting* is a thorough guide to independent consulting and an essential resource for independent consultants, whether new to college counseling or seasoned professionals. Its clarity will also help parents and high school counselors understand what independent consultants actually do."
— Joyce Vining Morgan, PhD, Certified Educational Planner; Co-author of *Admission Matters*; Walpole, NH

"No one has contributed more to the advancement of the profession of college consulting than Dr. Steve Antonoff. He has been a spectacular role model to hundreds seeking to become a guide and counselor to students entering the college search and application process. More than this, he has dedicated himself to raising professional standards by writing, speaking, guiding, leading, and teaching to ensure practitioners grow and become more knowledgeable and more ethical in their work.
This book marks a wonderful beginning for those who want to not just join the profession but also aspire to be among the best. Steve helps readers understand the role of consultants and much more. He explores counseling theory and the importance communicating effectively and building partnerships with parents. He makes it clear that being an IEC is not about 'admission' but about the student's journey of self-discovery. Steve shares with the reader the secrets that have made him and his practice the essential archetypes of the independent educational consultant. And while he underscores the need for ongoing training, workshops, and study, no one should doubt that this book is THE starting point for anyone beginning a journey in this exciting and fulfilling profession."
— Mark Sklarow, Chief Executive Officer, Independent Educational Consultants Association, Fairfax, VA

"Steve Antonoff is the consummate student of colleges and a tireless champion for the profession of educational consulting. Those of us who have ever taken a class from him, served on a committee with him, or listened to him speak know that anything Steve produces will be thoughtful, thorough, and sensitively presented, and this book is no exception. Here is a compendium of his sage advice for college counselors, whether they are just getting their feet wet or boast years of experience. You will refer to this invaluable resource again and again."
— Ann Montgomery, Certified Educational Planner, Houston, TX

"Amidst the noise of a vastly prolonged college prep process, Dr. Antonoff in his new book, *A Student of Colleges: Fundamentals of Independent Educational Consulting*, peels back the curtain of this highly mystified and often high-stakes system to reveal previously unseen opportunities and pitfalls for today's independent educational consultant. I marvel at his ability to cut through the cacophony inherent in college admissions and course-correct toward the first and best litmus test: college fit. Antonoff dedicates large swathes of this pioneering book to instruct new and tenured IECs alike on how to be both ethical and excellent service providers. Throughout the book, Antonoff focuses on best practices, employing the balanced critical eye that only a professional with more than three decades of experience, study, and research in this burgeoning field could offer. Ever the conscience of the independent educational consulting profession, Antonoff prompts all college admissions stakeholders to consider critically how we have fallen for the myth of prestige and irrational ranking and at what cost. This book answers the questions that we, as professionals, may not have been able to pose even a decade ago. It is so timely and necessary, given that this field has exploded in recent years. Reframing preconceptions, carving out space to help adolescents process uncertainty, and restoring peace throughout the college admissions process are just some of the countless areas for which Antonoff provides turn-key tips and sample scripts to foster client dialogue. Antonoff's unique pedigree as counselor, educator, and authority allows him to be the voice of reason in independent educational consulting and trends in higher education. This book enables consultants to bring professional development home. It is an indispensable compendium for IECs and a rich and robust reference text for even the most accomplished members of this field."
— Dr. Erin Croddick Avery, Certified Educational Planner; Avery Educational Resources, Fair Haven, NJ

"No one has made greater contributions to the field of independent educational consulting than Dr. Antonoff. This book, like the author, is a gift to our profession."
— Ethan Sawyer, Founder, CollegeEssayGuy.com, Los Angeles, CA

"*A Student of Colleges: Fundamentals of Independent Educational Consulting* is like having a mentor in your back pocket. Dr. Antonoff guides the new IEC through all the critical elements of a successful practice with his targeted and knowledgeable voice. His language and examples make it easy to incorporate good counseling skills into daily interactions with clients. This guide provides far more than fundamentals, as even more experienced IECs will find themselves challenged to re-evaluate their process and their interactions with students and families. Like Dr. Antonoff's previous work, this book will quickly become a dog-eared and book-marked essential in my resource collection."

— Katelyn Klapper, Certified Educational Planner; Instructor, University of California, Irvine; Founder, College Options, Sudbury, MA

"In a career as an IEC that has spanned over 30 years, Steve Antonoff has distinguished himself as a thoughtful, highly respected leader in a still young yet rapidly maturing profession. He has generously shared his wisdom and experience with others through his many roles including—but certainly not limited to—as a formal or informal mentor to countless colleagues, an inspiring teacher in both long and short workshops and programs for current and aspiring IECs, and an author of books designed to help families and colleagues with various aspects of the admissions process.

A Student of Colleges: Fundamentals of Independent Educational Consulting draws on all of this and more as the first textbook to focus on the fundamentals of independent educational consulting. Deeply anchored in the ethical principles that Steve believes should be at the core of the work of an IEC, *A Student of Colleges* provides a strong foundation for those seeking to enter the field as well as an inspiring refresher for others already working as IECs. It has a strong focus on practical matters that are unique to IECs, while also covering a broad range of topics essential to the knowledge base of any professional seeking to help families with the college admissions process. It includes a chapter focusing on how IECs can keep current in a field that is always changing. *A Student of Colleges* is a lasting contribution that makes Steve's extensive knowledge, experience, wisdom, and generous spirit available to anyone, anywhere. Our profession is indebted to him for writing it."

— Sally P. Springer, PhD; Co-author of *Admission Matters: What Students and Parents Need to Know About Getting Into College* (4th ed.); Associate Chancellor Emerita, University of California, Davis

"In every profession there is one person who, because of his or her experience, commitment to shared success, and interest in and love for the work, becomes the embodiment of that profession. In the field of independent educational consulting, Steve Antonoff is that person. As a pioneer in this field, Steve has a unique perspective on its development and growth. Of Steve's many gifts to generations of independent educational consultants through his teaching and writing, it is his generosity of spirit that defines him best, as evidenced in the pages of this book."

— Rachel B. Sobel, PhD, Certified Education Planner, Independent Educational Consultant; College Possibilities, Philadelphia, PA

"Dr. Steven Antonoff has made countless contributions to the field of independent educational consulting over many years. This book is a testament to the depth of his knowledge as well as his generosity of spirit, and it is an important milestone for the IEC profession. As the director of the IECA Summer Training Institute (where Steve serves as a founding and permanent member of the faculty), I have seen firsthand the profound impact he has on new IECs. This book is a tremendous resource for current and future consultants."

— Sue DePra, Deputy Executive Director, Independent Educational Consultants Association, Fairfax, VA

"Steve Antonoff expertly writes about the importance of parental involvement in a client's college planning. Parents know their children best and will always be their child's number one advocate. As Antonoff so clearly states, an IEC must be sensitive to that fact, providing respectful acknowledgment of a parent's role. Professional and ethical advisement alongside this respect deepens the viability of an IEC—client relationship."

— Deborah B. Davis, Certified Educational Planner, MBA; Davis Education & Career Consultants, Ridgefield, CT

"In *A Student of Colleges: Fundamentals of Independent Educational Consulting*, Steve Antonoff has identified the range and breadth of knowledge that a competent IEC needs to master. This text should have a prominent spot on every IEC's bookshelf. The content introduces a beginner to our profession, yet suggests possible new ideas to seasoned professional. Steve is the master statesman of independent educational consulting. His commitment to constantly improving our standards and ethics shines through each page of this book. I know I will reference the wisdom contained in these pages for years to come. Thank you, Steve, for what must have been nothing short of a labor of love."

— Joe Bernard, MAEd; Certified Educational Planner; Past President, Higher Education Consultants Association; Academic Directions, Portland, OR

"This is the right book at the right time by the only person who could have written it. Dr. Antonoff has been a champion of training for IECs for 30 years, and his passion is evident in his writing. This book is the seminal text for prospective IECs and for those who

need a refresher about why we do this work and how to do it ethically, with the student at its center. Steve's involvement in training, setting policy, and encouraging thousands of practitioners to do their best work and to share with each other makes this a must-read."
— Charlotte M. Klaar, PhD; Klaar College Consulting LLC, Fort Mill, SC

"For years Steve Antonoff has taught aspiring Independent Education Consultants how to become professional and solid college consultants. The insight he shares with future and tenured Independent Education Consultants is invaluable. I am a proud former student of Steve's from the inaugural class of the UCLA Extension Program for budding IECs. Steve was as inspirational twenty years ago as he is today. It has been stated that Steve has worked with approximately 3,500 students. I would beg to differ because by association he has also worked with each of the students we, his former IEC students, have worked with. Thank you, Steve, from the hundreds of IECs that you have inspired and from the students and families we have better served because of your mentoring. We are eternally grateful."
— Cheri Barad, Education Consultant; President, Higher Education Consultants Association; Cheri Barad Education Consultant, Wellesley, MA

"With his usual clarity and student-centered approach, Dr. Antonoff has provided a comprehensive view of the theory, practice, and art of being an independent educational consultant. This book deserves careful review by those considering entering the practice, as well as those with years of experience in this work."
— Patrick J. O'Connor, PhD; Author, *College Counseling for School Counselors*; College Counselor, Cranbrook Schools, Bloomfield Hills, MI

"I can think of no better person than Steve Antonoff to write this must-read textbook about independent education consulting. Readers will benefit from his years of experience, sage advice, and incredible insight about the profession. His description of IECs as managers of expectation, information, reframing, and uncertainty is spot on. He offers excellent advice and examples of how to do all of the above to ensure that IECs serve as the calm in the storm of college admissions. *A Student of Colleges: Fundamentals of Independent Educational Consulting* will become the go-to best-practices book for IECs just starting out as well as seasoned professionals looking for additional tips on running their practice."
— Lisa Bleich, Author of *Surviving the College Application Process: Case Studies to Find Your Unique Angle for Success*; Founder and President, College Bound Mentor, LLC, Westfield, NJ

"Dr. Antonoff has revolutionized the field of independent educational consulting by standardizing the expectations, qualifications, and credentialing of the profession. His in-depth knowledge and the high ethical and moral standards that he upholds are the foundation for this bourgeoning field. If you are contemplating this profession, then *A Student of Colleges: Fundamentals of Independent Educational Consulting* is a must-read, as it will be the industry's bible and gold standard."
— Caryl Frankenberger, MAEd; Head of School, The Greenwood School, Putney, VT

"Steve Antonoff's expert knowledge and broad experiences within educational consulting are reflected in this resource. *A Student of Colleges: Fundamentals of Independent Educational Consulting* is essential for anyone interested in pursuing the profession of educational consulting or in having a deeper understanding of the subtleties within the college search and application process. We are so fortunate to have Steve's wisdom and generosity at our fingertips!"
— Ann Rossbach, Past President, Independent Educational Consultants Association; Member, American Institute of Certified Educational Planners; Ann Rossbach Educational Consulting, Rumson, NJ

"This soon-to-be classic book on the multilayered profession of college advising presents well-researched and comprehensive information on every aspect of this growing profession. From helping parents and students understand the realities of college admissions to balancing different viewpoints to explaining popular ranking systems and what they really mean, *A Student of Colleges: Fundamentals of Independent Educational Consulting* provides actual solutions to college advising challenges—solutions based on extensive research and years of practical experience working both inside and outside the college and university system. Steve Antonoff has provided our growing profession with an easy-to-read and easy-to-use guide that puts everything the college advisor needs to know in one place."
— Bob Dannenhold, Past President, Higher Education Consultants Association; Collegeology, Seattle, WA

"Dr. Steven Antonoff, a mentor to so many in the field of college advising, has written a textbook that goes well beyond a basic introduction to the independent educational consulting profession. His approach to counseling students is instructive for even the most seasoned consultants and a reminder that we are perpetual students ourselves. How fortunate we are that Dr. Antonoff, the guru of our profession, has so generously shared his guiding principles, which I suspect will encourage many of us, new and experienced consultants alike, to reflect on our fundamental practices and how we communicate and engage with students and families."
— Jane Klemmer, MBA, Certified Educational Planner; Klemmer Educational Consulting, Briarcliff Manor, NY

"I can't think of a better person and educator to write a book about the fundamentals of independent educational consulting than Steve Antonoff. Fourteen years ago, when I first entered the profession, Steve was a faculty member at the Independent Educational Consultants Association's Principles & Practices Institute (now the Summer Training Institute). Since that time, he has been a mentor, respected colleague, and trusted friend. Steve is widely considered to be the 'father of educational consulting.'

Steve's dedication to his students—both teenage clients and fellow consultants—is unmatched. Steve set the standard for the profession and serves as a model for what independent educational consultants should be: students of colleges, ethical beyond reproach, and above all else, focused on the 'best fit' for their students. For over 30 years, he has devoted himself to helping all of us be better educational consultants, and I will be forever grateful."

— Barbara Pasalis, Certified Educational Planner; President, Independent Educational Consultants Association; Northcoast Educational Consulting, Cleveland, OH

"Whether you are someone considering entering the field of independent college counseling, a newer educational consultant, or a veteran of many years in the field, you will find *A Student of Colleges: Fundamentals of Independent Educational Consulting* to be an in-depth look at best practices and an insightful journey through the myriad situations and personalities encountered in working as a college educational consultant."

— Carl "Sandy" Behrend, Certified Educational Planner; Past President, National Association for College Admission Counseling; Behrend Consulting, Buffalo NY

"The name 'Steve Antonoff' has been synonymous with 'the best of the best' in the college consulting profession from its earliest days. In addition to being a knowledgeable, talented, and sensitive counselor to each of his students and their families, Steve has been extraordinarily generous in sharing his expertise with all of those in our growing profession through his unique books, his classes, professional leadership, and role modeling.

When I first started working as a college counselor, I thought, 'I want to try to be just like Steve.' But as I grew to know him, I soon realized that no one can do that simply because no one is as competent, responsible, ethical, and kind, or as funny, clever or generous as Steve. One can only aspire. Thank you, Steve, for setting the bar so high for the rest of us."

— Shirley Levin, MA, Certified Educational Planner; Author, *Summer on Campus*; Past Board Member, National Association for College Admission Counseling, Independent Educational Consultant Association, and American Institute of Certified Educational Planners; Educational Consultant, Potomac, MD

"No consultant has contributed more to the profession of independent educational consulting than Steven Antonoff. His years of experience, his devotion to teaching new consultants, and his leadership distinguish him as the foremost expert in the field. Steven's caring personal interactions and willingness to share knowledge have earned the respect of colleagues. His introductory textbook, *A Student of Colleges: Fundamentals of Independent Educational Consulting*, clearly identifies all the essential elements needed for an independent educational consultant as well as the ethical standards so important to the profession. With his vast knowledge and wise perspective, Steven has written a book of great practical value for new and more seasoned consultants."

— Judith Berg, Independent Educational Consultant, Little Silver, NJ

"*A Student of Colleges: Fundamentals of Independent Educational Consulting* is an invaluable resource for new IECs and seasoned practitioners alike. The world of college admissions changes daily, but our work needs to be guided by a clear vision of professionalism, honesty, and expertise. Steven Antonoff—one of our most respected, insightful, and eloquent 'students of colleges'—provides not just that powerful vision but also the tools and structure to help IECs gain confidence and grow as professionals."

— Joan Koven, Independent Educational Consultant, Academic Access, Havertown, PA

"As a nationally recognized college admission expert and one of the most well-respected IECs in the industry, Steven Antonoff is the perfect person to write a book addressing the fundamentals of independent educational consulting. Dr. Antonoff is our industry oracle, and I'm thrilled that he's written a guide that clarifies and defines our roles as consultants and the ethical guidelines that frame our work. Dr. Antonoff approaches educational consulting with an exceptionally calming and positive presence and makes it his primary goal to take the stress out of the college planning process for students and their parents. We are fortunate to learn from such a leader."

— Brooke Daly, Independent Educational Consultant; President, Higher Education Consultants Association; Advantage College Planning, Raleigh, NC

"Whether you're a newbie to educational consulting or a seasoned professional, *A Student of Colleges: Fundamentals of Independent Educational Consulting* sets the standard for books on establishing and running a flourishing practice. And it's backed by decades of wisdom and experience. Nobody has a better handle on what families need to know about colleges than Steve Antonoff, and nobody has done more to educate consultants through his writings and in seminars and presentations.

If you are thinking about starting a practice, you'll find a blueprint for how to do consulting right. If you're already expert, you'll find insights that enrich what you already know. Either way, *A Student of Colleges* is a must-read for those in the profession or for anyone who wants to know what consultants do and how they do it."

— Dodge Johnson, College Planning, Philadelphia, PA

"Well, Steve Antonoff has done it again! His latest book, *A Student of Colleges: Fundamentals of Independent Educational Consulting*, is much like his previous works in that it is insightful, well researched, and helpful in so many ways. A book on this topic is well overdue and will be incredibly useful to anyone thinking about becoming an IEC. This book will be an invaluable guide to understanding what it means and what it takes to be an excellent IEC—one who can truly assist families during the strenuous college selection process—and what it means to be ethical and always honest with the students and their parents. The book is well thought out and presented, and covers so many topics touching on an IEC practice. Steve has used his years of consulting with clients and teaching other consultants as well as all of his college travels and on-campus work to make this book not just a must-have volume for potential IECs, but an incredible learning tool they will refer to again and again. I wish a book of this caliber and knowledge—and with all Steve's hints and tips—had been available when I began my practice in the dark ages, before the internet! Thank you, Steve, for all you have done over the years to help our field progress in the right direction and for now shining a light for the next generation of IECs who want to join this wonderful, rewarding profession."

— Francine E. Block, MAT, Certified Educational Planner; Past President, Pennsylvania Association for College Admission Counseling; Board Member, Higher Education Consultants Association; American College Admissions Consultants, Bucks County, PA

"This book, like its author, is honest, insightful, and focused. *A Student of Colleges: Fundamentals of Independent Educational Consulting* anticipates the reader's questions and is a 'must-read' for educational consultants."

— Marilyn G.S. Emerson, MSW, Certified Educational Planner; Past-President, Independent Educational Consultants Association; Emerson Consulting, New York, NY

"With Steve's new book, *A Student of Colleges: Fundamentals of Independent Educational Consulting,* we are fortunate to get a detailed roadmap of his impressive mastery of the critical aspects of independent educational consulting. This book poses the questions and issues facing all dedicated college counseling professionals. As a counselor educator, I know that *A Student of Colleges* will be an incredibly useful tool in helping IECs assist their students in making better college choices."

— Esther B. Hugo, EdD; Adjunct Professor, San Jose (Calif.) State University College of Education; Distinguished Instructor, UCLA College Counseling Certificate Program, Los Angeles, CA

"Steve Antonoff has once again provided us with a treasure trove of knowledge about the profession of educational consulting in his newest book, *A Student of Colleges: Fundamentals of Independent Educational Consulting*—a must-read for anyone involved in the field of educational consulting! Through his writing engaging style, Steve demonstrates his long-standing commitment to the profession as well as his love for the work he does."

— Judith S. Bass, Certified Educational Planner; Chair, American Institute for Certified Educational Planners; Bass Educational Services, LLC, Olney, Md.

"Steve Antonoff writes with clarity, integrity, and authenticity about guiding young people in their transition to college. He does so with urgent support for the preparation of those who might work in private counseling, emphasizing the absolute imperative to be "certified" as an educational planner (CEP). His voice is one I trust, and his commitment to guiding and counseling students to find the right college/university fit is a shining model for the entire private college consulting industry."

— Richard H. Shaw, Dean of Undergraduate Admissions and Financial Aid, Stanford University, Stanford, CA

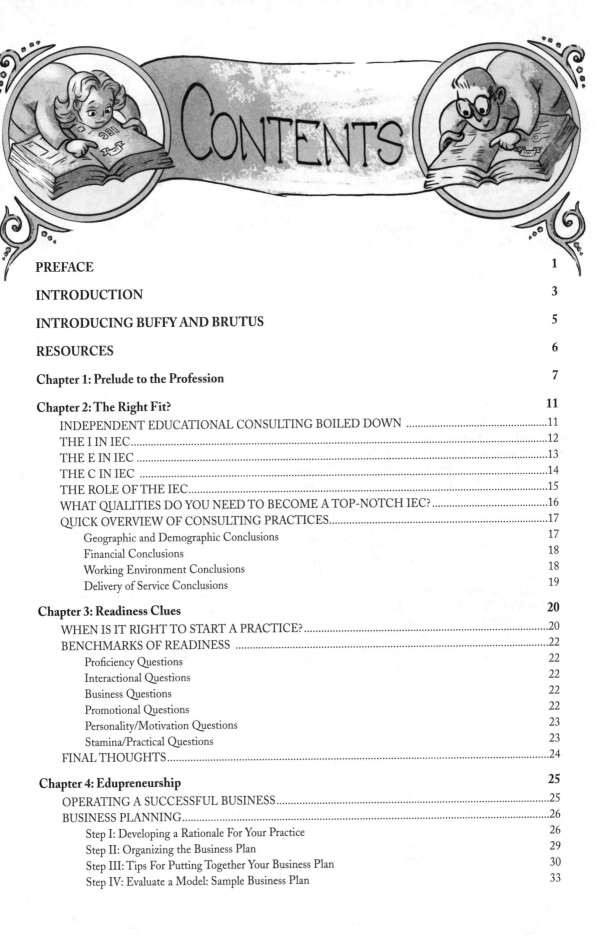

CONTENTS

PREFACE

After thirty-five years of professional practice as an independent educational consultant (IEC), I'm still learning. That's high praise for the field. As a diehard learner, I have never tired in this dynamic arena.

I've seen this profession grow from its infancy. I've been in the front row of many discussions about the future of the profession and in the balcony for others. I've both agreed and disagreed with professional directions and policies. With interest (and occasionally with involvement), I've watched as professional organizations took root, evolved, and prospered.

My life has been defined by my profession. It's taken me to colleges around the globe and into the lives of thousands of students and thousands of parents. Through decades of private practice, I've learned the right and wrong ways to deliver services. Interacting with hundreds of colleagues—both novices and veterans—informed me about practices I could analyze and synthesize to come up with the paradigms presented in this book. As the author of two college planning books designed for students and parents, I've studied and shared what works and what doesn't work as one goes through the hunt for a college. I gained further knowledge and perspective through teaching and training independent educational consultants and through giving presentations to student and parent groups. I've taught, and I've learned.

This book reflects these learnings. Much of what you will read was originally developed for classes I taught at UCLA and University of California, Irvine. I developed the syllabus for the first class on educational consulting offered through the UCLA college counseling certificate program. When the UCI certificate program in independent educational consulting began, I created the syllabus for the Principles in Educational Consulting course. I also taught the final course, the Practicum, for UCI. The original outlines of several chapters in this book were conceived from those courses and from materials that I designed in teaching at the Independent Educational Consultants Association (IECA) Summer Training Institute (formerly called Practices and Principles Institute).

This book is a lifetime in the making. When I was dean of students at the University of Denver, I learned how institutions affect students. I realized that colleges have a "feel." That is to say colleges are unique and serve different student needs. I then moved over to admissions and financial aid and gained a host of new perspectives. I learned how colleges market themselves, how college admission officials work with school-based counselors, and how important affordability and financial aid are in student and family decision-making. The university gave me insight into the minds of young people and the influence that adults can have on students who are transitioning and changing. I learned about how students choose a college and the factors affecting enrollment and retention. I also learned that I wanted to work directly with students.

Shortly after I began my career as an independent educational consultant, I joined IECA. I was active in IECA, and I encouraged others, both in and outside of college admission, to join. I became president of the board and worked on events that led to success: hiring a full-time executive director, developing a training program for prospective consultants, making college admission representatives participants in meetings, determining the basic core of principles that would serve as the basis of our profession, and so on.

And now I offer this textbook—the first of its kind—as a basic introduction to the field of independent educational consulting. It explores, analyzes, and explains many dimensions of the field. This book highlights the practices, principles, and tenets that define who we are, how we operate, and how we grow. I hope this foundational piece of writing serves as the basis for ongoing professional dialogue and sharing. I want to encourage leaders in the field to have a point of discussion for critical issues and perspectives. This book provides that beginning.

Having a point of reference for professional success is essential. It is my intent to standardize the basic and best practices in the field.

I'm not sure that this book could have been written a decade ago. It is only possible to write a "fundamentals" textbook after a field has established a body of knowledge, after ethical guidelines have been clarified, and after enough people have entered the field for there to be a standard of practice. Now is that time.

This book is designed to inform, and to keep it a reasonable length, I had to limit the information I wished to share. As with my prior books, the second edition will be more complete. Beyond informing, this book is intended to inspire. I wish to inspire readers to share my love of the profession of independent educational consulting. And I wish to use these pages to address what it means to be a student of colleges. It means to be an insatiable learner of college knowledge. It means to be a generous sharer of such rich knowledge. This book is my tribute to the world of higher education and its many students. We, as independent educational consultants, are lifelong students.

This book, first in my mind and now in your hands, was always called *A Student of Colleges*.

INTRODUCTION

Independent educational consulting has matured from a loose collective—a cottage industry—to an organized profession. When I landed on the scene in the 1980's, educational consulting was insular, cliquish, and, to some extent, floundering to find its mission. No longer. The field has grown because there is a need for the service. It has grown because it has worked from within to make itself viable and to establish an ethical core. The new generation of consultants brings energy and vision. The regular exchange of ideas makes each consultant stronger. Professions take decades to resolve tender issues, and the field is almost unrecognizable from the one I entered in 1981. I'm proud of my colleagues. I'm proud of their commitment to learning and to making their work meaningful in the lives of those they serve.

The most significant growth is in the area of the development of a community and camaraderie within our profession. The mission of the independent educational consultant is to be a student of colleges and a knowledgeable resource to students and families concerning the college admission process. That clarity of mission has united us. We guide students to colleges, but, more broadly, we help students define themselves and their relationship to information acquisition, knowledge, and to people. We help a young person through the college planning process and, in doing so, we serve as adult guides to a critical part of adolescent development. We are a community connected by our vision of building an informed, curious, and compassionate society.

Education unites. Ignorance divides. Independent educational consultants appreciate that distinction on many levels. We work to educate others; we commit to educating ourselves. We need to aid in national efforts to promote the value of education, particularly the formative years of undergraduate study. The notion of "fake news" calls for a learned electorate, a learned society. Learning during the undergraduate years provides ways to discern the fabricated from the actual. It enables one to separate the signal from the noise. These skills are more and more important in America these days. We need to help young people get to environments where they are challenged to think about assumptions and encouraged to problem-solve. The complex years ahead demand that we step up as a collective to help young people recognize the link between education and compassion, the link between education and humanity.

I'm heartened by the increase in membership in the professional associations from independent educational consultants practicing across the world. Canada and the United Kingdom have been represented for many years, but there is a sizable increase in IECs establishing practices in countries such as China, Hong Kong, Singapore, and Turkey. I believe that independent educational consultants bring promise to the world.

IECs have been instrumental in developing new resources for students and parents who want reliable information about colleges. We further education through publications, webinars, product development, and outreach. Our influence extends beyond the clients we see in our offices. Let's double and then redouble our efforts to reach students worldwide, to teach students worldwide. Knowledge should be accessible to all.

In terms of enhancing our own knowledge, I'm impressed with what the associations have done in the area of programming for professional development. The strength of the associations has contributed to the dramatic increase in learning opportunities. An area of learning that I'd like to see further emphasized is the counseling and interpersonal skills necessary for professional success. Specialists in communication and psychology should be recruited to present at national meetings. Our work is intrinsically tied to adolescent development, and we should always consider the human element of our educational services. Yes, we've circled back to compassion.

It is incumbent upon the profession to meet its lofty goals, to be all it is capable of being, and to be a respected voice in the enterprise that exists to help young people become educated, thoughtful, and cultured adults. So much rides on our work. Let's get rolling.

INTRODUCING

BUFFY AND BRUTUS

Instead of repeatedly referring to students by pronouns, I'll sometimes refer to Buffy and Brutus.

Buffy has been my go-to student name for many years. What started as a joke name quickly became associated with me. Over the years, I've been tempted to change Buffy to a name that is more multicultural and inclusive, but it was too late. Buffy had grown into my sidekick, so to speak. Please don't think of her as a preppy, yuppie cheerleader from an affluent family. The Buffy I refer to is also no vampire slayer, and her name has nothing to do with a component of blood. Why Buffy? I have no idea. Buffy could just as well have been named Betty, Tippy, Rosie, Lizzy, Sadie, Penny, Jenny, Bessie, Jessie, Flossie, Fanny, Skipper, or Toots. It is best to consider Buffy as a character created without symbolic representation. She's simply an adolescent who seeks sound advice.

As this book was being compiled, my editor and I felt the need for a male name so as to avoid the continual reference to a female student. Brutus, beyond being a B name, seemed both comical and unique. He defies generalizing. He's likely not brutal, bull-headed, or backstabbing. He may not have read Shakespeare or traveled to Rome. Brutus could easily have been Bruno, Buddy, Blotto, Braun, or Boone. Like Buffy, Brutus is an adolescent who wants to find a college that holistically suits his desires.

RESOURCES

The field of independent educational consulting has grown significantly in the last five years. With the increase in practitioners has come an inundation of new books, websites, and other materials. In gathering materials for this book, I realized that some of the resources I had listed when I began writing were already outdated by the end of the writing process. Further, throughout my research, I kept discovering even more great resources. I also saw the advantage of live links.

As a result, I developed a website, astudentofcolleges.com, that is intended to supplement the book you are holding. In addition to general references, you will find information about topics such as higher education, counseling, diversity, business management, software tools for the IEC, degrees and certificates available, and college tours. You will even find information about webinars, podcasts, and blogs.

Parenthetical notations throughout this book will guide you to resources listed on the *A Student of Colleges* website. Resources will be updated regularly.

In addition to resources, this website also allows for feedback and interaction—two qualities that are essential to the professional development of IECs. I welcome your input and encourage readers to engage in an ongoing professional dialogue.

CHAPTER 1

Prelude to the Profession

Let's start with the Dark Ages. No, not the period following the collapse of the Roman Empire, but the Dark Ages of educational consulting when headhunters brokered matches between students and boarding schools on the basis of financial kickbacks from schools. The dark forces of commercialism and profitability drove the matching process; the best interests of the children—merely incidental. To fight this unethical trend, a few wise souls got together, formed the Independent Educational Consultants Association (IECA), and made a claim for the best interest of the child. Their goal: find the right fit between child and school. Moreover, the Association felt that the process needed to be pure; that is, that families pay a professional to help them find suitable choices. To transcend the unprincipled practices of the Dark Ages, IECA professionals took fees directly from families, thus differentiating themselves from those who took money from schools. Once IECA ushered in the Enlightenment (all in a matter of years rather than centuries and without revolts and bloodshed), the ranks grew to include consultants who focused on finding the right milieu for struggling or at-risk teenagers or young adults. This area of specialization later morphed into a focus on therapeutic schools and programs. Today, a quarter to a third of IECA members work with these students.

Because the concept of fit had revolutionized the practice of boarding school placement, it struck some that the college scene required the same focus: help students find schools that are a good match for their interests and abilities. Approximately thirty years ago, independent educational consultants launched college admission as an area of professional concentration. Today, college consulting—now the largest specialty area in the profession—also comprises the largest segment of IECA membership.

But let's go back and add in another component of history in order to reach the roots of independent college consulting. Certainly, college advising has been a part of the fiber of private secondary boarding schools for decades. Prestigious schools in New England, for example, had especially attentive college counselors; were often in direct contact with college admission officers. After all, these schools were sold to parents as college preparatory. Independent day schools had a similar emphasis. In the 50's and 60's (and even before, according to some), public high schools, particularly in suburban and affluent areas, began to incorporate college advising into the responsibilities of the guidance office. Some public schools even relegated college advising to specific individuals whose job descriptions did not include many of the other duties that high school guidance counselors typically perform. Before the 1980's, students in public schools that did provide college advising generally turned to their high school guidance department for assistance with college admissions. Public school students whose high schools did not offer college advising services were generally left to field college admissions on their own. Back then, however, the higher education landscape was less complex.

And then the higher education landscape changed dramatically. The cost of a college education skyrocketed.

Additionally, over the past several decades, an undergraduate education became *de rigueur* in most parts of our society. As such, the percentage of graduates seeking higher education increased. Coinciding with the rise of college applicants, the Information Age brought forth a surge of information about colleges. In fact, college guidebooks became a growth industry in the 1990's.

At the same time, college admission became increasingly selective. This was not only true of the Ivy League colleges; in fact, hundreds of colleges, both public and private, increased in admission competitiveness. Moreover, colleges began recruiting aggressively, and college marketing billowed into a multi-million dollar industry. In order to increase applications and selectivity, colleges began to bombard potential students with marketing ploys. Adding to the college frenzy, the media hopped up the hype by covering colleges and college admission routinely. For example, a change in early decision procedures made the front page of *The New York Times*. Recently, reporters and bloggers nationwide piped in with opinions regarding the latest revamping of the SAT.

All of the above factors contributed to the dramatic growth of independent college consulting. The rising cost of college incited parents to seek professional advice in order to help ensure that the financial investment in their children's higher education was made wisely. The barrage of information, marketing, and media coverage led to a greater awareness of the admission process yet left some families overwhelmed. As such, they reached out to consultants to receive up-to-date, factual information. Families desired objective facts: the articulation of what the student experience is really like at College X and College Y. They turned to consultants to help navigate the increasing complexity and chaos of college admission.

Yet let's back up once again to make it clear that the pioneers of the profession didn't waltz effortlessly onto the college admissions scene. We didn't receive gilded invitations to join the college ball. In fact, in the 80's and 90's, many school-based counselors voiced concerns that perhaps it wasn't kosher for consultants to charge for college counseling. They saw business and education as being like oil and water. (Note that this was before colleges put their admission offices in the hands of marketers.) Worried that we'd offend school-based counselors, we made a concerted effort to prove our worth to them. Moreover, in the infancy of college consulting, many of us feared that we would not be accepted by admission officers. Initially, we fretted backlash and rejection from the established college admissions community.

However, a milestone in our quest to assume a unique and valued place at the college advising table came in 1985 when the major organization for school-based counselors and college admission officers, the National Association for College Admission Counseling (NACAC), approved allowing independent educational consultants to become full members of the Association. This was a major development as it "legitimized" the field, particularly in the eyes of school-based counselors.

Another milestone for the profession (though jumping into recent history) was my invitation to speak at the Ivy Plus Conference in 2007 at Stanford University. The Ivy Plus Conference is an annual meeting of admissions deans, directors, and staff of the schools in the Ivy League plus Stanford and MIT. This marked the first time that an IEC was asked to speak at Ivy Plus and further reflected our acceptance in the field, particularly among selective colleges.

In the spring 1989 edition of the *Journal of College Admission*, I wrote what was likely the first major description of the components of this new profession. "Educational Consulting: A Focus for the Profession," articulated a rationale for the profession of educational consulting. It was an early effort to establish the parameters of the new field and, in particular, to define it within the context of NACAC.

Here is part of my rationale for the profession included in the 1989 article:

"The expertise of the consultant is being sought by increasing numbers of families nationwide. Consultants are sought because there is a body of information about colleges that requires a full-time effort to be understood thoroughly, and that information is perceived as worthwhile in the marketplace. Such a body of information is the centerpiece for any profession."

Our body of knowledge is what keeps us in demand today. As our role became clearer, we've developed a body of consultant knowledge in areas such as counseling, college facts, understanding of admission processes, family dynamics, cultural differences, and learning profiles.

The following excerpts speak to the need for consultants as educators. Our role as educators defines a significant component of our work, both in 1989 and today.

"Despite the proliferation of information, there are many students in my practice who are simply uninformed and ill informed about such topics as career options, goals, and the purposes of undergraduate years and college adjustments."

I continued as follows:

"The college choice is neither incidental nor inconsequential. The professional literature suggests that the college decision represents the most important decision a young person makes; as important, this decision comes at a time when the student has had little experience in making important decisions.

"Effective college counseling, regardless of the setting or amount of time devoted, teaches students the skills and curriculum that contribute to thoughtful, appropriate decisions. And effective teaching, regardless of the subject matter, engages the student; it provides opportunities to test hypotheses and explore and clarify choices and their consequences."

And to further emphasize the value of independent educational consultants and the need for consultants to be welcomed within the larger scope of the college admissions field, I expressed the following convictions:

"Colleges, educators, future students, and society can benefit from the growth of the educational consulting profession. The educational marketplace is large enough to allow the growth of this profession without disrupting traditional counseling in the schools. In fact, the overall effect probably will be more time for more students in all of our offices. We will be better able to assist students if all of us—school counselors, admission officers, and consultants—can share information and interact with trust and openness."

The above has proven true.

"Consultants can expand the dialogue about important educational issues we face. Consultants can, and do, contribute by writing books and articles, contributing to panels at national conferences, conducting workshops, and working to clarify and even improve the transition from school to college. The extent to which the educational consultant can be accepted as a professional colleague is a measure of the self-confidence, pride, and honor we have in our profession—and in ourselves. Ultimately, I hope we also will benefit from the resultant professional growth and competence."

We have carved a niche; we have found a unique and valued place at the college admissions table.

And to voice my hopes for the growth of the field, I offered the following:

"I am still learning and growing as a knowledgeable counselor. But I see potential both within myself and within the field of educational consulting. There is potential within my profession to contribute to helping young people realize their dreams... "I hope that the field will expand on strategies that will lessen the tension some families feel as the college years approach. I hope that we can do an even better job of teaching self-knowledge that will lead to carefully articulated college choices and future successes. More than anything, I hope we can teach, by example, the values of helping someone reach his or her growth potential."

We have done just that.

CHAPTER 2

The Right Fit?

INDEPENDENT EDUCATIONAL CONSULTING BOILED DOWN

You wish to explore a new career, and, just as a student must look for a good fit in a college, you must look for a good fit in a career. Here's a framework: An independent educational consultant is "a student of colleges." I coined that term several years ago in trying to find a phrase that captured the substance of the work of the Independent Educational Consultant. Equally important, a student of colleges characterizes the IEC's commitment to studying colleges, a covenant that calls for a lifetime of learning. This chapter is designed to orient you to what the career of independent educational consulting involves and to what mindset a student a colleges embraces.

IECs create an environment rich in dialogue wherein parents and students can make thoughtful decisions about college attendance. Independent educational consulting is not therapy, tutoring, or life coaching. IECs do not solve adolescent problems, nor do we fix floundering students. IECs do not do the work that rightfully belongs with the student or parent. We do not guarantee admission, nor do we influence admission decisions. We provide informed, up-to-date advice and guidance and are compensated for our best judgment. IECs are expectation, information, uncertainty, and reframing managers (see Chapter 9). We advise, inform, teach, encourage, and empower. Specifically, we teach parents and students about colleges. By doing so, we educate students about decision-making, consumerism, the value of conducting thorough research, and independence. Importantly, we teach students more about themselves. Independent educational consulting is a niche with a clear mission. As students of colleges, we continually educate ourselves so as to better educate the families who place their trust in our services.

THE I IN IEC

The I in IEC stands for independent. It's easy to romanticize the concept of independence, especially if your current employer is tyrannical, condescending, grumbling, bumbling, or mind-numbingly dull. As an IEC, you set the rules and standards, you answer to yourself, and you own the clock. Does Fido need a walk every few hours? Leash him up! Prefer to sleep late and luxuriate over your morning coffee? No need to set an alarm clock. Frustrated with red tape? As an IEC, you are the organization and the departments; there is no red tape. Annoyed that your boss doesn't give you full credit for your success? Celebrate the success you've earned. Yes, independence feeds the soul for many who think outside the cubicle, so to speak.

But stay level-headed and carefully consider the flip side of independence: risk, unpredictable income, initial outlay of cash, no built-in benefits, no technical support, and no one has your back. If no panic button goes off, going into business for yourself might be the right track. If you're comfortable marketing yourself and building clientele off of your reputation, the I in IEC will be a draw rather than a drawback.

Let's clarify another important element about being independent. Independent educational consulting is not the same as school counseling other than the location of the work and the payment for services. Yes, it's true that college advising is similar to school advising, in that there is a foundation of similarity among all persons who advise students on the transition between high school and college. Wherever they practice, college counselors focus on what is best for the individual student; they must be sensitive and comfortable with young people. But while there are broad similarities, there are also some profound differences in philosophy and operation.

Of course, no two institutions (schools or colleges) are alike, and no two counseling practices are identical. The IEC's role is characterized by independence (maybe uncertainty); flexibility and freedom; financial limits and opportunities; interaction with students; the work reflects the consultant's own personality, style, beliefs, and attitudes; the consultant decides who to see and when and what to do; and success is a personal feeling of accomplishment. In contrast, the institution-based counselor's role is broadly defined by these characteristics: steady income, resource availability, multitasking, close friendships with colleagues, stability and predictability, the opportunity to see students in many roles such as in the school play or on the athletic field, and the pride of being part of a team.

These contrasts are intended to provide some focus for your thinking as you understand the profession of independent educational consulting. Certainly, they are generalizations. The role of the school-based counselor, in particular, is extraordinarily variable. There may be as much variation within a school counseling department as there is among independent consulting businesses. Good educational consultants need people on their team just as much as school counselors, but those players may come from different places. Rather than relying on a team within the institution, independent consultants must turn outward to connections within the associations and the profession generally: mentors, online resources, webinars, course attendance, connections with local educators, supportive family members, and others.

The scope of responsibilities of the school-based college counselor and the independent consultant also differ. The school counselor's tasks typically include providing guidance and direction on the college search process, completing transcript preparation and guidance counselor recommendations, remaining current on colleges, helping students sign up for appropriate academic courses, providing information on testing deadlines and college fairs, updating the school's written profile, offering parent/student conferences when appropriate, keeping all testing and school inventory records, sending materials to colleges, helping students develop a list of colleges, and handling calls from colleges seeking information such as first semester senior year grades. The school-based person is typically trained as a counselor. He or she may have other in-building responsibilities like personal counseling, testing, teaching, crisis counseling, and behavior monitoring.

The IEC provides personalized support and attention to individual students (and parents) regarding the college search process, works with both students and parents to assess strengths and weaknesses to begin to determine creation of the college list, helps students define college characteristics that are meaningful, provides knowledge of colleges based on being a "student of colleges," helps to mitigate stress regarding the college search and application process, and provides assistance on brainstorming college essay ideas and topics. The educational consultant focuses exclusively on college matters.

Most seasoned educational consultants consider themselves to be experts on colleges; their professional lives are focused on learning about colleges and learning about the admission process. Our expertise comes from networking, visiting colleges, taking courses, and so forth. Some have compared an independent college counselor to a math tutor. The math tutor isn't there (necessarily) because a student's math teacher isn't doing a good job—she or he is there to offer additional help. As such, educational consultants are sufficiently focused to provide the type of guidance that students and families need to make an informed higher education investment.

While there is overlap between the school-based counselor and the independent educational consultant, these are two valid, separate, professional tracks.

THE E IN IEC

The E in IEC refers to consultants' roles as educators. Consultants do not teach core or elective classes; rather, consultants teach fundamental life skills that prepare students to make critical decisions, recognize the value of parental input, and transition to independence.

IECs first educate students about the value of self-assessment. Before students start considering college options, they need to identify how they think, learn, study, and interact with others. Self-awareness is the backbone of finding the right colleges.

IECs teach students the components of effective decision-making: define the problem, brainstorm solutions, gather information, develop alternatives, weigh alternatives, embrace open-mindedness, limit boundaries, assess the validity of opinions and assumptions, and clarify priorities.

We keep students front and center and teach them to take leadership of the process.

As educators, consultants teach students to separate what's best for college admission versus what's best for mental health. Our students are often driven to exhaustion loading up on AP courses and extracurriculars in order to get in to brand-name schools. We teach that college planning is important but shouldn't dominate one's adolescence.

Moreover, consultants challenge the idea that only one school or group of schools can make someone happy. Colleges are not perfect, and we educate students of the need to be realistic rather than idealistic. Additionally, we impart the following knowledge to our students: You will be judged according to criteria that you will never again use to judge another person and which will never again be applied to you once you leave college. We teach students to understand and cope with the judgment involved in the admission process.

Additionally, consultants teach parents and students to work together through the process of researching potential colleges. I encourage Buffy to assign her parents particular parts of the research process. In other words, I might say, "Researching colleges is a family affair. Buffy, I suggest you start researching by using *College Finder* or *Fiske*. While you do that, allocate a parent to look at each school from a safety perspective and from a financial standpoint." A joint research effort then leads to a family meeting to discuss what each participant has learned. The options for parents and students to collaborate are many: one participant can look at online resources; one can take the lead reviewing printed guidebooks; one can hone in on premedical programs, merit scholarship opportunities, or location. Parents working together with students results in a more informed and educated choice. (See Chapter 12 for continued discussion.)

IECs also teach students about being independent of parents. As suggested above, the consultant tries to keep the student in the driver's seat. By assigning tasks to parents, the student is given the lead role. The IEC can encourage student independence in other ways. For example, in family meetings, consultants should direct eye contact with the student first. Ask Brutus about the progress he's made since the last meeting. In early meetings with a family, I discuss what taking the lead in the process means and what my expectations are for the student. I emphasize that the student should monitor deadlines, make the decision on test preparation strategies, keep his or her own Common Application password, and so forth. The IEC also educates students to self-advocate. The student takes the responsibility of approaching teachers in order to get letters of support, and the student checks in with teachers, if need be, to remind them of upcoming due dates. Self-advocacy is a life skill that students need to develop in order to be successful in college.

THE C IN IEC

The C in IEC establishes our role as consultants. IECs are paid to share their expertise and knowledge to help students attain goals and solve problems. As a person new to the family, the IEC views the situation from a fresh perspective. Because an IEC isn't beholden to any particular list of colleges or to the reputation of a school or college, he or she can act as the catalyst for change.

It is important to note that an IEC is not an agent. (Hence, there is no A in IEC.) The National Association for College Admission Counseling (NACAC) defines an agent as follows: "A company (agency) or individual (agent) contracted and paid by universities in other countries to advise and recruit students to those institutions. Usually, the agency/agent is paid by its partner university only if and after a referred student enrolls and begins taking classes. This payment is often a percentage of a student's tuition fees, or a flat rate, and is called a commission."

In contrast, NACAC defines an IEC as follows: "A professional hired and paid only by students and their parents for personalized advice on the university admission process, financial aid, and career possibilities." NACAC further notes that IECs are "independent from high schools and universities; they are not contracted or paid by these institutions." This distinction is critical because as IECs, we do not represent particular colleges, and our objective is to find good-fit colleges for our students, not to push colleges that foot our mortgages.

Our role is to guide the process of college planning, goal-setting, and awareness of appropriate options. No one else involved in the transition from high school to college has this unitary focus. (Even college counselors in boarding schools who exclusively deal with college admission matters may, to some degree, be concerned with the overall look of the "college profile" from their school's perspective. In other words, there may be concern for how the list of colleges where graduates attend "looks" to administrators and prospective families.)

There are persons who do this work on a part-time basis. Some are school-based counselors who see a few students a year outside of their school system. There are tutors and test preparation persons who share perspectives about college choice with their students. Similarly, there are "life coaches" who help with the high school-college transition. Some have estimated that there are several thousand of these "dabblers." I believe that these numbers may decline as families learn about the benefits of full-time, informed, knowledgable IECs.

We don't just provide time. We provide time in the company of a professional. We provide expert time. In my book (pun intended), "expert" is defined by at least these three variables: 1) a core set of skills (interviewing, listening, knowing about colleges, knowing about the process); 2) a core set of attitudes (about success, about the profession, about the value of a college education, etc.); and 3) a plan for growth, development, and networking. The "expert hat" will never land by itself on your head. Instead, you will grow more comfortable wearing it as you work in all three areas to become aware, sensitive, and informed.

THE ROLE OF THE IEC

- Provide personalized support and attention to individual students (and parents) regarding the college search process.
- Offer one-on-one time to students and parents who are in the college search process.
- Assume the role as main coordinator between student, parent and high school, if necessary.
- Encourage students to become actively involved in finding the right college.
- Work with both student and parent to assess strengths and weaknesses to begin to determine creation of the college list.
- Help student define college characteristics that are meaningful.
- Act as a cheerleader, encourager, and guide through the process.
- Provide knowledge of colleges.
- Help to prepare an individualized plan of action in the college search.
- Assess students' interests and activities.
- Prepare and present a list of colleges that meet students' criteria and admissibility.
- Help students and parents understand how to do further college research on the internet themselves.
- Help to lessen stress and family squabbles regarding the college search and application process by providing a buffer between parties.
- Provide assistance on brainstorming college essay ideas and topics.
- Give hints and tips on how to have a successful college visit and on-campus interview.
- Provide support and guidance for the student (and parents) once college decisions arrive.

WHAT QUALITIES DO YOU NEED TO BECOME A TOP-NOTCH IEC?

- Upright character: We are, in the end, role models and ethical weather vanes. Our families deserve to deal with consultants with a moral base and wholesome values. An educational consultant adheres to and surpasses accepted standards and rules without compromise and exemplifies moral character.
- Solid listening skills: Consultants need the ability to truly hear students. What are they really saying? What are their parents saying to you? We can't do a good job finding colleges, reducing stress, etc., if we can't hear what students need and want. That also means hearing what they don't say.
- Steady and even-temperedness: We need to leave our bad moods outside the door. A teenager should always be able to count on what our personality is going to be today—not sometimes nice, sometimes mean, but always kind and respectful. If we have to cancel an appointment because we are having a bad day, we do it. But don't bring moodiness into a session with a student.
- Approachability: Students need to feel comfortable enough to open up to us to share their dreams and fears. The consultant can't be another nagging adult; the consultant should be someone whom students can trust with feelings and plans.

- Organization: To juggle lots of kids, all with different needs, an educational consultant needs to have finely-tuned organizational skills. It is important to pay attention to detail. There is a vast amount of ever-changing information in this field that could become overwhelming without organization. Consultants need detailed, well organized information to be readily accessible.
- Knowledge: This is the one of the most important qualities. The desire to be a lifelong learner is important here. The learning necessary as an educational consultant is never-ending. A great consultant embraces the desire to learn. There is no substitute for intimate knowledge of not only college facts and admissions processes, but also the intangibles. For students in special groups, like learning disabled students, a consultant's depth of knowledge is essential. As educational consultants, we are responsible for learning an endless amount of information and are also responsible for conveying that information to our clients. Our job is to read, assess, take in, interpret, and convey as much as we can for our clients so that they can make better choices.
- Business savvy: Independent educational consulting is a business. It is up to the consultant to determine his or her own business goals and strategy to achieve them. We must be able to talk to families about services and attain solid contacts. We have to be constantly looking one, two, and three years ahead for new clients. Business development is crucial to the longevity of any practice and needs to play a central role in how we work. This quality also includes the need for the consultant to be interested in financial gain. The consultant is a professional, and professionals take money from clients because they deliver a valued service. The consultant establishes a fee structure that yields a reasonable profit margin.
- Knack for problem-solving: The whole educational consulting process is based on a consultant's ability to effectively make choices and solve problems. Every student presents a profile filled with strengths and weaknesses. Throughout the process, any number of issues may arise. It is the consultant's duty to utilize knowledge and experience to guide that student through the steps necessary to tackle problems.
- Flexibility: Each student is independent with different needs. No one solution fits all. Educational consultants must learn to apply their individual method while still attending to the specific needs of each student and his or her family.
- Passion: This job is not for the faint of heart. To succeed, we have to possess a deep ingrained belief in the potential of all young people and the opportunities that lay in education.
- Commitment: This relates to passion, but it is deeper. It is one thing to believe; it is another to be in it for the long haul. Kids can really see who is committed and who is not. For them to be successful in this process, they need to see that IECs want what's best for them. Too often in their high schools, students are confronted with people who talk the talk, but don't walk the walk.

- Compassion: The admissions process is one of the most stressful times in a young person's life. From this stress, great things can emerge, and terrible things can rise to the surface. This can be a triumphant time, but there are typically setbacks. The independent educational consultant goes into every relationship with what the Japanese call "both hands open." We are there to help students keep their eyes on the prize, but we are also there to help them up from a slip-up and to aid families as they help their children leave the nest. We are also students of the human condition. Most who enter this field *like* people. With fondness for people comes joy and pain, satisfaction and disappointment, encouragement and discouragement. An IEC must be willing to study and understand people.
- Gentleness: It's been said that there is nothing stronger in the world than gentleness. Being gentle doesn't mean being weak or lacking assertiveness. It means being soft-spoken and caring. Disarm people by the gentleness of your manner. You'll get much further in consulting. How you come across, your self-presentation, is critical for a one-on-one service professional.
- Self-direction: With no greater structure to back us up, IECs need to have their own internal engines. We have to carry the responsibility of our practice while setting and achieving our own personal goals.
- Optimism: This career is quite challenging, but we need to remind ourselves why we wanted to work in educational consulting in the first place: to help as many people as we can to realize their dreams of a better education and future.
- Responsibility: We must take responsibility for everything we do. If we have made an incorrect choice, we must own up to it and be responsible by dealing with the consequences that may come from that choice. Educational consultants must do their best for their client, but if we cannot for whatever reason, we must be responsible and do our best to correct the matter.

QUICK OVERVIEW OF CONSULTING PRACTICES

I've been observing consultant practices for several years through interviews, surveys, and anecdotal evidence. In addition, the Independent Educational Consultants Association (IECA) conducts surveys of its own, and the conclusions below reflect both sources of information.

Consultants are coming into this work from a wide variety of backgrounds. It is still common for consultants to have served as school-based college counselors or as college admission officials. More recently, folks have entered the field with business/management/marketing backgrounds. Beyond these fields, there are those whose experience is with community-based organizations, psychology, medicine, or law.

As the field has grown, so too have the numbers of IECs from diverse backgrounds (socioeconomically, racially, professionally, and ethnically).

Geographic and Demographic Conclusions
- About 40% of consultants in the nation practice in the New England/Mid-Atlantic area. While the other regions (Midwest/Great Lakes/Rocky Mountains, South, and Pacific) are fairly equally divided, California has had a disproportionately large percentage. Almost 10% of consultants practice internationally. The best marketplace for independent educational consulting services is generally a high-density area near a major city.
- A typical client these days is hard to define. Like others who provide a personalized service, IECs see many middle/professional and upper-class clients. But more and more consultants are targeting students from lower-middle class or working class.
- About half of consultants work with some students internationally. IECA reports that in the last three years, its members worked with students from at least 80 countries.

- Students working with an IEC are much more likely to go out of state. According to IECA, 20% of students nationwide do so compared to 69% of those working with an IEC. In addition, students working with an IEC are more likely to attend a private college (about 70% versus less than 20%).

Financial Conclusions

- The average comprehensive fee has gone up significantly as the profession has become more knowledge-focused. Fees vary as a result of years of experience, location of practice, and scope and duration of work. IECs in the New England/Mid-Atlantic areas typically charge higher fees than do IECs in other regions. Those practicing internationally also tend to charge more than their domestic counterparts. The average hourly IEC fee is often compared to the fee of a psychologist or a physical therapist. Decades ago there were reports of consultants charging tens of thousands of dollars. By charging exorbitant fees, these early consultants did a disservice to the profession. Fortunately, we seldom read about such outrageous claims these days, and families now can find consultants who offer a wide variety of series for a wide variety of fees.
- A great majority of IECA members with over three years of experience realized a profit. More than half of IECs with less than three years of experience realized a profit.
- Over 90% of IECs use a contract or a letter of agreement.

Working Environment Conclusions

- Two-thirds of consultants work full time, according to IECA. The average IEC works 36 hours per week. Over half see students on Saturdays and Sundays.
- Approximately three-fourths of clients pay the IEC through a comprehensive package fee. "Comprehensive" means that the consultant has a flat fee for a service. The service typically starts in the junior year. The comprehensive fee includes face-to-face time, research time, phone time, and e-mail and text time, etc. The primary alternative to the comprehensive plan is for the consultant to charge by the hour, and nearly three-fourths of consultants surveyed use hourly fees for some or all of their pricing. Note also that almost a third of consultants offer smaller plans, a third have "a la carte" services, about ten percent use a sliding scale, and almost 100% of consultants offer pro bono help.
- Approximately two-thirds of consultants hold between six and fifteen face-to-face meetings with their students in a comprehensive program. Fifteen meetings is the average. A typical meeting in a comprehensive package lasts 75 minutes. Many consultants have a longer (three hours in some cases) initial meeting.
- When asked in the IECA survey to report the "average number of new clients they are taking on this year," college consultants responded: 26.
- Approximately half of consultants see all or most of their clients directly (face-to-face). About 5% of consultants see clients only virtually. For distance advising, consultants, like other like professionals, use e-mail, teleconference platforms, Skype, text messaging, FaceTime, Zoom, video conferencing software, and webinars.
- About 50% of IECs work by themselves, and slightly fewer have a multiperson practice. This reflects a change from a decade ago when most IECs worked alone.
- About 30% of IECs see clients exclusively in their home office, and about 30% see clients exclusively in their commercial office. The rest either see clients in a combination of both, do not meet clients face-to-face, meet at a client's home or community location, or have no "typical" location.
- Most consultants use social networking tools as part of their business. LinkedIn and Facebook are the most common. In an IECA study, consultants also mentioned using Pinterest, YouTube, Instagram, blog, and Twitter. A small, but not insignificant, percent of consultants report using no social networking sites for their business.

- Most IECs work for a for-profit institution (their own business or a joint practice). Some work (full- or part-time) at a local private or religious school. A growing percentage of consultants work in community-based organizations, health care organizations, corporate/HR, etc.
- An industry has grown up around the profession of independent educational consulting. For example, database/office management systems like GuidedPath and CollegePlannerPro are commonly used in consulting offices. In addition, there are programs in areas such as essay assistance, career guidance, test preparation, learning disabilities, and shipping that are designed specifically for IECs.
- The vast majority of consultants allow unlimited face-to-face meeting time, particularly if it is defined as including time spent via phone, e-mail, text, etc. As noted later in the book, I don't believe this is a good practice. I believe professionals should provide a ceiling on the number of meetings or number of hours of professional contact.

Delivery of Service Conclusions
- Consultants spend about one-third of their total time with their students talking about specific colleges. Another third is spent talking about the application itself, the essays/personal statements, financial aid advising, and career exploration. The remaining time is spent talking about the process, such as academic course planning, timetables, how decisions are made, getting things done, meeting deadlines, etc. It is still common to find an IEC doing preparation for SAT and/or ACT.
- Most consultants put a significant focus on financial concerns as well as application completion and essays.
- Other primary uses of an IEC's time include summer placement and programs; résumé discussion and creation; academic course selection; testing schedules and test prep; and discussion of progress, expectations, and grade goals. Increasingly, IECs advise younger students (even middle school students) on steps necessary to prepare for a successful college admission process.
- Consultants also spend time with students on matters pertaining to campus visits; careers; interviews; time management; assessment of values, personality, aptitudes and interests; rapport building; motivating; anxiety counseling, and family dynamics.
- There are consultants who specialize. Primary areas of specialization include career advising, test preparation, gap year advising, advising student athletes, graduate students, therapeutic camps and programs, homeschooled students, students with learning disabilities, international students, and visual and performing artists.

CHAPTER 3

Readiness Clues

WHEN IS IT RIGHT TO START A PRACTICE?

When are you ready to charge for your services? It may be sooner than you think! It's no different than earning an undergraduate or graduate degree and applying for a job. I don't imagine that any one of us accepted our first job without compensation, and yet we may have had no real experience in the field. Instead, we presented a background, and the prospective employer/institution had a choice whether or not to hire us.

Professional knowledge increases with experience. When should you consider yourself knowledgable enough to begin a career as an independent educational consultant? That's hard to say. But the answer is not just how much you know about College X or College Y. The answer comes from addressing questions such as:

- Have you visited colleges?
- Do you understand the general admission and match processes?
- Do you present yourself in a trusting and confident way?
- Do you demonstrate an interest in learning about higher education?
- Are you devoting time to learning and to the profession?
- Have you started talking with other consultants?
- Are you attending professional meetings?
- Are you working toward membership in IECA? HECA? NACAC (local and national)?
- Are you reading voraciously about the field?
- Are you taking classes to learn more?

Above are the types of benchmarks that indicate preparedness. Take it slowly but steadily as you meet your knowledge needs. Getting up to speed is a marathon, not a sprint. Like our students, we each have our own style of learning and our own learning curve.

We all have strengths. Some may have experience working in a high school counseling office. Someone else might be able to interpret career tests. Another may be great at giving presentations. The next person might have a business background and be comfortable with the marketing, social media, and financial aspects. Others may be knowledgeable about a particular population of students. Another person may have extraordinary skills at rapport building or researching. Acknowledge the abilities, sensitivities, and perceptions you do have. Use your strengths as the starting point for your professional success.

The following are some of the skills that you may need as an independent educational consultant:

- accounting and finance
- administrative
- advertising
- analytical
- change management
- communication (written, oral, and nonverbal)
- computer office applications
- creative
- counseling
- interpersonal
- language
- learning
- legal
- listening
- marketing
- mathematical and money management
- motivational
- multimedia
- negotiation
- organizational
- people management
- problem-solving
- public relations
- sales
- technical
- thinking
- writing

Many of these skills are discussed throughout the book. Others are inferred. It is important to be honest about which skills you may lack and consider how you will handle these areas. It used to be sound advice to caution those entering the field to keep their day jobs and enter the field gradually after honing skills and visiting colleges. It is still true that starting a business takes time and financial investment, but as more people are aware of IECs, it is generally quicker to establish a practice than it was a decade ago. Of course, if this is a second income in a family, the financial considerations may be less daunting.

Each individual must decide: Is this a career that suits me? If yes, then when is the time to enter the field? The second question comes through consideration of such factors as confidence, marketability, and passion. More variables will be identified to help make these decisions as we move along.

BENCHMARKS OF READINESS

Below are some questions that can serve as benchmarks of readiness for a career as an independent college counselor.

Proficiency Questions
- Am I professionally competent?
- Have I seen and evaluated enough colleges? Can I describe what they're like? (Here's an example: "Can I describe Harvard without regard to its reputation or academic rigor?")
- Do I stay current with developments in higher education?
- Do I enjoy visiting colleges?
- Is learning about schools most people have never heard of appealing?
- Do I know enough about adolescents to understand their needs and perspectives?
- Am I ready to call the shots? (You will be the one families turn to for the answers.)
- Do I see ongoing learning as an important part of my professional life?

Interactional Questions
- Can I hold my own against an assertive parent?
- Am I a good listener?
- Am I a keen observer? (For example, am I able to pick up subtle cues during a campus visit?)
- Do I enjoy interacting with young people? Am I good at it?
- Will teenagers listen and respect my point of view?
- Will parents listen and respect my point of view?
- Do I respond positively to setbacks?

Business Questions
- Am I looking at being an IEC as a career as opposed to a hobby?
- Am I ready to develop an initial operating budget?
- Am I starting my IEC business to make money and to do what I love?
- Am I self-disciplined enough to focus on the needs of my consulting business?
- Do I have the financial resources necessary to establish my practice? Can I afford the financial uncertainties of quitting my day job, or can I moonlight on my current job, if necessary?
- Do I have a pretty good idea about funds needed to start my IEC business?
- Will my consulting business support the lifestyle I want?
- Can I afford the time it will take to build a stable consulting business? Do I have 12 to 18 months of living expenses in the bank, or am I willing to downsize my spending before making the switch?
- Can I afford the costs associated with travel?
- Can I afford the costs associated with learning (professional development, etc.)?
- Do I know where to turn for answers?
- Can I develop milestones for my business over the next year?
- Do I have the smarts to realize and deal with my business deficits?

Promotional Questions
- Do I envision myself as an entrepreneur?
- Can I convince people to pay for my services?
- Can I pinpoint my market?
- Can I explain how my work as an IEC is different from work offered by other consultants?
- Can I get in front of people and articulate why they need me?

- Have I developed a strong network of potential clients or people who might refer to me?
- Am I comfortable charging people for my time and expertise?
- Am I knowledgeable or interested in learning about new marketing techniques?
- Am I comfortable networking with other professionals?
- Am I comfortable with social media and/or willing to learn ways it can help me build my business?
- Am I comfortable calling everyone on my contact list to ask them to consider me if they have college planning needs?
- Do I have a name for my business (or some really great ideas)?
- Do I have ideas about how to drive traffic to my website for my business?

Personality/Motivation Questions
- Can I deal with limits (such as recognizing that a case is beyond the scope of my training) and be willing to refer to others even if it means less income?
- Am I ready to give the required time, resources, and capital to succeed?
- Am I convinced of the value of using an IEC?
- Can I adapt to a new situation?
- Am I willing to ask for help?
- Do I function well in the midst of uncertainty?
- Am I the independent entrepreneur type? Am I comfortable with independence?
- Do I like the idea of controlling my own work instead of having someone else control it for me?
- Am I an ethical and responsible person?
- Am I willing to meet the needs of students even when they are contrary to my advice?
- Am I a risk taker?
- Do I have a strong drive to succeed?
- Am I ready to work as hard as or harder than I have ever worked before?
- Is my self-image strong enough to work through the ups and downs of establishing a new business?
- Am I sure I am not changing careers to run away from a job-related problem?
- Do I like to laugh?

Stamina/Practical Questions
- Does being with young people each day seem uplifting and rewarding?
- Am I physically prepared for long days (or, as often, nights) and the demands of consulting?
- Do I possess a high level of energy that is sustainable over long hours?
- Am I willing to give up evenings and weekends to accommodate student schedules?
- Will my family accept my focus of time and energy toward my profession?
- Do I have the support of my significant other/family?
- Is the timing right for me to start my business?
- Do I have a plan for measuring success?
- Can I break things down into small pieces?
- Can I identify the sacrifices and risks involved in being a successful businessperson? Am I prepared to make/take them?
- Do I like to travel?
- Am I comfortable in an environment where I may have no control over admission decisions?
- Can I deal with the uncertainties that are a part of elite college admission?

It's good if there are a lot of "yes" responses to these questions, but keep in mind that answering "no" to some does not mean you are unsuited for a career as an independent educational consultant. Rather, "no" responses may identify areas or skills that you need to develop or improve.

FINAL THOUGHTS

Being a good independent educational consultant combines lots of qualities—ability, energy, and humanness are among them. Knowledge of the student, knowledge of colleges, and knowledge of human interaction are key. Additionally, you need to understand student records: testing, achievement results, and transcripts. You should also know technology and be able to balance human interaction with technological innovation. You need to allow time for seeing your students, time to market, time to follow up with your students, and time for yourself. Thus, you need to be a good time manager. Whew! It's not easy, but it's doable and well worth it if you are committed.

CHAPTER 4

Edupreneurship

OPERATING A SUCCESSFUL BUSINESS

"I'm in education, not business!" the consultant may be thinking. The two, however, interconnect. To best maximize time spent with students, the IEC needs to make good business decisions and run his or her office effectively.

I became an IEC because I didn't particularly want to be in my family's commercial real estate business. In fact, I remember my eyes glazing over when my dad (and later my brother) talked about the excitement of being in real estate development. Not only was I unimpressed with the prospect of being a real-life Monopoly player, but I was also uninspired by the wheeling and dealing involved. When I became a consultant, I had to swallow some of my aversion to the business world to develop a successful practice.

IECs must have a business plan, or a blueprint, or a strategy for beginning their practice. Business planning involves careful thought about the intersection of the time, money, learning, and happiness axes. If specific steps in your new enterprise have not been firmly established, your business plan can be rudimentary, or if specific steps are intact, it can be more comprehensive. However fleshed out, your plan provides the opportunity to think through issues and to commit decisions to writing. Such a strategy is necessary for the long-term health of a new practice.

Step I: Developing a Rationale For Your Practice

An educational consulting practice is an independent venture designed to meet your needs for professional satisfaction and financial success. But what are your goals and perspectives? What are you trying to accomplish in your educational consulting practice? Such questions lead to the development of a business plan.

Before you put pen to paper, ponder the following principles of independent educational consulting. First, consider what qualities people look for in an IEC. By recognizing the qualities that make a good IEC, you will be able to establish an effective and successful business plan. Parents look for an IEC who is knowledgeable about colleges, the admission process, and student development; visits colleges regularly; is involved with a professional organization (at least after he or she has been practicing a few years) knows his or her limits; guarantees nothing other than informed, current knowledge and information about colleges and the admissions process; and allows the student to be the leader of the process. Second, consider some common misconceptions that have a bearing on conceptualizing a business plan.

Misconception #1: The key to good consulting is providing a list of colleges.

No. Not really. The key to good consulting is learning about the student and establishing a baseline for making college choices. It requires identifying the characteristics and the real and perceived needs of the young person with whom the consultant is working. The independent educational consultant must develop his/her counseling skills so that he or she can accurately read both what's on the page—transcripts, reports, test scores, and the like—and, importantly, be able to ask the right questions to find out the sort of environment where the student will thrive. That ability to identify and to understand allows the consultant to use his or her skills to match person with institution. The college list is the result of these other explorations and identifications. (Chapter 6 is dedicated to building the college list.) Your business plan should reflect ways you will assess student needs and should articulate how you will meet such needs.

Misconception #2: Consulting is an art.

No. That's not complete enough. There are skills and knowledge necessary to be a consultant. There is a body of literature to be learned about the dynamics of the counseling process, the psychology of children and adolescents, the value of education, the factors involved in decision-making, and the issues relevant to understanding family interactions. IECs are knowledgeable about the variety of problems young people face: social pressures, depression, drugs, pregnancy, and so on. The information base must extend in many directions, and good consultants take the time to keep up with the literature in education, psychology, sociology, and related fields. Above and beyond foundational knowledge, IECs add verifiable, objective knowledge about what specific colleges are like. With such a robust knowledge base, educational consultants' practices are ordered rather than random. IECs allocate time and money for travel, books, networking, etc. Consulting is more than an art; thus, your business plan should cover ways of learning and approaches to building knowledge.

Misconception #3: Principally, what educational consultants provide to a student and family is time.

This is untrue. Similarly, it is also untrue that the more time spent with the student, the better. The main commodity that an IEC provides relates to information: offering objective information about a multitude of colleges and eliciting relevant information from the student. Giving and gathering information allows the IEC to make appropriate recommendations. This, I feel, is the difference between a process-focused consultant and a knowledge-focused consultant. As discussed in Chapter 7, the process-focused consultant provides a warm, caring environment and is primarily concerned with meeting the student's needs to complete the college application process. A knowledge-focused consultant, on the other hand, centers his or her practice on information. The consultant is focused on the student, but knowledge-driven information about colleges, summer programs, graduate schools, etc. is at the core of the practice. Your business plan should describe your approach to consulting and should consider how much time you feel is appropriate to meet the student's needs without taking over the process.

Misconception #4: Business skills should take a back seat to counseling skills.

No. The bottom line ought to be important to any professional: IECs ought to be okay with charging appropriate fees and turning a profit. A good college consultant is a worthy investment. What the IEC provides is valuable and needed. Over the long haul, the profession needs to be able to attract people who view consulting as a full-time commitment. Business professionals should be able to earn a livable wage. A professional image and a livable wage will attract the right type of people to educational consulting. Your business plan may be the first formal effort to begin to detail how the mechanics of your operation will unfold.

Misconception #5: Independent educational consulting is the sure route to fortune.

The profession has come a long way in terms of income generation. The advice I used to give was to "keep your day job" as you explore consulting as a career. While doing both takes focus and balance, it can be done, and it is the right approach for many. Starting your business while still maintaining a paycheck will help cushion the transition between your day job and your new business. While you are still employed, you can test your materials and your skills, talk to lots of people about your new venture, test marketing and social media ideas, and attend national association conferences, etc. It is still true that independent educational consultants rarely turn a profit after a few months. In fact, it can take several years to develop a profitable practice. But it is easier to start today as compared to 20 years ago. Since more people are aware of educational consultants, new practitioners can focus on how they are different from other local IECs. Also, more and more consultants are starting in an existing practice; these folks begin with the tools and the resources that provide a better chance for early success. For the sake of all of us, each consultant needs to do a better job of marketing the profession and thus increasing the number of people who seek consulting services. And each consultant must get better and better at his or her work each year. Both your fee structure and your marketing strategy should be addressed in your business plan. While this profession is not the sure route to fortune, hard work and mentoring can make that goal a lot closer.

Misconception #6: The best educational consultants are able to offer expertise in areas such as undergraduate colleges, graduate colleges, financial aid, schools for "troubled teens," psychological issues, learning disabilities, athletics, and test preparation.

No. The best IECs know their limits, and those limits are spelled out in the business plan. Consultants can't be all things to all people. IECs don't just deal with the problem child, the child with a learning difference, or the marginal student. It's fine, of course, for consultants to deal with challenging kids, but consultants should be as comfortable if they want to deal only with high-achieving college students, graduate students, artists, or athletes. The skills required to deal with psychological issues are typically beyond the scope of IECs. Consultants must know when to refer a potential client to someone else, particularly to therapeutic consultants who work with at-risk teens. IECs must know when to help most by not helping. Clearly state your scope of practice in your business plan, including the clients you intend to serve.

Misconception #7: Independent educational consultants fix student weaknesses.

Problem-solving is a part of professional life. IECs are tasked with responding to issues and dilemmas on a daily basis. But IECs should see themselves as listeners and facilitators, not as fixers of student weaknesses. We acknowledge student strengths and encourage students to capitalize on their strengths. Consultants take the student/family situation as it is and direct it as appropriate. For example, the issue that Brutus has low test scores that might hinder admission to certain schools is not the consultant's problem to fix. IECs should help and even mediate when appropriate, but our job is to advise. Our role is to work with the student we see in front of us. Sure, we can suggest test prep, and we can help brainstorm personal statement ideas, but we're not hired to turn Brutus into Mark Antony. Our work is focused on finding the gifts that Brutus possesses and to use those gifts in the pursuit of identification of good fit colleges. The rationale for an IEC's practice—the business plan—explicitly or implicitly puts priority on the roles of guide and facilitator, not problem fixer.

Misconception #8: Independent educational consultants exist because public school counselors are ineffective.

No. Some high school counselors are ineffective; some are good. Some IECs are ineffective; some are good. Just because a family decides to use a private psychologist doesn't necessarily mean the school psychologist is inept. This is the nature of the marketplace. It is the nature of society in the 21st century. Each profession has its focus and its place. Your business plan offers you a chance to state how your service will differ from services offered in public or private high schools.

Misconception #9: Independent educational consultants work by themselves.

Sure, many IECs work alone; however, over the last few years, there has been a marked increase in IECs working together. The work of the IEC is enhanced by sharing with others. Independent educational consulting demands interaction; it demands that IECs actively seek out perspectives, impressions, and techniques from colleagues across the country. It took me five years to join a professional organization. One reason I got into the field was for the independence and, by golly, I meant to be independent. How much better a consultant I could have been in those early years had I joined a professional association sooner! I would have been a better consultant because I would have been able to share perspectives with colleagues across the country, attend meetings, and learn from specialists. I would have had a formal and congenial network of active minds and informed people with whom to interact from the get-go. Be sure your business plan allows the reader to understand how you expect to interact with your colleagues as your begin your consulting practice.

Misconception #10: Independent educational consultants give rich kids another advantage.

This is a dated generalization. Of course, like many generalizations, there is historical truth to this perspective. Independent educational consultants have often thrived in higher income neighborhoods. Twenty years ago, the average student receiving counseling was from a middle to high income family. That is no longer the case. Yes, there are IECs who cater to students from higher income families, but it is also common these days to find the consultant who works only with first-generation students or with blue-collar families. And as discussed later in this chapter, many IECs see clients on a pro bono basis. Also related here is the notion of packaging candidates for admission. Part of the folklore of IECs was that we wrapped garden-variety students into shiny boxes of college acceptances so that they could gain entry to prestigious colleges. That is folly. Given the complexities of college admissions, there is no formula or package that unlocks the doors to selective colleges. In fact, IECs have become the *anti-packagers*. That is,

IECs know that each student is different and unique. Your business plan should reflect the steps that you will take to share your expertise with a wide range of college shoppers and should express that you will not put a glittery bow on Buffy in attempt to catch an admission officer's eye.

Misconception #11: There will always be a need for the independent educational consultant.
I believe that there will probably always be a need for help with the college search process, but that advice could come from the school counselor, a computer program, a website, franchise college counseling offices, and so forth. Thus, to do away with the complacent conception that our services will always be in high demand, each IEC needs to market his or her services to make people aware of the valuable services offered. The profession will grow and thrive only if work is done to make it grow, and it will thrive only if there are people who care about the profession. IECs need to actively seek out the right people and encourage their contribution. The profession needs experience as well as youth. As society recognizes the importance of the right fit between student and college, and as it appreciates the fact that success comes from a student being in the right environment, the demand for the profession will increase. Further, as education on all levels becomes more and more expensive, as the willingness to travel for the right fit continues to grow, and as the population becomes more and more discriminating about educational options, the need for IECs will continue to climb. Again, the profession cannot be complacent. Each consultant must assume responsibility for keeping practice standards high and for furthering the reputation of the field. The field will grow not by professional associations or one or two good IECs; rather, it will grow by hundreds of people being respected in their communities and by positive word of mouth among parents that the best way to learn about colleges is by hiring an IEC. What's important is that we work to make a case for the value of the profession. Your business plan should include a statement as to the value of your service as an IEC and a recognition that the growth of this profession is the responsibility of all involved.

Step II: Organizing the Business Plan
Below are major sections used in business planning relevant to the IEC.

Summary: An overall statement of your business plan. This is really the essence of your plan. Typically this is the paragraph that you could share with anyone who wants to know about your new independent educational consulting business venture.

Mission: This is your philosophy, your commitment, your reason for going into the field of private college advising. The mission statement is typically filled with feeling language and is the place for the consultant to share hopes and dreams. Remember, the personality of your company is your personality. Is it structured and no-nonsense? Is it caring, creative, and compassionate?

Location and Facilities: Where will your practice operate?

Services: What services will you provide your clients? It is important to be as specific as you can about the nature of your proposed practice. It may be helpful to think of this not as a list of every service your offer; rather, it is a list of benefits you will provide to the family. In addition, consider the limits of your practice, and clearly note them.

Objectives: These are more specific goals. What will you actually do in the next few months (or immediately after you start your practice)? How many clients do you hope (need) to have? Even a rough guesstimate will get you headed in the right direction.

Milestones: These are key events in the early life of your firm. When will you see your first (or tenth) client? Do you have a specific date that you will open your practice? Do you want to visit a certain number of colleges by an upcoming date? Will you have materials produced by a certain date? Do you have a target date for developing a website?

Keys to Success: What are the absolute essentials to your being a successful IEC? Is it self-confidence? Is it time? Is it knowledge? Is it work ethic?

Marketing Analysis and Plan: You want to explore five elements here: 1) Identify your market; 2) Consider your competition and your approach to dealing with that competition. Either name these individuals or discuss competition in general. Is your competition counselors in public schools? Is it books and websites? Is it lack of knowledge that educational consultants exist?; 3) Analyze your strengths and weaknesses as an IEC; 4) Explain your specific marketing strategies. You should try to be as specific as possible with your marketing strategies and approaches; and 5) Talk about how you will evaluate your marketing approaches.

Materials: If you are going to use printed or electronic materials, what will they be? What sort of materials do you think are necessary to get started? Do you want to create a college planning binder for each student? What materials will you need immediately or within a year?

Pricing and Money Issues: Where will your cash flow come from? What sort of earning do you need? Can you afford to be a full-time consultant now? If not, when? What will you charge? Or, alternatively, how will you determine what you will charge? Will you offer a package of services or work on a per-consultation basis?

Technology: What will you need to keep records, to stay in touch with your clients, and, generally, to have a modern, professional operation?

Legal Issues: Will you incorporate? Are business permits required in your city? Are you going to need partnership papers? Do you have copyright permission for materials you will use? What other legal issues do you need to consider? College pro

Contingencies: This is a description of "Plan B" strategies. In other words, what are your alternate paths to meeting your overall goals? What in your business plan is most apt to be problematic? How would you deal with those problems?

Feelings: It is important for you to address any feelings or biases you may have. Consider these when you meet with families. For example, if you like to be liked, parents who challenge you may be prove difficult. Or you may have a bias in favor of small, liberal arts colleges.

Future Services: What would you like to do (if anything) in phase two or phase three of your business? Are there new areas of service you intend to provide? (Chapter 18 provides information about ways to expand your practice.)

Step III: Tips For Putting Together Your Business Plan

A Google search for "business plans" results in millions of hits. You will be able to find many examples of business plans and insights into the elements of a good business plan. Instead of providing another template here, I want to focus on 12 key elements of business planning for the IEC.

1. A business plan isn't a "school assignment." As educators, it's easy to try to fill in the blanks instead of making the plan workable and practical. You don't need to have 20+ sections that "everyone I know" has included in his or her plan. How are you going to realistically get your business off the ground? How are you going to realistically make money?

2. Substance takes priority over form. A perfectly formatted business plan is no better than one without all of the bells and whistles. In other words, what are the key things you need to do today to make your practice successful? Do you have a reasonable approach to dealing with expenses, pressures, and risks? Do you have a clear plan for making money and keeping your business alive?

3. Focus on time management. No IEC practice is possible without a significant commitment of time. Clients won't just show up. A new website will not, in and of itself, be the answer. Having a Snapchat account will not be the answer. Your business plan needs to forcefully articulate the actual hours you will put in per week to make your practice work. I believe that 20% of time must be devoted to marketing. If you don't have time to make your business a success, it will not be a success. Period.

4. Seek simplicity. There is no reason to overcomplicate your plan. Some of the best IEC business plans I've read are one or two pages. If you spend more than about half an hour looking for templates on the internet, you've wasted time. Get to the action steps immediately. You know yourself like no one else does. Use that knowledge to personalize your approach.

5. Stay confident! I find that lack of confidence is the primary reason new practitioners struggle during the first stages of business planning. Lack of confidence often surfaces as the business plan is unfolding because you are *forced* to think about the number of clients you want to serve, the money it will take to travel to a conference or to visit colleges, and so forth. Confidence here doesn't mean unfettered optimism; rather, it means giving yourself credit for the positives you bring to the consulting table. And it means confidence in the fact that starting an educational consulting business, while challenging and time-consuming, is not overly complex. It is relatively low tech, and the only "product" being produced is intellectual and personal. Remember also that motivation matters a lot! While experience is important, it is also important to remember that commitment and perseverance are, in the long run, better antecedents of business success.

6. Don't let being uninformed about social media pull you down. While we must be attuned to new media (and social networking particularly), business development and growth in our world relies largely on word-of-mouth recommendations and person-to-person marketing. Further, there are lots and lots of ways to learn about the marketing potential of Facebook and other platforms.

7. Remember to beg it, borrow it, and buy it. These are three ways of building know-how. "Beg it" means to learn through another person's established business. "Borrow it" points you to use approaches and materials readily available on the open market. For example, worksheets from *College Match* are available on my website for anyone to use. Plenty of materials are readily available and not restricted in use. "Buy it" means to hire someone with experience or perhaps to pay for a mentor who can spend time showing you the ins and outs of the consulting business.

8. Control what you can and don't dwell on any perceived negatives. Work to enhance your service offerings, and don't get buried in minor issues or those over which you have no immediate control. For example, one of the goals of the IEC is to work with college counselors in schools. We need to encourage our students to stay in touch with their school counselor, and to reach out to these colleagues in all possible ways. But we shouldn't fixate on the fact that a particular school counselor "doesn't like independent educational consultants." Seek students from another part of town, or do more work virtually. Focus instead on what you are doing to be a valuable colleague. Focus on working hard to help your students in their quest for a great college.

9. Be very specific in terms of time line for meeting your goals. It is not enough to say that you want to visit colleges in the next three months. A better option is to say that you plan to make 10 visits in the next three months. That's achievable as a result of visiting three colleges locally in May, visiting three colleges while on a trip to Philadelphia in June, and visiting four colleges on the Finger Lakes Counselor Tour. Such timelines also serve as motivators. Use your plan as a way to constantly push yourself to act. Check yourself against your business plan frequently as a sort of guidepost to build upon. By placing a specific guidepost every so often, you'll continue to grow and see your work develop into a more complex, successful, and inclusive business.

10. Recognize and deal with your weaknesses. After building a solid business plan, you can begin to understand where you might be weak. No one knows it all, and if you are weak in an area, your business plan should provide specific steps you will take to deal with the problem area. It may be that attending an upcoming national conference can provide the chance to talk to people about ways they have resolved similar problems. It may mean reading more, attending webinars, or spending time on the phone with a mentor or someone you trust. There are some issues that require you to be in touch with other IECs. There are other issues, like whether a home office is better than renting outside space or who to help design a website, that you can ask any other solopreneur. Another option is to outsource your weakness. For example, if you need help initially setting up a website, it may be that you hire a high school student in your community for a few hours to help you.

11. Plan for the cyclical nature of being an Independent Educational Consultant. IECs tend to be busiest in the fall when seniors are working on applications and personal statements; however, summer tends to be relatively quiet. The cycle of your business will depend on your location, your focus, and your preferences. You will want to take these matters into consideration as your business plan evolves. Considering cycles also means considering your response to an economic slowdown, a loss of population in your community, and other social or cultural changes that may impact your business.

12. Have a roadmap. Each of us needs to determine whom we want to serve and how best to do so. That's our curriculum. Some IECs see students for a limited number of hours, charge less, and depend on volume to bring in the income they desire. Some IECs see students for more hours, charge more, and depend on a smaller number of students to meet income needs. The first model seems to be particularly common among consultants who want to their practice to focus on less affluent clients. Whatever you do, you need a roadmap. Would you drive in a random direction in search of a completely unknown address? Of course not. You would have a tech tool (a GPS app, for example) provide you the most direct route, or you would pull out your old-school, coffee-stained foldable map and follow a course. Yet there are business startups that tootle along randomly, going in every direction. Avoid getting lost by charting your initial path and staying with it.

Step IV: Evaluate a Model: Sample Business Plan

Please note that the following example is fictional. This sample business plan is not provided as a model of genius; rather, it is included as an evaluative tool.

CollegeFitMatchConsulting
Annalise Durham

Summary

CollegeFitMatchConsulting is an independent educational consulting firm that helps guide students through the college search, application, and selection process.

CollegeFitMatchConsulting helps students and their parents understand the multitude of options available after high school that can lead to educational and career success. Through personalized counseling, students are able to make informed choices, successfully complete the application process, and achieve their individualized goals.

The firm is headed by Annalise Durham, an expert in the field of educational advising. Annalise holds a degree in education from the University of Virginia, is a graduate of the University of California, Irvine's Independent Educational Consulting Certificate Program, an Associate Member of IECA, and a member of HECA. Annalise also brings her expertise in the field of standardized test prep to her practice. Annalise worked closely with and was mentored by Daisy Lee Hufnagel, a well-respected consultant with over 20 years of experience. Annalise still maintains access to Daisy's expertise and occasionally consults with Daisy on difficult or interesting cases.

Annalise intends to work full-time in the practice, averaging over fifty hours per week during peak season (September, October, November, and December) and closer to forty hours per week during the remainder of the year. Annalise will spend approximately 25% of her time traveling to visit colleges and attending professional conferences. Every month, Annalise will attend a three-hour meeting with local IECs.

Mission

Annalise is committed to helping families explore all higher education options. CollegeFitMatchConsulting offers a broad range of personalized services, which directly address the needs and interests of high school sophomores, juniors, seniors—and their parents. Annalise educates her clients about the college process and, through a series of discussions, helps students explore and understand their academic and social preferences so that they ultimately choose a college environment that is a good fit for their needs and interests. Annalise draws upon her knowledge of college programs, campus cultures, admissions procedures, and educational trends to suggest colleges that could be a good match for her students.

Annalise's mission is to help student's understand that because they are unique in their talents, strengths, and learning styles, they should choose a college that offers a program that matches their interests and provides a cultural community that feels comfortable. Throughout the consulting process, Annalise's focus is to help students find a college that is a good fit, in other words, an environment where they will flourish both academically and socially.

Ultimately, Annalise's goal is to help students find their way through the sometimes stressful and scary process of applying to college. She enjoys facilitating self-awareness, guiding students through the college research process, and helping students visualize themselves at different college campuses across the country.

Annalise will strive to become a trusted confidante, consultant, partner, teacher, guide, and resource for students and their families.

By working ethically and responsibly with students and their families, Annalise hopes to help college-bound students with the entire college selection and application process. In order to generate a list of "good fit" institutions, Annalise will get to know each client well and will continually visit colleges to expand her knowledge in the field. Annalise wants to make sure that students are comfortable with the decisions they make, and she will manage the expectations of both the student and the parents. She will join professional organizations and stay abreast of current topics and news in the college counseling and consulting field.

Location and Facilities

CollegeFitMatchConsulting will operate from a home office. Annalise met with a local independent consultant who is currently practicing in her area, and the established consultant described the layout of her own home office: two chairs set up around a coffee table facing a couch. She and her partner sit in the chairs and the student (and parents) can sit comfortably on the couch. On the coffee table, she places a bowl of candy so the students can have sugar pick-me-ups if the meetings go long, and she feels like she's losing their attention. Annalise plans to adopt a similar setup. Additionally, Annalise will have a shelf filled with resource books and materials helpful for the college search and application experience. She will also have a computer station set up so that she and her clients can view and take virtual tours of schools together. Annalise will also make sure to stock notepads and pens on the table for the students and parents to take notes. She has a laptop that she will use with students who are working on essays or need help knowing how to research colleges.

Services

CollegeFitMatchConsulting offers a broad range of personalized services, which directly address the needs and interests of high school sophomores, juniors, seniors and their parents.

CollegeFitMatchConsulting typically meets with students on a comprehensive basis, although hourly services are available.

CollegeFitMatchConsulting services include, but are not limited, to:
1. Determine schools that are a good match for each student based on grades, test scores, personality, concerns, and finances; match criteria will also take into account the schools' selectivity, location/weather, proximity to home, diversity, academic environment, size, majors and departments, strength of curriculum, and the social environment on campus.
2. Help students generate a balanced list of schools to which they may want to apply, and narrow down the overwhelming number of options out there. Select at least three highly-selective (low chance of admission) schools, four with a 50/50 chance of admission (medium chance of admission), and three safety schools (with a high likelihood of admission). List building includes taking into consideration academic and pre-professional goals, financial considerations, and personal/extracurricular/athletic interests and needs.
3. Teach students how to search for colleges and how to self-identify good fit colleges.
4. Help students understand admission policies, requirements, terms, and their own responsibilities.
5. Explain the different types of institutions, including public vs. private, universities vs. colleges, national vs. regional, single-sex colleges, Historically Black Colleges and Universities (HBCUs), military colleges, professional colleges, international colleges, community and 2-year colleges, and religiously-affiliated institutions. Determine which types of schools may be the best fit for clients.

6. Make sure students are comfortable with the decisions they will make, and manage realistic expectations of both the student and the parents.
7. Set up a library of resources and materials for learning about individual schools and the application experience as a whole; join mailing lists for universities, create a file for each school, and consistently update each file with new school information; buy resource guides and books, have materials on-hand that students can access and borrow.
8. Assist with high school course selections.
9. Access and refine the student's academic and extracurricular credentials. Inform students about creative summer activities, employment opportunities, and internship programs.
10. Create timelines and due dates for assignments to keep students on track, and abide by each college's deadline.
11. Help generate and then review essay topics. Provide minimal editing services for students' personal statements and essays. Make sure essays reflect something the student is passionate about, and make sure that he/she wrote all text by himself/herself.
12. Advise students about standardized testing and organize an optimal testing schedule, including referrals to qualified tutoring services, as necessary.
13. Explore students' academic interests and related career directions.
14. Visit and tour colleges and universities nationwide in order to gain personal perspective and impressions about individual institutions.
15. Keep abreast of current trends, changes, and new policies in the college consulting profession and industry by engaging with IECA and HECA; attend annual conferences, and journals.

In terms of limits, Annalise plans to be a generalist when working with college-bound students, and she will probably not specialize in one particular aspect of the college process. For example, she can discuss learning disability programs, but Annalise will refer to another IEC if she feels that the case is beyond her expertise. The same is true in the area of financial management, athletic programs, and students seeking a conservatory.

CollegeFitMatchConsulting services do not include the following:
- Guarantees of admission into any particular college
- Advocacy for the students at college admissions offices
- Planning travel itineraries (for student college visits)
- Continued "nagging" to complete application materials
- Contact with admission directors on behalf of a student.

Objectives
CollegeFitMatchConsulting will work to serve 30 to 40 students per class per year. The goal in the next 12 months is to work with 15 juniors. Most students begin their college consulting process during fall of their junior year.

CollegeFitMatchConsulting offers both a process-oriented and a knowledge-oriented service.

The following are Annalise's thoughts about objectives and services:
Students will complete and we will discuss an Introductory Questionnaire. Questions are organized around the following areas: 1) personality strengths and weaknesses; 2) likes/dislikes; 3) passions and hobbies; 4) goals and dreams; 5) academic interests; 6) academic strengths and weaknesses; and 7) fears and concerns about college.

CollegeFitMatchConsulting believes that the first couple of meetings are especially important. These initial meetings set the flow and expectations for the remainder of time together. Annalise will go over what she can offer clients and what her expectations of students and parents include. She will present clients a binder containing her contact information, a calendar, a selection of good articles to read, and timelines for admission materials. Annalise will also give parents a questionnaire to fill out about their child, including questions about how they would characterize their child's personality and questions about their concerns and hopes for their child. While CollegeFitMatchConsulting's first priority is to make sure the students' needs are met, Annalise will also take into account the parents' views and perceptions.

Most of Annalise's students will be high school juniors and seniors. For underclassmen who seek Annalise's services, she will develop curriculum to support their specific needs. The exact number of meetings per student will depend on the student's year in school, individual needs, and own schedules. But, on average, Annalise anticipates meeting with most students approximately once every two to three weeks during the spring semester of their junior years and fall semester of their senior years.

Annalise believes it's never too early to start thinking about college and working hard in high school to ensure options for college. But her philosophy is that too much college planning focus in high school is excessive. Annalise will be open to meeting with freshmen to get them on track, but she does not plan on meeting with them more than once or twice a semester.

Moreover, Annalise is open to doing some pro bono work to help students and families who can't afford traditional private consulting fees. She will donate time to local fundraisers both as a way to support worthy causes and to get her name out to the local public. Annalise realizes that much of this career will be based on referrals, and she is comfortable starting out with lower fees in order to generate business and create a name.

Milestones
Annalise Durham's CollegeFitMatchConsulting was launched in [date]. Annalise attended IECA Summer Training Institute in [date], and she earned a certificate in independent educational consulting from the University of California, Irvine in [date]. Annalise is a member of HECA and an Associate Member of IECA. As of [date], Annalise has visited [blank #] of college campuses.

Milestones for future: Obtain Professional Membership in IECA [date], and obtain CEP designation [date]. Visit Wisconsin schools (COWS) [date], attend NACAC meeting [date], and visit colleges in Pacific Northwest. Visit as many of these colleges as possible: Manhattan College, Sarah Lawrence, Fordham, and CW Post, and visit Ohio colleges [date], including Ohio Wesleyan, Wittenberg, Kenyon, Denison, Miami of Ohio, Ohio University.

Keys to Success
Annalise's success will be measured by her ability to effectively manage a caseload of 40 students. "Effectively" is defined by feeling minimal or low levels of stress during peak business times (August through December), supporting all clients with adequate personal contact, and maintaining an active personal/social life. In addition, success means continuing to abide by all ethical standards as outlined by IECA, NACAC, and HECA.

A combination of factors is essential to becoming a successful consultant: knowledge of colleges, good time management, attention to detail, organization, good follow-through, the ability to put people at ease, determination, confidence, honesty, and experience.

Marketing Plan: Market Analysis

The market consists of upper-middle to upper-class families in the suburbs of Baltimore, Maryland. The area has several magnet high schools (IB) and many competitive public and private high schools. The typical public school guidance counselor has a caseload of approximately 600 students and does college counseling along with all other aspects of high school counseling. Many of these students will seek private consultants. Students who attend private schools in the area where the counselor caseload is significantly lower and a designated college counselor typically exists may also seek assistance outside of their schools. There is a mixture of needs among the population: high achievers who focus on the most selective institutions in the country, low achievers who have motivational issues, and learning disabled students who are in need of colleges with special programs or strong support services. Many students are interested in attending college out of state and most are interested in staying east of the Mississippi River.

Given the rising number of high school graduates and the subsequent increase in the number of college applications over the next few years, along with the diminishing number of high school guidance counselors in the suburban Baltimore community, Annalise is hopeful that her foray into independent educational consulting comes at a time of need.

Annalise feels a special obligation to handle high-income families appropriately. These families tend to be able to afford private services like tutors and educational consultants, but many of these individuals are also consumed with status. Here, Annalise anticipates a challenge, as her fundamental goal is to help each student find his or her best fit school rather than to generate generic lists that are identical to those of other prestige-seeking students.

Marketing: The Competition

There are at least 50 IECA or HECA college related educational consultants in Annalise's general vicinity. In addition, there are at least an additional 15 who do not yet have IECA, HECA, NACAC, or CEP credentials. Yet, Annalise does not believe that the market is saturated. In fact, most of the reputable consultants in the area are at caseload capacity. For the most part, the independent educational consultants in the greater metropolitan area are open and friendly with each other, eager to share information, and include one another in college presentations. Annalise has strong relationships with about ten other consultants in the area.

Annalise believes that there is enough business for everyone and that clients, when they know of availability, may choose CollegeFitMatchConsulting after interviewing several consultants. At this point, Annalise does not think that high school counselors are great sources of competition. Annalise brings a unique perspective, excellent preparation, and genuine enthusiasm to the field, which she believes will make her highly marketable.

Marketing: Strengths and Weaknesses

Annalise's strengths include her dedication to her clients and her knowledge about the industry, her commitment to visiting college campuses, her service-minded attitude, her flexibility with scheduling (including availability on weekends and evenings), and her warmth of personality. Annalise is encouraging and always has an optimistic attitude. She puts people at ease and facilitates harmony among family members. Annalise brings out the best in people by highlighting their strengths and suggesting ways that they can improve on their weaknesses. She has a solid understanding of the material on all standardized tests and can help students decide which test can best highlight their strengths. Because of her expertise in testing and long-standing relationships with tutors, Annalise can also make suggestions for appropriate test preparation.

Annalise is an excellent public speaker and is able to connect well with an audience. Annalise's client base comes from repeat families, client referrals, tutor referrals, and public speaking engagements.

Annalise enjoys all aspects of independent educational consulting: traveling to visit colleges, attending conferences (she attends at least two per year), meeting with students and parents, developing college lists, and brainstorming essays.

Writing is not one of Annalise's strengths, and it takes her a very long time to compose correspondences. Annalise sends out a monthly newsletter and follow-up letters after the initial intake meeting, and those letters take an inordinate amount of time to compose. Another weakness is Annalise's lack of a budget planning. She will need to curb her consumerism. Additionally, Annalise has been lax in contacting referrals and must actively pursue potential clients.

Annalise admits that her biggest weaknesses have to do with marketing herself online and starting up a business. While she is comfortable using the computer and internet, she is not comfortable with designing a website, which is critical in today's internet-age. She anticipates having a website that shows up on searches and hopes to initially include at least biographic information, contact info, and a bit of company history. Once this is established, Annalise hopes to one day introduce interactive features on the website. Her initial plan is to either scout the local community college for a student she can hire to get a website up and running or to enlist computer-savvy friends to help get her started.

As Annalise has always worked for other people's established businesses, she will have work to do in terms of setting up a business. She plans to set up an LLC, create a contract, acquire appropriate insurance, set up a billing system, and secure a business license.

There is one additional area that causes Annalise concern: She is in her mid 30's and doesn't know if age is going to be a strength or a weakness. On the one hand, Annalise is concerned that her age may be interpreted as inexperienced, but she tends to find her youth to be more of an asset than a liability. She hopes to bring youthful energy and a recent personal experience with applying to college to her practice. So many IECs in Annalise's market have learned a lot about the college application experience through their children, while Annalise personally went through the process just ten years ago. Annalise hopes to put a positive spin on this detail so as to counteract any potential of seeing age as a disservice.

Marketing: Specific Marketing Strategies
Annalise's marketing strategies include public speaking at local high schools and the Jewish Community Center. Most of Annalise's clients will be word-of-mouth referrals. Annalise will explore new avenues for marketing such as creating a website, joining local chamber of commerce groups, follow-up phone calls for potential for clients, and brown bag lunch presentations for corporations in the area. Annalise feels that as a result of new industry coming into town, corporations may be in the market for expert opinions about a wide range of topics, including college planning.

Specific marketing strategies:
1. Consistent advertising in local community newspaper and publications.
2. Advertise in local synagogue bulletins and newsletters to notify parents of services.
3. Leave cards with local offices and places teens frequently visit (doctors' offices, Starbucks, Barnes & Noble, dance studios, p\Pilates or yoga studios, gyms, etc.).
4. Donate mini packages of services to fundraisers.
5. Join NACAC and other professional organizations to stay on top of current news and events and to qualify for listing on professional websites.
6. Create promotional materials on paper and online, unified with a consistent logo and brand.
7. Email monthly newsletters to current students and potential students.
8. Tell everyone about the practice.
9. Find colleagues in the community with whom to establish cross-referral networks (financial aid consultants, test prep instructors, tutors).
10. Write an introductory letter to new members of the community (advertise in a local "New Home Services" guide).
11. Develop a professional business page on Facebook.
12. Once website is operating, update content regularly, posting resources and links to helpful information.
13. Check out Instagram or Snapchat to see if either platform would fit into marketing approach. Develop a social media presence.

Marketing: Evaluating Marketing Success

Annalise will look at business patterns and compare each month in the current year with the month from the previous year. Annalise will also look at the categories of expenses each month and compare them to the previous month. She will create a yearly budget for travel and office expenses. This is a priority as the business side of things has been mentioned as a weakness.

Materials

In addition to an electronic brochure, Annalise will prepare printed handouts. During the initial meeting, each client will be given a pocket folder with the following materials:
- CollegeFitMatchConsulting business card
- Several IECA brochures including: "Why IECA Members Are a Cut Above Other Independent College Consultants," "Top Ten Strengths and Experiences Colleges Look for in High School Students," and "10 Important Ways IECA Members Are Unlike Other College Consultants"
- Fast Web Quick Reference Guide
- Comparison Chart SAT/ACT
- "CollegeFitMatchConsulting: List of Favorite Internet Sites"
- "CollegeFitMatchConsulting: Favorite Books"
- "CollegeFitMatchConsulting: Making the Most of College Visits"
- "CollegeFitMatchConsulting: "College Visit Evaluation" sheets
- "CollegeFitMatchConsulting: "Client Fee Agreement"
- "CollegeFitMatchConsulting: "Why Are You Going to College?" questionnaire

Additional materials about college fairs, recommendation packet information, packing list, etc. will be provided during different points in the consulting cycle. All materials will be updated periodically.

All clients will receive a CollegeFitMatchConsulting monthly newsletter highlighting college admission trends, important reminders, and new information. This newsletter will be delivered both electronically and by postal mail.

Pricing and Money Issues

Most clients will hire CollegeFitMatchConsulting on a comprehensive basis. The fee is [$fee]. This fee will go up to [$fee] in six months. Throughout the admissions cycle, as time permits, CollegeFitMatchConsulting will take on hourly clients. The starting rate is [$fee]; it will go up in six months to [$fee].

The comprehensive fee includes preparation time, summary of progress report, and any other time needed to meet student and parent needs.

CollegeFitMatchConsulting will be clear about describing the differences between the two types of services. Some of these differences include: hourly clients will pay at the time of service; comprehensive clients will typically pay in two installments (half at the initial meeting, half during September of senior year); during busy season, hourly clients will be scheduled after comprehensive clients and may wait several weeks for an appointment; hourly clients will get billed for phone and email time whereas that time will be included in the fee for comprehensive clients; comprehensive clients receive unsolicited follow-up phone calls and email, and hourly clients will not.

Cash flow will be in the form of new client deposits, hourly client payments, and senior year (September) client payments.

Annalise hopes to transition her current job into a part-time position in order to begin to direct more of her time and energy (other than weekends and weeknights) into getting her practice up and running. However, she needs to generate immediate income and cannot quit her current job until her private practice shows signs of sustainability.

Technology

The office will maintain one desktop computer, one laptop computer, one landline, one mobile phone, and a copy/printer/scanner machine. Student records will be maintained in paper student binders. Each student binder will have dividers marked as follows: notes, transcript, standardized testing, activities resume, college list, applications/essays, client contact and other. The other category might include psycho-educational testing results, career assessment results, and client contract information. The face sheet for each client will contain demographic information on the client. A computer database will be maintained for each student which will include: name/address/phone numbers/parents' contact info/email addresses. A separate database will be maintained for group emails and will serve as a distribution method for the monthly newsletters.

CollegeFitMatchConsulting will use a web-based personality/career assessment. Students will be given access to the website and will self-administer the assessment in their homes.

Data on colleges will be kept on Word documents. In addition, hard copies will be kept in binders, and standing file cabinets will house college brochures and view books. All computer documents will be backed up on a portable hard drive.

Financial records will be kept in another database, and income/expense updates will be made daily, weekly, or monthly as needed and will be backed up monthly.

Legal Issues

The CollegeFitMatchConsulting Client Fee Agreement will contain the following disclaimer: "I understand that CollegeFitMatchConsulting will make every effort to be of assistance but cannot guarantee admission to any school. I will not hold CollegeFitMatchConsulting responsible for my child's success or happiness."

In addition, if the student, family, or Annalise Durham deems it necessary/important to contact another professional associated with the client (guidance counselor, therapist, or pediatrician), a "Release of Information and Waiver Form" will be required of the student and parent.

CollegeFitMatchConsulting, at this time, does not maintain any liability insurance. Annalise Durham plans on obtaining this insurance by [date].

Annalise will definitely have a contract that she will provide to students and their families at their first meeting. And, in materials outlining her services, she will indicate that she will not write essays for the student, nor will she fill out his/her applications.

Annalise will look into acquiring a business permit and any other permits or licenses needed to operate business out of her home. She will work up a contract with her uncle (who is an attorney) to help make sure that both she and the student(s) are on the same page with regard to what services she will offer within the fee.

Contingencies

There is no need for any business contingencies at this time. However, possible changes in business operations include:
- Fee collection (three installments, second or third installment in August rather than September)
- Distribution of newsletter in email form only
- Purchasing liability insurance
- Developing a blog
- Consider moving into leased space

Feelings

Although Annalise Durham is a pleaser by nature, she is aware that her consulting services cannot please everyone all of the time. She is relatively confident about her skills and the value of the service provided. Nonetheless, when she encounters a difficult parent, she will be eager to seek advice/support from colleagues who have more experience.

Annalise has no particular bias in terms of large/small colleges or liberal arts/pre-professional programs. Annalise believes that the important focus is choosing a college that is a good fit for the individual.

Future Services

There is some chance of expansion within the next three to five years, which would take the form of adding another consultant to the CollegeFitMatchConsulting practice. If, during the next three years, at least ten clients are turned away, such expansion will be more likely to occur. In addition, Annalise plans on obtaining the Myers-Briggs Type Indicator certification, and that training might bring in new clients. Finally, Annalise was a tuba player in her high school and college days. As such, she may learn more about admission to conservatories and begin to market her consulting services to these students as well.

*****

Is this CollegeFitMatchConsulting business plan excellent or perfect? No. But it is typical of a fairly comprehensive business plan. It provides an outline that is easy to follow and presents language that might be useful for any IEC to consider while developing a business plan. But this is her plan, not your plan. For example, Annalise is spending 25% of her time traveling. That's high for most IECs. She's creating a monthly newsletter that may or may not be in your initial business plan. Annalise is using "hourly"; I prefer "per consultation." Annalise is fairly optimistic about the number of students she will have during her first year, particularly since she is transitioning from her current job. She's keeping her records in both paper folders and electronic form while most have gone to all electronic filing systems. Further, this is a business plan of a consultant who is spending a lot of time with each of her students. As pointed out elsewhere in the book, more time with a student does not always lead to better consulting, and it definitely does not always lead to better college choices for the student. Her decision to start out with lower fees is a point worth discussing. Sometimes this strategy works; sometimes it suggests the IEC's lack of confidence. Annalise's targeting "upper-middle to upper-class families" is fine, but I wish she would give more attention to middle-income families.

BUSINESS CONTRACTS

Dealing with adolescents can present challenges. There are few rules, and each situation is different, but let me offer a few thoughts to get us going. Like so much in consulting, a critical element is your contract and your understanding with the family. It is important to be explicit about the role of everyone in the process, particularly the student. You want to be clear that you are not the parent and that you have no ability to get Buffy moving and meeting deadlines. You also want to explain that you are not responsible for Buffy's missed deadlines. That said, I try every persuasive technique I can think of to get Buffy to show up and do her work. I try to stay many weeks ahead of her deadlines. If a deadline is November 1, I begin to deal with it as if it were a crisis on October 1. I will always try to work directly with the student at first, but then (and this is known to everyone in advance) I will contact parents to tell them of an upcoming deadline, a delay in getting a draft essay done, or whatever. Throughout my years of doing this (recall that I started shortly after the Civil War), my persuasive strategies have had a 95% success rate. If I'm at the end of the line and neither Buffy or her parents are responsive, I fire myself. After all, I don't wear a badge and thus have no enforcement power. I will work hard to track Buffy down and try my best, but I can only do so much.

Reasons a Contract Is Essential:
- It's better to err on the side of caution than leave yourself exposed to possible lawsuits and contractual disputes.
- Damage control is much more expensive, stressful, and time-consuming than preventive action.

Contract Tips and Advice:
- Even though most IEC contracts are pretty straightforward, it is always advisable to run them by an attorney.
- Your contract should anticipate and address issues that could arise, regardless of whether a potential misunderstanding or disagreement seems likely to happen. For example, include specific actions that will be enforced in regard to delinquent accounts.
- To steer clear of misunderstandings, false assumptions, and ambiguity, the contract terms should be clear and concise.
- One method of assuring that all parties fully understand the intent and meaning of contract provisions is to include definitions of important terms in the document. For the IEC, that means "comprehensive program" might be defined and explained. The same holds for terms such as "essay help" or "availability."

- I don't feel it is advisable to use a stock or generic contract found on the web. Contracts reflect who you are as a person and who you are as a businessperson. We advise students to find their voice in writing personal statements. Similarly, we need to find our own voice when we write a contract. You can certainly use generic contracts for ideas about which points you need to cover.
- One important detail IECs sometimes overlook is whether a contract should be executed by an individual or a business entity, such as a corporation. Most typically, the IEC should sign the contract in the name of his or her business. Such action limits clients or customers from interfering with your personal assets.
- Some IECs don't like the idea of signing formal contracts with people they consider good friends or with whom they have a long-standing relationship. However, even in these cases, a written contract is advised.
- Begin by clearly stating the scope of the service or work you offer, as well as the timeline that you propose for the work to be completed.

Organization of a Typical Contract:
- Name of the parties (the IEC, the parent or guardian, the student)
- Scope of the services to be offered
- Approximate length of time for completion of services and the fees per services
- Comprehensive/per consultation/etc. (delivery model)
- Payment schedule
- Ability of both parties to part ways amicably
- Sign and date demonstrating that both parties are satisfied with the terms and conditions of the contract

Sample Business Contracts

Please note that the following examples are fictional.

Sample Contract #1

Penny Pinsky, LLC
Educational Consultant
15 College Street
Mt. Caramel, SD 88421

Educational Consulting Agreement

This agreement is made, effective as of (current date) between Penny Pinsky, LLC and the following party(ies) for services to be rendered by Consultant for the benefit of (name of student).

Name/relationship to student:

The parties agree as follows:

1. Consultant is engaged to render the following services and the responsible party agrees to pay the applicable fees indicated:
    a. Package Work: College search: assessment of records: investigation of pertinent colleges; interview, visit, application and essay advising, student and parent conferences. [fee stated here]
    b. By Consultation Work: Educational consultations: Any and all time spent working on the student's educational planning will be clocked and billed. [fee stated here]
    c. Other Work Plan: [nature of services and fee stated here]
2. For Package Work, a fee of [$fee] is due prior to commencement of services by Consultant. The balance is payable in full within one month or upon receipt of billing statement. By Consultation and Other Work Plan payable at time of service.
3. Consultant will make every good faith effort, utilizing her knowledge and expertise, to effect a suitable college placement. However, results cannot be guaranteed, and the designated fees are payable whether or not placement or other desired result is accomplished. Fees are to be paid in full even if the Consultant is instructed by the responsible party to terminate her efforts. The Consultant will be available for telephone consultation for one semester after college placement. Any consultation for transfer will necessitate an additional fee.
4. Interest on overdue account balance is payable at the rate of 1 and 1/2% per month. If it is necessary and reasonable for Consultant to engage legal counsel for consultation or other representation in connection with any dispute arising out of this Agreement or the services to be performed hereunder or the collection of any delinquent account balance hereunder, responsible party agrees to reimburse Consultant for all legal fees and related costs and expenses actually paid or incurred by Consultant in connection herewith.
5. It is the student's/family's responsibility to schedule college visits, complete and mail applications, write essays, maintain steady communications with Consultant to facilitate placement and monitor status of application, and notify schools of intentions.

Responsible Party (signature here)
Responsible Party (signature here)
Consultant (signature here)

Sample Contract #2

Contract for Independent Educational Consulting Services

Parties:
This agreement is between Sonia Swarm, Independent Educational Consultant, doing business as College Expert, Inc., and _____, in the capacity of parent, guardian, or guarantor of payment, for services to be rendered by Consultant for the benefit of _____, a high school student currently in the _____ grade.

Payment:
Parent, guardian, or guarantor of payment agrees to pay Consultant a sum of $_____ for a package of maximum twenty-five hours of professional consulting services provided by Consultant as described below. Payment in full is due at the time the Consultant is retained, unless an alternative payment schedule is agreed upon.

These are the services Consultant **will** provide for the student:
- Represent the student accurately, based upon a professional evaluation of circumstances and requirements of each client's educational and social needs.
- Provide the most current information about colleges and best judgment about options available.
- Respect the integrity of the consulting relationship, and of all relevant information protecting the privacy of the student and family.
- Offer support and structure for the family.
- Evaluate the student's record, including high school transcript, standardized test results, extracurricular activities, athletic activities, and special talents.
- Assist in selection of high school academic curricular choices and plan extracurricular activities, including meaningful summer activities.
- Assess career and possible college major interests.
- Explain and provide guidance through the college planning process (discussion of standardized tests, testing options, application deadlines, etc.).
- Clarify student's priorities and requirements for his/her college experience, understand the selection criteria of specific colleges or universities, and research and select appropriate schools to generate a long list of good match schools.
- Create a list of target of schools for the student to visit and prepare student to conduct meaningful visits.
- Refer to resources for test preparation and academic tutoring, if necessary.
- Develop student interview skills and confidence through mock interviews.
- Assist in narrowing down the "long list" of good match schools to a shorter list of best match schools, with varying degrees of admission difficulty, to which the student will apply.
- Discuss and evaluate early decision, early action, and other decision options.
- Assist with preparation of activity list and/or résumé.
- Assist with selection of recommendation letter writers.
- Assist with essay writing—primarily including topic development and critique.
- Assist with preparation of supplemental materials.
- Assist with application preparation—including organizational assistance, time and stress management, and making suggestions for the order of information to be included on the application.
- Assist with application follow-up procedures.
- Respond to emails and phone calls in a timely manner.
- Assist with final decision concerning which college to attend.

- Assist with wait-list or appeal process, if necessary.
- Assist student and family with transition-to-college process.

These are things the parent/guardian should do:
- Support their child throughout the process.
- Understand the pressures on the student.
- Assist in helping keep student on task.
- Allow the student to take the lead in college planning decision making.

These are services Consultant **will not** provide:
- Consultant does not guarantee that student will be admitted to any particular college or university.
- Consultant will not write student's essays or fill out admission, financial aid, or scholarship application forms.
- Consultant will not write the counselor recommendation—this is done by the high school counselor.
- Consultant will not select a college major for student.
- Consultant will not accept compensation from schools in exchange for placement.
- Consultant will not contact admissions officers to promote admission.
- Consultant will not assure that deadlines are met and will not "track down" students who miss meetings.
- Consultant will not be on call 24/7.
- Consultant will not text or advise via any social networking site.

These are things the Student must do for him/herself:
- Put full effort into the process.
- Do the very best academic work possible.
- Cooperate fully with Consultant.
- Meet all deadlines required for testing and completing applications.
- Request letters of recommendation and transcripts in a timely manner, pursuant to the procedures established by student's high school.
- Ask questions when things are unclear.
- Take the initiative to call or email Consultant when s/he needs an appointment, has questions, or has essays ready for review.
- Keep appointments.
- Enjoy the process!

Signatures:

This Contract for Education Consulting Services has been read, understood, and agreed upon by the following:

Parent, Guardian, or Guarantor of Payment
Parent, Guardian, or Guarantor of Payment
Student for whom services are provided
Education Consultant, College Expert
Date:

*****

Please do not use either of these contracts as your own! There are just too many differences from one IEC to the next, from one state to another, and even from those practicing in the US versus those operating outside. They are presented here to prompt you to think about areas of practice that are important to any contract. Further, each of these contracts has positives and negatives. Penny is particularly clear on the ethical side but shy on having a clear description of the services she will provide. Sonia, on the other hand, has a comprehensive list of her services, and I think that her list of dos and don'ts for the IEC, the student, and parents is appealing.

In addition to the legalities involved, having a clear, logical, thorough contract is essential to the delivery of your services. Much as a blueprint tells the contractor and the subs what goes where, the IEC's contract tells the student and the parent about expectations, costs, limits, and scope of the service. A good contract saves time, money, and energy through the college planning months.

(See resources at astudentofcolleges.com for additional information on business tools.)

PRICING: LET'S TALK MONEY

Pricing is so complex that it can fill a book of its own! Here, let's grapple with some of the major concerns that an IEC must address when starting a private practice.

Determining What Your Services Are Worth

The process of determining how much to charge for your services is often fraught with uncertainty and apprehension. Charging too much may seem unjustified on the basis of inexperience. Charging too little may signal lack of confidence. When initially assessing the monetary value of your services, keep in mind a few key points. First, inexperience doesn't mean lack of knowledge. It may mean lack of *lots of* knowledge—particularly about specific colleges. However, don't forget the importance of the process side of our work. (See Chapter 7 for the distinction between process-oriented and knowledge-oriented consulting). Don't minimize the value of your life experiences in being a successful IEC. Similarly, don't downplay the need that parents have for a great process consultant. In other words, even as a novice, you likely have a great deal to offer. Second, remember the importance of your personality. Lynn O'Liam, the veteran IEC across town who has visited over 200 colleges, might be painfully dull. Families might prefer to be in your presence. Yes, newer consultants often charge less (and are upfront about the reasons), but don't sell yourself short.

When I left my salaried position at the University of Denver in 1981, I had to determine a reasonable fee for my consulting services. There was nothing scientific about my decision. I arrived at a comprehensive fee of $1,500 based on several factors: discussions with other consultants (for example, I felt I couldn't charge as much as colleagues on the East coast as the profession was much older and more well known there), my experience in college admissions, my sense of the value I would add to the college planning table, and my guess as to what people might be willing to pay for a service that was not well known at the time.

In those days I didn't fret *will anyone pay $1,500 for my college counseling advice?* Rather, I pondered *where will I find parents who will pay me $1,500 for my college counseling advice?* That motivational perspective allowed me to keep pushing and keep working to make my practice successful.

Note that I set an end date for the $1,500 fee. In other words, I established from the outset that I would not be forever bound to my initial comprehensive fee. I launched my practice with a personal goal that the $1,500 fee would be valid only for nine months. Come nine months, I could elect to keep the fee the same or change it.

Over the course of a career spanning three decades, I've changed my fees perhaps 15 times. Some years my fees increase, and some years they decrease, depending on many factors: how many meetings are included, how busy I am, the demographics I'm seeking in my office, and so forth. You can, and often should, change fees as your experience increases, as you alter the format of your services, or as your market changes. You can increase your service charges again if you are successful at the new rate, whether it be a new per consultation rate or a new comprehensive fee package.

Tips to Help New IECs Determine the Monetary Worth of Their Services

- One way to determine how much to charge is to do an appraisal of your background, readiness, and skills. Relevant factors to keep in mind include education, prior work experience, motivation, and commitment. Compared to a novice with zero experience, how much is your time worth? Some say you should charge $5 per year of school or experience, some say you should charge $10 per year of school or experience, and some say you should charge on a scale from $0 (novice) to $100 or even $1,000 (the best of the best).
- Another way to determine worth is to compare yourself to other IECs in your area. Professional associations can give you collective data. IECA, for example, frequently surveys its members and publishes average comprehensive and hourly fees. These are often listed according to region. Calling IECs randomly and asking what they charge is rarely successful. A few IECs have fees listed on their websites, but more are willing to talk to you about pricing as a part of a larger discussion of state or local issues related to a consulting practice, service delivery models, and so forth.
- You can also assess your relative worth based upon how much other professionals in your community charge. For example, research similar occupations that require comparable levels of education or experience. Some examples include director of admission, nutrition advisor, tutor, or career counselor.
- Also consider what service professionals in your community charge. For example, how much is a 60-minute massage? If it costs $100 for a massage, how does your expertise stack up against those of the masseur? How much does a private fitness trainer charge? How much do people pay gardeners or pet sitters?
- Spending some time browsing salary websites can be helpful: payscale.com and salary.com are two of these. For example, salary.com gives you how much a career counselor in Chicago makes in a year. You can find annual salary as well as hourly and can also see how variables such as number of years of experience affect salary.

Factors to Consider Before Establishing a Fee Structure

Setting an informed initial price for the services you offer involves several considerations. Step one in forming a fee structure is to come to a clear understanding of your financial needs and your work style preferences. Play with the key variables: income goals, work schedule (hours per week, weeks per year), methods of delivery options (hourly versus comprehensive). Think about these questions: How much money do I want to earn per year? How many hours per week do I want to work? How aggressive do I want to be about adding more clients?

It is also important to assess your efficiency. If you are 20% more efficient than a competitor, you'll work 20% faster, meaning you'll log 20% fewer hours and will wrap up 20% sooner.

Additionally, realistically consider how much behind-the-scenes time consulting requires, especially for a novice. For example, when I started my practice, I spent approximately five hours building each college list. I researched in every way I could from calling colleagues for advice to reviewing view books (when I started, I had a library of college view books, alphabetized by state) to rereading notes from my maiden campus visits. Of course, I did not bill clients for excessive hours that I myself acknowledged as "learning the ropes" time. As a new IEC, you may need to "eat" some preparatory hours until you get into a groove. The key in starting a practice is to arrive at a method of charging that respects the value of your time and covers the worth of the time you have taken to visit colleges and to become a helpful advisor. (Note that over the years, the time I needed to generate a list has decreased. That's because I've visited more colleges, attended more conferences, and learned ways to research more efficiently. More than anything, I now know where to look for answers.)

Each IEC will need to gauge how many behind-the-scenes hours to build into a business day (and into a consulting curriculum). While I'd like to provide an absolute number, there are too many idiosyncratic factors involved. I can, however, point you to the ballpark. See the sample comprehensive programs in Chapter 5. You will note that one of the comprehensive delivery samples suggests 12 meetings and the other 18 meetings. For the 12-meeting model, it is reasonable to expect to log double the number of hours provided in order to account for all non-contact time: research, phone, text, etc. This figure also takes into consideration that some meetings will last longer than one hour. For the 18-session model, the IEC might expect to log an additional 12 hours of non-contact time. Having more face-to-face meetings often slightly reduces behind-the-scenes hours. Understand, please, that these proportions are illustrative only. What you need to do is make your price point realistic in terms of the work required that the student and/or parent never sees.

Let me offer an analogy. The travel service Kayak used to display "We're searching" while checking to find the best hotel deal. "Wow!" a user might say. "Look at all of this work that Kayak did for me." IECs are the Kayaks of college planning! We need to let the student and the parent know that our identification of good fit colleges is the result of the huge database in our minds and in our files.

The point is that much of what we do for a student is hidden. That is, it is not obvious. So, for example, if it takes me 15 minutes to come up with a great list of colleges for Buffy, what is not obvious are the years of visiting colleges, studying colleges, and knowing colleges that factor in to my ability to come up with an on-target list quickly. Here's an illustrative connection: During a remodel a couple of years ago, one of my favorite oil paintings was damaged. Something hit the piece, leaving a noticeable mar. I took it to a framer to see if he could repair it. He said yes, and I returned a couple days later. Miraculously, the damaged area looked like it did before the accident. The repair was perfect. I couldn't even tell where the damage had been. When I asked what I owed him for the repair, he said, "You don't owe me anything. It only took me five minutes to repair." I replied, "No. It took you a lifetime to fix it." What I meant was that he had developed his knowledge of paints, color, and oil on canvas over the years. In the wrong hands, the piece could have been ruined. I owed him a fee commensurate with his knowledge, not on the basis of how long it took him to do the work.

Pricing Models
An IEC may elect to set a pricing structure according to one of the three models below:

1. The Per Consultation/Hourly Model
Common sense suggests that starting with an hourly rate is the best way to break in. I, however, have not found that to be true. The hourly model works well for some professionals yet not as well for others. Psychologists have operated on an hourly basis for decades. For IECs, however, the hourly model is more difficult, although not impossible. There are consultants whose students are best served hourly, but most of our clients don't always know what they need. They might think, for example, that meeting once and getting suggestions on colleges (a knowledge base that takes years to develop) is worthy of only a one-hour fee, or they might not realize that college planning is a process that involves sequential steps and is

best carried out over several encounters. From a practical standpoint, meeting hourly means much more billing and "money time" than I personally want to take. Alternatively, advertising chunks of time packaged together is another popular approach. Having a "college list" package containing up to three meetings and up to five hours of contact time (phone, email, etc.) for a set fee might work. If you choose an hourly model, be sure that clients are aware that you will include behind-the-scenes time in your invoices.

2. Percentage of Tuition Model

One way to set your comprehensive fee is to calculate your price according to a percentage of the annual cost of attending a college or university. For instance, in a recent year, the average total cost of attending a private college (including tuition and fees, room and board, books and supplies, personal expenses, and transportation) was approximately $50,000. This is based on College Board averages as follows: tuition and fees $33,480; room and board $11,890; books and supplies $1,230; and personal and transportation $2,720. Some IECs choose this approach because they reason that if a client is planning on spending $50,000 a year on college tuition, it is worth it for the client to make a 5 to 10% investment in IEC services. A possible advantage of this model is that as tuition costs go up, so will the IEC's salary.

If the IEC charged 5% or 10% of the annual average cost noted above, the comprehensive fee would be somewhere between $2,500 and $5,000. Alternatively, the total cost for students attending public colleges or universities out of state is approximately $40,000. This means that an IEC fee at 5% would be $2,000 and at 10% would be $4,000 for public out-of-state schools. The average cost for in-state residents attending public universities was approximately $25,000, meaning an IEC fee of 5% would be $1,250 and a fee of 10% would be $2,500 in-state.

IECs should not raise or lower an established set fee based upon the college that Buffy ultimately attends. The model is designed to help IECs gauge a reasonable pricing structure in relation to the larger cost of college attendance.

3. The Juggling of Variables Model

Alternatively, consider calculating a comprehensive fee based on the number of clients you intend to serve and the salary that you want to make. This formula stipulates that the price for a comprehensive plan for a single student should equal the sum of your expected salary and your expenses divided by the number of students you will serve each year. For example, if you wish to net $25,000 and your expenses total $12,500, the sum of the two figures is $37,500. If you work with 15 clients, the comprehensive fee per student would be $2,500; using the same net salary and total expenses, if you work with ten clients, the comprehensive fee would be $3,750 per student.

The formula is restated here:
(Target Salary + Expenses) / Number of Students = Comprehensive Fee

When considering these variables, be sure to create a manageable quota of hours for each comprehensive package. Without a limit on the number of hours that you will see each student, you will jeopardize your profit potential and your life outside of your work. It is also important to make an estimate of your unbilled hours.

Budgeting in Accordance with Pricing Models

As a beginning consultant, you may only have five students and may not net any profit. In fact, you may incur a net loss if your expenses exceed your profit. It's difficult to get started in private practice, and you must be willing to brave the waves until your practice grows. To help prevent a tsunami of unexpected expenses, I provide the worksheet below. The worksheet illustrates common expenses associated with private practice as an IEC and allows you to estimate expenses, gauge the likelihood of fluctuation, and strategize how to keep expenses manageable. It's critical to estimate expenses before embarking upon any type of private practice. The worksheet below is applicable to all three of the above pricing models.

Note that when you use the worksheet, you may need to adjust your expenses in relation to the number of students you plan to serve annually. Frequently, there are costs associated with an individual student, such as office materials, fees for software, and so on. In addition, advertising costs will vary as a result of geographic location, years of experience and referral base, comfort with online and free advertising, and so forth. Business textbooks recommend that 4% to 12% of annual revenue be spent on advertising.

Common Expenses	Estimated Annual Expense if Applicable	Startup Expense or Recurring Expense?	Strategies to Minimize Expenses
Health Insurance			
Liability Insurance			
Advertising/Website			
Office Space			
Office Supplies			
Management System			
Travel			
Professional Association Dues			
Conference Fees			
Accounting and Legal Fees			
Vehicle			
TOTAL EXPENSES:			

General Pricing Rules (The Antonoff Pricing Bible)

I have two steadfast rules of pricing:

1. Thou shall put an expiration date on fees to allow for change. For example, stipulate "Prices are current through August 31, [year]."
2. Thou shall not offer unlimited time in a comprehensive package. Comprehensive packages, as described in Chapter 5, should be priced with a clear statement of number of meetings and total number of hours to be spent with a student. For example, "My comprehensive fee for all of the services listed is $X. The fee includes up to Y direct student and/or parent meetings and up to Z hours of consultant time. Consultant time includes meetings, email, phone, text, research, and any other work on behalf of the student." The IEC can always go over the number of Y or Z hours, but put families on notice that you are not available 24/7 for an indefinite period of time.

General Pricing Tips

- Avoid being tentative when you talk to parents about your fees. Be confident and assertive.
- Pricing should be kept simple. It is typically best to pick one or at the most two ways to be compensated for your services. Picture your fee structure on a price sheet and consider whether it is easy to understand. Do not confuse potential clients. As it is, clients for college consulting services seldom know what they need. Further, they may not realize the work that goes into the development of a college list.
- If you choose a per consultation/hourly structure, it is important to remember that as your number of hours per week decreases, your hourly salary will have to increase to make up the difference. Also remember that in order to make charging hourly a successful business structure, you will need to charge for all of the time spent working on behalf of the client (research hours, email or text hours, phone time, and so on).
- Regardless of what fee structure you may choose, try to extrapolate what you intend to make annually (in dollars per year) to obtain a more tangible estimate of how your fees can affect your profit and salary.
- In-person time is just as valuable as virtual time. As such, I encourage you to charge the same amount for each mode of meeting.
- It is not atypical for new IECs to have a net loss in the first year because of the traveling, campus tours, office equipment, and overall steep learning curve. Plan wisely for this.
- Charging on a sliding scale, in my opinion, tends not to work. Frankly, I don't like to intrude that much into family finances. Consider instead the alternative option to offer half or full scholarships for your services.
- It is better to have a fairly tight fee schedule and make exceptions, if necessary, rather than to have one that is too lax. For example, it is normally better to have a set fee and then discount for professional colleagues, family members, or whomever.
- Your fee structure needs to be priced high enough to allow for you to make a living.
- I firmly believe that giving away 80% of your knowledge for free makes a lot of sense. Give away timetables for college planning, essay writing tips, and lists of affordable test preparation tutors. The reason I give all of that away is to get clients to pay for the very significant other 20%: the matching process. No matter how many handouts you distribute or how many speeches you give for free, none gives away your bread and butter: the knowledge of colleges that really fit Brutus!
- It's up to you to create value for your work. Here's an example. A customer says he is not going to use your services because you are too expensive. He claims that $100 for college counseling is too much, and he can't afford you. Let's say your retort is this, "Okay. Then I'll work with you for $50." Most clients will still not buy into your service! The initial hesitancy—couched in financial considerations—may not be the real reason that the customer doesn't want your service. Perhaps he just doesn't like you! (That's okay!) Or maybe you have not made it clear why you are a value added.
- Note that fee-setting is a dynamic process. It evolves as one grapples with the realities of the market, business goals, and professional considerations.

How to Bill

A component of pricing is how to bill. Be vigilant about fees when you start. This means to bill quickly and perhaps collect before or during the early stages of work with a family. For comprehensive programs, I generally bill three equal payments. One-third of the comprehensive fee is due at the time a contract is signed, one-third is due before the final college list is delivered, and the remaining third is due before major work begins on college essays. I have always had individualized payment options. For example, some families pay me monthly. Indeed, I'm eager to make whatever reasonable payment plan makes sense for a family.

Nonpayment is rare in my practice (and for most consultants). It happens, but fortunately not often. I have had very few delinquent accounts over the years. After a few years, most of your clients will come by word of mouth, and these referrals tend to be good about payment. This is particularly true if the person who referred paid promptly. As noted previously, be sure to include a stipulation in your contract that addresses delinquent accounts.

In my recent study of consultant practices, I found that while some consultants accept credit or debit cards or PayPal, most prefer to be paid by check. Be sure to consider the fees that you will incur if you accept payment that is not in the form of a check.

Fee-related Conflicts

IECs deal with the public, and there will be unhappy clients. Our goal, of course, is not to have dissatisfied clients! Strive to under-promise and over-deliver. Practicing in accordance with such a maxim minimizes the potential for conflict.

When I do face conflict, it's fairness that guides my actions. If I feel that a refund of half of my comprehensive fee is justified, I give it. If a full refund is justified, I give it. Likewise, if I feel strongly that a disgruntled family is treating me unfairly, I pursue money due. I operate according to fairness, yet I also try to minimize the time it will take me to fight for payment.

Even early in my career, it was more important for me to concentrate my efforts toward doing a great job for other students than toward devoting the hours and energy necessary to go back and forth in a dispute with a family.

If after signing a contract I fire myself due to unforeseen ethical conflicts that arise such as a parent who encourages Brutus to fabricate his extracurricular involvements or a parent who insists on writing Buffy's essay, often, but not always, I return money already paid. There are no rules for how to handle such circumstances. Yes, a business contract should stipulate terms of conflict resolution and should be upheld. Ultimately, the IEC may decide that the easiest course of action is to refund payment, cut losses, and move on.

Tips to Avoid Conflict

- Clearly stipulate expectations and limits on a business contract.
- Never guarantee that Buffy will get in and be happy and/or successful at her chosen college! Such guarantees are not only unrealistic and unethical, but they may also result in loss of payment or in litigation.
- Remember the importance of record-keeping. Keep detailed records of the dates of your contacts with students and parents, the topics discussed, the advice you provided, and action steps you promoted. These notes can be particularly helpful if a client begins to complain.
- Look for red flags. If you haven't heard from a student or a family in a few weeks, call to see what's up and how to get back on track. Call if a student misses a meeting or two or if a payment is missed.
- Request an evaluation of your services now and then. In other words, an email with "I've met with Brutus two times, and I want some feedback on how I'm doing" is useful. (As a common courtesy, do not bill for feedback.)
- Warn families when/if they are nearing the maximum allowed hours of a comprehensive plan. In my statement of fees, I note that if the number of meetings or the number of hours is close to being exceeded, I will notify the family and we will, together, determine how to proceed. (Be aware that the number of hours I choose is high enough to ordinarily not be exceeded.) At such a point, we can agree

to an additional fee for additional time, we can agree to meet fewer times in upcoming weeks, or we can agree to convert to a per-consultation plan. Or, particularly if it's the spring semester of the senior year, we can agree to continue with no further charges. Avoid potential conflict by keeping families abreast of their accounts.

BUSINESS MISSION: PRO BONO WORK AND TARGETING UNINFORMED AND/OR UNDERSERVED POPULATIONS

Pro bono ("for the good of the people" in Latin) is defined as working without charge and carries the connotation of work that is undertaken because of the recipient's low income. Most veteran IECs work with clients in this way, and I hope that continues. In my mind, it's not enough, however, for IECs to be receptive to helping a housekeeper's daughter or the niece of the manicurist. That's fine and admirable, but pro bono work can and should have a greater impact upon community and society. Pro bono work in this profession (and in countless others) can change lives. We can reach a broader spectrum of the population through pro bono work and can enlighten youth and families to the value of higher education. As a credit to the profession and a boon to communities both local and national, let's make a commitment to giving.

As a component of your business, create a specific plan to provide outreach. Explore connecting and/or partnering with underfunded and/or understaffed high schools. Such an exploration, moreover, ought to include nonprofits such as I Have a Dream Foundation, local Latino/Hispanic organizations, etc. IECs can make contact with the counselor/principal/director at one of these schools or programs and suggest conducting workshops, sharing college visit information with public school counselors, or even helping to organize a summer "Boot Camp" for first-generation students. Publicize your willingness to help. In other words, it's best to be pro-active in your willingness to work pro bono; make pro bono work part of your professional identity.

If a family cannot pay, we should be able to make room for them in our practices. But let's remember the difference between *inability* to pay and *unwillingness* to pay. Obviously, there are families with real financial woes. Again, let's provide for them. Recognize, however, that there are families who know that Buffy will go to State U and don't want to invest in exploring other options. And there are families who can afford a comprehensive program but don't put a priority on college planning (and thus don't see a need for our services). As a profession, we should embrace giving our services to those who are *unable* to pay.

Beyond pro bono work, a component of your business mission should be to seek out clients—students and families—who are uninformed or underserved. Uninformed needs to be defined broadly to include any populations that would not "automatically" search for an IEC. It is not just the rich, the bright, or the private school student who should have access to great college advising. In fact, while I understand how significant it is for a student to decide between Tufts and Northwestern (two schools of roughly similar admission standards), my heart aches for the student who doesn't know she can get a scholarship to any four-year college or the student who thinks, because of cost, he will not be able to go to college at all. Consider how rewarding it is to inform a lower-income Latina student that she doesn't need to "settle" for the in-state option *without even considering other choices*. There is nothing inherently wrong with choosing an in-state option, but there is plenty wrong with not knowing that you really do have options. Working with these populations may be without charge or at a lesser charge, but no assumptions should be made. With increasing frequency, consultants are choosing to focus their energies on these populations. Some IECs target specific underserved populations, forming nonprofit businesses, or providing college consulting through a nonprofit or community-based organization.

I also include in this category a middle or upper-class family who is just not aware of the ins and outs of the college planning process. For example, I see students from South Dakota. Most are white and seemingly fairly affluent—but they are not admission savvy. Many are not aware of the value of looking nationally to find good match colleges. Many are unaware of the prevalence of test prep to help assure as many college options as possible. Many haven't heard of merit scholarships. These students need to be served just as much as lower income or first-generation students. I hope that you will make your services available for these less savvy students.

For those IECs who wish to expand their client base to include lower-income students, know that the reward is invaluable. To embark on such a mission, consider the following strategies:

- Lower your prices. To make up the income, see more clients. To make that work, alter the number of hours you spend with each client. At least consider having more than one "price point" for your services.
- Have more than one service option. Comprehensive services are typical, and they are fairly easy to maintain. But you may attract an entirely new client base by adding a shorter comprehensive program that is less costly.
- Consider group meetings for some students in your practice. Add hourly or per-consultation options to your price list.
- Reach out! Consider your marketing techniques. Is your marketing focused only or mainly on attracting affluent clients? If so, it's time to reconsider. Targeted marketing can be effective in generating more buzz for your services among these student groups: first-generation, Latino/a, African American, homeschooled, gay/lesbian students, "dreamers," students from the "other side" of your town, and on and on. (Note that many included in one or more of these groups are able and willing to pay your regular fee.)
- Take your college knowledge on the road. Have lunch college planning programs at an industrial park or a local factory. Put on a program for a local Native American organization or a local nonprofit that offers college scholarships.
- Consider forming a nonprofit. It's worth exploring the pros and cons of starting your own educational planning nonprofit organization. Very, very broadly, if the point of your business is to make money, then the business should, generally speaking, be for-profit. If the point of your business is to give away services, then being a nonprofit should be considered. Some form a nonprofit if they don't feel the business can be viable in five years. People also form a nonprofit if they feel that they can raise the capital to build their consulting practice and serve students via individuals, philanthropists, foundations, and other nonprofits. The legal and tax laws vary from state to state. Some states, for example, give nonprofits benefits such as tax exemptions. Instead of the owner receiving the profit (as is the custom in a for-profit business), any money that's left after the organization has paid its bills is put back into the organization in a nonprofit. Despite these restrictions, you can still receive a salary, but your nonprofit would have to report significantly more information about your organization's finances because of financial transparency regulations. You should also note that the legal fees for creating a nonprofit are significantly more than those associated with creating a for-profit company and may even require a lawyer to file for tax exemption.

MARKETING

Effective marketing promotes sales (for IECs, that is generally more clients) and profit. While always important, a marketing plan is particularly important as most forecasts show a decline in college enrollment over the next decade. Marketing your business is central to success. At the very least, you need to know your market. This includes an understanding of your competition and your approach to dealing with that competition. Sometimes competition is from other consultants, sometimes from books and websites, and sometimes it's from counselors in public schools. Suss out the competition. You will also need to analyze your strengths and weaknesses. Are you a good speaker? Are you comfortable making calls to friends about yourself and your service? Finally, consultants need a specific plan for marketing. What will you do to either get the numbers of clients you want/need or to reshape your clientele into the students/parents you feel you best serve?

Here are ten tips about marketing:

1. This is not *Field of Dreams*. Just because you open a practice doesn't guarantee that the clients will come. They will come if you sell yourself. When I left the University of Denver, I thought people would flock to see a former dean of admissions and financial aid. Not only did clients not flock, but they also didn't assemble at all. I needed to market my services aggressively. I needed to call friends, relatives, former colleagues and everyone else on my contact list. I needed to write articles and speak locally. In other words, I needed to aggressively say, "hire me." That was tough as I'm not inclined to be that brazen. But I knew that if I ever wanted to be successful as an IEC, I needed to make my business known.

2. While search engine optimization is important, it is only one tool in your marketing arsenal.

3. Marketing needs to fit your style and reflect your mission statement.

4. Timing is important. Just because a marketing approach didn't work last May doesn't mean it is not worth trying again in January.

5. In areas with many consultants, you need to think through how your practice will be different from others'. Maybe you'll spend more time with each student than other consultants do. Maybe you'll spend more time talking about colleges and less time talking about applications. In other words, your model of delivery is very much a marketing decision. Consider what it is that you find easy to do that others may find hard, and concentrate on that aspect of your business. If you are a great speaker, for example, go above and beyond to market your talents in that area. Also related to the above is the notion of being comfortable with your discomfort. As an introvert, try going into a crowd and telling everyone what you do. Recognizing and trying to deal with discomforts is essential to IEC success.

6. Networking is important and can be accomplished in many settings. Network at meetings and use the services of the people that you network with so that they will in turn refer or use you.

7. Always have business cards with you, and distribute them liberally.

8. Beat your competition with service. Answer phone calls and emails within 24 hours. It is amazing how we have all gotten used to bad service and then are so delighted when we get treated in a reasonable manner. Let your personal service be a marketing point. Work to convert potential clients into actual clients. A high conversion rate is often the easiest way to increase business. If a family makes contact with you, respond multiple ways (email, phone, second email, second phone, send an interesting article about college admission, etc.).

9. Don't just talk about what you do. Talk about the *benefits* of what you do.

10. Be able to give a 30-second business card description of your services. I call this a 30-second elevator speech. Thirty seconds is, theoretically at least, the length of a typical elevator ride.
    - The elevator speech to avoid: *I am an independent educational consultant. My office is at the corner of Hollywood and Vine. I work with high school students on college readiness and planning.*

I review high school courses and test scores to help a student decide on his or her college options. I help all the way through the process.

- A better one: *I can take the stress out of college planning. Parents and students can be at odds during the college admission process. I can help bring sanity and order to your household in the year before your son or daughter leaves for college. My knowledge of colleges will result in less confusion and more focus on colleges where your student will thrive.*
- Another example: *As a student of colleges, I can direct you to college options that are affordable. I can help you find great colleges that cost less, colleges that give out lots of money to students, and colleges that offer a good return on your investment.*
- Another: *I'm a private college counselor with the time to really get to know your student and help [her] find a great college match. I research and study colleges for a living. Working with me can help you identify colleges where Buffy will be happy and successful.*

Digest the ideas above and remember that, most important of all, financial success depends on sheer number of hours per month spent on marketing your business. Consulting businesses are built with dedication, patience, know-how, and hard work. Mainly, the latter. To be more precise about the hours needed to promote your service, my observation is that someone who wants to be successful in this career should spend as much as 20% of his or her time marketing. This doesn't necessarily mean working on a new website. It means active, ongoing cultivation of clients: contacting friends, relatives, and colleagues; speaking or writing; and otherwise making one's expertise known in a community.

As mentioned earlier, it is fair to say that it takes most consultants three to five years to develop a private practice. I don't want to be pessimistic, but anyone who thinks they can make a living from the start as an IEC is being unrealistic. Have a game plan and stick to it. Consider working full- or part-time at your current job while developing consulting clients. Have confidence in yourself and confidence in what you are doing.

Remember also that your best marketing strategy is to do a super job consulting students! The more you under-promise and over-deliver, the more likely you are to get referrals. It's easy to blame social media or your webmaster for your lack of business. That may be true, but it also might be true that your product is flawed. Consider the case of Emmett Smoot, owner of The Margarita Hut, a local taco restaurant. Emmett gets bad publicity because his customers report seeing mice. The restaurant is becoming known on social media as The Mouse Hut. Emmett may consider the fact that he has few returning customers to be a marketing problem. In other words, he can say that if he only added a professional page to Facebook, more customers would return (and bring their friends!). Or Emmett may think that he needs to have someone stand on the street corner beside a sandwich board, proclaiming, "Best margaritas in Margaritaville!" But at some point, Emmett needs to realize that he does not have a marketing problem; he has a mouse problem!

Similarly, you need to think carefully about the reasons you are not getting the number of clients you want. Perhaps you are too impatient. Perhaps your persona is turning students off. Perhaps parents are confused by your complicated pricing system. Perhaps you haven't been explicit about your what families can expect as a result of working with you. Whatever the issue or the problem, your careful diagnosis is the first step in finding the cure.

(See resources at astudentofcolleges.com for additional business and marketing resources.)

SOCIAL MEDIA: LOG ON

Social media (and Facebook in particular) is today's newspaper. People use social media to get updates from friends, give updates about their careers and families, find jobs, get recommendations for local businesses and professionals, and share interesting/noteworthy content.

Maintaining an active social media presence is important for many different reasons. Regularly posting content and publishing blogs is a significant way to build your credibility, strengthen relationships with students and parents, and improve your website's search engine rankings. What is important is having a plan and coming up with stellar content. If you are not sure what to write about, put yourself in a client's shoes. If you were a parent with a high school sophomore who is thinking about college, what would you want to know?

By publishing noteworthy, helpful, and shareable content, you offer valuable information to your clients. If they find your content to be particularly interesting or beneficial, they may share it with their friends, families, or coworkers. When you consistently offer this type of helpful content, you not only position yourself as an expert in your field, but you also make your practice accessible to your clients.

Remember that there are so many businesses and individuals vying for attention in news feeds, and thus, your postings should stand out.

Tips for Getting Started and Establishing a Social Media Presence

1. Build relationships with influencers. It's best to start by looking for journalists and bloggers who write about education, colleges, higher education, and admissions. Read, comment on, and share their posts, if appropriate. Connecting and developing relationships with influencers and experts in our field will help you down the road. Should you approach them later, they'll be more likely to recognize your name, or at least be receptive, because it's obvious you know what they cover. (See resources at astudentofcolleges.com for lists of influential bloggers.)

2. Stay up to date. Find out who's talking about what, where they're talking about it, and start listening. Figuring out where to find your target market on social media takes time and involves searching for people who are talking about topics that are important to you.

3. Find your audience. If you haven't taken the time to build your networks and develop relationships ahead of time, figure out which social platforms are best to reach your target market. (See descriptions below). Then study those platforms and, when possible, take your targeted advertising to those platforms.

4. Be "follow worthy." Make your profile worth following on social networks. Run a contest, have a live Twitter debate using your own hashtag, or post the best picture from your top followers on your Instagram or Facebook feed. Don't just put up posts to try to grab attention. Work to make your postings interactive and fun.

5. Realize that, generally, social media isn't for selling. Pushing sell message after sell message will likely not be effective. Clients thinking about the services of an IEC don't want to be sold to in the traditional sense. They want to engage with your practice and build a trusting relationship. Once this foundation has been established, they will be more likely to come to you when they need college consulting. Reach out warmly to those whose interest you've piqued.

6. Know that effective social media marketing takes time. Social media isn't like traditional forms of advertising where you can invest a few hours designing your ad and then sit back and let it do its thing. In order to be successful, social media requires an ongoing investment of time and energy. Set a schedule, and share new content consistently.

Social Media Platforms

Twitter: Twitter is the dominant democracy of the social-sharing economy. Relevancy, personality, and brevity are the keys to making your voice heard. Start, join, and lead conversations; interact directly with your community. (See resources at astudentofcolleges.com for feeds worth following.)

Instagram: Instagram invites brands with visual content (lifestyle, food, fashion, personalities, luxury brands, etc.) into their customers' zone-out time. Create and post content accordingly. Share visual content, including short videos.

LinkedIn: LinkedIn is the online analog to old-fashioned networking. People—and connections to people—are everything. Most consultants, even those with a minimal social media presence, find LinkedIn essential.

Facebook: Of all social networks, Facebook is best equipped to linearly share responses to a post, ask a question, or spark conversation. Friends of your followers receive your comments, thus spreading the conversation. Facebook offers personal connection and an enjoyable distraction amidst the work day, but use typically peaks outside of work hours. Consider advertising or paying to promote your page on Facebook. Inspire conversations and shares—and be sure to ask questions. Facebook Ads are sometimes used to market IEC businesses. They allow you to target a specific demographic. Facebook Live is a way that some IECs communicate with their clients. Live can be used in multiple ways. For example, a review of recent posts across all of one's social media channels can answer the question: what are people asking frequently? These questions may be answered via Facebook Live.

Google+: As Google's proposed alternative to Facebook, keywords and search engine optimization are central to the appeal of Google+. Link often to content on your own website to direct this search boost where you want it most.

YouTube: Google treats its own well, and YouTube (owned by Google) is a good example. YouTube videos feature prominently in Google search results. YouTube is huge—it has over one billion users. That's more than a third of all people on the internet! It is the third most visited site on the internet after Google and Facebook. It is known for a wide array of videos and it offers immense potential for IEC offices who have a visual presentation to share.

E-newsletters as a Social Media Niche

IECs can use e-newsletters creatively in promoting their business and in making students and parents more informed about consulting and admission issues. Here are some ways to do it:

1. Determine what kind of online newsletter you want to send. Too many newsletters are scattered and not focused. Pick one topic and stick to it. Don't get caught up in discussing multiple topics in one newsletter.

2. Create unique content. Your consulting business is unique, so your newsletters should be, too. Create content that is compelling and educating. This will make your consumers want to read it. Providing unique content is a must (remember copyright laws) and will give your e-newsletter a professional presence.

3. Determine your readers' needs and adapt your newsletter to them. Figure out what your readers want to know, and let them enjoy it through your e-newsletters. Address frequently asked questions. Do your research and determine your target market. Try taking a poll with your current clients and simply ask them what they want to know more about.

4. Keep it precise. Keep your e-newsletters to the point. If you have more information you would like to cover, add a link to your website and enter the additional information there. Doing this will allow your readers to scan the e-newsletter quickly and then go to your website for more information. That is the goal. Getting more people to your website is key to growing your IEC business.

5. Add a fresh design. Nothing spruces up an e-newsletter like a fresh design. Not only do creative graphics help, but also how you format your text will affect your readership. People will continue to view your e-newsletters if they look professionally designed and formatted. Allowing poor looking e-newsletters to go out is a good way to lose credibility. Potential clients want to know that they are working with a professional consulting business that's serious about its work.

WHERE TO SET UP SHOP

About half of consultants work from their home office; the others in rented space. But there are lots of possibilities. There are consultants who drive to the home of the family for each meeting. There are those (particularly some who are beginning their practice) who meet at a library, church, or coffee shop. There are those who rent space from a psychologist or lawyer or some other professional who may have space available in the evenings and/or on weekends. There are also "executive suites" in large cities that make small offices available for rent.

Below are thoughts regarding the benefits and drawbacks of where to set up shop.

Home Office
Benefits:
- A home office saves a lot of money, particularly during the first months or years of setting up your IEC practice.
- IECs may be able to deduct a portion of their house and related expenses as a home office deduction and may thus save on taxes.
- It's easy to care for children and pets.
- We fill our homes with belongings that mean a great deal to us. Sharing those belongings with clients can be rewarding.
- Home offices are often friendly and warm environments. In a field such as independent educational consulting, that warmth can add to rapport building and ease of communication.
- Some IECs have the ability to separate office space from living space. For example, some IECs can see students in a room right off of the main entrance. Others can set up a basement or a upstairs area as professional office space. A private entrance, if available, can be helpful.

Drawbacks:

- The freedom to work anytime can be stressful for some. A home office may not provide a sufficient divide between work time and personal time.
- The freedom to work any time also comes with the possibility of procrastination or workaholism.
- Bringing students and parents into your house is to share your values and your personality. Your home may tell students and parents a lot about your values, your opinions, and your priorities. Visitors may pick up on religious and political views.
- An in-home office means keeping the porch free of leaves and the house clean and neat. This may present a problem for some IECs.
- While I don't think it's true, some IECs think they are viewed as less professional because they don't have a "real" office.
- A home office may elicit concerns with safety, volatile clients, and the necessity to protect yourself from claims of unethical behavior. To deal with this, some consultants ask students to bring a friend to meetings, particularly if they are meeting after dark.
- Family members, pets, neighbors, music, children's play, et cetera may interrupt meetings.
- Clients may feel like they're imposing by entering your space.
- IECs tend to be busiest after school, evenings, and weekends. Those are the very times one's family may require attention.
- Parking availability: Do you have three cars parked in front of your house all day? Would your neighbors or your HOA take any stance against this?
- Number and accessibility of available restrooms may be a consideration.
- Running a home-based practice often involves additional attention to zoning, tax, and insurance considerations.

Rental Space
Benefits:

- A rental office offers a separation of the home and work, creating a clear divide between the two locales and giving yourself space from the distractions of home.
- Further, it's easier to set boundaries with family and friends, who may see a rented office as more legitimate than a home office.
- There is a feeling among some parents that having an out-of-home office is more professional.

Drawbacks:

- Expensive! Having an office space means considerably higher startup costs.
- Unfamiliar. You might not be used to the space, and your clients may see a rental space as less personal as compared to a home office.

Co-working Spaces
Benefits:

- Co-working spaces offer month-to-month lease terms and variable office arrangements, saving the IEC the cost of furniture, cleaning, etc. Some options include: Davinci, Regus, Impact Hub, Industrious, Spacious, Kettlespace, and WeWork. For example, WeWork provides space options such as a private office, a dedicated desk, and a "hot desk" (guaranteed workspace in a common area). Options for all noted co-working spaces vary according to geographical location. Co-working spaces offer a community environment and may offer comforts such as food and beverages in-house.
- Co-working spaces may resonate with teens as many of the designs range from hip to ultra-hip.

Drawbacks:

- For those who work best in private, quiet environments, sharing space may not offer such an atmosphere.
- May be uncomfortable for specific clients.

Meeting Students in Their Homes
Benefits:

- Oftentimes, the IEC is introduced to neighbors, family, and friends of both the student and the parents, and some will ask for your business card so their teens may consider using your services.
- Word of mouth referrals spread quickly when they see how well the consulting process is working for Buffy.
- This model adds a uniqueness to your practice.
- You don't have overhead for rental costs.

Drawbacks:

- Travel is time consuming and may cut into your profits.
- Most of us use materials (guidebooks, forms, etc.) in our office, and taking materials from house to house is cumbersome.
- Finally, there is the question of professionalism. There is something legitimate about seeing students in your personal professional space.

CONSULTANT RECORD KEEPING

Managing an independent educational consulting practice has become way easier than it was when I opened shop. The technology available to the IEC today is incredible. (Keep in mind that I originally sent bills via carrier pigeon.) Now the profession is big enough for companies to develop resources just for us. As such, an IEC office can easily be an efficient enterprise, one that allows us the time and energy to earn a respectable wage.

Two of the popular business management tools designed for the IEC include CollegePlannerPro (collegeplannerpro.com) and GuidedPath (guidedpath.net). A third is Cialfo (cialfo.co). (See Business Resources and Tools at astudentofcolleges.com for in-depth descriptions of business management platforms.) Note that management tools offer a thirty-day free trial.

New web-based and software options are cropping up all the time. Being a member of professional associations is one way to keep abreast of new time-management and record-keeping options. (See resources at astudentofcolleges.com for a list of additional business references.)

For those who prefer to do record keeping the old-fashioned way, I share with you my system. (Note that I set my carrier pigeon free.) I keep physical file folders for each of my students and organize them as follows: On a yellow sheet, I date and write notes of every meeting. On a separate page, I keep a running list of the student's courses and grades. Using the student's transcript, I create a simple grid with the names of academic subjects (English, math, etc.) on the left and columns for each semester in high school at the top. The grid helps me see course sequencing. I also recompute the GPA on a 4.0 scale counting grades in English, math, science, languages, and social science. In addition to the note sheet and the grid sheet, I write a to-do list after each meeting (or when substantial discussions have taken place via email or phone). At the end of the meeting, the student gets the original to-do list, and I keep a copy. Some consultants send copies of this list to parents after each meeting (having discussed this with students in advance).

REFERRING CLIENTS FOR ADDITIONAL SERVICES

Business relationships with test tutors, et cetera are individually arranged. You want to determine whether the relationship is more of a partnership or more of a trade-off. Most consultants recognize those who refer with a simple note (or maybe a gift card at the end of the year). It's not common, but if a consultant hires another person for a particular service and that service is part of the college consulting process (as would be the case for essay work or list building), then the consultant pays the person for services performed (either a percent of the comprehensive fee or a straight dollar amount for hours of work). In this context, remember that most consultants are jacks-of-all-trades. The knowledge to help with essays, for example, comes with practice, reading, talking to colleagues, and so on. Finally, I advise all of my students to run their essays by their English teacher. I'm a consultant and not an expert on word choice or grammar. I help students most by thinking about topics and organizing ideas, not by proofreading or by perfecting English mechanics.

A FINAL BUSINESS TIP

If any of the above business considerations still seem out of your realm, you might wish to hire a business coach. Some consultants have found their money well spent by seeking such guidance. However, as anyone can call him/herself a business coach, you need to check references carefully and be clear on your specific needs, for example, help with marketing strategies, search engine optimization, technical issues, business planning, accounting matters, expansion. (See resources at astudentofcolleges.com for business references and tools.)

CHAPTER 5

It's All in the Delivery:
Service Models

THE IEC's CURRICULUM

Determining the way to deliver services to students (how time is spent) is the IEC's curriculum. Just as classroom teachers and professors determine their curriculum prior to the start of the academic year or term, the IEC must organize a thorough curriculum—a game plan, if you will—prior to seeing clients. Teachers and professors typically stick to (or do their best to stick to) an organized plan, often structured in the form of a syllabus. Similarly, the IEC maps out solid curriculum and adheres to it throughout the course of service with a given client. Curriculum equates to organization; no curriculum equates to disorganization. If the IEC is not clear as to what he or she can and intends to do, clients won't know what to expect.

In Chapter 4, I discussed curriculum as related to the business plan, contract, and fee structure. This chapter is designed to walk IECs through the process of designing curriculum. I do wish to note that over the course of a career, curriculum will likely change. To get started, certain fundamentals must be established; a structure must be in place. I present in this chapter a discussion of paths that the IEC can follow in order to organize effective curriculum.

GETTING STARTED WITH CLIENTS: INTRODUCTORY MEETING

To orient clients to my practice, I routinely have a free introductory meeting with families. This meeting is valuable from both sides. Families meet me and learn about my approach, philosophy, personality, etc., and I learn about their attitudes, their values, and their expectations.

I talk extensively with families about what I do and don't do. I don't accept those who want me as an influence peddler or if values are radically different from my own. For example, a family might be obsessed by name and might not seem to buy in (on any level) to the notion of fit and match. I have less tolerance for that attitude than some of my (equally good) colleagues. While name is important to many families, I need to work with families who are malleable enough to consider Buffy's happiness in college over the name of Buffy's college. Another scenario involves a student who is completely focused, for example, on a trumpet program, and that one factor alone might drive the decision. In such a case, I'm not likely to know enough about Buffy's trumpet ability (even after reviewing data on competitions won, etc.) or to know enough about specific trumpet programs at specific colleges for a specific year to be of great assistance. I need to be sure that I'm an added value; I want to be an advisor worthy of my fee. And my worthiness comes from the family who is reasonably open to the central college planning tenets I possess.

If I am not the right consultant, I encourage a family to find someone who is a better match. I explain that the fit between consultant and a family is important and that I think the family will be best served by another IEC. That said, I turn down very few clients. Over 95% of families come to me for the right reasons, and the relationship is ultimately a good one.

Note that an introductory meeting is not, here in my office at least, a counseling/consulting session. There is a difference between *describing* services and actually *helping* Buffy with her specific concerns. For example, Mrs. Jones wants to know whether I think Buffy should do test prep, I honestly say that it would be unprofessional of me to offer an opinion as I don't know enough about Buffy.

MAJOR SERVICE DELIVERY MODELS: OVERVIEW

The decision of how to deliver your services to students is complex. Many issues are involved in deciding how to use time: educational philosophy, income needs, family needs, efficiency, communication skills, work ethic, and so forth (Some of these issues were addressed in Chapter 4.)

There are two primary ways of providing services: comprehensively and non-comprehensively. Over two-thirds of IECs offer a comprehensive package. At the same time, most offer less extensive (and less costly) options. These options (called non-comprehensive or hybrid models) include condensed time plans, per consultation or hourly rates, and/or a sliding scale.

COMPREHENSIVE PACKAGES: THE GOOD, THE BAD, AND AVOIDING THE UGLY

Comprehensive packages are by far the most common way of delivering services and tend to be the best way to deliver services, particularly in the beginning. A comprehensive plan is one in which the consultant offers a service (a number of meetings) for a fixed fee. This approach works well because it is clear to families the services you are providing and at what cost. While comprehensive packages come in many shapes and sizes, they typically involve working with the student from the beginning of the junior year through the senior year and may involve 10, 15 or even 20 meetings. To use a medical analogy, this is the continuous care model.

There are several advantages of the comprehensive model. First, these models make billing issues relatively simple. Everyone is clear on what is provided, and the consultant can decide whether to bill up front or in installments. A major advantage of the comprehensive package for the consultant is that parents often don't know what it takes to find a good college match. They might have grown up in an era when "brilliant" students went to Harvard or Amherst, and the others packed their bags and went to the good ole state university. Comprehensive programs illustrate the value of time. The IEC gets to know the student, gains the opportunity to witness changes that are typical for adolescents, and can explore college options in a slow, deliberate manner. Mostly, time allows the wisdom of fit and match to sink in. Adopting such a mindset takes time to process and internalize. As noted throughout this book, we're attitude changers, and attitude change requires repetition and time.

I don't feel, however, that consultants should advertise unlimited time to potential clients. It's not educationally sound. Students and parents should assume responsibility for some of the process, particularly since we are dealing with young adults who are about to leave home. The unlimited time approach encourages handholding, a stereotype of educational consultants that we must work to overcome. (While a bit exaggerated, I've often thought of "unlimited time" as being similar and equally harmful to the concept of "unconditional love.") If a consultant charges on a package basis, he or she should have a maximum number of hours associated with that package. (Please refer back to The Antonoff Pricing Bible in Chapter 4 and allow me to reiterate.) Clearly state that the fee schedule includes "up to X number of meetings" and "up to Y number of hours." In other words, for a student on a comprehensive program who signs up in the fall of the junior year, you might say to the parents, "This comprehensive fee includes up to 12 meetings and up to 25 hours. "Hours" include any time involved in work for that family: face-to-face, research, email, phone, even texting. That way, the IEC is free to see the student for different meeting lengths over the months of service and has extra hours built in for behind-the-scenes work. Comprehensive packages give a clear blueprint to the family of what college planning entails.

Be aware, however, that comprehensive plans may have drawbacks. For starters, parents and students can misinterpret a package plan with a "I paid you for your time and by golly you're mine" plan. Parents can expect that the consultant will be available at all hours. Second and related, the consultant may become more than an advisor and may take over the college planning process. Sometimes in an effort to get things done, it is easier to "just do it" for the students rather than putting the onus on them. Unless the consultant is careful, consulting becomes coaching and that, in turn, becomes dependency. We must be careful to always maintain a healthy relationship with students and their parents by presenting realistic expectations at the onset.

Again, determining how best to structure time with students is not easy. We need to be fluid enough to allow for individual differences yet structured enough to get the job done. As an overwhelming percentage of consultants use a comprehensive approach, it says to me that experience validates this type of consulting. On the other hand, I think for consulting to grow, we also need variability in practices for at least two reasons. First, it's important to accommodate the increased diversity of backgrounds of those entering the field. Second, I think the public benefits from various price points. As a consumer, I should be able to find a consultant who provides a "soup to nuts" service (that is a reference to the IEC providing all of the options typically associated with our work) and a consultant who does things a bit (or a lot) differently.

SAMPLES OF COMPREHENSIVE PACKAGES

Below are two sample comprehensive programs. These samples illustrate ways to organize a sequence of meetings (referred to as sessions below) with students. Sample One includes 18 sessions. Sample Two includes 12 sessions. Sample One has 8 sessions designed for application/essay work. Sample Two has 2. Sample One includes the administration and the discussion of a career inventory. Sample Two includes a spring session to discuss the final college choice and another session later in the senior year or in the summer to discuss strategies for success in college.

Both samples start with the assumption of a signed contract with the family. Both assume that the student begins to work with the IEC in the fall of the junior year.

The length of sessions can vary. In my office, they are typically 75 minutes. That's the expectation, and I stick to it. If there are sessions where more time is needed, I schedule accordingly and adjust meeting length to meet the tasks necessary. For example, the first session in Sample One includes a lot of activities and may require 90 or even 120 minutes. The second session, the student and parent interviews, may take 120 minutes (one hour with the student and one hour with the parents).

Note the following points as you read the two samples:
- These samples are instructional. While both provide specific tasks for each meeting, seldom are things as clean-cut.
- I don't know a consultant who follows the exact same meeting sequence for each student. Even if a contract specifies a meeting-by-meeting plan, changes are made as the process unfolds to meet individual needs.
- The overlap of topics is not fully reflected in the written meeting sequence here. For example, sharing information about colleges can start at the first session and can continue all the way through service.
- When a comprehensive plan begins is variable. There are consultants who start working with students early in high school and some who start working with a student in October of the senior year. Some of this variation is the result of consultant preference, and some is the result of market demand. (Further discussion is provided later in this chapter.) I recommend not to start a comprehensive program before the junior year and to see ninth and tenth-graders on an hourly basis.
- The time that IECs devote to topics varies. Some spend more time discussing colleges and less time addressing applications and essays. Some do the opposite. There are consultants who spend a few sessions on career/vocation matters and others who touch on this topic briefly.
- Students vary widely in their needs. Some students need more help with applications and essays; some students need more help with career alternatives or cost issues. Some students need more contact hours; some need less. Some students need help with early decision issues; others need help completing the Common Application.
- Parents vary widely in their needs. Some families are college-savvy, but others don't know how the process works.

The permutations and combinations are endless. In other words, there is an individuality to consulting relationships that these samples do not reflect. Even with the limitations of presenting the following static samples, I hope they prove useful in getting a feel for consultant activity.

DELIVERING SERVICES COMPREHENSIVELY: SAMPLE ONE

Session 1: September or October, Junior Year (or earlier). Potential agenda: 1) Get acquainted/ get organized; 2) Develop a college planning timetable; 3) Discuss "essentials": courses, testing, recommendations, activity list, summer activities, and so forth (See Chapter 15 for further discussion.)

Session 2: November, Junior Year. Potential agenda: 1) Get to know student and parent(s): individual time with the student and with the parent(s). (The IEC may choose to schedule two separate sessions or incorporate one of the individual sessions into Session 1); 2) Suggest some colleges to research and/or react to any choices brought to the table by the student or parent(s).

Session 3: December, Junior Year. Potential agenda: 1) Timetables/organization/ideas for college visits; 2) Activities list/résumé (See Chapter 16 for further discussion.); 3) Suggest ways to keep track of college information, deadlines, etc.

Session 4: December or January, Junior Year. Potential agenda: 1) Discuss factors important in choosing a college (See Chapter 6 for further discussion.); 2) Organize (note that a component of all sessions is a discussion of student organization and movement toward goals).

Session 5: January or February, Junior Year. Potential agenda: 1) Discuss colleges: While colleges would have been discussed previously, this is a thorough discussion of college options. At this point, semester junior year grades and ideally at least one set of test scores (or preliminary scores) are available to bring clarity to the discussion. Also, the student has had a chance to think through the qualities that he or she is seeking in a college, and parents have also had time to digest the college selection process from both fit and admission perspectives. 2) Possible additional topics: visiting colleges, financial matters, careers and majors, résumé writing, summer activities, brainstorming essay topics.

Session 6: March, April, or May, Junior Year. Potential agenda: 1) IEC hears student's report on colleges researched; 2) Discuss college options; 3) Possible additional topic: explain early decision/action options; 4) Set goals: a) 70% of college choices established by end of next session; b) student brings in essay prompts that are already known.

Session 7: Spring, Junior Year or Summer between Junior and Senior Year. Potential agenda: 1) Discuss college list; 2) Answer questions about application submission process; 3) Review the student's application deadline list; 4) Discuss process to be followed in working with IEC on applications and personal statements/essays (See Chapter 16 for further discussion.); 5) Tips to stay ahead of the process: how to navigate the Common Application, Coalition Application, Naviance, and other software tools that the IEC will use; 6) Set goals: a) 85% of college choices established by the end of summer; b) work on application completion and personal statement (ideal to complete over summer).

Session 8: September, Senior Year. Potential agenda: 1) Discuss applications and essays (part 1 of 3 sessions): application list review—enough reaches? Enough back-ups? Financial safety school?; 2) Review activity list; 3) Get up to speed in terms of the personal statement and supplemental essays (See Chapter 16 for further discussion.); 4) Review student's application deadline list; 5) Set a specific goal and write it down. For example, complete as many applications and essays as possible by Halloween.

Session 9: October, Senior Year. Potential agenda: 1) Discuss applications and essays (part 2 of 3 sessions): continue addressing items noted in Session 8; 2) Parental support: direct efforts to elicit parental support, particularly in regard to cost/finances.

Session 10: November, Senior Year. Potential agenda: Discuss and review completed applications and essays (part 3 of 3 sessions).

Session 11: April, Senior Year. Potential agenda: Discuss final choice: At this point, students have been admitted to several colleges, and they seek the consultant's counsel in terms of making a final choice. Topics include discussing or re-addressing the criteria to use in making the final choice, whether final visits to colleges should be made, how to handle financial aid offers, and other related issues.

Session 12: End of Senior Year. Potential agenda: 1) Success in college: During this final meeting, issues related to beginning college success and happiness are addressed. Discuss student's concerns, help the student assess how he or she will choose freshman classes, understand how a core curriculum works, etc. At this meeting, the consultant might help the student think through ways he or she can become involved on campus and point out how extracurricular involvement increases the sense of connectedness a student feels in college, thus boosting happiness; and talk about success variables—dealing with roommates, how to be a better time manager, how high school is different from college, etc. (See Chapter 17 for a full discussion.); 2) Get feedback on services; 3) Establish a method of keeping in touch with the student while he or she is in college.

DELIVERING SERVICES COMPREHENSIVELY: SAMPLE TWO

Session 1: September or October, Junior Year. Potential agenda: 1) Orientation and overview: student and parent interviews, state or restate limits, and discuss issues such as best ways for student/parent to communicate with IEC; 2) Evaluation of "essentials": courses, testing, recommendations, activity list, summer activities, etc. (See Chapter 15 for further discussion.); 3) College planning timetables: discuss at all upcoming meetings; 4) Introduce factors important in choosing a college (including finances); 5) Introduce campus visits (perhaps identify a few colleges to visit close to home); 6) Career assessment: assign student to complete an inventory on his or her own.

Session 2: October or November, Junior Year. Potential agenda: 1) Career assessment discussion/review; 2) Introduce the Common Application and/or discuss Coalition Application, Naviance, standardized IEC management systems like CollegePlannerPro or GuidedPath; 3) Discuss factors important in choosing a college: generate a list of written factors and perhaps identify few more colleges to visit/research (See Chapter 6 for further discussion.).

Session 3: November or December, Junior Year. Potential agenda: 1) Discuss expectations and goals of work with IEC: how time will be used, what resources will be used (and how to use them), careers and majors, etc.; 2) Brainstorm essay topics (See Chapter 16 for further discussion.); 3) Organize activity list; 4) Discuss campus visits; 5) Mock interview practice.

Session 4: December or January, Junior Year. Potential agenda: 1) Continue brainstorming essay ideas and/or review and discussion of essays and personal statements; 2) Further discuss factors important in choosing a college; 3) Present additional colleges; 4) Discuss campus visits; 5) Set goal: two to three essays complete by spring break.

Session 5: February or March or April, Junior Year. Potential agenda: 1) Discuss colleges (see Session 5 in Sample One); 2) Teach how to research colleges (if not covered previously).

Session 6: March or April, Junior Year. Potential agenda: 1) Results of student research; 2) Further discuss colleges; 3) Work on activity list; 4) Continue work on essays.

Session 7: April, May or June, Junior Year. Potential agenda: 1) Financial aid; 2) Continue work on activity list or essays; 3) Further discuss colleges; 4) Review college websites; 5) Work on the Common Application.

Session 8: Summer prior to Senior Year. Potential agenda: 1) Continue as per above; 2) Set summer goals: a) 80% of college choices established; b) complete Common Application, including finalization of activity descriptions; c) complete the personal statement and as many supplemental essays as available.

Session 9: September, Senior Year. Potential agenda: 1) Further discuss colleges; 2) Review/discuss applications and personal statement; 3) Develop timetables for upcoming application/essay work; 4) Set goal: complete at least three applications by October 15.

Sessions 10-18: Rest of Senior Year. Potential agenda: 1) Continue to meet biweekly (or weekly) to complete all application materials; 2) Set goal: submit all application materials by Thanksgiving; 3) Final meeting: success in college (see Session 12 in Sample One).

NON-COMPREHENSIVE MODELS

While the comprehensive model is common, there are many ways to deliver services. What's important is to understand your market, your income needs, your availability, and your skills and to find the approach that best meets your needs.

"Hybrid" is the term used for any model that does not follow a traditional comprehensive approach. The hybrid model includes both "mini comprehensive models" and other ways of organizing to help students. Here are some examples:
- The consultant meets with the student and the family four times only. These meetings could be structured as follows:
    1) Meet student and parent(s) individually, discuss the process, and develop a timeline.
    2) Discuss colleges and how to research and make campus visits.
    3) Assist with application/essay.
    4) Determine final college choice and discuss success in college.
- The "Right College Fit" package: offer two or three meetings with a goal of arriving at a final list of colleges.
- The "College List" package: meet with the student in the sophomore and junior years to discuss which colleges to visit and research and then meet again in the junior (and perhaps senior) year to arrive at a final list of colleges.
- The "College Application/Essay" package: provide two or three meetings to help with application and essay concerns and issues.

A colleague uses the following curriculum that incorporates fixed and variable sessions. The plan offers eight total sessions. The consultant sets the content of four sessions: initial/fact gathering session, overview of the college search process and organization session, college list session, and essay/application session. The student's needs dictate the other four sessions. Additional sessions could cover topics such as review of colleges visited and revision of the list, essay review, mock interview, and addressing college costs. A student may want three essay review sessions instead of additional meetings to talk about his/

her list of colleges. This consultant counts review of emailed essays and review of online applications as separate sessions.

Another approach involves group meetings or workshops. The consultant schedules specific times to talk to a group of his or her students about the college admissions process, college essay writing essentials, researching, and so forth. Workshops for brainstorming essay ideas, as well as for venting feelings about the process, for example, can be very helpful. There are endless varieties in this (as well as the other) ways of delivering services. For example, the IEC can offer a group session to discuss the factors important in choosing a college and then follow it up with individual meetings to identify appropriate colleges for each student. Potentially, delivery of service in this way allows the consultant to see more students. It also has the advantage of peer-to-peer support. Lastly, peer-to-peer nudging is often more effective than consultant-to-student nudging! A general limitation to the group model is its inherent lack of personalization. Parents, in particular, may expect the consultant to work one-on-one with their child.

PER CONSULTATION/HOURLY

Providing services by the hour appeals to some consultants. This model, typical of professionals such as lawyers and psychologists, essentially says, "I'm a professional with a level of expertise and you can buy my time as you need/want it." Those who provide hourly services charge for all time—face-to-face, phone, research, and so on. This approach often results in less abuse of the consulting relationship. That is, if parents want to call all the time, or if there is need for multiple meetings (e.g., for essay help), the consultant is compensated based on the hours of service provided. (In contrast, comprehensive programs are much like a retainer, in that once a fee is agreed upon, the consultant continues to provide service.)

The limitation of the hourly plan for the consultant is that detailed records for billing must be kept. It can be unpleasant to charge for small segments of service (e.g., a 20-minute phone call, research, or spending five minutes writing an email). The consultant may not get to know the student as well; thus, the essential components of building rapport and suggesting the best fit colleges may suffer. In addition, families may not know when they need additional help. That is, they may be naïve to the college planning process, key events, and timetables. They may hesitate to call, believing it might not be worth the charge to ask a question. Thus, instead of using the term "hourly," try using the words "per consultation." The latter terminology allows you to offer blocks of service and also to value substance over minutes.

VIRTUAL CONSULTING

Virtual consulting (visually connecting with students via the camera on your computer or mobile device) is well worth considering as a delivery model. (Note that virtual consulting is also referred to as e-consulting, online consulting, web consulting, video consulting, and internet consulting.) I note elsewhere in this book that I feel that face-to-face consulting is the preferred method of delivery. What I believe more strongly, however, is that the profession of educational consulting needs to expand its reach. There are oodles of students who need and want consulting services but do not have access to local options. When the alternative is to wing it due to lack of professional guidance, the utility of conducting college consulting online seems obvious. Moreover, virtual consulting allows IECs to see students outside of their local area. Now, an IEC in Laramie, Wyoming (or another low population city, state, or country) can build a successful practice. Note that virtual consulting can also—geography allowing—be combined with face-to-face consulting to make a more inclusive and varied experience.

For IECs contemplating virtual consulting as a primary or secondary mode of service delivery, consider the following positives and negatives.

- Many of the students we see are proficient at technology and have been online all of their lives, virtual consulting seems particularly well-suited to our work.
- Virtual consulting may allow for greater flexibility in scheduling, especially when different time zones come into play. Night owls can accommodate students outside of standard business hours.
- Working online affords the IEC the chance to use creative approaches for mixing and matching text, sound, and visuals. The virtual consulting modality lends itself well to multimedia presentations, video vignettes, flash and static slides, interactive slides, etc. The IEC can go over features about colleges collectively and can visually illustrate methods of researching colleges. Such presentations can pack a punch.
- The online platform works well for brainstorming essay ideas or editing written work. Google Docs, or example, allows for online collaboration.
- Importantly, working online pushes the IEC to embrace a love and respect for the spoken word. Time has a different meaning online: the immediacy of the communication system encourages instant response. The impact of words used alone may be more powerful than in face-to-face communication. The IEC may need to choose words that are warmer, more sensitive, more caring than might be necessary face-to-face.
- Virtual consulting is not an ideal modality for everyone as not everyone is comfortable with technology. Even people who are normally good presenters may underperform when working with the limitations of virtual meeting technology.
- Time may be required to become familiar with the tools and techniques of working online. IECs need to know enough about technology to fix a problem that develops with visuals or sound during a meeting.
- Time may be required to test-drive how one comes across when using a virtual meeting platform. The IEC needs to look visually prepared and professional.
- Reading nonverbal cues when the client is shielded by the technological screen of the internet may be challenging. The IEC must be acutely aware of body language and emotional cues.
- The IEC also needs to be acutely aware of the nuances of his or her facial expressions, body language, make-up, apparel, and voice inflection as these elements may be magnified in work online.
- Working via the web can increase the IEC's sense of isolation.

Ultimately, IECs doing work electronically need to prepare themselves to meet added responsibilities. For those up to the challenge, virtual consulting may be the next wave of service delivery.

CONSULTING LATE ARRIVALS: WELCOME ABOARD OR ABANDON SHIP?

Scenarios often occur wherein students seek college consulting services late in the game, thus throwing the IEC's curriculum off-kilter. This section addresses positives and negatives of accepting late start students and how the IEC might best accommodate such students if accepted.

First, most IECs have room for late arrivals and are happy to assist a student starting college planning in the fall of his or her senior year. Some IECs who have a limit on the number of students they see annually plan for a certain number of "late" clients. That is, they may hold space for such students.

Other consultants are conflicted about whether to take such a student. Supposing the IEC could squeeze the student in, is that the best move? After all, much of consulting is based on building rapport, and there is less time to do so if the student starts late. Further, parents may have unreasonable expectations of what the IEC is capable of doing in a short amount of time. Then again, the student might be super motivated and a pleasure to work with. An introductory meeting will help shed light on whether welcoming a late arrival might be a burden or an unexpected joy.

My advice is for the IEC to evaluate each situation based on his or her needs and the needs of the family. These situations require a clear-cut contract with realistic expectations on both ends.

For the IEC who cannot squeeze the student in, simply explain that the curriculum requires a more substantial time commitment and that it would be unprofessional to provide Brutus a rushed service.

If the IEC feels that he or she can offer Buffy quality consulting, what does the curriculum of that service look like? Start by looking at all the items typically included in a comprehensive package to determine the essentials. For most students, the essentials are the development/implementation of a clear time frame for testing, development of the college list, and application/personal statement completion. If it's possible to cover all elements of the curriculum at a much accelerated pace, do so. If not, here are some other options:

- Offer a short package geared to Buffy's individual needs.
- Offer services on a per consultation basis, focusing on Buffy's major concerns.
- Offer only essay editing help.
- Offer assistance strictly with building the college list.
- Offer a late college application boot camp for two or more late arrivals.
- Offer to help after November 1 (or some date in the future) with the assumption that some students, like those applying early decision, will be finished, thus allowing the IEC time for Buffy.

Ultimately, the curriculum will likely need adjusting; it is up to the IEC to determine the best course of action.

The late-arrival scenario warrants a brief discussion of how much to charge. While it is justified for the IEC to charge the full comprehensive fee (based on the fact that overtime work will be needed to complete all of the college planning steps necessary in a short amount of time) the IEC may set a lower fee. Or charge a higher price! In other words, one may feel that the extra burden of doing the work required is deserving of a higher comprehensive fee.

ORIENTING THE STUDENT/FAMILY TO THE PROCESS

Once a contract has been signed, the consultant orients the student and the family to the environment they are about to enter. Here are some of the ways we do that:

1. We orient to college admission. This includes how colleges make decisions and how students prepare to present themselves to admission officials. In addition, we provide general advice about the admission process. For example, we may talk about how admission is different than marketing, how recruitment differs from admission, and how finding a good match instead of the biggest name means less tears and more smiles over the college planning months.

Here's what I tell my students:

"It is important to remember that colleges are evaluating pieces of paper about you, not you personally. There is a big difference between the two. Remember that this is not a contest to see who can get into the most prestigious school; it is a very personal decision about where you want to spend your college years, and there is no right or wrong answer. Relax and have fun with it!

"Remember that you are the consumer. You are in control. Four years is a long time to spend somewhere where you don't fit. Imagine how ridiculous I would look walking down the street in a bright orange dress that clashed with my red hair and was two sizes too small and three inches too short. 'It's a Vera Wang!' I would say proudly. 'Who cares? You look like an idiot!' should be your response. Choosing a college only for the label is just as misguided. It's all about being an educated consumer.

"As your independent educational consultant, I am your trail guide, but I cannot walk it for you. Turn to me for guidance and direction. I am with you for the journey. There are many trails and paths, but there is no set destination. Some may be well tramped but turn out to be dead ends. Others will bring you back where you started. You may have to hunt for the entrance to a few. That is just part of the journey."

2. We orient to the idea that preparing for and applying to college involves several distinct steps. In other words, a good college choice involves several different decision points and each requires time and attention. An important point here is to tell students that they are coming with us on a journey and that we, as consultants, are going to try to make that journey as positive and exciting as possible.

3. We orient to the difficulty of decision-making and emphasize that there are few easy answers.

4. We orient to the idea that everyone has a role to play (student, parent, consultant, school counselor, grandparent, etc.).

5. We orient the student and the family to who we are as educational consultants and how our services will aid the student in the college planning months.

Orienting means that the consultant takes control of the consulting process, not control of the decision-making or control over getting tasks completed. Rather, it is important that you establish—early on—that you can relate to teens, that you know the current admissions scene, and that you know colleges. Without such early orientation, you may lose control over the consulting.

GENERAL CURRICULUM AND TIME MANAGEMENT TIPS

Regardless of which delivery model(s) the IEC offers, utilizing the following time structures can greatly improve efficiency.
- Time can slip away in a meeting without the necessary attention to essentials. I might say something like this at the start of the session, "We have 75 minutes, and I want to use the time we have efficiently. As you know, today's topic is X, and so let's spend Y minutes discussing the pros and cons of X. Then we'll have Z minutes left for any questions."
- The last five to ten minutes of a meeting are especially important. That's when the specific action steps are outlined for the next meeting. Provide the student a detailed list of what he or she must prepare for or accomplish by the next meeting. This list should be written, and both the IEC and student should have a copy. Teaching students to be accountable for their share of tasks helps them build life skills and helps the consultant manage time efficiently.
- Practice front-loading. Front-loading is a time management technique that keeps the IEC ahead of the curve. The IEC tries to move the consulting process along as efficiently as possible. Experience with the admissions process gives the IEC the power to assist the student in planning and anticipation. The IEC knows, for example, that a student doesn't have to wait until college choices are selected to begin working on essays. In other words, the IEC accelerates the process so that the student stays on task with academics, activities, and college admissions tasks.

- It doesn't take much math expertise to determine that if one spends a hundred hours with each student, there will not be time for many students, and therefore business may not operate profitably. As emphasized throughout this book, more time with a student or a parent does not necessarily mean better consulting. It does not mean that the student will have more or better college choices. It does not mean that the student or the parent will be happier with your services. Deliver curriculum in a way that brings about effective and efficient consulting, maximal college choices, and happy clients.

- Optimize phone, email, text, virtual conversations, and social networking time. Hours can be stolen from the day if one is not careful about their use. If necessary, tell families in advance that phone time is generally limited to ten minutes per call and that if more time is necessary, an appointment should be made. Feedback on essays or general college planning questions can often be handled via telephone or email. Such time counts as a session or as an hour.

- Great consultants learn to prioritize their time. For example, each morning, the effective IEC determines the goals and priorities for that day. Those might be as follows: identify colleges for Buffy and Brutus, respond to the request of the committee chair to provide input on colleges that should be included in an upcoming tour, finish the PowerPoint needed for an upcoming conference session, and learn more about financial aid for divorced families. Then focus the day's work on those activities only (except, of course, in the case of an emergency!).

- Discipline yourself to be aware if you are entering a "not a priority for the day zone." A "not a priority" item includes anything other than the tasks that were identified as priorities. Spending time on social media, email and/or the internet, working to identify colleges for Jason or Jennie, and reading *The Chronicle* fall into that category. The point here is that the effective IEC puts time into those activities that most reflect actual priorities. Without such discipline, days get away from us: today turns into tomorrow and soon enough, we're hitting a deadline to get the PowerPoint submitted and rushing to build a list of colleges for Brutus who's coming in tomorrow. Frenzy generally does not yield the best-quality work.

- To improve time management, I employ general strategies. For example, I don't check my email or voice messages in the morning because doing so may interfere with the tasks that are a priority for the day. I also recognize that time can get away from me in web surfing or going on Facebook. Recognizing this weakness, I try to limit my general browsing to a few times a day. If I need to go onto Twitter, for example, for a particular reason, I get off of Twitter as soon as my business is complete.

- Consider investing in a service that provides computer-generated transcriptions of voice messages to improve your efficiency.

- Consider using an online scheduling service so that students or parents can simply select appointment times from your available slots.

- Billing software is a quick and fairly cheap way to save time sending statements.

- To save time explaining your philosophy to prospective clients, prepare a statement of your consulting philosophy. In it, share what you do, how you do it, and the reasons that make working with you productive and valuable.

- Designate at least an hour each week as "IEC recharging" time. Do an inventory of primary tasks for the upcoming week. What *must* you get done? What projects are most going to help you be a more successful IEC during the next week?

- Structure your work schedule to best suit your internal clock and body rhythm. Keep in mind that being your own boss grants you the flexibility to break from the traditional 9 to 5 workday. If you do your best college planning once the moon rises, schedule accordingly. Both night owls and early birds can serve Buffy and Brutus well. It's important to understand and honor the factors that allow you to capitalize on productivity and develop a structured routine.

CHAPTER 6

IEC as Architect:
Building the College List

INTRODUCTION

IECs help students have a successful transition from high school to college. Finding the right colleges to consider and the right one to attend is the key way we help increase the odds of a successful college experience. A most important task for the IEC is to help students think through what they are looking for in a college and, ultimately, to come up with good match colleges.

I want to share a story: Not too long ago, a college friend called and left me a message that more or less said the following: Steve, I know you know colleges, and I just want two minutes of your time to tell me which colleges my daughter should look at. She has a 3.6 average, a 25 ACT, and is into every activity there is at school. She wants to major in pre-med or pre-law. Please give me a few names of colleges that she should be apply to. I really value your advice.

The above reflects a common misperception that grades, test scores, and a potential major are the only variables involved in college choice. My friend thought that the process was relatively straight forward and surely he had given me enough information to help make college planning decisions.

I called him back and asked a lot of questions about his daughter: Was her 3.6 weighted or unweighted? What level are her courses? Is she in an IB program? Has she taken any AP classes? What is her high school like? What specific activities is she involved in? Is she a member of everything, a leader of everything, or somewhere in between?

More importantly, I asked: What is she like? How much does she want to go to college to be a student versus going to college for the experience? (Most students want some of both, but the discussion is often illuminating.) How much is cost an issue in her choice? Would she be just as happy in the middle of Manhattan, New York as Manhattan, Kansas? What level of intellectual life is right for her? (It's not a matter of how smart she is; the question is how curious she is.) Would she be comfortable at a school with many alternative, free-spirited students? How about a campus where most students participate in athletics and/or fraternities and sororities? The answers to these questions, and, more importantly, a discussion with the student, led me to the point where I could give some reasonable, viable college choices.

Chapter 10 provides in-depth discussion of how the IEC can go about getting to know students. I address building the list early in this book because aspiring and novice IECs are often especially eager (and often anxious!) to learn about building the college list. Please use the story above to reinforce the necessity of knowing students before sharing college knowledge.

IECs must know that finding good match colleges for students requires three elements: 1) knowledge about the student and his or her needs; 2) knowledge about what the student is looking for in a college and the trade-offs/balances involved in college choice, and 3) knowledge about colleges themselves.

While there are many dimensions to a good match, among the most important are: 1) where the student will be pushed but not shoved; 2) where he or she can engage with friends, become more mature, make wise decisions, and be more self-aware; and 3) where the student can prepare for a successful and productive life.

In an ideal world, the best list comes from the student's knowledge and articulation of what he or she desires in a college. Aha! The student visualizes and verbalizes; the IEC drafts a blueprint. Let the architecture begin! Ah, if only consulting were so simple! Realistically, it's worthwhile and productive to think about how to work toward this goal.

Remember that colleges are normally discussed from the first meeting onward. Buffy (and/or her parents) may come to you with a group of schools she is considering. Perhaps they are legacy colleges (where Buffy's parents attended). Perhaps they are high-profile or big-name colleges. Perhaps they are schools where siblings or friends have enrolled. From that point, the IEC adds colleges to the table as appropriate. Sometimes the IEC starts seeing a student in the second semester of the junior year, and the family has already planned a college visit trip over spring break. On such occasions, the IEC provides suitable schools to visit on the basis of what he or she knows about the student.

PRELIMINARIES TO BUILDING THE COLLEGE LIST: IDENTIFY, EVALUATE, AND CONCEPTUALIZE

Before discussing any particular colleges with students, IECs guide students to **identify** factors important in choosing a college, IECs **evaluate** the student's appeal from an admission perspective, and IECs formulate ways to **conceptualize** characteristics of colleges. (Yes! Another play on IEC!)

I. Identify

The first step in the list building process is to guide students to identify factors that they should contemplate and weigh in order to hone in on good match colleges. An examination of factors provides a template from which the match process evolves. Some factors—like size, location, and cost—are clearly on every list because they are standard considerations. We'll look below at basics and at more complex factors. As an author, I have long grappled with the way to list "Factors Important in Choosing a College." Over the years, I have added and removed characteristics. Even now, I keep looking for ways to help students understand how colleges vary. The following characteristics (essentially from *College Match*), are those that I think best form a template of salient factors to consider.

Factors Important in Choosing a College

1. Size of College/University
Includes issues such as:
- Need for accessible teachers
- Relationship between size of classes and grades
- Student/faculty ratio (note that though the ratio may be listed as 20:1, that includes a wide scope—counting one-on-one tutorials—and thus the ratio may be misleading)
- Preference for discussion versus lecture classes
- Desire to be a participant versus desire to be more anonymous in classes
- Need for academic/career advising

A consulting issue involving size relates to the sheer numbers of institutions with varying enrollments. About 60% of all colleges enroll less than 2,500 students, about a quarter enroll 2,500 to 9,999 students, and a little over 10% enroll 10,000 or more students. At public institutions, a third or so enroll less than 2,500 students, a bit under half enroll 2,500 to 9,999 students, and about a quarter enroll 10,000 or more students. At private institutions, over 80% enroll less than 2,500 students, less than 15% enroll 2,500 to 9,999 students, and less than 5% enroll 10,000 or more students. As such, if a student wants a college bigger than his or her high school, and if the high school has 2,800 students, the student is eliminating practically two thirds of colleges. As IECs, we need to make these points clearly as we need a "playing field" rather than a "closet" within to work.

This is particularly an issue with a student without a stellar record. That is, if Brutus has a C+ GPA and average test scores, he has fewer options than Buffy who has better credentials. Thus, Brutus has fewer colleges from which to choose from an admission standpoint. If he insists on a college with more than 20,000 students, he limits his potential college options even further. IECs should engage students and parents in this discussion if size is a significant, central factor.

2. Academic Offerings and Careers
Includes issues such as:
- Pure liberal arts and science versus more direct career preparation (or, exposure to many academic subjects versus more career-directed courses)

- Subjects the student would like to learn more about and/or academic majors of interest
- Strength in a specific department (plus, specific schools for photography, film, etc.)
- Type of college (public/private/trade, etc.)

(Please see a discussion of academic majors and careers later in this chapter.)

3. Coeducation or Single Sex

While over 90% of all the colleges in the United States are now coeducational, there are also a small number of single-sex schools, a few for men and more for women.

4. Religious and/or Ethnic Orientation

Includes issues such as:
- Emphasis on religious life
- Desire to be around students who share religious/ethnic/racial heritage (or, varied mix of student backgrounds versus one's own background)

5. Student Body Characteristics

Includes issues such as:
- Description of personality, character, or academic traits of other students
- Significance of fraternities/sororities, spectator sports, participating in a specific sport/activity
- More independence versus more rules and regulations
- Desire for lots of school spirit versus an average amount of school spirit

This is an important variable. Does the student want an "artsy" student body? One that's unusually diverse? Politically conscious? Outdoorsy? What we're asking students is about the sort of classmates whom they are most likely to be happy around. We're asking them to think about the student culture.

6. Academic Environment

Includes issues such as:
- Intellectual/scholarly versus an academic and social life balance
- Extent of academic pressure
- Significance of study abroad, internships, learning disabilities support, etc.

7. Activities Available

Here, the IEC is identifying which activities (such as clubs, fraternity/sorority life, concerts, and sports) are important and/or essential to the student.

8. Prestige

What drives the student's college search: big name or best fit? We recognize that when a student (or family) is fixated on a big name school or prestige, such a one-track focus can derail an otherwise solid college planning process. Let me stress that there is nothing wrong with a top student wanting a big-name college. But when brand name in and of itself takes over the hunt, fit and match can be displaced. As students of colleges, we know that there are at least 100 elite colleges in the US, not merely a handful. We need to be sure that our students know this. We need to be sure that families realize, for example, that Washington University in St. Louis is accepting the same students in terms of GPA, test scores, etc. that Dartmouth was accepting ten years ago.

An eye-opening resource that I like to share with prestige-focused families is Harvard Law School's publication of the list of undergraduate colleges from which it draws its class. It's illuminating to point out the great variation of colleges—particularly all of the state universities—included. A search of "Harvard law school undergraduate colleges" gets you to the list.

Also well worth mentioning here are families who are so unconcerned about prestige that they need to be reminded that applying to selective colleges may be a good option. The factor of prestige goes two ways!

9. Cost/Availability of Financial Aid

A key question here is how cost-driven the choice process is. These days, practically all college decisions have a cost component. Most commonly, the questions center on ability to pay. These discussions involve exploring need-based and merit-based options.

As finances are a concern, students need to have "financial safety schools" on the list. These are colleges that the family feels are affordable, whatever might happen in terms of financial aid.

10. Admission Selectivity

This factor is salient for all students. Students must question how competitive they are as applicants. How do their grades, scores, etc. stack up against others?

11. Need for Academic/Social Recognition

To what extent does the student want to be recognized for achievements? For example, there are students who will be happiest at a less intense college where they can shine.

12. Location

Includes issues such as:
- Relative importance of location to other factors like size or academic program
- Salience of being close to home and close to family
- Regional geographic preference, if any
- Particularly appealing states
- Significance of being close to a city or preferring a rural location
- Weather

Something I like to point out to students is that some colleges in the Rust Belt and some in the Midwest routinely spend more on student life in comparison to colleges in highly desirable locations like Southern California. Of course, that's hardly a hard and fast rule. While location is a salient factor to many, I encourage students not to overlook schools in Schenectady or Worcester or Detroit. After all, students are not picking a vacation site!

13. Academic Success in College

This is a wide ranging factor that might include any variable that leads to student success. Examples include tutors, learning disability support, or special facilities or services.

14. Real-world Opportunities Including Internships, Cooperative Education, Practical Capstone Projects, Experiential Learning, and Hands-on Research

Includes issues such as:
- Percentage of students who receive internships annually
- Existence and quality of a cooperative education program
- Encouragement to learn about careers
- Used and appreciated career planning office

- Time to work and/or explore career options
- Opportunities for campus leadership
- Professors, when appropriate, add a career component to classes
- Evidence of students being employed when they graduate

15. Fitting In/Being Comfortable in College

Here the IEC is using knowledge and intuition in considering any other variable that will lead to a positive collegiate experience. Examples include campus beauty, privacy considerations, residence hall facilities, dining options.

16. Risk

Finding a good match for our students involves dealing with the concept of risk. In this sense, risk refers to a college choice that is adventurous—one that diverts (a little or a lot) from the student's stated criteria. For example, a student might want a student body that is heavily into sports and where most students join fraternities or sororities. College A fits perfectly. The student body at College B, on the other hand, is a little less athletic and not as Greek-oriented. College A is the better choice if the student is not comfortable with risk. Because the IEC has taken time to get to know Buffy, he or she can advise around this issue.

Fit and match can (and probably should) include some risk for each of our students. We should push the envelope in creating a list for students. Encouraging students to think broadly is one of our key tasks.

Consider the following scenario: You know that Brutus is not very confident and feels that he would have a hard time making his way at a college that is not Christian. Brutus comes from a very religious home. In this instance, the IEC might be cautious in suggesting colleges that deviate too much from those that fit the bill. That doesn't mean to refrain from pushing the envelope in identifying colleges for Brutus; rather, it simply means knowing how far to push. On the other hand, Buffy is confident in her religious ideas and is more likely to be successful at a school that deviates from her religious preferences. You might be more inclined to identify (or even promote) colleges that are more mainstream on the religious life perspective for her.

Risk doesn't mean identifying colleges that are totally in contrast with a student's preferences. It means knowing how to use risk in the course of the consulting interaction and knowing which student is suited to handle risk. (See Chapter 17 for additional discussion on risk as it applies to the final decision.)

17. Additional Factors

The factors below enter the choice process depending on individual needs and desires. For most students, they are not central factors. Rather, the consultant may introduce them to meet specific preferences and/or to broaden the universe of factors to consider.

Often important:
- Retention rate from freshman to sophomore years
- Focus on programs/personnel to support students of color
- Strength in a varsity sport
- Strength in undergraduate teaching
- Study-abroad offerings

Sometimes important:
- Local, two-year colleges, no housing
- Beauty of the campus

- Campus safety
- Military
- Hearing impaired supportive
- Physical handicap supportive
- Calendar
- Size of library
- Faculty salaries

The factors above are not exhaustive, and there are overlaps. Size is often related to academic success, for example, and obviously location is related to cost. But they are important because they provide discussion points. They are the template upon which students' needs are assessed, and the answers form the base of our recommendations of appropriate colleges. The template paves the way for the IEC to help a student grapple with both the factors themselves and also the nuances of each factor. For example, if Buffy wants a college that is liberal politically, what does that actually mean? How liberal is liberal? If Buffy wants religious influence, how much influence? Additionally, after the IEC ferrets out Buffy's perspective on these matters (knowing that she is a growing and changing teen), it's essential to encourage her to compare one factor to another. If Buffy wants a small school in a big city, which does she value most highly: the small size or the big city? Through dialogue, the student defines and refines her needs, eventually arriving at choices that are informed both intellectually and emotionally.

Finally, I want to emphasize the importance of considering as many factors as possible in our work with students. I consider the most important factors to be "anchors," and they change for each student. If cost considerations are paramount (meaning that few or no colleges will be considered without assurance of either need-based aid, merit aid, or lower cost), then that is an anchor factor. If religious considerations are vitally important (meaning that few or no colleges will be considered without assurance of good fit religiously), then that is an anchor factor. But having one or more anchor factors on the list doesn't mean the others are unimportant. As important as cost or religion or major or whatever may be, we need to help Buffy with college options where she will be happy and fit in. So we need to consider as many factors as we can—what the student is like, what academic resources are available, the culture of non-competition, et cetera, in our building of a list for her. The problem with online college searches is that they deal with very discreet variables (selectivity, cost, location) and do not deal with the more subjective variables that IECs juggle. As subjective variables experts, IECs deal with trade-offs and ambiguities. We rarely find perfection, but we can verbalize the trade-offs involved and engage the student and the family in discussion of a wide range of factors. Trade-offs are a central component of building the college list and should be addressed throughout the consulting process. The IEC should initiate and take careful note of all trade-off discussions. (See further discussion of trade-offs later in this chapter and in Chapter 17.)

Additional Ways to Help Students Identify College Priorities

Please see Appendices C, D, and E for additional resources that prompt students to reflect upon their college priorities. The "College Planning Values Assessment" in Appendix D asks students to identify and prioritize what they most want from college. When students are introspective and acknowledge their college-going values, the IEC can better peg potential college matches. Additionally, see resources at astudentofcolleges.com for a listing of ways to get to know students. I also recommend that you look at Corsava cards and materials (corsava.com), a method that Seattle-based IEC Anne Wager developed to determine the qualities students are looking for in a college.

II. Evaluate

Prior to developing the college list, consultants evaluate the student in terms of admission. The key element to that evaluation is the student's high school transcript. Grades are pertinent to being realistic about admission chances. When I get a transcript, I recompute GPA using an unweighted standard. Unweighted GPA is the standard 0-4 scale for grades A-F and applies to all courses, no matter the difficulty. Weighted GPA considers the difficulty of a course, such as honors or AP. Some high schools weigh classes to determine class rank. In some schools, a 4.0 GPA means half Bs and half As because of weighted grades. Though some colleges primarily consider unweighted GPA and some weighted, almost all of them go beyond the stated GPA on the high school transcript (or self-reported) to determine rigor of classes. I have students in suburban public schools who claim that because they have a 4.0 GPA, they are Ivy bound. If they have taken vigorous classes, that may be true. But I need to be able to differentiate the student with the most competitive classes and the highest grades from the student with the most competitive classes and less stellar grades.

After I recompute the GPA, I evaluate the coursework. Is it excellent, very good, or standard? I evaluate the 5 major subject groups. (I go through this exercise for all students, looking at the level they have reached in each area juxtaposed with what's offered at their school.) For example, how does the student's math and science and social science courses stack up with what's offered at his or her school? Has the student taken accelerated classes? How academically solid is the student's senior year schedule? In English, is Buffy taking the highest level class possible in senior year? Recomputing GPA and evaluating coursework help me determine admission chances.

In addition to evaluating a student's transcript, IECs also use existing test scores (Pre-ACT, PSAT, SAT, and/or ACT) to determine the chance of admission. Buffy may swear that she's studying like crazy for the SAT and is sure she'll improve by leaps and bounds. That's fine, and the IEC should hope she does. But it's important to use what we know (not Buffy's projection) as the determiner of admission odds.

IECs also need to think about and evaluate other qualities that may be assessed during the admission process. That includes—but is not limited to—factors such as strength of extracurriculars, writing ability (based on writing we request from the student), positive interview potential, articulateness and energy, special categories that might be involved in the decision (legacy, underrepresented group, athlete, artist, learning disability, and so on). If available, it's a good idea to also review a recommendation letter. Sometimes students have reference letters at hand for a summer experience or to join a school group such as the National Honor Society.

Further discussion of evaluating a student's admission profile is presented later in this chapter. Please see "List Building Steps."

III. Conceptualize

Our visits and our research give us raw data about colleges that is essential. But what is most important is taking the information we glean from these sources and organizing it so we can provide a list of colleges that meets the needs of each of our students.

Consultants can help students understand differences between colleges in many ways. Many factors important in choosing colleges were identified above. As an additional way to think about this process of identifying college variables, a characterization design called "The Axes of Comparing and Contrasting Colleges" is introduced below. Using the design, IECs can well articulate the "feel" of colleges and can demonstrate to students and families the wealth of educational opportunities available in higher education.

These axes include distinctions such as openness to different ideas, academic interactive potential, extent to which an average student desires an academic (versus social) experience, intellectual intensity, spirit, career focus, and the extent to which the center of student life is on or off campus.

What follows is, in every sense, a model. It is a way of conceptualizing various elements that are present at colleges and universities. The examples provided in each of the categories are still in their alpha stage and are in no way exhaustive. I have not yet carefully considered which colleges should be included in each category. What I would like you to get out of this section is a conceptualization of ways colleges can be differentiated from one another. Thus, I discourage focus on the examples provided. What I encourage is that you refine the examples, adding or deleting in accordance with your perspective of strong examples (perhaps in the beta stage!).

Further note that the model does not take into account the variability within and among colleges. For example, consider the distinction between intellectual intensity and intellectual mellowness. This is a construct. No actual distinction is quantifiable. Yet as we visit colleges and explore them, we can draw assumptions and conclusions. Just because Lehigh is listed in the more "intellectually relaxed" category does not mean that it is among the least intellectual schools in the nation. Far from it. It means that students have reported to me over the years a lack of intellectual vigor when compared to schools listed in the intense category. Further, there are intra-university differences. For instance, an engineering student at Lehigh may have more of an intense experience than a student enrolled in the liberal arts.

Moreover, colleges handle various student band sizes. In other words, some colleges have a fairly narrow band of students who will likely be happy, and some have a more expansive one. Evergreen State, for example, has a narrow band. It's a special fit type of school. Although I've found that many "types" enjoy their Evergreen experience, those who didn't particularly enjoy high school, those who didn't quite fit into their high schools, and those who identify with a more alternative approach to life seem happiest. Do you have to be high on pot and listen to Umphrey's McGee or Phish to enjoy Evergreen? No. But it wouldn't hurt if you were a bit left of center, had a unique way of seeing the world, were turned on by interdisciplinary studies, and were fairly confident in your approach to life.

Also, it should be stated that it is easier to distinguish traits at smaller colleges. Trying to identify "collective" factors in mega-universities is difficult.

What matters most in consulting with students is the interrelationships between these variables. For example, if a school is intellectually intense and if the interactive potential with faculty members is low, then that school might be right for the independent, scholarly student. Others would be cautioned against considering such a school. Again, focus on the axes themselves and not so much on the examples.

The Axes of Comparing and Contrasting Colleges

I. The Academic Culture
1. Liberal Arts or Vocational Focus
Vocational focus includes colleges with more practical (as opposed to theoretical) courses, applications of material, emphasis on "what it means to your future," internships, and hands-on learning opportunities. It is not related to getting a job after graduation. Vocational focus, as used here, does not include vocational schools per se, so Fred's School of Photography would not be included. It can also be seen as "many majors" versus specialization.

Liberal Arts: Bard, Bates, Beloit, Colorado College, Columbia U, Deep Springs, Dickinson, Furman, Grinnell, Hillsdale, Northwestern, Rhodes,Wellesley, Wooster.

Vocational Focus: Alfred, Art Center College of Design, Bentley, Champlain, Claremont McKenna, College of the Atlantic, Columbia College (IL), Embry-Riddle, Harvey Mudd, Ithaca, Johnson and Wales, Julliard, Kettering, Menlo, Montana Tech, Northeastern, Northland, Renssalaer, University of Cincinnati, University of New Haven.

2. Intellectual Intensity (rigor, high academic expectations, less grade inflation, etc.)

This is a variable that has a number of dimensions. Challenging intellectual and creative work is central to student learning and collegiate quality. Components of academic challenge include the nature and amount of assigned academic work, complexity of cognitive tasks presented to students, and standards that faculty members use to evaluate student performance. Is memorization emphasized? Or higher order, complex cognitive skills? How much time do students spend preparing for class? What does the campus do to encourage students to spend significant amounts of time studying and on academic work? What do faculty and staff do to challenge and support students so that they work to their potential? How hard does the student want to work? Does the student want peers who have taken all AP classes and received As in high school? Are one's study habits and time management skills strong enough for intellectual intensity? How much of a scholar is the student? Does a student want to be at a school with a high risk of burnout? (Not included in either category are schools with little or no intellectual rigor.)

Intellectually intense: Amherst, Barnard, Carleton, Grinnell, Johns Hopkins, New School (NY), Oberlin, Pomona, Reed, Sarah Lawrence, St. Johns (MD and NM), Swarthmore, Thomas More, University of Chicago, Wellesley.

Intellectually relaxed: American, Catholic, Montana State, Rider, Rollins, Southern Illinois University, Southern Methodist, Texas Christian, University of Colorado (Boulder), University of Hartford, University of Montana, University of San Diego, University of the Pacific, University of Tulsa, Willamette.

3. Academic Interactive Potential, Support, and Collaboration (extent to which an average student receives an opportunity to interact with teachers and thinking students, a feeling that professors care, the perception of professors and administrators as collaborators, good advising, mentoring and engagement)

Students perform better if they feel that professors are working with their best interests in mind. Students are motivated when they see faculty and administrators as part of their "team." In general, the more contact students have with their teachers the better. Working with a professor on a research project or serving with faculty members on a college committee or community organization lets students see firsthand how experts identify and solve practical problems. Through such interactions, teachers become role models, mentors, and guides for lifelong learning. Variables to ponder in this distinction include how often/where students meet with faculty outside of class, how the institution promotes such contact, and the number of students who collaborate on faculty research.

Academic interactive potential also includes peer collaboration. In what percentage of courses do students work in teams to complete assignments, solve problems, or apply course content? When students collaborate in solving problems or mastering difficult material, they acquire valuable skills that prepare them to deal with the messy, unscripted problems they will encounter daily during and after college. Small colleges generally have more interactive potential than bigger schools, but there are variations, particularly among the liberal arts and sciences schools.

High interactive potential: Bethune-Cookman, College of Idaho, Elmira, Knox, McDaniel, Mt. St. Mary's, Pitzer, Prescott, University of Montana Western, University of Nebraska.

Neutral on interactive potential: large universities generally, Clemson, Trenton State, University of Miami, University of Toledo.

4. Sensitivity to Learning Style Differences

This often means the level of academic support for students with learning differences; however, a wide range of services, facilities, and sensitivities exist.

High sensitivity to learning style issues: some of these schools have specific programs and others are especially open to and responsive to learning differences: Adelphi, Beacon, Curry, High Point, Hofstra, Landmark, Lesley, Linfield, Lynn, Marist, Mitchell, Muskingum, New England College, Otterbein, Ripon, Schreiner, St. Andrews Presbyterian, University of Arizona, University of Denver, Westminster (UT), Wittenberg.

Neutral on sensitivity to learning style issues: most Ivy league schools, most colleges in the US (Note: It's not that colleges are uninterested in offering services; rather, some schools do the minimum to meet federal law, and students are on their own to find resources.)

II. The Student Culture

5. Accepting Differences in Ideas

The general climate of the school is accepting of different lifestyles and perspectives.

Accepting of differences in ideas: Bard, Bryn Mawr, Clark, Eckerd, Goucher, Hampshire, Smith, University of Michigan, Vassar.

Neutral on accepting of differences in ideas: Grove City, Hollins, Millsaps, University of South Carolina, Washington and Lee, William Jewell, Wofford.

6. Spirit (student life, gung-ho attitude, high interest in college events such as athletics)

In general, bigger universities have more interest in campus events. For example, many students go to athletic events, and the spirit for football or basketball teams is high. In the traditional sense of spirit, big universities have an edge, but campuses of all sizes can be spirited.

More spirited: Baylor, Clemson, Colgate, Dartmouth, Duke, Gettysburg, Lehigh, Louisiana State, Notre Dame, University of the South, Williams.

Neutral on spiritedness: Antioch, Barnard, Belmont, Bennington, Goddard, Ramapo, Santa Clara University, Trinity U (TX), University of Pittsburgh, University of San Francisco, Wheaton (IL).

7. Political Awareness and Involvement

The extent to which a student is able to engage in issues of the day. In recent years, the US has been divided politically, and most would agree that that has contributed to gridlock and stagnation, particularly in Washington. It seems obvious that breaking down these barriers will foster openness, understanding, and progress. We can help our students see the value of that dialogue in picking a college match. We will increasingly face political issues with our students and their parents including questions regarding the prevalence of "liberal teachers," freedom of speech on campuses, and encouraging Buffy to attend a college where she will not be influenced by those on the opposing side of the political fence.

More politically aware: American, Franklin and Marshall, George Washington, Macalester, Mills, Oberlin, Washington College, Yale.

Neutral on political awareness: Creighton, Oglethorpe, Regis (CO), Stephens, Stetson, Susquehanna.

8. Socially Liberal/Conservative
Religious colleges and/or colleges in the Bible Belt states tend to be more conservative.

More liberal: Clark University, Earlham, Naropa, New York U, Scripps, University of California-Berkeley, University of Wisconsin, Madison, Wesleyan.

More conservative: Creighton, Hillsdale, Monmouth (IL) Ripon, Seattle Pacific, Taylor, University of Dallas, University of the South, University of Tulsa, Westmont, Wofford.

9. Extent to Which a Sense of Community Exists
A community feeling is defined by a sense of "we-ness," as seen in closeness among students, group interaction, and a set of activities students generally participate in. Student life is focused inward, meaning the campus is the hub and heart of daily life. Colleges with large commuter populations often have less of a sense of community. All commuter student colleges wouldn't register on this continuum. Schools with a sense of community often are not overly bureaucratic. Large universities vary in the amount of runaround students encounter.

More feeling of community: Bowdoin, Cornell College, Denison, DePauw, Howard, Humboldt State, Kenyon, Knox, Mt. Holyoke, Pitzer, Point Loma Nazarene, Smith, St. Olaf, Washington and Lee, Washington College.

Neutral on feeling of community: Fordham, Hawaii Pacific, Marquette, Rider, Temple, University of North Carolina-Charlotte, Xavier (OH).

10. Comfort: "Preppy" or "Alternative"
Certainly, these are two general and stereotypical ways of viewing the student body. While most schools have students in each of these categories, some schools have a pronounced majority in one camp or the other. Of course, a student could want neither, both, or a combination. The point is that a college's vibe is a salient feature in distinguishing schools.

Comfort for a more preppy/traditional/clean-cut: Agnes Scott, Christopher Newport, Citadel, Trinity (CT), Tulane, Vanderbilt, Washington and Lee.

Comfort for a more free-spirited/alternative/individualistic: Alverno, Bennington, Brown, Clark University, Earlham, Emerson, Goddard, New College (FL), Oberlin, Reed, Warren Wilson.

III: Other Variables
11. Being a Learner Versus Having an Experience
Is the student looking to go to college primarily to be a student, i.e., primary motivation is learning in the classroom, exchanging ideas in and out of the classroom? Is the student interested in concepts, ideas,

and interrelationships between lines of inquiry, or is the student going to college primarily for the student experience, i.e., plenty of time in college to be with friends, grow up socially, engage in college life (the camaraderie, activities, spirit, etc. that has traditionally marked one's college days)? Most students want both; where they put the emphasis, interestingly, is not always a function of how well they've done in high school. Most colleges have students who want both, but colleges differ in the sort of students they generally attract.

More academically-focused students: Bates, Bryn Mawr, Cornell (liberal arts), Haverford, McGill, Rice, St. Johns, Swarthmore, University of Chicago, William and Mary.

More experience-focused students: Davidson, Elon, Emory, Pepperdine, Southern California, St. Louis U, Syracuse, University of British Columbia, Wheaton (MA).

12. Cost and Value

The definition of a college's value is elusive. What is a great value for one family may be less so for another family. Further, value has several connotations: Is it always good value for the money? Are the relevant variables limited to quality of education and cost? Are we talking about return on investment? Is good deal the same as good value? We don't really solve the puzzle by looking at value from a "what colleges are just as good but cost less" perspective. The same can be said for the "most bang for the buck" definition.

It's clear that value in a college education is heavily influenced by cost, but it's not the only factor. Rather, value is influenced by life experiences, images (even stereotypes) of colleges, and images parents have of their sons and daughters.

While it's a slippery construct to define precisely, IECs can have very fruitful discussions with students and parents about how they define value. IECs should pay close attention to clues of family values and priorities and help students and families understand the various ways value can be defined. (See Chapter 14 for further discussion about the worth of higher education.)

Given all of the subjective factors here, let me generalize and suggest that most large state universities are pretty good values for those who live in that state. To be more specific, flagship schools in each state are less likely to be good value colleges when compared to others in the public sector within each state. I also find, generally again, that schools in the Midwest and the South are priced more reasonably as compared to colleges on either coast.

As far as schools that are priced lower than what one might expect on the basis of the quality of the education, I would mention these: Agnes Scott College, Albion, Beloit, Berea, Centre, Clark University, Gustavus Adolphus, Hillsdale, Miami (OH), Rice University, University of Kansas, Ursinus, Valparaiso, Wofford.

13. Undergraduate or Graduate Emphasis

This may be the factor that is most likely to be missing in the college search. If not missing, this factor may not be given the weight it deserves in determining a great match. Colleges that have both undergraduate and graduate programs differ in terms of the emphasis given to each. At some universities, graduate studies and graduate students do not bother the undergraduate experience. At other schools, the most distinguished teachers spend the majority of their time with graduate students. This is also a very difficult factor to measure, particularly in monolithic ranking systems that assign a "score" for the university, often combining undergraduate and graduate sides together. While hard to define precisely, IECs should ask admission officers and students about the focus on undergraduate education. Specifically, ask admission officers to provide a few examples of the college's best professors who teach freshman classes. Additionally, while browsing a college website, look at a department or two. Scan for clues that undergraduates are valued. Are there undergraduate research opportunities? Writing contests for undergrads? Looking at traditions during the undergraduate years can be revealing. For example, a college that has annual freshman or sophomore events is apt to be focusing on these students. Finally, looking at the percentage of freshman coming back for a second year can be insightful.

Undergraduate emphasis: Most small liberal arts and sciences colleges (all of the college resources go toward the undergraduate experience), Baylor University, Brown and Dartmouth have the highest percentage of undergraduate-to-graduate in the Ivy League, Clemson University, Pennsylvania State University, Texas Christian University.

Graduate emphasis: (Inclusion of schools here should not suggest that the undergraduate experience is inferior. It is merely a reflection of a dominant graduate enrollment.) Columbia University, Duke University, Northwestern University, University of Kansas.

BUILDING THE COLLEGE LIST: A FRAMEWORK

There is no set formula as to how IECs should approach the process of developing the college list. It's no easy task. It requires that we put into play both knowledge of an individual student and knowledge of perhaps hundreds of colleges. (Don't panic!) Yes, we have limited time to learn who Buffy is and what she most desires in terms of her education, her college experience, and ultimately her career. (Keep in mind that Buffy herself may not know exactly what she wants!) Yet we have more time—whole careers—to build our college knowledge base. As students of colleges, we study and learn the particulars of colleges and thus become highly confident of our knowledge to help orchestrate Buffy's journey. No one hands us college lists "brought down from the mountain" and tells us how to guide Buffy; likewise, most IECs don't hand students a scroll inscribed on parchment. Developing the college list is an interactive process that is best undertaken in sequential steps, though there is no commandment to do so.

Throughout my career as an instructor at both UCLA and UCI, certificate students have regularly sought a how-to guide to developing a college list. I don't presume to deliver the gospel. However, I am happy to share what has worked well for me.

I follow—to a general degree—the three steps below.

List Building Steps
Step 1: Generate an accurate articulation of what Buffy is "like."
Throughout the first step, I don't have a guidebook in sight, and my computer is not busy browsing a search engine. Instead, I ponder who Buffy is. I reflect upon what I've learned about her from her responses to "Self-Survey for the College Bound" (provided in Appendix C) from *College Match* and what I've learned about her from our discussions.

What is she like as a person? Does Buffy engage well in conversation? Is she articulate? Is she interesting and interested in the world around her? Does she have a wide range of interests? What do Buffy's electives suggest about her? Is she a person who is likely to develop new interests quickly over the college years? Are Buffy's activities focused, or are they diverse? Is she cerebral? Cultured? Sheltered? Well rounded?

What motivates her? What intimidates her? What sort of students do I envision Buffy being surrounded with in college? Nailing this step requires acute observational and listening skills (as discussed in Chapter 7). Questions designed to get to know students are noted in greater detail in Chapter 10. (Also see resources at astudentofcolleges.com for tools to get to know a student.)

While I'm still in pondering mode, I think next about Buffy's writing ability. Are her early writing samples insightful? Overly descriptive? Trite? What do her writings reveal about her personality and her view of life? Is Buffy a person whose personal statements are likely to wow admissions officers?

Overall, does she have that "certain something" an admission officer is likely to detect? If I were an admission officer, would I be impressed with the totality of her presentation and qualifications?

Finally, I put my impressions of Buffy in writing and date my notes. When I discover new facets of Buffy's personality, I add to my character sketch.

Step 2: Inventory what Buffy is looking for in a college.
I begin this step by reflecting upon Buffy's self-discoveries. Let me explain. In early meetings with Buffy, I encouraged her to think about herself and her learning priorities. Let's say that this guided thinking led Buffy to believe that small classes are essential. And let's say that this thinking led her to recognize the need (and want) to be the smartest student in a classroom. These conclusions helped enable Buffy—on her own—to dismiss schools like Harvard and Yale for being too big and too intense academically. Such give and take with a student is growth producing. In this example, Buffy realized what a good-match college looks like. As noted earlier in this chapter, when Buffy can articulate criteria for her best-fit colleges, I have an easier task ahead of me in building her list. (It's important to note that the magic of consulting is not necessarily delivering the list; rather, the magic lies in showing students how to figure out the ways that they themselves can identify good-fit schools.)

Furthering this step, I evaluate Buffy's responses to the student worksheet, "Qualities Important in Selecting a College," from *College Match*. (Whether you choose to use this or other instruments, take the time to thoroughly understand the sort of collegiate environment that will be best for your students.) I use the worksheet as a tool to start thinking broadly about college environments that will provide Buffy a setting where she can succeed academically and thrive socially, where she can build confidence and humility, and where she can grow and be the person she's most capable of being. I contemplate the overall landscape before diving into the details. (One secret to good consulting is to keep the general in mind before the specifics.)

Here are some of the general qualities of the overall landscape that I evaluate:
- Does Buffy have a need to interact with teachers, or does she prefer to be anonymous?
- Should the school be Greek-oriented?
- Should sports rule?
- Is diversity important?
- Is a friendly atmosphere important?
- Is Buffy a more "traditional" or "preppy" student or one who is a bit (or a lot) more "spontaneous" or "alternative"?
- Does Buffy desire a "community" where students are close-knit?
- Is Buffy seeking a strictly academic experience in college, or is she seeking more of a college experience? (Or does she desire some combination of the two?)

- In terms of major, how solidified is her choice of what to study? Is Buffy fixed on major, or is she fishing, discovering, and/or trying to decide? (At this point in the process, I'm not too concerned about major.)
- Does Buffy understand the difference between a college major and a career choice?
- In terms of geography and climate, how open is Buffy? (Early in the list-building process, I don't focus too much on geography and climate.)

If a college doesn't have all of the factors Buffy is seeking, but I feel that it has the atmosphere to further her growth and development, I include it in my initial brainstorm of potential colleges. It's the overall climate I'm seeking. For example, let say Buffy doesn't want a "party hardy" place. I know, however, that there are parties everywhere (or at least most everywhere!), and so I merge this facet in with the others to arrive at good-fit schools. Important to note here is that IECs should and do "turn students on" to colleges that they may never have considered. (Many of these colleges and universities, by the way, are independent.)

At the end of this step, I hone in on more specific factors that Buffy included as important in her selection. If Buffy wants a college that offers a Japanese program, for example, I include a school or two in that category. If Buffy has a particular interest in the Pacific Northwest, I include schools in that region.

Of course, the factors that Buffy deems important in a college may change during the consulting process, but I always make sure that Buffy, her parent(s), and I have a "blueprint" of what we are looking for. I compile this blueprint as I inventory Buffy's college criteria. (Note that later in this chapter I address adding and deleting colleges from the list.)

Step 3: Compile an actual list of appropriate colleges.
Now, with a good sense of who Buffy is and what she is looking for in a college, I turn to my college visit notes. I scan a list of 400 or 500 colleges and consider potential matches for Buffy. (No new IEC will have such a list. As discussed throughout the book, IECs visit colleges over time. Use whatever resources—guidebooks, websites, colleague input, etc.—that you have available at this point.) My goal here is to find a good blend of colleges for Buffy to research. I compile an initial list knowing that not all will make the final cut of schools to which Buffy will apply. I'm not building the ultimate list yet. Rather, I want a list of appropriate colleges for Buffy to check out.

First in my mind as I scan is considering where can Buffy grow. Where will she discover more about herself? Where will she be encouraged to try new things? I think about the students I've met at particular schools and gauge whether I feel that Buffy would fit in and learn from them. I look for schools where Buffy will be challenged academically; where she can engage with friends, become more mature, make wise decisions, and be more self-aware; and where she can prepare for a successful and productive life.

In a less abstract sense, I also scan according to clusters of colleges: arts and sciences oriented, vocationally oriented, religious affiliation, etc. I look for schools that fit both my perception of Buffy and her general college criteria. I scan by region and size. If Buffy has expressed that she only wants small colleges, I push the envelope a bit at this point in the list-building process because she is eliminating a majority of the colleges in the nation from the get-go. I certainly tell her that. (My experience suggests, by the way, that big schools can seem a bit smaller if one is in a smaller college within a big university, like a School of Engineering or an Honors College; broadly, however, a large university, in terms of its general interactive potential, is often still a large school, particularly in the first two years.)

As I sift through my college notes, I list potential matches. Again, the list is large and fairly broad at this point. It is important to note that I need to create a balanced list in terms of likelihood of admission. In other words, I search for schools with a high chance of admission, a few with a low chance of admission, and most with a medium chance. Having evaluated Buffy's admission profile, I can more clearly gauge how many colleges Buffy should have at various selectivity levels. For example, I will err on the side of a few more "low chance of admission" colleges if I feel that Buffy's personal attributes or qualities might supersede her grades and/or her test scores. The other side is the student with great grades and scores but lacking in such personal qualities. (As a side note: I prefer to refer a school as a "low chance of admission" school as opposed to a "reach." I also prefer the phrasing "high chance of admission" school instead of "backup." I feel that "backup" sounds like a booby prize! I call colleges in the Ivy League Athletic Conference, Stanford, Duke, MIT and a few others "wild cards" because they are so selective, and admission decisions are unusually difficult to predict.) Further discussion regarding a balanced list is presented later in this chapter.

When I'm satisfied with my compilation, I put the list away and revisit it in a couple of days. I look again at Buffy's factors, the notes in my files (particularly from early meetings where students are often most spontaneous and I learn a lot about their passions, feelings, and values), her parents' feelings, and other documents in her file. My objective here is to confirm that I have a fairly accurate fix on Buffy's personality, motivations, and goals. If so, I make no changes; if not, I adjust accordingly. There you have it: a framework for building the college list.

OTHER LIST BUILDING APPROACHES

You have just read the steps that I use in list building, but there is certainly more than one way to play a tune. The process of building a college list is not rigid. Each IEC will discover his or her groove. Part of the beauty of being an *independent* educational consultant is being free to find and practice methods that fit your unique style, and I wholeheartedly encourage you to do so.

Below are three other approaches that IECs commonly use to construct a list of colleges.

Consultant A, Macdonald Berger, might spend a whole session talking about the differences between a large school and a small school and end that discussion with a couple of colleges in each category for the student to research. At the next meeting, Macdonald might discuss the pros and cons of an isolated location and again identify colleges. (The process continues.)

Consultant B, Casey Deeyah, might identify the 200 colleges that a student is most likely to consider. Using the list of schools included in *Fiske* or drawing from his own list of colleges, Casey will go through the colleges on that list with the student and parents present and will give families an individualized list at the end of the meeting. This technique has the advantage of the family hearing the rationale for inclusion/exclusion of various colleges. In other words, the consultant might say, "Okay, let's look in Vermont. Middlebury doesn't work because it's way too small and remote given what you told me about an ideal college, and the University of Vermont doesn't have the student qualities you've described. I don't see any other schools in Vermont to explore, so let's move on to colleges in Virginia. Let's see . . . Lynchburg and Roanoke aren't right, but, aha! The University of Richmond has the qualities you want, particularly the type of student you described, so let's write Richmond on our list. Now let's see if there are others in Virginia . . . " And so it goes until all states (if the consultant's list is divided by state) or all colleges are explored. Using this approach, the consultant teams with the student and parents to generate the list.

Consultant C, Shanda Lear, might prepare a list of colleges in advance and use a meeting to describe the listed colleges and to give the rationale for each. For example, "I put this one on your list mainly because the words you used to describe ideal students—spontaneous, alternative, funky, scholarly—are totally true of College X."

Whatever approach is used, I want to emphasize that identifying colleges for students is a time-consuming process. Indeed, it is the essence of being a student of colleges.

LIST BUILDING: HOW MANY COLLEGE APPLICATIONS TO SEND

Again, the college list is not brought down from a mountain, and no official number of colleges that IECs should give students to review is chiseled in stone. Rather, the number of colleges given depends on the student. It has been my experience that some students can handle more colleges and don't necessarily get overwhelmed. The number also depends on when the list is presented. If it's in the end of the sophmore year, I'll give more colleges as compared to the number that I present in October of his or her senior year. Further, the number depends on the variability of the student's search parameters. If a student's interests are more regional, the number of schools will be less when compared to a review list for a student who is conducting a national search. If I sense that a student is super prestige-oriented, I'll give more colleges to consider because I need to assure enough less competitive choices. Finally, I typically don't wait for one meeting to give students colleges to research. I might suggest visiting state universities early in the process, and so I'll talk very early in the junior year about which in-state schools are a good fit. Other times, the family will be in Chicago or LA or Philadelphia or wherever for other reasons and, if time allows, I suggest a few colleges to visit as part of that trip.

Equalizing all that, my average initial list, which I usually give in the middle of the junior year, is about 20 to 25 colleges. That's a lot, but the list is narrowed throughout the reviewing process. For a student who will ultimately apply to ten colleges, having two or three times that number of colleges to consider and research seems right. Applying to eight to ten colleges is average at my office. My experience suggests that once the number gets over 12 or so, either not enough research has been done and/or too much emphasis has been placed on brand-name colleges.

Well worth bringing up here is a work that I often refer to in my courses at UC, Irvine, *The Paradox of Choice: Why More Is Less*. Author Barry Schwartz postulates that too many choices can lead to bewilderment and loss of satisfaction when a decision is made. The Schwartz construct presents questions for us to consider in our practices: How many college choices are too many? Too few? Are we adding to stress through the process, or are we neutralizing it? Does giving Buffy lots of choices make her believe that a perfect college exists for her? Each IEC will likely grapple with this conundrum and will need to find his or her own comfort zone as a deliverer of choices.

PRESENTING COLLEGES TO STUDENTS

The presentation of colleges meeting is a very important one. During this meeting, the consultant demonstrates his/her training and expertise and shares his/her knowledge of colleges. A common method to "deliver" the list is to present colleges at a "college list building" meeting. Using this delivery method, the consultant shares the pre-prepared list of colleges. It is important for the parents to be present at this meeting because a great deal of information is conveyed, and the more ears, the better. During the meeting, the consultant talks a little bit about each college and why it was selected. The consultant strives to make the colleges come alive by discussing the facts as well as the atmosphere or culture of each school. A student is more likely to remember a quirky tidbit about a school than a cold statistic or general fact. For example, if presenting Boise State U to a student, I might say that their football stadium has blue turf. Additionally, it's important to emphasize that part of delivering good match options means delivering ideas about *types* of colleges. For example, for a cost-conscious family, I might suggest looking at a couple of honors colleges. The student may not have even known about this option. Or I might convey to the family know that liberal arts colleges most often include strong science programs. Ultimately, it's best not to suggest that the list is "perfect"; rather, impress upon families that the foundation of the list is good match options.

Having a carefully laid out plan for presenting colleges to students is essential. Consultants often provide written materials to go with their recommendations. Many consultants give a sheet of description on each college presented. Some give students a page from *CADS* (from Wintergreen/Orchard House) or *College Handbook*. Helpful websites include Fiske Interactive Online (collegecountdown.com) and College Data (collegedata.com), the latter offering a printable page of data. There are consultants who give an Excel spreadsheet of statistics (as presented in *US News*, for example) with additional categorization in terms of admission selectivity. Others give a Word document in a table format with school name/website and descriptive information (five to six pieces of relevant information as to why the consultant included this school).

Or you can create a Powerpoint presentation of the college list. Slides can relate to what the student and parents are looking for in a college, the student's strengths, a college list separated by admission difficulty, college descriptions (name, pictures of the college, core attributes of the school that make it a particularly good fit such as a great student-faculty interaction or an excellent neurobiology department, key statistics like size and male/female ratio, admissions statistics, etc.). Slides can also address next steps, outlining the research process. Some consultants give each student a binder with printed information and/or a portable file case with hanging folders for each of the schools recommended.

Before I present a college list, I carefully consider in advance how to organize the schools. I may categorize according to selectivity: low, medium, and high chance of admission. (Some common ways to phrase on the basis of selectivity include: stretch, target, likely; reach, likely, sure bet; unpredictable, possible, foundation; tough admit, good admit, likely admit.) I may organize schools geographically (clustered as West, East/Mid-Atlantic, etc.) or perhaps by size. I may create a separate list of colleges with high merit scholarship potential. Ultimately, I organize the list in accordance with what I believe best fits the student's search criteria. I generally title the list "Colleges to Consider" and include the date. Importantly, I note that the list is tentative and explain the reasons why it's tentative (for example, no SATs, no subject tests, no sixth or seventh semester grades). Another option is to present the colleges alphabetically.

In lieu of a designated college list meeting, the consultant may opt to present colleges over the course of several meetings. The extended approach has several options. For example, the consultant can give the student a few colleges at the end of the sophomore year or early in the junior year for the purpose of jump-starting research. Or the consultant may want the student to get a head start visiting colleges. Perhaps the consultant wants to talk to students about low chance of admission schools at one meeting and high chance of admission schools at another (or schools on the East Coast at one meeting and the West Coast at another). This approach may be especially beneficial for students who need to process information in small doses.

THE BALANCING ACT

The college list is dynamic. Schools are added or deleted as the process moves along. Students change their minds, and consultants should develop early lists that account for unpredictability. Moreover, there are often many reasons why the consultant should revisit the list: receipt of new test scores or grades, the student's impression of a college following a visit, and so on. Remember that the student and the parents have a lot to think about. They are wrestling with distance from home, finances, the value of a small school versus large, and so on. In turn, we as consultants wrestle with our best judgment as to match, fit, and admission. After several meetings I may feel that Buffy should consider more small schools. I push the envelope, tell her my rationale, and present new schools to her. Perhaps her grades shoot up, and I feel that another couple of low chance of admission colleges should be added. In other words, list building is a process that evolves over months.

None of our students should be left without college options. While we don't guarantee admission, we work to ensure that our students have choices. I have never worked with a student who ended up with only denials and wait lists. Part of the reason is assuring that students and parents who hire me understand the parameters of my work. Specifically, my goal is to provide options, and part of the deal involved in contracting with me is the willingness to appreciate what's happening in college admission these days and to apply to schools at all levels of selectivity. When consulting students with outstanding grades and test scores, I emphasize the obscene numbers of applications that the elite colleges receive. In a recent year, Stanford received almost 50,000 applications but enrolled only about 2,000 first-year students. UCLA received nearly 100,000 applications yet enrolled 6,000 first-year students. We want to discourage families from applying to four low chance of admission schools and one high chance of admission school. One of the greatest roles we play as IECs is as identifiers of schools on the middle list.

As a practical exercise, consider the following apply lists and determine if they are balanced: Stanford, Yale, Princeton, and the University of South Carolina. Balanced? No balancing act here. The list is comprised of three low chance of admission schools and a sure bet. Now, let's take a deeper look at balancing. Brutus has a 3.8 unweighted GPA, has lots of AP classes, a 1520 SAT score, and great activities and recommendations. Is Brutus' apply list of Stanford, Harvard, Amherst, Chicago, Washington U (St. Louis), and Pomona acceptable? No. The list contains too many schools in the low (5-20%) chance of admission category and in the medium (20-45%) chance of admission category and none in the high chance of admission category. In such a scenario, I would need to work with Brutus to find acceptable options in the 50%+ category (and I would try to go beyond the State U). This can take time, energy, attitude reformulation, and jawboning. But, by golly, that's my job. And it's my job in October, not April.

For many students (not Brutus in the example above), applying to a local high chance of admission school—a state university or perhaps a community college—is the way to assure an admission. And many students are on board with this strategy. Even after working with hundreds of students, I still err on the side of encouraging more than one sure bet. If I'm uncertain, I share that uncertainty with the student and the family and do my darnedest to convince them to add more choices. In 95% of the cases, my recommendations to add more sure bets are heeded, and we're safe. If every effort is met with resistance, I document my efforts to avoid a disaster and bow out. I am forced to fire myself. Firing myself is the action of choice if and when my efforts to reason with students and parents fail and my advice is repeatedly rejected.

Another potentially disastrous scenario to be avoided is when a student "coronates" a school. Let's say that Buffy has declared Duke as *her school*. If Duke is a reach, I need to work to help her find other good match colleges that are a bit less selective.

If a student has coronated a college from the very beginning of our work together, I talk to the student and parents about the problems inherent in this approach to college planning. I can't stop Buffy from coronation, but I can point out pitfalls and limitations. Parents who don't want Buffy to be disappointed can help. No one can "force" Buffy to be happy with less competitive choices, but with time to let the process unfold, Buffy may come to important realizations herself. I try to counsel so that Buffy feels as much happiness and optimism as possible. But I normally don't tangle with the hardwiring of teenagers.

GUIDING STUDENT RESEARCH AND CAMPUS VISITS

Student Research

Just as we hit the highway or take to the sky to visit college campuses, our students need to do so as well. Campus visits are an integral part of students' college research. For many, the campus visit is a significant step in compiling a college list. A visit can help answer the critical question: "Can I see myself as a student on this campus?"

During campus visits, students observe the undergraduate population, interact in the college community, and get a sense of the prevailing spirit of a college. Perceptive students can learn a lot on a visit, especially if they explore beyond group tour and information sessions.

I tell students that they need to actively investigate potential colleges. Investigation involves researching colleges to gather facts, organizing the agenda, exploring and experiencing colleges through on-campus observation, recording observations, and reflecting on findings. Essentially, IECs prepare students to become investigative college reporters. Most IECs provide materials designed to help students through both initial research and the visiting processes.

To direct students' initial research, I point them to "College Fact Finder" in *College Match*. There are similar worksheets in other general college admissions guidebooks. The "College Fact Finder" worksheet provides prompts geared toward assembling an overview of each college on the initial list. IECs should encourage students to read subjective reviews from *Fiske Guide to Colleges, Princeton Review*, etc., scour each college's website, and take virtual tours. Virtual tours are available at sites such as Campus Tours (campustours.com); eCampus Tours: (ecampustours.com); YouniversityTV (youniversitytv.com); and YouVisit (youvisit.com/colleges). (Also see resources at astudentofcolleges.com.)

You might copy, date, and file completed worksheets in students' binders. I recommend that consultants set a due date for research. (Remember that parents can assist students with the research stage. Teamwork is encouraged!)

As students research, I tell them to focus on the following:
- Academic factors: Where will you be pushed, not shoved? Where will you be able to get the best grades? Where is the learning environment that best fits your learning style?
- Social factors: Where will you be comfortable? Where will you fit in? Where will you have many friends?

As students arrive at good-fit colleges, I encourage them as follows:
- Do not focus too much on major.
- Do not focus too much on cost.
- Do not focus too much on location.
- Do not focus too much on prestige.

Finally, I ask students these questions and follow with wisdoms:
- Are colleges included on your list because they fit on the basis of your reading and your general analysis? Your colleges should be more than just "names." Keep in mind that college planning is not just about getting into a top school—it is, more importantly, about fitting in and being happy.
- Does your list of schools represent a good match between your interests and talents and the strengths of the colleges?
- Do you have some appealing high chance of admission colleges? Having solid backups is important, especially in these days of increased college selectivity. Some students spend a great deal of time deciding on their low chance colleges and relatively little time choosing their safety schools. Safety schools are important to good college planning. A balance is what you are looking for in terms of admission selectivity. Let's assume you apply to ten colleges. In that case, you will want one or two schools from your low chance of admission list, four or five from your medium chance list, and two or three from your high chance list.
- Do you have a financial safety school? This is the college (perhaps a local state university) where cost is agreeable (or at least more reasonable) with your parents.

If Brutus tells me that the answer to any of these questions is *no*, I ask him to rethink his college selection criteria. This is a good time for us to have a conversation about decision-making! On the other hand, if his answers are *yes*, I congratulate him and tell him that he's on the road to a good college choice.

Campus Visits

Families often ask for our thoughts on when Brutus should begin visiting colleges. I tell families that it's fine to visit a college any time after a student enters high school. I note, however, that visit goals for underclassmen compared to those of upperclassmen are different. Ninth and tenth graders (and even some eleventh graders) visit models of colleges to help determine ultimate fit. For example, as a freshman, Brutus may find it enlightening to visit a small liberal arts and science college and a large state university.

While I encourage visits early in the process, many families postpone visits until after students receive admission letters. The wisdom behind such timing extends beyond saving money. As an admitted student, Brutus will likely pay great attention to the feel of a campus and will likely be especially invested in sussing out the student body, facilities, organizations, and the surrounding locale. In other words, Brutus may accept his mission with great integrity.

Families are also apt to inquire if Brutus should take time off school to visit colleges. IECs can put campus visits in perspective. As helpful as campus visits are, good college planning often calls for students to spend time working to keep their grades up.

Tips for Organizing the Campus Visit:
- Plan travel several months in advance (if possible).
- To minimize expenses, organize travel plans to visit several schools in the same region.
- Visit colleges when school is in session. It's important to get a feeling of what the campus is like with students there.

- Set up tours, interviews, classroom observations, meetings with campus staff, coaches, professors, etc. prior to travel.
- Use college websites to determine if it is possible to stay overnight in one of the residence halls. If this option is available, jump on it!
- Prior to visiting, scan club and organization web pages or their social media outlets to connect with students and schedule in-person chats.
- Look on college websites for special visit opportunities prior to booking travel: "Engineering Days," "Discover Days," "Be a Student for a Day," "Transfer Student Day," and so on.
- Parents are welcome to join in the tour and visit. Plan accordingly. Note that the student should take the lead. Parents should avoid speaking for their student.

Exploring and Experiencing Colleges

IECs should arm students with tips to make the most of their time on campuses. Many consultants provide printed lists of questions that students may wish to consider asking during campus visits. For particular lists, consult *College Match*. Below is a broad list of visiting tips that IECs can share with students.

Visiting Tips for Students
- Allow plenty of time to stroll the campus and observe.
- Ask questions of several random students. Different opinions help provide a clearer picture of campus life.
- Pick up a campus calendar to see what events are taking place on campus.
- Pick up a campus newspaper to discover hot topics.
- Look at bulletin boards and posters around campus.
- Collect as much written information as possible. Take handouts, pamphlets, publications.
- Eat a meal in one of the campus dining facilities.
- Tour a residence hall or two.
- Attend a social, athletic, or cultural event if possible.
- Visualize how well you would "fit in" among the students you observe and interact with.
- Keep the following factors in perspective:
    - Weather: Try not to let the weather affect your opinion of the college or campus. Weather is important, but so is getting along with students and being in a place that will help you grow, learn, and have a successful life.
    - Tour guides: Do not judge the student population solely on the basis of the tour guide. You would likely have had a different tour guide if your tour was an hour later.
    - Location: You are not picking a vacation site. Consider location, but more so consider the specific qualities the campus offers that will enable you to be successful. Make sure to check out the neighborhood around campus. Also note how long it took you to get to the college from home. Consider if the distance feels comfortable.
    - Bookstore: A large selection of (or many people buying) sweatshirts, mugs, and other branded insignia items has nothing to do with whether the school is a good fit for you. If the bookstore has a lot of books on interesting subjects, that is a positive!

Recording Observations

It's not common for most students to put pen to paper while touring a school. However, students can easily snap pictures and even dictate quick observations into their mobile device. It is important that students document thoughts about a school immediately after the visit. I direct students to "Campus Visit Notes" from *College Match* and send them off with an observation sheet for each school. If students visit more than one school on the same trip, it's easy for them to forget what they saw at each college or university. Encourage students to write questions to be answered by the IEC upon return.

Reflecting on Observations

Upon return, students should review their recorded observations and reflect. Did they make the most of their visit? Were there any particular circumstances that may have tainted their impression? What was their gut feeling about the school? What resonated with them and why? What was off putting and why? How well do they envision themselves fitting in? What uncertainties about the school should be further investigated? Where might the school land on an apply list?

Some IECs have students generate pro/con lists. Others have students create a mind map. Depending on the student's aptitude, numerous reflection techniques are possible. Ask your students what reflective strategies work best for them.

TRADE-OFFS

As noted above, IECs, unlike search engines, guide students to evaluate subjective variables in their college choices. Trade-offs are the nuts and bolts of an IEC's toolbox. At this point in the college searching process, we refine the student's priorities. We might ask questions like these: "Is size a more important variable than location? Even though your preference is for a large college, would you go to a small one if you got a merit scholarship?" We encourage a student to look at his or her college selection as a process of trade-offs. We need to help students consider what factors are most important as they learn about colleges. What's negotiable? Would smaller size be acceptable if that would mean getting into a "better" college? Discussing trade-offs is an essential component of counseling and consulting. The IEC must take note of and be responsive to changes in students' openness to trade-offs as the college search process takes shape. (See Chapter 17 for additional discussion of advising students to weigh trade-offs.)

WORDS OF ETERNAL WISDOM

No school should be on the college list that the student wouldn't attend if admitted. Further, no college should be on the list that parents wouldn't allow their student to attend for whatever reason, including a feeling that the school is not worth the price. Talking over various perspectives will save confusion and disagreements in March and April of the student's senior year.

ACADEMIC MAJORS AND CAREER ISSUES

IECs decide the right time to discuss academic majors and career issues. Both may have bearing upon the students' apply lists, and IECs should weigh for themselves the significance to place on each.

Too often, students—and especially parents—believe a significant factor in college planning is finding a college that offers a particular major. College is a huge financial expense, and deciding on a major simplifies the process. If one looks at the number of entries on the NACAC listserv, it is clear that counselors are feeling the heat to make the proposed college major a primary selection criterion. But research shows that the decisions made during high school regarding careers have a short life. Further, studies show that college students change their major at least once during their collegiate career. As important as career choice may be, I admonish most students not to "chase a major." Indeed, there is only a one in ten chance that a person will be doing anything connected with his major ten years out of college.

Still, while in most cases we shouldn't fixate on it, we should include a discussion of a school's academic strengths when we address college lists. Gauging the quality of academic undergraduate programs, however, is a difficult task. There are so few quantifiable variables. One can look at the number of research papers authored by students, but for some students authoring is not important, and for some majors, it's irrelevant. You can look at strength in teaching, but we know how difficult it is to reliably measure instructional strength. And, even if we could measure it, one college would rate teacher effectiveness differently than the next.

As far as career planning, I've changed my view. A few years ago I was content to say that most kids change majors, so parents need not worry too much about careers. Maybe that's true, but it's not enough. Yes, some students (and parents and consultants for that matter) are okay with the ambiguity of not having a life direction and believe that *not* knowing one's desired career assures a substantial dedication to the liberal arts and sciences as an undergraduate. I myself am a staunch advocate of the liberal arts and sciences because such classes prepare students for citizenship, for parenthood, and for lives based on reason. Being in a classroom with a sharp professor and intellectually curious peers pushes students to think clearly, to engage wholeheartedly, and to speak rationally. Understanding oneself and how one fits into the world of ideas and people is a by-product of liberal arts education.

However, some students (and some parents) see career matters as defining and feel that a good match is not found unless Buffy knows what she wants to so with her life (or at least has a good idea). According to the annual UCLA student survey, significantly fewer students attend college to "develop a meaningful philosophy of life" as compared to 20 years ago. (In the era of "fake news," I especially consider the trend to veer away from the liberal arts a shame.) The reasons for attending college have shifted to the career arena and to financial success. Whether I agree or disagree with today's college-going mindsets, there is a need to arm our students with factual data on careers.

While I state that I am not a career counselor (that is, I explain that I am a student of colleges and not a student of careers), I try to find a blend of these approaches in my practice. I have a responsibility to keep up on career matters, and I encourage thought and attention to career options, not necessarily so that one's college major can be found, but rather to begin an exploration of the world of careers. Long-term, substantive career planning in our society is woefully lacking. As a result, students must take it upon themselves to learn about careers, gather information, and establish some career planning goals. IECs can help ease this burden.

There are several ways to engage students in a discussion of careers, vocations, and life planning. For example, IECs can have students write about their "ideal job" or "perfect career." Prompt students to fantasize that there are no limitations (i.e., degrees or training needed, funds available, etc.). Ask them to describe a typical day rotating around the "perfect career." Guide them to be very specific in their description—what time they would wake up, the kinds and numbers of people with whom they would interact, the kinds of projects they would work on, etc. Such write-ups are usually about one page. The IEC can analyze the write-up, looking for patterns, goals, values, and themes to come up with jobs/careers that would satisfy the factors identified in the fantasy job (i.e., creativity, independence, personal contact with others, etc.).

I encourage high school students to do a bit of legwork on their own: read books about career options, look at career websites, shadow people who do different things, etc. Students might want to consider taking some pencil-and-paper interest inventories, often given in high schools or local community colleges. "Do What You Are" is a web-based career and guidance package that uses personality type to help students develop a path toward career insights. Other popular career inventories are Strengths Finder 2.0, YouScience, and I Start Strong Inventory.

To engage parents and students in talk of career issues, consider drawing attention to two schools of thought that Bill Mayher addresses in his classic *The College Admission Mystique*. Mayher juxtaposes the following viewpoints: 1) Young people should settle down and figure out what path to take in their lives. Keep them on the straight and narrow to begin with—which for many means going into the family business, and 2) The happiest and most successful adults are those who discovered an interest on their own and pursued it vigorously. Opening these viewpoints for discussion may be quite enlightening for all at the table.

Ultimately, the expectation of IECs in the career area is changing. We have an obligation to stay attuned to career information, career inventories, and job prospects. The goal is not necessarily to help Buffy "find" a career; rather, the goal is to provide a place where students learn more about themselves, and that includes a focus on life and career planning. Administering a career inventory and talking to students about career interests can both be useful. After all, things move quickly when one is in college, and it is helpful if students have some options before they begin their college years.

(See resources at astudentofcolleges.com for more information about careers and majors).

FINAL THOUGHTS

Finding the right college is a lot like house hunting—this is, after all, going to be Buffy's "home" for the next four years. When you looked for a house, what was the first thing you did? You probably looked at a website to get a sense of options in your price range. You likely filtered the search according to some specific parameters, and you looked at the pictures posted and the description of those houses. But you can't make a decision just by searching a website. You need to learn what the neighborhood is like, determine how safe it is, consider the school district, know what the demographic is, etc. You need to think about how close or far it is from other aspects of your life: your commute for work, parks, entertainment, grocery shopping. You and your realtor put together a short list—houses you want to see in person as well as some that the realtor thinks might work for what you based on your criteria. You might not have considered some of the listings that your realtor compiled. When you tour the options, one of the spaces you had thought would be perfect for you may end up not being at all like the pictures and descriptions, or it may require more expense to make it what you want than you can afford. It's also possible that you walk into a place that you didn't even want to look at and something just clicks, and it feels like home. And sometimes, you aren't ready for the house of your dreams, and you need to start with something smaller or less upscale and start looking again in a few years. Ultimately, you have to weigh all the factors and decide places to put offers on. The decision may not be easy, but with careful thought and the guidance of a trusted realtor, you can make a wise choice and have no buyer's remorse.

And so with the college choice. Creating the right list for each student is imperative to the work of the student of colleges. Our focus on fit and match demands that we know both the student and the colleges. If we operate with a one-size-fits-all mindset, we do Buffy a disservice and are not a value added. Students working with an IEC deserve to have college recommendations that are based on current and reliable information and that will offer an environment wherein they can be successful and happy.

CHAPTER 7

Three C's: Consulting, Counseling, and Communicating

One of the joys of being an IEC is interacting with—and often laughing with and learning from—young adults. We'll look at elements of that interaction in this chapter. The first part of this chapter identifies the process-oriented from the knowledge-oriented consultant and suggests that success comes when the two approaches meld into a cohesive whole. The discussion of communication theories and strategies takes up much of the chapter because insightful IECs go beyond the obvious presentation to understand what makes Buffy Buffy. The chapter also covers specific approaches to communication such as person-centered counseling, motivational interviewing, and nonverbal communication. Finally, since our work often involves attitude change ("Yes, Buffy, Rice University is really that good!"), we'll explore some counseling theories that will help Buffy see the value of options she may not have been open to. The chapter ends by putting many of these components together with a tool designed for IECs to evaluate their communication skills.

PROCESS-FOCUSED AND KNOWLEDGE-FOCUSED CONSULTING

Within the college consulting field, there are two tracks of focus: process-focused and knowledge-focused. The process-focused consultant guides a student through the steps necessary to make reasoned choices and to have a successful transition to college. He or she lends a hand, an ear, and, perhaps even a shoulder to cry on. He or she helps manage the process of applying to college. In a pure sense, the person working as a process consultant typically is attuned to the emotional well-being of the student, meets the needs of the student, and assists the student through a series of steps leading to an educational outcome. Process-focused consultants are not just sympathetic ears and hand-holders; rather, they are people who primarily manage the process of applying to college. They control the flow of information, assist in comprehension, and reduce the tendency of the student to become overwhelmed. Important background credentials for the process-focused consultant are an awareness of adolescent issues, an understanding of counseling theory and practice, an understanding of the general landscape of the subject matter, and a passionate heart. This person primarily relates to students as a partner. This style of consulting focuses on the student.

The knowledge-focused consultant, in contrast, understands the collegiate landscape as well as the recruitment, application, and selection processes. The knowledge-focused consultant targets his or her work primarily on providing information regarding educational options. The interaction between consultant and client is more directive, informational, and less focused on meeting emotional needs. He or she is focused on providing information about colleges. Important credentials for the knowledge-focused consultant are number of visits to colleges and schools, staying current with trends and practices, and being on the cutting edge of institutional knowledge. The consultant primarily relates as an expert to the student. The style of consulting focuses on institutions.

The process-oriented consultant typically meets students and families more frequently than the knowledge-focused consultant. Commonly, the focus of the meetings is different. The rapport building and the process-orientation often translates into a need for more contact time. The knowledge-focused consultant is slightly less concerned about rapport and has a different attitude about delivery of service. The "pure" knowledge-based person, for example, might see his or her expertise as providing information about colleges and developing an appropriate college list. As a future IEC, instead of meeting many times for application/essay work, the knowledge-focused consultant may meet more times to discuss colleges exclusively.

Which perspective will likely drive the future of independent educational consulting? The short history of the field leads me to think that the future of the profession is going to be on the knowledge-focused side. Every consultant will be expected to be able to handle the process side efficiently. Certainly, the tools of consulting (counseling techniques, listening skills, caring, etc.) lay the foundation for practice. However, a caring, supportive advisor who lacks the ability to help a student understand the difference between Oberlin and Hobart, for example, is less than effective. Knowledge of colleges and the admission process is the reason for the success of the field in the last few decades. In some ways this also emphasizes the word *consultant* in our profession's name. "Counseling" will always be our base. That is, the student comes first. Quality independent educational consulting rests firmly with our ability to relate, empathize, challenge, expose, and engage with young people. That said, the profession is flourishing not because of the counseling we are doing—it is flourishing because we know colleges and understand the admission process. We need to understand the specifics (admission selectivity, deadlines, admission procedures, etc.) but, more importantly, we need to understand the infrastructure of admissions. We need to understand how market forces and economic conditions affect the process. We need to be aware of the ways consumerism affects admission. We need to be able to understand the influence state legislatures have on the success of public universities and be aware of the ripple effect of changes in the public arena on private colleges. The profession of independent educational consulting will grow when knowledge is the driving force of its need and purpose.

I am not diminishing the process side of our role. If we lost that focus, the profession would truly lose its way. However, it is my conviction that the knowledge we acquire over the years will distinguish the advice of the educational consultant from the advice offered in the schools, in magazines, in newspapers, and on websites.

PERSON-CENTERED COUNSELING

Whether process or knowledge-oriented, consulting involves a lot of counseling. While consultants are not therapists, counseling theory is relevant as we work to understand our students and to help them make important choices. Carl Rogers and Robert Carkhuff provide perspectives that are useful to educational consultants, and the following material comes directly from the work of these two theorists.

The Rogerian approach to counseling is based on the belief that people have the capacity and the right to move toward self-actualization. As such, people are considered rational, forward-moving, and realistic beings. Because people can regulate and control their own behavior, the counseling relationship is a means of tapping personal resources and developing human potential. Rogers first called his approach *non-directive therapy*, because he discouraged giving advice, asking questions, and making interpretations. Later he adopted the term *client-centered* because of the responsibility given to clients for furthering their own growth. Finally, Rogers embraced the term *person-centered* in hopes of further humanizing the counseling process.

A person-centered counselor practices in accordance with the following principles:
- a person has worth and dignity and therefore deserves respect
- a person can identify his or her own values
- a person has the capacity and right to self-direction; when given the opportunity, a person can make wise judgments
- a person has the capacity to deal with his or her own feelings, thoughts, and behavior
- a person can make constructive use of responsibility
- a person has the potential for constructive change and personal development leading toward a full and satisfying life.

Rogers believed that the counselor becomes an objective, unemotional mirror who reflects the person's inner world with warmth, acceptance, and trust. This mirroring allows people to judge their own thoughts and feelings and to begin to explore the effects of emotions and cognitions on behaviors. To effectively facilitate the mirroring role, the person-centered counselor must possess three special qualities:
1. Congruence: genuineness and honesty with the client
2. Empathy: the ability to feel what the client feels
3. Respect: acceptance and unconditional positive regard towards the client

In regard to independent educational consulting, the consultant is likely more directive than the person-centered model identifies as ideal for a counselor. Still, our warmth and acceptance create an environment that facilitates trust and willingness to share. When the consultant is nonjudgmental, the student is free to explore and discover his or her values, which should lead to better decision-making and to more productive behavior.

Robert Carkhuff (in *The Art of Helping, The New Science of Possibilities* and other books) expanded on Rogers' three qualities noted above and postulated seven skills important to the work of the counselor. In the outline below, I apply Carkhuff's postulations to fit the IEC-student dynamic:

1. Empathy
   - The IEC strives for an accurate sense of the student's experience and point of view.
   - The student should feel that the IEC understands, relates to, and accepts his or her thoughts and beliefs.

2. Respect
   - The IEC conveys caring for the student.
   - The student should feel that he or she has the capacity to lead the consulting process and to ultimately make wise decisions.

3. Concreteness
   - The IEC avoids abstractions and communicates using specific language.
   - The student should be able to connect with the specifics that the IEC communicates.

4. Genuineness
   - The IEC expresses a sincere desire to engage with and help the student (clearly demonstrating the IEC loves his or her work).
   - The student should sense the IEC's authenticity and trust the IEC's genuine desire to help.

5. Immediacy
   - The IEC discusses openly his or her concerns as they arise, focusing on the present.
   - The student should trust that the IEC is engaged in the here and now.

6. Confrontation
   - The IEC points out incongruent thought patterns and discrepancy between words, feelings, and actions.
   - The student should feel not feel defensive as if under attack; rather, the student should consider the feedback as an invitation to examine the behavior and change it if necessary.

7. Self-Disclosure
   - The IEC communicates an openness to volunteering personal information in accordance with the student's interests and concerns. The IEC refrains from force-feeding personal anecdotes.
   - The student should recognize that self-disclosure on the part of the IEC is given as example, not dogma.

While it is not necessary for the IEC to adopt the thinking of Rogers, Carkhuff, or any other theorist, it is essential that the IEC sees himself or herself as a counselor and that the IEC maintains a curiosity about this area. I find the concepts of person-centered counseling to be especially relevant to our interactions with students and parents. Our words matter. Every dialogue with a student and a parent has a goal: assisting the student to find a good fit college. Every dialogue impacts the degree to which clients develop trust in our knowledge and judgment. To be effective in our component as counselors, IECs would do well to employ the fundamentals of person-centered theory: empathy, genuineness, respect, etc.

Some IECs come into the field grounded in counseling theory and only need an occasional brush up. Others need to take the time to learn basic principles. I often go to a college bookstore and find the textbooks used in counseling classes in graduate school. Until a book is written on counseling for the IEC, I encourage practitioners to explore the works of authors compiled on my website. (See resources at astudentofcolleges.com for counseling references.)

MULTIPLE INTELLIGENCES

Howard Gardner's *Frames of Mind*, published in 1983 and in 2011, postulates the theory of *multiple intelligences*. Gardner's theory contends that there is not a single measure of intelligence (like the traditional IQ) but rather that people possess a range of intelligences. Essentially, what Gardner calls intelligences are competencies or talents. Some people are conscious of their intelligences and capitalize on their core strengths; others may need guidance to uncover or discover the area(s) in which their core competencies lie. Originally, Gardner identified seven distinct intelligences; he recently added an eighth intelligence, all of which are outlined below. It's possible that Gardner may soon add a ninth intelligence: "spiritual" or "existential," relating to a person's ability to see the big picture. Note that Gardner's theory also encompasses learning styles that align with each intelligence.

The theory of multiple intelligences is a tool we can use as we think about our students; it allows us to view our students (and to encourage our students to view themselves) with more dimensions than merely their SAT or ACT scores. Buffy may be a word wizard while Brutus is music maestro. Our students all have their own set of *smarts*.

The information below has been compiled from (multipleintelligencesoasis.org) and (institute4learning.com).

The Eight Intelligences Outlined
1. Visual-Spatial ("picture smart")
- Likes to draw, build, design/create, daydream, look at pictures/slides, watch movies, technology
- Is good at visual arts, imagining, sensing changes, mazes/puzzles, reading maps and charts
- Learns best by working with images (pictures and colors), spatial organization (mind mapping), visualizing, imaging, drawing

2. Bodily-Kinesthetic ("body smart")
- Likes physical activity, touch, and talk: uses body language
- Is good at sports, dance, acting, hands-on projects
- Learns best by processing knowledge through bodily sensations, movement, touch, hands-on, creative dramatics, dance

3. Musical ("music smart")
- Likes to sing, hum, tap, listen to music, play an instrument, respond to music
- Is good at picking up sounds, remembering melodies, noticing pitches/rhythms, keeping time
- Learns best by rhythm, melody, patterned sound, songs, rap, spoken word

4. Verbal-Linguistic ("word smart")
- Likes to talk, read, write, tell stories
- Is good at written and communication, memorizing (names, places, dates, trivia)
- Learns best by reading, writing, speaking, listening

5. Logical-Mathematical ("number/reasoning smart")
- Likes to conduct experiments, figure things out, work with numbers, ask questions
- Is good at math, science, reasoning, logic, problem-solving
- Learns best by working with numbers, exploring abstract patterns/relationships, classifying, categorizing

6. Interpersonal ("people smart")
- Likes to have lots of friends, talk to people, join groups
- Is good at understanding people, leading others, organizing, communicating, mediating conflicts
- Learns best by sharing, comparing, relating, cooperating, interviewing, teaching

7. Intrapersonal ("self smart")
- Likes solitude, self-reflection, pursuing own interests
- Is good at understanding self, focusing inward on feelings/dreams, following intuition, being original
- Learns best by working alone, working intuitively, individualized projects, self-paced instruction

8. Naturalistic ("nature smart")
- Likes conservation, outdoor activities, wilderness, animals, exploring natural surroundings
- Is sensitive toward nature and the world; feels renewed by natural, outdoor settings
- Learns best by observing, classifying, labeling, categorizing information, and recognizing patterns

How to Use Multiple Intelligence Theory to Better Serve Students
We can make use of Gardner's theory during our meetings with students by tapping into as many modalities as possible. We may not know which *smarts* our students excel in but when we break from our standard routines and mix up the dynamics of our sessions, the likelihood of creating an engaging atmosphere in which students feel comfortable and learn best increases. Our offices are places where we can use cooperative learning, role play, multimedia, inner reflection, and so forth. Below are some specific techniques that we might employ in each of the areas.
- **Visual-Spatial:** Create visual analogies; use charts, graphs, and photos to illustrate concepts; create visual story maps to bring our college visits to life for our students.
- **Bodily-Kinesthetic:** Dramatize when sharing college insights, engage in hands-on activities when working with students to build college lists, change room arrangement, use cooperative groups.
- **Musical:** Play background music and allow students to pick the musical genre, let students get into a *groove*.
- **Verbal-Linguistic:** Give presentations both verbal and written, generate lists of adjectives with students in order to describe and help classify colleges, encourage students to journal and share their thoughts about colleges they research and/or visit, listen attentively to and note the student's words.
- **Logical-Mathematical:** Help students organize their thoughts about colleges through the use of categorizing and classifying techniques, use logical equations to help problem solve, use graphs to measure and sequence, employ critical thinking, predict logical outcomes.
- **Interpersonal (people smart):** Practice cooperative learning, encourage students to share their stories, suggest that students interview you about a particular insight of yours that they wish to learn about, engage in group work, practice social awareness, brainstorm with students actively leading the way.
- **Intrapersonal (self smart):** Ask students to reflect on college research and visits, provide personal responses, engage students in individual study, encourage students to articulate in whatever manner they choose their hopes and dreams, emphasize personal goal-setting.
- **Naturalistic:** Sit outside (especially practical if you have a home office with private patio space), use natural lighting in your office, suggest a walk if the student seems stifled by a long session indoors, encourage students to snap photos of natural settings during campus visits, create and share scrapbooks of scenic campuses you've visited.

Finally, Gardner's theory is also helpful as we talk to students about careers. Many adults find themselves in jobs that do not make optimal use of their most highly developed intelligences; for example, consider the bodily-kinesthetic individual who is stuck in a desk job when he or she would be much happier in a career that involved movement, such as a recreational leader, a forest ranger, or a physical therapist.

The theory of multiple intelligences gives young people (and adults) a new way to look at their lives, examining potentials and opportunities.

EMOTIONAL INTELLIGENCE

While Peter Salovey and John D. Mayer were the first to introduce this concept, emotional intelligence (EQ), a behavioral model, rose to prominence with Daniel Goleman's 1995 book *Emotional Intelligence*. Gardner's theory of multiple intelligences certainly influenced Goleman's work.

Emotional intelligence is the ability to recognize and understand emotions in yourself and others and to use this awareness to manage your behavior and relationships. Emotional intelligence is another tool we can use in our approach to our students. It helps make clients more trusting; in turn, trust leads to good rapport and increased satisfaction. I also feel that emotional intelligence can help make us more resilient to the stresses of the profession and less likely to experience burnout.

The essential premise of EQ is that the effective awareness, control, and management of one's own emotions and those of others is critical to success. EQ embraces two aspects of intelligence: 1) understanding oneself, one's goals, intentions, responses, and behavior; and 2) understanding others and their feelings.

Outlined below are competencies and skills that Goleman posited as key to working well with others:

Self-Awareness
- Recognize one's emotions and their effects
- Welcome candid feedback
- Develop new perspectives

Self-Regulation
- Manage disruptive emotions and impulses
- Maintain standards of honesty and integrity
- Build trust through reliability and authenticity

Self-Motivation
- Strive to improve or meet a standard of excellence
- Seek information to reduce uncertainty
- Pursue goals despite obstacles and setbacks

Social Competence
- Listen well and seek mutual understanding
- Foster open communication
- Orchestrate win-win solutions

Empathy
- Show sensitivity and understand others' perspectives
- Take an active interest in others' concerns
- Communicate acceptance

How I Use EQ in My Practice

Consulting is a dialogue between the IEC and the student. IECs need to work on their own emotional intelligence as well as learn to deal with varying levels of EQ in our students.

Remember that everyone is growing as a person, and it is common for adolescents to be low on the EQ scale. Be on the lookout for students (and, not uncommonly, parents) who exhibit these types of traits:
- trouble reading/regulating their own emotions

- inability to use emotion to facilitate thinking
- difficulty understanding how emotions progress
- blur the progression between emotions (for example, the progression from irritation to frustration and the progression from frustration to rage)

More broadly, students or parents who lack EQ may struggle with the following: self-awareness, self-regulation, self-motivation, empathy, and effective relationships. In addition, here are signs of lack of emotional intelligence: being overcritical, seeking to blame others (including the IEC), thinking in terms of absolutes such as *always* or *never*, and focusing on or presupposing negative feedback.

IECs, as a general rule, are empathic people. Thus, dealing with someone who is not empathic can be a particularly troubling. As consultants, we need to help our low-EQ clients see the world in ways other than just black and white. This means understanding that some people cannot read and respond to other people's emotional currents. We need to focus on behavior and issues and not try to "fix people."

Here are some practical approaches to dealing with clients who lack EQ:
- Use as many modes of communication as you can. The low-EQ person has a hard time picking up on nonverbal cues. Find many ways of saying the same thing using verbal messages, tone of voice, repetition, and writing.
- Combine formal meetings with informal meetings and with email.
- Be careful about your use of sarcasm. Some people with low-EQ can't pick up sarcasm.
- Use quantifiable data when you can. You need to give emotionally unintelligent people a fuller sense of the data that they are missing. Repeat and clarify information often. If Brutus can't read your emotions, he won't get all the information you're sending.
- Set boundaries. Some of those with low EQ don't have the ability to know when they are going beyond common norms in dealing with a professional. It's important to stand your ground.
- Don't take it personally! Clients with low emotional intelligence often find themselves reacting with frustration and anger when they aren't immediately understood. If a student or parent becomes angry for no rational reason, it may be time to pause for a second or two, and move on to another topic if possible. Further, those with low emotional intelligence tend to blame others; it's always someone else's fault when things go wrong. Low emotional intelligence people have difficulty seeing flaws in themselves; thus, they frequently attribute failings to external sources.
- Be your own therapist. You can't control what other people do or say. However, you can control your own actions. Be emotionally self-aware, too. Stop occasionally throughout the day and check in with yourself. Are you calm? Stressed? Are you coping?

IECs who are high in emotional intelligence are able to admit they don't know, prioritize and complete daily tasks, and recognize and deal with both positive and negative emotions. Those high in EQ are able to do an inventory of their emotions. That is, they recognize that their brain is where all of the facts about colleges, students, the admission process, etc., are housed. But they also understand that all of the facts in the world don't help us be *emotionally present* for our students and parents. It's important to pay attention to our emotions and recognize that they affect interactions with clients.

MOTIVATIONAL INTERVIEWING

Motivational interviewing (MI) is a communication technique designed to motivate change. The interviewer, in dialogue with the interviewee, consciously crafts conversation so as to elicit, rather than impose, change. Through the practice of MI, the interviewer develops acute listening skills and a heightened ability to empathize with the interviewee. The interviewer does not assume the role of an expert imposing advice; rather, the dialogue prompts the interviewee to self-reflect and consider the personal value of change.

Here, let's look more closely at the central tenets of MI and how the IEC can employ MI to help facilitate change.

First, I wish to establish that change is a key component of decision-making and thus an important part of the work of the IEC on behalf of the student. Some of the many circumstances in which the IEC works to motivate change include:

- The student (or parent) who believes a prestigious college is the only way to go
- The student who believes she can't be happy at any school that is not huge
- The student who believes that since he hasn't received all As, he will have to *settle* for a lousy college
- The student who is not engaging in the process of college planning
- The student who doesn't associate better high school grades with more college choices
- The parent who doesn't see that his or her intrusive behavior is having a negative effect on Buffy's college planning

As the interactions between people influence change, the IEC is in a pivotal position to help students rethink and switch gears.

The practice of MI begins with a clear understanding of the stages of motivation to change:

Pre-contemplation: At this stage, the individual is not aware that a thought process or course of action may be detrimental to future success. This stage is also known as denial. Here, Brutus may be under the illusion that as a legacy, he is a shoe in at Stanford and no extra effort needs be taken to prepare for application and no backup plan needs be established.

Contemplation: At this stage, the individual recognizes that his or her thoughts or actions are faulty but is not yet ready to commit to or act upon change. Here, Brutus acknowledges that he may not be accepted to Stanford but doesn't wish to do anything proactive either to improve his odds of admission or generate a backup plan.

Preparation: At this stage, the individual considers options to remedy the problem but does not commit to immediate action. Here, Brutus admits that he ought to step up and get to work crafting a stellar personal statement and adding more colleges to his list, but he doesn't wish to put the pedal to the metal quite yet.

Action. At this final stage, the individual commits to change and is ready to roll. Here, Brutus gets his creative juices flowing, drafts his personal statement, and welcomes the IEC's additions to his college list.

To help students move to the action stage, the IEC can utilize the fundamentals of MI as outlined below.

- Establish a collaboration with the student, grounded in the student's point of view and experiences. To get the most from motivational interviewing, the IEC should not act as an authority figure. The relationship should be more like a partnership or companionship than an expert/non-expert dichotomy. Collaboration builds rapport and facilitates trust in the helping relationship.
- Draw out the student's own thoughts and ideas. Commitment to change is most powerful and durable when it comes from the student. No matter what reasons the IEC might offer to convince the student of the need to change behavior, lasting change is more likely to occur when the student discovers his or her own reasons and determination to change. Encourage the student to take the lead in developing a *menu* of options as to how to achieve the desired change.
- See things from the student's point of view, even if you disagree.
- Express empathy. It is a means of effecting change. Expressing empathy towards a student shows acceptance and increases the chance of the IEC and student developing rapport.
- Encourage the student to make his or her own choices. Do not argue that the student has a problem and needs to change. Do not offer direct advice or prescribe solutions to the problem without encouraging the student to make his or her own choices. MI doesn't work when the IEC does most of the talking, functions as a unidirectional information delivery system, or imposes a label. Do not point out to Brutus that his issue is commonly called *having no backup choices*.
- Listen for and appreciate the student's ambivalence about change. Ambivalence—feeling two ways about behavior change—is a natural part of the change process. As an MI practitioner, the IEC needs to be attuned to student ambivalence and *readiness for change*. To broach ambivalence with teenagers, consider the following: in "Use Motivational Interviewing to Change Teen Habits" (*Family Practice News*, May 23, 2012) Sherry Boschert, journalist and blogger, posits, "A good way to start is by talking about ambivalence, a word that adolescents love once you explain what it means." Boschert continues, "You're kind of not sure. You feel two feelings, and it's kind of crazy. You feel one thing and you think the other." That usually clicks with teenagers "because that's their life, really," according to Boschert.
- Reinforce change talk. Change talk covers five categories: desire, ability, reason, need, and commitment, or DARN-C. A part of the process of learning MI is coming to recognize and reinforce change talk because when people talk about change themselves, they are more likely to change than if someone else talks about them. In this way, change talk is self-advocacy. Learn to listen for the subtleties of meaning in each of the five categories.
- Try using the questions below to elicit change talk:
    - Desire: Why do you want to make this change?
    - Ability: How would you go about initiating such change?
    - Reason: What are the three best reasons to support the change?
    - Need: How and why is change important?
    - Commitment: What do you think you'll ultimately do?
- Guide students to perceive differences between their current situations and their hopes for the future. A discrepancy between present behavior and important goals motivates change. Consider the student who visits ten colleges and likes none. Point out the discrepancy: "So we have a gap between schools you like and your stated need to have a completed apply list by November 1." This conversational technique helps students examine their behavior and develop an awareness of consequences.
- Facilitate discussion through open-ended questions that are not easily answered with a "yes/no" or short reply containing only a specific, limited piece of information. Open-ended questions invite elaboration and thinking more deeply about an issue. By asking open-ended questions, you encourage a student to tell his or her story. Your goals are to gather information, learn what's important to the student, allow the student to listen to him/herself, and to provoke thought and consideration.

- Use open-ended questions such as:
    - "What are your dreams?"
    - "What are your ideas?"
    - "What steps can you take?"
    - "How do you feel about that?"
    - "What does 'Buffy college' look like?"
- Probe for more information:
    - "Please elaborate on—"
    - "Tell me more about—"
- Avoid questions that begin with "why" because they may sound judgmental or threatening.
- Practice skillful, reflective listening. Help the student listen to him/herself. You can demonstrate that you understand a student's issues or feelings by reflective listening. This listening might prompt the student to see his or her inconsistencies. Reflective listening also helps a student clarify misinterpretations or add depth to the thoughts and feelings expressed.
- Repeat or rephrase the student's words. This is one level of reflective listening.
    - Student: "I feel like I won't be happy unless I go to Yale, Stanford, or Princeton."
    - IEC: "It sounds like it's difficult for you to go beyond the biggest name colleges as you think about being happy."
    - Student: "Yes, I think it's because—"
- Other ways to respond:
    - "So you feel—"
    - "It sounds like you—"
    - "You're wondering if—"
    - "What I hear you saying is—"
- Paraphrase the student's words. This is another level of reflective listening.
    - Student: "I know I should have more backups on my list; it's just that I can't seem to find any I like."
    - IEC: "You are aware of all the reasons you should add backups, but it sounds like it has been hard to find the motivation to do that."
- Reflect the student's feelings. You may be able to tell what a student is feeling (from verbal or nonverbal cues) and give him or her words for those feelings.
    - Student: Appears sad.
    - IEC: "How have you been feeling? Do you feel as if you won't find the right college?"
- Practice the technique of simple reflection. The simplest approach to responding to resistance is with nonresistance, by repeating the student's statement in a neutral form. This acknowledges and validates what the student has said and can elicit an opposite response.
    - Student: "I don't plan to add any backups to my list."
    - IEC: "You don't think that having backup colleges on your list would make sense for you right now. You are okay taking a risk that you may not get into any college."
- Practice the technique of amplified reflection. Here, the IEC repeats the student's statement in an exaggerated form but without sarcasm. This can move the student toward positive change instead of resistance.
    - Student: "I don't know why my parents are worried about this. Lots of students I know don't have their essays completed."
    - IEC: "So your parents are worrying needlessly?"
- Practice the technique of double-sided reflection. This strategy entails acknowledging what the student has said but then also stating contrary things that he or she has said in the past. This requires the use of information that the student has offered earlier, although maybe not at the same meeting.

- Student: "I know you want me to look beyond the big-name schools, but I'm not going to do that."
- IEC: "You can see that there are some problems with your list, but you're not willing to add some of the other schools now."

- Summarize the student's statements. A summary gives you an opportunity to make sure that you understood what the student has told you, and it gives the student an opportunity to correct you if you have misunderstood something. The example below pertains to using MI with a parent.
  - IEC: "Let me make sure that I understand. You are very concerned about your daughter's college list, particularly that she add some small schools, but whenever you ask her to do that, she refuses and a fight ensues."

- Provide the student with regular affirmations. This helps to set the correct environment open, understanding, and nonjudgmental. Affirmations also help support and build a student's confidence (or self-efficacy). Even simple responses can promote or erode the supportive environment. A student may say that he has put the University of Colorado on the list as a backup. One response could be, "Yes, but would you go there?" A more affirmative response would be: "That's super! Now you will have a great backup on your list if you need it." Everything the IEC says can contribute positively to an environment conducive to change.

- Empower a student by helping him or her recognize strengths and see him/herself more positively. You can use affirmative and positive language such as:
  - "I'm really glad you brought that up."
  - "Trying to reorganize your time so you are not so tired when you study is very difficult. I'm really proud to be working with you on this."
  - "I appreciate that you are willing to talk about this."
  - "That's a good idea."
  - "I enjoyed talking with you today."
  - "You have struggled with grades this semester, but you have had some real successes in determining the priorities in your life."
  - "You are clearly a very resourceful person."
  - "If I were in your shoes, I don't know whether I could have managed nearly so well."

- Reframe behaviors or concerns as evidence of strengths. For example:
  - "So many people avoid seeking help from teachers when they need it. It says a lot about you that you are willing to take this step."
  - "You've had a setback in math, but you are really trying. Look at the progress you are making."

- Ask questions to prompt the student to give self-affirmations. For example, with a student who is struggling to add realistic choices to his college list, you might say, "What have you noticed about your college list in the last couple of months?"

MI skills should be in the IEC's toolbox since, at its heart, MI is a conversational enhancement. William R. Miller and Stephen Rollnick's *Motivational Interviewing: Preparing People for Change* is a good introduction.

SELECTED COUNSELING THEORIES THAT PROMOTE ATTITUDE CHANGE

The successful IEC knows that, in many ways, our work is grounded in attitude change. Think about it: Our work is designed to move students from one point to the next. For example, we show sophomores how their class selection for the junior year will affect the sort of admission options they wind up with. We encourage students to get or stay involved, to be good citizens, to work to become better conversationalists, and so on. Each of these tasks involves changing students' attitudes.

We do not, however, twist students' arms. (At least not most of the time!) Instead, we mount arguments that lead students (and parents) to see another side of an issue, to expand their knowledge of the world of higher education and their knowledge of themselves.

Three theories of attitude change are discussed below: cognitive dissonance, social judgment, and functional. There are many more, and I urge readers to learn about others. I chose these three because they have tenets that are especially appropriate for the IEC. Beyond gaining practical knowledge about these theories, my hope is that these paragraphs will encourage you to think about the words you use and how those words can have a strong attitudinal change component.

Cognitive Dissonance Theory

Cognitive dissonance (or disharmony) is a state of conflict in the mind, whereby a person simultaneously holds opposing views. According to cognitive dissonance theory, people tend to seek consistency among their cognitions (i.e., beliefs, opinions). When there is an inconsistency between attitudes or behaviors (dissonance), something must change to eliminate or reduce the dissonance.

Cognitive dissonance is normally strongest when a person thinks about himself/herself in a certain way and then does something to oppose that belief.

To manage cognitive dissonance, a first option is to change one or more of the attitudes, behaviors, beliefs, etc. so as to make the relationship between the conflicting elements a consonant one. When one of the dissonant elements is a behavior, the individual can change or eliminate the behavior. However, this mode of dissonance reduction frequently presents problems for people, as it is often difficult for people to change well-learned behavioral responses (e.g., giving up smoking).

A second cognitive method of reducing dissonance is to acquire new information that outweighs the dissonant beliefs. For example, thinking that smoking causes lung cancer will cause dissonance if a person smokes. However, new information such as "research has not proved definitively that smoking causes lung cancer" may reduce the dissonance.

A third way to reduce dissonance is to reduce the importance of the cognitions. People could convince themselves that it is better to *live for today* than to *save for tomorrow*. In other words, they could tell themselves that a short life filled with smoking and sensual pleasures is better than a long life devoid of such joys. In this way, they would be decreasing the importance of the dissonant cognition (smoking is bad for one's health).

Let's use an example in our field. Let's say Buffy is sure she will get accepted to and belongs at Harvard, yet she isn't able or willing to take challenging classes during her senior year. As a result, there will be a great amount of tension in her mind. To reduce this tension, she might change her beliefs or attitudes, or blame, deny, or justify. Buffy might deal with the dissonance by asserting one of the following statements:
- "Harvard is overrated, and I don't want to go there anyway."
- "My college counselor must be wrong because I know that Harvard will accept me and won't care about my senior year classes."
- "My happiness is more important than getting into any one college."
- "Even though I'm not taking the hardest classes, my teachers are the best in the school, and Harvard will know that."

Although Buffy might have originally disagreed with these statements, her mind is open as she struggles with ways to reduce her dissonance.

Here is another example:
Brutus sees himself as an artist and thinks that a top art college would be perfect for him. He even thinks that perhaps he should learn French and study art at the Sorbonne as he heard the school has a great art program. He's been known to dress like Michelangelo in his high school art class. He enters his high school art contest. After two days of judging, he places last out of 10. Here are some possible ways he could respond to this dissonance:

- "The contest judges are idiots. It's clear that they don't know great art when they see it."
- "I would have won if I had spent more time on my project. I'm a good artist, but I didn't prepare well enough."
- "I guess I'm never going to be an artist. I heard that being an anthropologist is cool."
- "Colleges will like the fact that I entered the contest; though I didn't do very well."

Like Buffy, Brutus might have disagreed with these statements originally. But he is struggling to resolve the dissonance he feels.

From the theory, we know Brutus' mind will lead to him to reduce the dissonance he feels. Maybe we can suggest other ways for him to make sense of this. Perhaps encouraging Brutus to enter another contest might give him another point of reference as he considers his future. If and when the time is right, we might suggest minoring in art or perhaps encourage him to complete a career inventory so that he can learn more about art careers (including working as a curator or art writer) and more about other fields, including anthropology. Being aware of Brutus' dissonance, however, doesn't mean we know precisely how to proceed. Rather, it gives us some conversational directions; it is an invitation to provide him with options that he may not have considered.

Social Judgment Theory

Social judgment theory emphasizes the role of prior attitudes in shaping attitude formation and change. Attitude is seen as a kind of spectrum with a *latitude of acceptance* surrounding a current attitude; a new position is more likely to be accepted if it falls within this latitude and less likely to be accepted if it does not. This theory suggests that change in attitude position might be greater in response to the presentation of a moderate persuasive position than to a more extreme message.

The key point of the social judgment theory is that attitude change (persuasion) is mediated by judgmental processes and effects. Put differently, persuasion occurs at the end of the process when a person understands a message then compares the position it advocates to his or her position on that issue. A person's position on an issue is dependent on the following:

1. the person's most preferred position (the anchor point)
2. the person's judgment of the various alternatives (spread across his or her latitudes of acceptance, rejection, and non-commitment)
3. the person's level of ego-involvement with the issue. Ego-involvement is how important an issue is to our self-identity.

Consider Brutus: a student who puts emphasis on attending a big name college and is reluctant to accept your suggestions for backup colleges. You engage with Brutus about which college to add to his list; in other words, which college will he accept as *good enough*? The IEC has a goal of adding at least one less selective college to Brutus' apply list. In other words, the anchor point is that Brutus wants a big name college.

Colleges that fall under Brutus' latitude of rejection are schools that you feel you will have no chance whatsoever of convincing Brutus to apply. Almost no IEC will be effective in persuading Brutus to add these colleges. Further, the more ego-involved Brutus is to go to a name-brand college, the larger the latitude of rejection will be. That is, these colleges will appear to be further away from Brutus' anchor point than they actually are. That's not good news for the would-be persuader.

Now consider the colleges that Brutus really doesn't have an opinion about, that he doesn't have positive or negative feelings toward. Those colleges fall in the latitude of non-commitment. It's possible that someone could persuade Brutus to enroll in one of these colleges, but Brutus would have to learn more about the college first, at least enough until an opinion, or judgment, is formed. The latitude of non-commitment can be the IEC's friend as it opens the door to potential possibilities.

Now, consider the schools Brutus sees as acceptable to add to his list. These schools fall in his latitude of acceptance. But he may not be totally convinced and some persuasion may be necessary. In other words, Brutus might see the University of Rochester as a great, acceptable school from a name and prestige perspective, but he dislikes its location in New York. An IEC with solid arguments and perseverance may be able persuade Brutus to add this school, especially if, in Brutus' mind, Rochester has more positives than negatives and meets the primary goal of a *top quality* school.

If Brutus is persuaded, then the further a message's position is away from his anchor point, the larger his attitude change will be. But remember that it is very unlikely that Brutus will be persuaded out of his latitude of rejection. So, once a message enters that region and moves away from his anchor point, the amount of his attitude change decreases.

This theory of attitude change is different from other consistency theories in two ways. As its name suggests, it is a model of judgment, which means that it declares that the student interprets (judges) a message. Specifically, a student judges how much the message agrees or disagrees with his or her own attitude. Second, social judgment/involvement theory holds that a student's involvement in the topic of the persuasive message that is, how important is attending a *great college* to this student, will be important to attitude change.

Functional Theory

Functional theory suggests that attitudes serve a variety of psychological needs and that changing an attitude requires an understanding of its purpose in the life of the individual who holds it. It is based on the idea that attitudes develop to satisfy certain functions, e.g., needs or goals, for the individual. According to this theory, attitudes reflect the underlying motives of the individual; thus, the theory is sometimes referred to as a motivational approach to attitudes.

Consider the following statement uttered by dear Brutus: "I really want to be happy at my choice of college, and 'match' is really important to me. But I also want my friends and families to be impressed when they hear the name of the college I was admitted to." Which cluster of attitudes will be most salient in the student's thinking?

Ponder Buffy's declaration: "I know how important essays are to my college application. But I'm really busy with my senior year classes and with my boyfriend, and I don't have lots of time to spend writing." Is Buffy's need to have first-rate essays greater than her need for a social life?

Now, apply functional theory to the following student sentiment: "I know I'll do better at a small college because personal contact with teachers and the ability to speak up in class will help me succeed. But I see college as a big place where everyone goes to the Saturday football games, where there are hundreds of students playing outside on nice weather days, and where Greek life rules." Which of these potentially conflicting values will be most important as this student picks schools to apply to?

Let's consider another of Buffy's quandaries: "Two of the most important factors in choosing a college are that it is prestigious and that it is co-ed. I've done well in high school and deserve to go to an esteemed college. I'm also really social and enjoy the company of men. But my IEC says I can get into a 'better, more prestigious' women's college." How can the IEC employ functional theory to encourage Buffy to rethink her opinion about women's colleges or her opinion about the value of an "esteemed" college?

The key for the IEC in dealing with these issues is to expose the underlying attitudes and talk to the student about them. Some students, when they hear that women's colleges are, indeed, prestigious, take another look. The persistent IEC can help alter the student's perception of the salience of certain factors. In other words, the IEC might redirect the need for prestige into the need for happiness in college.

COMMUNICATING WITH BUSY BUFFY OR BLAH BRUTUS

Dealing with an unresponsive student (one who is not meeting college planning goals) tests an IEC's communication skills. What's important is navigating those waters well before the problem escalates. Before a contract is signed, there is an understanding that the student wants to engage in the college planning process: it simply does not work if Buffy is not actively involved or if Brutus is disengaged. If/when the situation arises that a student is not coming to meetings, then a procedure that has been discussed in advance is put into effect. That typically means trying X times to reach Buffy or Brutus and then turning to the parents to take next steps. Most students are responsible and responsive, but they are also busy. Communicate using a gentle, positive nudge: "In terms of your essay, I'm worried that you're not showing the colleges what an insightful person you are." Recognize that parents may toss out a flippant gibe: "What's the matter with you? Don't you know how important this is? You're throwing your life away?!" The IEC must express concerns in a manner that will motivate, not antagonize.

NONVERBAL COMMUNICATION

IECs spend most of their professional time communicating. Indeed, the more the IEC considers his or her communication style, the more success the IEC tends to have in achieving educational planning goals. While we tend to think primarily about verbal communication, IECs also need to assess nonverbal communication, a range of communication elements responsible for much of message transmission. Nonverbal communication includes tone of voice (timbre, volume, and speed), gestures, facial expressions, posture, shrugs, foot tapping, drumming fingers, eye movements, use of interpersonal space (arrangements of people at the consulting table, the distance between speaker and receiver, etc.), use of time, smell (may be particularly noticeable if, for example, an IEC is wearing heavy perfume), sound symbols (grunting, mumbling, or using "communication fillers" such as "mmm," "er," "ah," "uh-huh"), position of the body, stance, clothing, jewelry, and hairstyle. Even silence (pausing and waiting) can be communicators to students and parents.

Our work is accomplished as a result of the exchange of messages from sender to receiver and back again. Our interactions are open to distraction, noise, and uncertainty. Conversations are quick. These reasons, among others, require us to focus not only on the verbal side of communication, but also on the nonverbal.

Here are a few key points about nonverbal communication:

- Be conscious of both your verbal and nonverbal signals so as to avoid sending the wrong message.
- Various aspects of speech itself are particularly rich in terms of communication impact. Factors such as accent, tone of voice, and speed of speaking are highly communicative.
- When our nonverbal message conflicts with our verbal message, the nonverbal message will be the one that is believed. Actions can often speak louder than words.
- Emotions are expressed mainly through the face, body, and voice.
- The establishment and maintenance of relationships is often done through nonverbal signals, including tone of voice, gaze, and touch.
- On the grounds that "It's not what you say, it's the way that you say it," there is much to be said for focusing on nonverbal behavior in considering how to be a better communicator.

An IEC who doesn't regularly self-evaluate communication may be missing out on desired clients. Have a colleague sit in on a meeting with a student and give you some pointers on your nonverbal communication strengths and weaknesses. (See Communication Evaluation at the end of this chapter.)

Facial Expressions

Students pick up facial expressions more than they do any other communication mode. Consider the information that can be conveyed through different smiles (a smirk, a grin). Think of the ways we register facial behaviors as cues to give us information about a student's interest in the consulting meeting, reaction to a particular college suggestion, and so forth. Just as we detect Buffy's dislike of rural regions through her grimace, Buffy senses our sincerity by reading our faces. It's been said that smiling even while on a phone call affects how communication is received. A simple glance at another person can indicate a range of emotions including hostility, interest, and attraction. People also utilize eye gaze a means to determine if someone is being honest. Normal, steady eye contact is often taken as a sign that a person is telling the truth and is trustworthy. Shifty eyes and an inability to maintain eye contact, on the other hand, is frequently seen as an indicator of lying. Keep your face in mind, and present the countenance you want clients to register.

Gestures

Common gestures include waving, pointing, and using fingers to indicate numeric amounts. In courtroom settings, lawyers have been known to utilize different nonverbal signals to attempt to sway juror opinions. An attorney might glance at his watch to suggest that the opposing lawyer's argument is tedious or might even roll his eyes at the testimony offered by a witness in an attempt to undermine his or her credibility. Such nonverbal signals are so powerful and influential that some judges even place limits on what type of nonverbal behaviors are allowed in the courtroom. Think about what you do with your hands and what you may be communicating without intention. Posture and movement can also convey a great deal on information. Be conscious of gestures such as arm-crossing, leg-crossing, nail biting, placing your hand on your cheek, tapping or drumming fingers, nodding your head, and various other expressions of interest or boredom.

Paralanguage

Paralanguage refers to vocal communication that is separate from actual language. This includes factors such as tone of voice, loudness, inflection and pitch. Consider the powerful effect that tone of voice can have on the meaning of a sentence. When something is said in a strong tone of voice, students might interpret approval and enthusiasm. The same words said in a hesitant tone of voice might convey disapproval and a lack of interest. Simply changing your tone of voice might change the meaning of a sentence. A friend might ask you how you are doing, and you might respond with the standard, "I'm fine," but how you actually say those words might reveal a good deal about how you are really feeling. A bright, happy tone of voice can reveal that you are actually doing quite well. A somber, downcast tone would indicate that you are the opposite of fine and that perhaps your friend should inquire further. Paralanguage is an extremely important part of our interaction with students. In many situations, the words themselves matter less than the tone used to say them. Studies show that as much as 60% of interpretation comes from the tone in which it is said.

Think of the many ways that the following statement can be said: "You have until October 15 to complete these three essays." Tone of voice has the chance of communicating, "This is an exciting time, and you only have three essays left," or, it may communicate the following very different message: "Geez. Only three essays complete? You are way behind and need to get on the ball."

Proxemics

People often refer to their need for "personal space" or proxemics, which is an important type of nonverbal communication. The amount of distance that we need and the amount of space we perceive as belonging to us is influenced by a number of factors including social norms, cultural expectations, situational factors, personality characteristics, and level of familiarity. For example, the amount of personal space needed when having a casual conversation with another person usually varies between 18 inches to four feet. On the other hand, the personal distance needed when speaking to a crowd of people is around 10 to 12 feet. One important variable for an IEC is office setup, specifically where you sit in relationship to your student. I have found a round table works best as no one is at the head of the table and all parties are equidistant. Sitting behind a large desk can intimidate students and parents alike. If the seating arrangement between you and your student is such that one person appears to look down on another, an effect of domination may be created.

It's interesting to note that every culture has different levels of physical closeness appropriate to different types of relationship, and individuals learn these distances from the society in which they grew up. Keep cultural relativity in mind when working with diverse populations.

Haptic Considerations

Communicating through touch is another important nonverbal behavior. There has been a substantial amount of research on the importance of touch in infancy and early childhood. Touch can be used to communicate affection, familiarity, sympathy, and other emotions. We shake hands and agree that that is socially acceptable. While boundaries need to be clear, I don't have a problem with a consultant who pats a student on the back for getting through a particularly turbulent part of the admission process. Indeed, a friendly hug can show that you value your student and that you understand his or her plight. Of course, touch can be misconstrued, and it should be used thoughtfully.

Appearance

Our choice of color, clothing, make-up, hairstyle, and scents are all communication vehicles. Research on color psychology has demonstrated that different colors can evoke different moods. Appearance can also alter physiological reactions, judgments, and interpretations. Just think of all the subtle judgments you quickly make about someone based on his or her appearance. These first impressions are important, which is why, even if we work in a home office, we need to *dress up* for work each day.

Artifacts

Objects are also tools that can be used to communicate nonverbally. On an online forum, for example, you might select an avatar to represent your identity and to communicate information about who you are and the things you like. People often spend a great deal of time developing a particular image and surrounding themselves with objects designed to convey information about the things that are important to them. I use stress toys as artifacts in my consulting practice. Students and parents seem to like the little gizmos that I place at the center of my consulting table. These devices don't require thought and can be manipulated easily; thus, they are helpful throughout the meeting process. Many small artifacts like fidget spinners and Rubik cubes are too attention consuming to be useful as practical artifacts.

Having a tablet in front of me during a student meeting is also an artifact. Taking notes lets students and parents know you value what they are saying and that you are engaged in the conversation.

Final Thoughts on Nonverbal Communication

Nonverbal communication plays an important role in how we convey meaning and information to others, as well as how we interpret the actions of those around us. The important thing to remember when looking at such nonverbal behaviors is to consider the actions in groups. What a person actually says *along with* his or her expressions, appearance, and tone of voice might tell you a great deal about what that person is really trying to say. The IEC needs to be continually alert to the nonverbal cues of students and parents. The student who says that everything is okay but has a blank stare or an angry tone might just have something to say if prompted correctly.

Also recall that silence is communication. IECs do not need to fill every moment with words. There is power to silence; it gives students the chance to think and react after deliberation.

It's also important to keep in mind that, without even knowing it, we can give nonverbal cues that may not send the right message. For example, I don't jump in jubilation if a parent says that his or her daughter got into Stanford. I smile and look happy, but I don't do a jig. As a profession, we need to be cautious about talking about the value of fit and then expressing nonverbally (or verbally) that some schools are better than others. Our nonverbal language should convey the same message whether a student is accepted to Stanford or State U.

For more about the importance of nonverbal communication in communication with students and parents, some helpful books include: *Nonverbal Communication in Human Interaction* by Mark L. Knapp, Judith A. Hall, and Terrence G. Horgan; *Nonverbal Communication in Everyday Life* by Martin S. Remland; *Talk Less, Say More: Three Habits to Influence Others and Make Things Happen* by Connie Dieken, and *Nonverbal Communication: Science and Applications* by David Matsumoto (Ed), Mark G. Frank (Ed), and Hyi Sung Hwang (Ed).

COMMUNICATION EVALUATION

Independent educational consulting is very much an interactional occupation. IECs are *positive change agents* who consciously use knowledge of communication to effect change. We are often called upon to introduce new concepts (the value of *fit* comes to mind) and to transform perceptions and attitudes that may limit our students' higher education options. As such, making use of the counseling and communication theories and strategies discussed in this chapter is critical to your success as an IEC. In order to gauge the effectiveness of your communication skills, I offer the practical assessment tool below.

To objectively measure your communication skills, ask a professional colleague to observe a session (or even several sessions) and to note and rate the efficacy of your communication. As you interact with a student, the observer will assess the essence of the communication with regard to nine specific qualities. Prior to the observation, be sure to have your observer familiarize him/herself with the communication skills/strategies described below. Inform your observer that not all scales are appropriate for all communication interactions. Use N/A if not applicable to the session observed. I recommend that you provide your observer with both a physical copy of the assessment criteria and the assessment itself so as to facilitate ease.

Finally, it's best practice to inform the student in advance that an observer will be present at an upcoming meeting. Assure the student that the purpose of the observation is to provide you with critical feedback valuable to your practice. Should the student express discomfort, schedule the observation with another student who voices no objection.

Communication Evaluation Criteria

1. Active Listening
How well does the IEC concentrate on what is being shared? Is the IEC simply hearing the message, or is he/she employing verbal and/or nonverbal signs to show active listening? (These signs can include smiling, nodding, eye contact, saying 'yes,' 'hmm,' etc.) It's fascinating to observe have much concentration it takes to pay attention to someone. Some people are gifted, almost innate listeners. Others of us need to work at it.

2. Information Exchange
Information giving is delivering data without attention to the needs of the listener. It might be explaining something broadly and without reference to the specific needs of the student. *Information sharing*, in contrast, requires one or more of the following: summarizing, demonstrating empathy, building rapport, demonstrating active listening skills, or signposting. Signposting gives the student a map of what's to come, thereby helping the student to feel in control. The following is signpost language: "I want to learn a little bit about you before we begin to talk about colleges, so we'll talk about you today. Next time, we'll talk about what you want in a college. By our third meeting, I'll be ready to give you some colleges to research."

3. Communication Dynamic
While there are certainly times when the IEC needs to be the authority/expert, communication theory suggests that more productive communication occurs when the IEC guides and counsels as a partner. The point here reinforces the person-centered counseling approach as well as motivational interviewing discussed previously.

4. Promotion of Rational Thinking
Rational thinking helps students make the best possible decision. To what extent does the IEC encourage the student to think outside of the box, think critically, and most importantly arrive at a rational decision to support his or her choices? Does the IEC help the student use the information at his/her disposal to develop a logically sound solution to a problem?

5. Percent of Talking by Student Compared to IEC
IECs have information to disseminate and should be doing lots of talking. On the other hand, good counseling means that there is a dialogue, not a monologue. Both parties should have a chance to explain and react.

6. Allowing Silence
Strong communication benefits from silence. Related to the percent of talking variable, this scale suggests that filling every opportunity with verbosity works against the value of strong dialogue.

7. Using Righting Reflex

The righting reflex is the instinct to correct an action when one perceives another to be moving in the wrong direction. If an IEC acts upon the righting reflex, the student may instinctively resist such attempts at persuasion and continue on his or her previous path.

8. Rolling with Resistance

The idea behind rolling with resistance is to help the student change negative behavior. This can be achieved by avoiding an argument, demonstrating understanding of the student's position, focusing on the problem and not the student, evaluating potential consequences of the student's behavior, and encouraging the student to discover his or her own solutions to the problem. In other words, Buffy is not a bad person just because she does not have enough backups.

9. Emotional Attentiveness

Emotional attentiveness is an important skill and, in the long haul, develops empathy and builds richer, higher-quality relationships. IECs who are emotionally attentive tend not to be distracted, tend to focus on the student's communication needs (need for reinforcement, need for ego boost, etc.), attend to only one message at a time, and focus eye gaze on the target of the communication.

10. Influence of Nonverbal

This scale allows the observer to comment on the ways in which nonverbal signals either add to or distract from the flow of communication. Examples of nonverbal signals that add to communication include the IEC looking and acting in ways that promote constructive conversation and encourage the student's voice; leaning in, and/or "looking" engaged; using a tone of voice that is reassuring and supportive; sitting in a position of equality with the student (and not, say, behind a huge desk); using appropriate gestures to make points; dressing professionally, yet not stiffly.

Consultants as Positive Change Agents: Communication Evaluation

Date:

Active Listening

Low	1	2	3	4	5	High

Information Exchange

Information Giving	1	2	3	4	5	Information Sharing

Communication Dynamic

Authority / Expert	1	2	3	4	5	Guider / Counselor

Promotion of Rational Thinking

Passive	1	2	3	4	5	Active

Percent of Talking by Student Compared to IEC

Low	0%	20%	40%	60%	80%	100%	High

Allowing Silence

Few Pauses	1	2	3	4	5	Uses Silence Effectively

Using Righting Reflex

Tries to "Right" Concerns	1	2	3	4	5	Counsels Toward Resolution

Rolling with Resistance

No Acknowledgment / Bed of Roses	1	2	3	4	5	Rolls with Resistance

Emotional Attentiveness

Low	1	2	3	4	5	High

Influence of Nonverbal

Nonverbal Adds to Productive Communication Flow	1	2	3	4	5	Nonverbal Distracts from Productive Communication Flow

CHAPTER 8

Knowledge: The Holy Grail

UNEARTHING THE ANSWERS

It is very important that we walk the walk and talk the talk of confident, caring, and intelligent educational consultants. Does that mean we'll have all the answers to every possible question at the tip of our tongues? No. It means we'll have the intelligence to know when we need to do some additional research on a question, the grace to say, "That's an interesting question. Let me do a little further study on that one and get back to you," and the knowledge, resources, and ability to conduct necessary research and get back to the questioner in a timely manner. We shouldn't have that "deer in headlights" look when we're asked something we don't know right off the top of our heads. I cannot begin to tell you how many times I say, "I don't know." In some ways I'm proud to say, "I don't know." To me, it signals that I'm a professional, that I care enough to find out, and that I'm not full of myself.

Still, not having the answer burdens many IECs with guilt. That's primarily due to the characteristics of people who choose this profession: they are caring, sensitive folks who are often people pleasers. Thus, not having an answer can seem to signify either inexperience or lack of knowledge.

My hope is that you move beyond the guilt. The name of the game is your learning potential, not what you know today. You build your knowledge gradually over time. I'm a huge advocate of the learning and visiting that is necessary to be a great IEC. That's why I teach classes and training programs. People who want to do this work and are willing to put in the effort to learn should be encouraged to begin consulting. There is a world of need out there. Think of a lawyer who just graduated from law school and takes on her first job in a general law practice. You can bet that she will need to do research for her first case and may still be doing research on her hundredth case. Law school gave her the framework and the resources. Her experience and curiosity will give her the rest. Yours will, too.

So be cool, calm, and collected when you need to unearth an answer, and rest assured that you know a heck of a lot more about colleges than any of your clients—students or parents.

DEVELOPING A LEARNING PLAN

Every profession worth its salt has a body of knowledge that is required of practitioners. In our field, that body of knowledge includes knowledge of students and families, knowledge of post-secondary options and the admission process, and knowledge of colleges. I encourage you to focus on a learning plan instead of dwelling on lack of college knowledge. When I started (think dinosaurs), the professional associations were weak and unhelpful, and there were few ways to learn. Now there are oodles of ways to develop the knowledge base of a great consultant.

As students of colleges, we need to be well versed on a wide range of colleges. It means we need to visit college campuses. It means we need to test our college perceptions and our impressions with colleagues. It means we are able to articulate distinctions between colleges that look, from the outside at least, very similar. Importantly, students of colleges means that we are students! As emphasized throughout this book, that means that we are lifelong learners. It means we know more next month than we know today. It means we have a plan to learn more.

Learning about colleges and learning about their selectivity takes time. In *The Outliers*, Malcolm Gladwell says that the key to success in any field is a matter of practicing a specific task for a total of around 10,000 hours. I'm not sure 10,000 hours is necessary here, but Gladwell's point is well taken. There are no easy answers and no "CliffsNotes for College Knowledge." It's about developing a plan of learning, connecting with the professional associations, and attending training seminars. The more you read, talk to colleagues, and visit campuses, the more the collegiate landscape opens up to you. Learning and keeping up with the literature in the field separates the professional from the novice.

It is important that consultants offer their clients up-to-date information about colleges. Without such knowledge, the service offered by the consultant is more properly called coaching, tutoring, editing, or nudging. None of these functions is unimportant. But the field has grown to the point where there is an expectation of knowledge—or at least a responsible, ongoing plan for learning. Consultants who take money without having the requisite college facts hurt the profession. Remember the distinction noted between knowledge-based and process-based consultants. For a profession to thrive, there must be a body of information, and there must be encouragement for the knowledge-focused side. If the consultant cannot explain differences from one campus to the next, if the consultant is not able to articulate how these differences affect the student experience, or if the consultant is not versed in the *culture* of specific colleges, then that consultant is operating against the principles necessary for independent educational consulting to grow and flourish as a unique, specialized profession.

We live in a world where there is no shortage of opinions about colleges. Pseudo-experts are everywhere. The hairstylist, the neighbor, the sister's cousin's brother's wife are all glad to share an all-knowing perspective: "I went to Dartmouth, so I know the Ivy League," is a common refrain. Or, "As a Smith alum, I know women's colleges." Right! And because I know Elvis Presley's music, I know the Rolling Stones, or, by extension, I know all music. And there are those who feel that because they have helped their own kids through the process, they are qualified professionals (these are the so-called I-helped-my-kids consultants). We need to be different. Our opinions must be grounded in well developed and well researched knowledge. Knowledge separates the opinions of the professional consultant from the rest. Colleges are complex and defy simple generalizations. IECs are uniquely positioned to be college knowledge experts.

When do you have enough knowledge? On one level, the answer is that there is always more to learn. On another level, the answer comes from the ability to say that you are immersing yourself into the field and that you have a game plan for learning. The ability to differentiate among hundreds of colleges is a lifetime in the making; the knowledge required to truly go beyond *The Fiske Guide to Colleges* and know differences among collegiate environments is immense. The stone is never completely polished. As students of colleges, we actively consume college knowledge. For most of us, the challenge of mastery is amazingly fulfilling.

What follows in this chapter is a discussion of the many ways that we build our knowledge base. IECs have a smorgasbord of options to fill their hunger for knowledge. Step up to the table!

VISITING COLLEGES

Visiting colleges is the primary way we build our knowledge base. Yes, independent educational consultants can learn about colleges from guidebooks, view books, websites, phone conversations, and professional exchanges. We can get "facts" fairly easily. We're a Google search away from knowing enrollment numbers, campus acreage, percent of faculty who hold Ph.D's, and the number of student organizations for just about every campus. More obscure, however, is what a campus "feels like," what students are like, and what makes one liberal arts and science college different from another. Where will I look up the subtleties of campus life at, say, Penn State when compared to Michigan State? A case can be made that the more information is available at a simple click, the less students and their parents really know about colleges (and the more likely they are to be misled). Therefore, IECs must take all the facts available and convert them—via visits—to concepts that set professional knowledge apart from Google.

Consider the following analogy: I can teach history by reading the books and knowing the facts. But my credibility depends on the feeling and conviction in my voice when I talk about standing in the middle of the battlefield at Gettysburg or seeing the Chartres Cathedral. As a historian, my visits make me a more credible source of information, and my words become more powerful. For independent educational consultants, personal visits have the same effect on credibility and power.

When I left the University of Denver in 1981, I quickly learned how little I knew about colleges. Even though I was Dean of Admission and Financial Aid, my knowledge of other campuses was rudimentary at best. What I knew about various colleges was largely determined either by naïve assumptions or by whether I liked the Director of Admission! Yale had to be intellectually intense. Right? Well, I learned after my first visit that the answer is "sort of." And the University of California, Berkeley had to be wildly liberal. Right? Well, again, the post-visit answer is "sort of." Because I didn't have the knowledge of colleges necessary to provide students with a firsthand, objective sense of the culture, the feel, and how a particular college fits into the higher education landscape, I hit the road and took to the sky to become a student of colleges. And I quickly discovered that I love learning about colleges. I love getting a sense for the culture, the ethos, the feel of a college campus. What's more, I like turning students on to places they never would have considered.

Commitment to travel (and ability to do so) is truly a defining feature of the successful consultant. We are students of colleges, and that moniker comes with a critical assumption: that we visit colleges regularly, talk to admission personnel and other administrators, and that we talk to students. The consultant gives up billable hours to travel because the building of a solid knowledge base is so important. There are good ways and better ways to visit colleges. We've all heard of active listening. (Recall that active listening was addressed in Chapter 7.) When you visit, take the tour and walk around; practice "active seeing." What can I learn about this place that I cannot learn by knowing the school's admission standards? What is the ethos? The vibe? What types of students seem to be happiest? Which majors are most popular? Which activities have the greatest participation? Take the analogy of the diplomat. Diplomats may go to a country to assess the state of affairs, the sensitivities, the opportunities for interaction. Subsequently, they share their impressions and the decisions that are made as a result of their onsite observations. The same general approach is true of the consultant. The consultant listens, observes, and assesses. It is vital to talk to students—both individually and in groups—in the quad, the dining hall, the library, etc. Find out what it's like to be a student at that college. Later, those impressions are communicated to your students and your families so that they can make good decisions.

College visits can take many forms. Visits can be made individually by calling the admission office and making arrangements. IECs often travel together, again making arrangements with each college.

As previously noted, the cost of visiting colleges needs to be built into the budget of anyone working as an IEC. Many IECs make visits before they start seeing students; others start soon thereafter. Typically, IECs visit local colleges first for two main reasons. First, many students will be looking at in-state options, and second, it keeps expenses down. After these visits, most IECs branch out; many visit colleges before or after national conferences or before or after a family trip. And if the conference or family trip happens to be in a city like Boston where there are over 60 colleges to choose from, travel expenses again stay down. The professional associations organize group tours, both connected to their national meetings and stand-alone. IECA and HECA have tours before and/or after their national meetings, and these are quite popular. Another way to learn about tours is to join regional associations outside of your region of residence. Members are often the first to be invited to tours.

Colleges also sponsor tours. These are largely by-invitation only and some are for school-based counselors only and/or counselors from particular states or regions of the country. Typically, participants pay to fly in and out of a central location, and the college(s) involved pay for housing, meals, and transportation. To be included, consultants should establish relationships with admission personnel. Meeting and talking to a college admission official at a national conference is one way to be noticed. Consultants can write to individual colleges or organizers to inquire about being included in an upcoming tour. If you have a college that you are interested in visiting, try calling the Office of Admissions and ask if the institution provides tours for counselors. (See resources at astudentofcolleges.com for a list of some of the more popular multi-college tours.)

Campus Visit Tips for the Independent Educational Consultant

The best way to understand a college is for you to schedule a personal visit, observe students, and record your reactions. Here are some questions and answers about college visits.

1. How should I prepare for campus visits?

You need to have a college visit plan. The plan may be to visit local colleges in your first year of practice or to visit schools around professional or personal travels. But you should decide, by research in advance, which colleges you want to visit. Needless to say, travel plans are dictated by time and resources. You also should consider the sorts of colleges that you need to visit. Who are your clients or prospective clients? Should you focus your visits on selective colleges? Colleges popular with students from your city? Major universities within your state? Where are voids in your college information? What do you know about your clients that might help you develop a plan?

2. When should I visit colleges?

As stated in question #1, your visits depend on time and resources. Recognize that *A Student of Colleges* puts a priority on college knowledge. The primary method of college knowledge is to regularly visit (and learn from) college campuses.

Of course, the best time to visit colleges involves a number of considerations and will vary for each consultant. Don't just head West (or any other direction, for that matter) to visit colleges in a willy-nilly fashion. As stated above, visit colleges that are appropriate for your practice.

If you want to gain a real sense of campus life—meet some students, sit in on classes, and participate in some typical activities—then you should schedule your visits during weekdays of the regular school year. While some admission offices are open on Saturday mornings, most campuses are fairly quiet on weekends. Also, to get a good sense of a campus and its people, you want to visit on a 'normal' day, so avoid exam weeks, big football game weekends, etc.

3. How many colleges do I need to visit?

That depends on your location, your goals, your budget, your experience, and so forth. A factor to consider is that professional membership in IECA and HECA both require (among other criteria) a specified number of college visits. Note that these numbers are subject to change.

4. I am visiting several colleges in one trip. How much time should be spent on each campus?

You should try to spend as much time as possible at each college. An overnight stay in the college city is ideal. Most independent consultants need at least half a day for each visit.

5. What arrangements should I make before I visit?

You should arrange for your visit by calling or emailing the admissions office at each school you plan to visit. Tell the admissions counselor about your visit, your visit goals, and how long you have to spend on campus. At some colleges, you will be asked to make calls to other offices to arrange features of your visit. Some consultants will meet with athletic personnel; others will want to see the learning resource center or the studio art facilities. Your visit depends on your needs and the needs of your students.

You will also want to arrange a meeting with students. If you know a current student, contact him or her and ask to spend some time together. Even better would be for the student to arrange for a group of his or her friends to meet with you as well.

6. What are the parts of a typical visit?

There is often a set routine that is typical of college counselor visits. Sometimes it is possible to tell the admission office what you would like to do during your visit—take a tour with prospective students and parents, meet with a member of the admissions staff, attend a class, meet with someone from the activities office and the director of financial aid—and the office will arrange it.

When you call or email the school, ask if they would send you a parking permit and a campus map. Also ask the admissions office for recommendations about nearby lodging.

Most importantly, read about the college before you arrive. Carefully peruse the college's website as well as information about the college in both subjective and objective guidebooks.

7. What should I do when I get there?

Spend time in the student center (perhaps have a meal there), pick up a student publication (a great way to get a sense of "hot" issues on campus), and, most of all, observe students. Do they seem happy? You can learn a lot just by watching student interactions. Also pay attention to bulletin boards as another clue to campus life.

8. How do I get students to talk with me?

What I've found is that college students are delighted to talk to those whom they perceive to be safe, trustworthy, and sincere. I go up to individual students or groups of students and say that I'm an independent educational consultant who wants to learn about their school. I ask, "Can I take five minutes of your time to ask you some questions about your experience here?" Students generally love to be a college reviewer. I say we can do it right there standing up (I always have paper and pen on hand or a device, much like a reporter) or we can go somewhere else. I truly don't take more than five minutes typically, because I want to talk to as many students as I can during my visit. The more students, the broader my perspective will be. There are lots of times when students don't have time to talk. (They are rushing to class, or to meet a friend, or they just don't want to talk to me.) But another group of students is usually nearby.

9. What sort of questions should I ask?

The purpose of your college visit is to increase your awareness of the programs and the people at the school. Plan a list of questions that will enable you to find out as much as you can during your visit. Some of the questions may be general and apply to every school you visit; other questions will be specific to each school. You will gain the most insight into the school you visit if your questions go beyond the obvious that are answered in the factual materials available from the college. Don't hesitate to ask the nitty gritty questions.

- Why do students apply to this college?
- What do students on campus rave about?
- What do students complain about most?
- What type of student seems happiest?
- What are the most popular majors?
- What are the most popular extracurricular activities?
- What are the opportunities for extracurricular participation?
- What are student traditions? (These can be serious traditions like guys wearing coats and ties for football games at Vanderbilt to more frivolous ones. For example, at Texas Christian University, legend has it that if students rub the nose of the six-foot-tall wrought-iron statue of TCU's mascot, the horned frog, good luck will accompany them during their final exams. At the University of the South, when a senior takes comprehensive exams, friends will typically "comp" the student's car, writing on the windshield with paint or soap. Sometimes, the message is a phrase related to the person's major. Other times, it's a bawdy joke.)
- What types of services exist for personal and career counseling?
- How is the faculty advising for selecting classes and meeting requirements?
- How are roommates chosen?
- What is the school's assurance that freshman merit aid will continue to other years?
- What safety services are available to students?

- Is there an admission officer assigned to my state/region? Are there local programs for students and parents? Are alums active in the area?

More questions (These questions are specifically for students):
(Note: Questions should be asked of several students on your visit for better sample representation.)
- What do you like best about your college? ("Do you like it here?" is seldom helpful in differentiating colleges.)
- When did you last meet individually with a professor?
- Do you know one or two professors well enough to ask them for a work or graduate school recommendation?
- What is the "glue" that binds social life? Is it fraternity/sorority life? The outdoors? Academic major? Clubs? Athletics?
- What happens around here on weekends? Do students stay on campus?
- What was happening on campus last weekend?
- What events draw a crowd?
- Does a particular group dominate the social scene?
- What is the balance between spending time on academics and spending time on personal and social life?
- What did you learn about this college that you didn't know before you arrived?
- Is there anything that really surprised you about this college?

Still more questions (These questions might be asked of admissions officers or professors):
- Do students use laptops in most classes? Are examinations available online?
- How would you describe the "personality" of the student body?
- What do you like to emphasize about your institution when you talk to groups of prospective students?
- What are the standout attributes or features of your college?
- Why should a student select your college from other similar colleges? (What colleges do you consider similar?)
- What is new at the institution in the last year or two?
- What is the freshman year like in terms of such things as requirements, traditions, and orientation programs?
- Are there categories of students you work particularly well with? (For example, some schools can provide a positive environment for kids who need an active learning center, or students of color, or recreational athletes.)
- What percentage of students study abroad? What percentage are involved in internships? (Most colleges have study abroad and internship options. Thus, it is important to know the extent of the abroad or internship programs, rather than their existence.)
- What are typical course requirements—how many exams, papers, etc.?
- What range of GPAs/test scores are you looking for in applicants? (I typically give admissions people a hypothetical student profile a bit lower than what they've described. For example, would a student from Prestige High School with a 3.2 and 1300 SAT score have less than a 50/50 chance of admission?)
- How do you weigh factors such as quality of high school, GPA, rank, scores, activities?
- Who teaches introductory courses—professors or graduate students?
- What arrangements are made for advising and tutorial help?
- What opportunities exist for independent study?
- What departments are considered outstanding and why?
- What percentage of graduates go to graduate school? Get a job?

- What constitutes a typical freshman-year program?
- What if students are unsure about their major? Is this a good place to explore?
- If you had only two minutes to describe your college (and get the student interested enough to contact you) what would you say?

10. What other tips do you have about visiting?

Don't be distracted by unreliable cues. Consultants are human, too, and can be influenced by perception of quality, personality of the admission officer, and even weather the day of the visit. Keep in mind what you have heard and read about the college ahead of your visit. View the visit as one important way to assess a college, but not as the only way. Here are a few other suggestions:

- Record your observations diligently. Take notes on a screen or a notebook.
- Talk to students on every campus.
- Analyze the whole school, not just one part (for example, not just one field of study).
- Read the student newspaper.
- Roam the campus—look for clues about the types of students who might be happy there.
- Walk or drive around the community surrounding the college. Note walkability and safety.
- Check out public transportation. (Is it easy for a student to get around if he or she does not have a car?)
- Go to the student activities office. What clubs are most popular? Are first-year students able to get involved in most organizations? Does one type of activity—sports, Greek letter organizations, the local bar scene—seem to dominate?
- Look for or ask about traditions. For example, Bucknell has an interesting candle lighting ceremony, Carleton students go "traying," and Hope has an annual tug-of-war. These tidbits humanize a college.
- Look at bulletin boards and other places where there are postings. What's happening on campus?
- Take pictures of what you want to remember about the college. Begin with a picture of something with the college's name on it.
- Spend a lot of time looking around campus. Observe what you see. What's happening on campus?
- Pay attention to the physical upkeep.
- Try to determine what makes the place special/unique/interesting.
- Do not let perceived quality or academic reputation affect your feelings about the school.
- Do not judge the college solely on the basis of impressions made on your visit.
- Judge schools after you return home and have time to process all of your visits.
- Do not make snap judgments.

11. How can I remember my impressions of each college?

Record and write them down. You should review your impressions—both the day of the visit and a couple weeks later. I have both paper and electronic folders filled with notes from my college visits. I keep a file of word documents, one document for each college. The folder is always available on my desktop via iCloud and Dropbox. When I started, I used notes from my reading of *Fiske* and other subjective guides. Now, I add and delete notes after attending a conference, talking to a colleague, reading an article, etc.

I organize my visit notes around these points:

- Basics
- Academics
- Admissions
- Cost
- Student Life / Campus Life / Culture
- Location
- Tidbits / Other

JOINING PROFESSIONAL ASSOCIATIONS

IECA was the first professional organization exclusively for educational consultants. Created in 1976, IECA is the oldest voice of the independent educational consulting field. As introduced in Chapter 1, IECA began as a result of the need for a "student first" philosophy as families were contemplating enrollment in boarding and other selective secondary schools. In those early days, it was not uncommon for schools to pay "agents" to seek placements for students, a philosophy that the founders of IECA solidly oppose. IECA, by its early guidelines, made a key point: Advice is best when free of institutional involvement; what is important is simply what is best for an individual student. These consulting pioneers developed Principles of Good Practice, the first document to articulate ethical standards for the profession. (See Appendix A.)

When I joined IECA in 1981 after my stint as Dean of Admission at the University of Denver, I was outnumbered in the early years by those doing boarding school consulting. Over time, that emphasis shifted to the college side, and the overwhelming majority of IECA members now work in the college sphere. IECA also serves consultants who work in the therapeutic area. These consultants help families with troubled or struggling teens or young adults (those with emotional and/or behavioral difficulties) find suitable solutions via therapeutic schools, residential treatment programs, wilderness programs, outdoor therapeutic programs, and home-based residential programs.

IECA's full-time staff (about eight professionals) allows the association to coordinate a wide range of services including two annual conferences, stand-alone educational training programs, college tours, webinars, leadership training, an active talklist, a professional directory, a nimble website with millions of hits annually, referrals to members, insurance, an efficient board of directors with active committees, and an extensive and informative newsletter. For over 20 years, Mark Sklarow has forcefully directed the professional association. He has influenced the growth and the direction of the Association. IECA's premier training program, the Summer Training Institute (STI), often held on the Swarthmore College campus, is a serious and successful effort to orient prospective consultants to the practices and philosophies that guide successful and ethical consulting. As a founder and regular faculty member, my comments about STI are not without bias. IECA also offers two national conferences annually that are open to non-members and brings together hundreds of consultants, college, school and therapeutic program admissions officers for professional development and networking. IECA states, "There are many organizations professionals can join, but none provide the rewards, support, and commitment that have distinguished the Independent Educational Consultants Association for more than 30 years."

Yet as the field of college advising prospered, there were those who longed for an association whose members solely focused on college work. And there were those who felt, for various reasons, that a new organization could offer a vision not addressed by IECA. To that end, Cyndy McDonald of Visalia, California founded the Higher Education Consultants Association (HECA) in 1997. McDonald felt that the emphasis on college work exclusively (and thus not school and therapeutic consultants) would make for a worthy professional association. McDonald credits Bob Dannenhold, Joe Bernard, Paul Kanarek (then with Princeton Review) and Mark Corkery with their part in the early creation of HECA. Members join primarily due to the camaraderie and the inclusiveness that HECA offers. HECA sponsors an annual conference and college tours, makes marketing materials available for new consultants, coordinates a talklist, provides an online directory of members, and has developed a database of tools and resources on the members-only side of their website. HECA prides itself on being member-driven. With a limited number of paid staff, HECA's business rests with committed members, officers, and committee chairs. HECA's website states: "The Higher Education Consultants Association (HECA) is the premier professional organization for consultants who focus exclusively on helping high school students realize their full potential. Our mission is to support independent education consultants as they work with students and parents during the transition into higher education by providing professional development, advancing ethical standards of conduct and promoting equity and access to higher education for all students." (See Appendix A.)

Another organization IECs are welcome to join is the National Association for College Admission Counseling (NACAC). This is a large organization (over 16,000 members) made up principally of college admission officers and high school guidance counselors. NACAC's Statement of Principles of Good Practice is a central document that affects how the college admission process functions. (See Appendix A.) For example, the Statement provides rules about how colleges use early decision, how testing is best utilized, the procedure for release of confidential information, and so on. Much of the work of NACAC takes place in state, regional, and international affiliates. To become a member, consultants need three years of college admission counseling experience in a secondary school or college as well as recommendations from colleagues or employers. NACAC sponsors many special conferences and learning opportunities. One is the *Tools of the Trade* program held prior to national conventions. Regional ACACs are very active and can be joined at a relatively low cost. Some of the regional associations offer mentoring opportunities and often sponsor summer workshops and institutes for counselors.

A final organization is the National College Advocacy Group (NCAG). According to their website, "The National College Advocacy Group (NCAG) is a non-profit networking educational organization providing educational and resources for independent college admissions and financial aid professionals, financial advisors, students and families. We are dedicated to providing training and education regarding the ins and outs of college planning." This organization is most frequently seen as focused on financial matters.

I am concerned that too many educational consultants don't affiliate with the profession. The lack of affiliation allows all sorts of people to merely hang out a shingle and start work. These individuals (we might call them "rogue consultants"), some of whom have no background in either college admission or high school counseling, remain out of bounds for standards, guidance, and training. While guarantees are impossible in any profession, the benchmark for the educational consulting profession must be affiliations and training. I hope that those looking at the field from outside (and school-based counselors and admission officers) will make a distinction between a person who has demonstrated competencies by being admitted to one of the professional groups and one who has not. Further distinction ought to be made between a person who has taken the time to attend professional meetings or training opportunities, who has taken relevant classes, or who has become a Certified Educational Planner and one who has not.

As for the associations, they have the responsibility to provide leadership, forge bridges, and work to include a higher percentage of qualified consultants into their ranks. They also must do more to promote the profession and train leaders and spokespeople. The associations need to embrace growth and inclusiveness. IECA and HECA need to cooperate between themselves and with NACAC. Membership in more than one of these organizations should be encouraged. Consultants need to work together—as a consulting collective—to fight incompetence, unethical practice, and simple answers.

EARNING A PROFESSIONAL CERTIFICATE

The first program in college counseling was developed through the University of California, Los Angeles. UCLA Extension's program was designed for school-based college counselors and continues with that focus. The UCLA program started as a classroom-based program in 1995 and transitioned to an online format in 1998. While applicable to IECs, none of the core course requirements focus on issues specific to IECs. In the last 15 years, however, UCLA has offered a course (The Business of Educational Consulting) as an elective in their program.

There are other programs as well. The University of California, Berkeley offers an on-campus certification program, the Certificate Program in College Admissions and Career Planning. The University of California, Riverside offers a Professional Certificate in College Admissions Counseling, and the University of California, San Diego offers a short online Program in College Counseling.

In 2010, the University of California, Irvine, through its Division of Continuing Education, started an online Independent Educational Consulting certificate program—the first program designed specifically to suit the educational needs of IECs. In fact, the University of California, Irvine consulting program heralded our job title: Independent Educational Consultant. Decades ago we were labeled as "private college counselors." Sometimes, we were known as "independents." One still hears that label. I think it's time to retire that work title. After all, being an "independent" is not only ambiguous, but it also doesn't say anything about the nature of our work. Independent educational consultant fits the bill and has become the standard title. We need to stay with it.

Recognizing the unique nature of the IEC's work, UCI's online program consists of courses on principles and practices, use of college resources, and developing a business. Students are also required to complete a practicum. Electives include courses on transfer, summer, and gap year consulting; marketing; learning disabilities; international student counseling; and social media. This program provides the foundational knowledge essential to embark on a career as an independent educational consultant. Since its founding, over 400 students have earned the certificate, and at least double that number have taken classes within the program. Having a major university single out this profession as one large enough and significant enough for a certificate program is a major achievement for the profession.

ATTENDING PROFESSIONAL MEETINGS, INSTITUTES, AND SUMMER PROGRAMS

In addition to taking advantage of the learning opportunities offered through the professional associations discussed above, some independent educational consultants also attend national and regional meetings of the College Board or the American Counseling Association. Some consultants attend meetings of the American Psychological Association and similar academic associations. (It's amazing what you can learn about undergraduate life through faculty members, student activities personnel, housing staffs, and so forth.) Others attend meetings of foreign student advisors or learning disabilities groups.

Summers provide opportunities to attend a myriad of institutes and programs. State and regional NACAC and College Board groups have extensive summer programming. (Some of the College Board institutes grant academic credit in addition to Continuing Education Units (CEUs).) The NACAC website lists professional development opportunities for counselors. NACAC occasionally offers online courses.

As noted above, the IECA Summer Institute provides an excellent introduction to consulting. I was instrumental in founding the IECA program almost 20 years ago, and I've been on the faculty of this program in recent summers.

The Cape Cod Institute is a summer series of week-long courses, many of which have an educational bent.

Texas ACAC (joined by College Board) has a well respected four-day Admission and College Counseling Institute. Similarly, the Potomac and Chesapeake Association for College Admission Counseling (PCACAC) sponsors a summer mini-institute for novice and experienced high school and independent counselors.

For those who wish to further their knowledge of learning disabilities, ADHD, and autism spectrum disorder, Landmark College in Putney, Vermont offers its annual Summer Institute for Educators. The training combines hands-on, multi-day workshops, research presentations, and a student panel. In 2018 Landmark offered a workshop titled "College Transition: What Do You Mean It's at Least a 10-Year Process?".

WORKING TOWARD PROFESSIONAL CREDENTIALING

In 1996, in an effort toward licensing, the American Institute of Certified Educational Planners (AICEP) was established. AICEP awards the CEP credential to professionals working independently or in schools. Although the credential was established by IECA (since it was the only professional association at the time), it is now more widely available. Only the most experienced counselors qualify to become CEPs. To become a certified educational planner, candidates must
- hold at least a master's degree in a relevant educational field
- submit five professional references who can attest to experience and expertise
- pass a written (and peer-reviewed) assessment that provides insight into one's ability to interpret student needs—including data from relevant testing—and recommend appropriate colleges. The assessment focuses on two areas—institutional knowledge (knowledge of colleges) and professional knowledge (knowledge of standard, ethical procedures involved in working with high school students and families).

The CEP application process includes a thorough review of education, training, expertise, and professional activities. Consultants are certified for five years and then are eligible for recertification. Recertification requires both continuing education hours (professional meetings, workshops, seminars, classes, etc.) and college visits. As the profession has expanded, knowledge has increased, and standards have risen, it should be the goal of every IEC to become certified.

All professional experiences (association membership, conference/workshop attendance) "count" in the certification process. Certification is an important step in the right direction of accreditation. Should states eventually require licensure to practice as an independent educational consultant, those who are certified by AICEP will likely face less scrutiny obtaining licensure than those educational consultants without nationally recognized credentials. More information is available at aicep.org.

PURSUING ADVANCED DEGREES

Many folks are enrolling in classes and even earning advanced degrees. Most consultants have a master's degree. Programs in college counseling, counseling psychology, family dynamics, student affairs, and education provide potential majors. Completion of a graduate degree is required, for example, for many careers in education. IECs might wish to consider master's degree programs in guidance and counseling or higher education. Georgetown University offers a Masters of Professional Studies in Higher Education Administration and a Master's in Global Higher Education. The programs are offered both on campus and online. IECs interested in further formal education should check local colleges and universities for options. Like we tell our students, there are options for everyone—"traditional," extended weekend, online, and so forth. Schools of Education often make it relatively easy for students to work and earn a degree. Colleges like the University of Calgary, Capella, Argosy, Regent, and Walden have offered online programs in the past; some even offered doctoral degrees. The University of Missouri offers an online Master's of Education with an emphasis in mental health practices in schools. (See astudentofcolleges.com for additional learning opportunities.)

EARNING SPECIALIZED CERTIFICATES

Myers-Briggs Type Indicator (MBTI) Master Practitioner
The MBTI Certification Program provides participants with the tools to administer and interpret the MBTI assessment. MBTI is based on Carl Jung's thinking. The assessment takes less than 30 minutes to administer, and it is worthwhile for our students as it helps them understand themselves and others. The MBTI assigns a combination of eight letters that suggest both interactive and personality characteristics.

In addition to certification, the program provides all recipients with access to the MBTI Master Practitioner Referral Network, a network designed to connect professionals with practitioners. The MBTI Master Practitioner course is a four-day program offered in the United States and Canada. Information: mbtimasterpractitioner.org

Strong Interest Inventory Certification
The Strong Interest Inventory is an assessment designed for students to discover personal interests as well as potential educational and career opportunities. The Strong Interest Inventory has been a staple in the interest inventory business for several decades. This certification can potentially drive traffic to the IEC, especially to those who provide (or wish to provide) career advising. The certification provides another tool to assess a student and help him or her discover personal preferences and options for higher education. The Strong Interest Inventory Certification Program is typically three days and usually ranges from $800 to $1,000. Information: https://www.cpp.com/en-US/Products-and-Services/Certification-and-Training/Strong-Certification

Certified Career Counselor (CCC) Credential
The Certified Career Counselor credential, offered by the National Career Development Association, is a certification for professional, experienced career counselors with a graduate or master's degree in an educational counseling related field. The CCC program focuses solely on the relationship between career knowledge and counseling. This credential can distinguish an IEC as a career counselor. Information: https://www.ncda.org/aws/NCDA/pt/sp/credentials_faq

Murphy-Meisgeier Type Indicator for Children (MMTIC) Certification
The MMTIC assessment is a test that has been "developed to measure children's psychological type preferences," and is marketed towards children aged 7-18. The assessment utilizes a shorter and simpler form than the comparable MBTI instrument. The MMTIC Certification provides the skills to teach children how to become better communicators and to be more effective at using social skills to promote healthy relationships. The course is marketed towards professionals with a four-year degree who are over 21 years old and are looking to assist children with personal and social development. The cost for the certification program is $595. Information: https://www.capt.org/assessment-mmtic/home.htm?bhcp=1

Learning Differences and Neurodiversity with Specialization in Executive Function and LD

Landmark College in Putney, Vermont specializes in providing educational opportunities for students with learning disabilities. They provide an online, post-baccalaureate certificate program for those working with diverse learners. Educators can elect to take individual courses in the "Executive Function and LD: Integrating Strategies, Study Skills, and Technology" program or complete the entire program (five courses) to earn the certificate. Graduate credits are available at additional cost. Information: https://www.landmark.edu/research-training/

ACCESSING WEBINARS, BLOGS, PODCASTS, AND TWITTER

There is no excuse for professional stagnation! There are more opportunities than ever to be lifelong learners. The most accessible ways to learn are in front of our computer screens: webinars, blogs, podcasts, and Twitter. Webinars have become particularly abundant. Over the last few years, they have become better organized and targeted. Each IEC needs to think carefully about his or her learning needs. For example, if learning about basic counseling theories is identified as a need, Google that topic ("webinars about counseling theory" or "blogs about counseling theory"). The same goes for topics such as "tours of colleges in Wisconsin for counselors," how to help students select a college major" and "marketing ideas for a small businessperson." (See astudentofcolleges.com for resource lists.)

RESEARCHING (NON-TRAVEL)

Books about colleges have proliferated in the last decade or so. There have never been more opportunities to learn about colleges and the college admission process. I remember reading *The Fiske Guide* whenever I was on my treadmill, yet because of my inherent aversion to exercise, I had to designate other times to read *Fiske* and other college guidebooks. I remember going through the descriptions of certain colleges in *The College Handbook*, looking for certain data such as the percent of students in housing, or the percent of out-of-state students. I made lists based on whatever data I could find. (These lists, by the way, resulted in the publication of *The College Finder*.) I read everything I could about student loans, or early decision, or Catholic colleges. All of this taught me that the consultant needs to stay immersed in college material and needs to be a good researcher.

Browse through the college guides at Amazon or in a bookstore—if you can still find one! Review the options, noting similarities and differences. Which of the books is easiest to use? Which seem written for accuracy, and which seem written simply to sell books?

I have provided the resources I find most useful on the website that complements this book: astudentofcolleges.com.

While they are far from perfect, I would begin my research with two or three of the "subjective" guides. *The Fiske Guide* is in that category as well as *Colleges that Change Lives*. Others are *College Finder, Cool Colleges* (by Asher), *Creative Colleges*, and any of the books related to good value colleges and/or colleges for the B student. These are the books that provide a page or two description of colleges. When reading these subjective reviews, I pay particular attention to student qualities such as the popularity of clubs and other data that give me insight into the sort of student life available, and, by extension, students who will fit into that particular culture. As far as the "facts," *The College Handbook* and *College Admission Data Hyper-Handbook* (Wintergreen Orchard House) are those that I pick up most often. I also find the data in collegedata.com to be valuable. The Common Data Set is the result of a joint effort by the College Board,

U.S. News, and Peterson's. It was created to improve the accuracy of college facts and figures and gives information specific to admission and financial aid.

You can commit to study a "college of the week." During the week, read the description of your chosen school in a few of the books listed above, check out the college's website, and maybe even call the admissions office to talk with a counselor. Keep a record of your research. I have a folder on my desktop that holds research and visit notes for each college I research.

The final tip regarding researching is to stay out of the weeds and prioritize. I try to spend my research time on the major topics that I need to know about. For example, I pay more attention to a new database of college facts than on nuances of early decision. I am most attuned to the "vibe" or "culture" of colleges and universities. I can simply check on a college website for an answer that I don't have to a question about early decision policies, majors, or merit scholarship options. My research time is devoted to the broad view.

TALKING, LISTENING, AND SHARING

Good consultants talk to one another. They talk to friends and colleagues who are counselors at high schools or colleges. They talk to students who are in or have attended college and listen intently to their stories, gaining knowledge through students' experiences. IECs take note of students' perspectives and share valued feedback with other students and parents. IECs who crave knowledge actively engage in conversation with parents about their child's experiences. Talking, listening, and sharing perspectives can take place formally or informally; the goal is to adopt a mindset that knowledge can and will be found through taking advantage of one's curiosity and communication skills.

WORKING WITH A MENTOR

Though working with a mentor is included at the end of this list of ways to increase your knowledge base, it is perhaps one of the most important. Mentorship can take many forms and can develop into lifelong associations and friendships. If there is someone in an established practice whom you trust and admire, ask about shadowing, mentoring, and other interactive possibilities. You might also consider a long-distance mentorship. Think about the value of meeting via Facetime/Skype/Zoom every Monday morning with someone who is willing to talk about your practice issues. Note that both IECA and HECA have mentoring programs available to their members.

FINAL THOUGHTS

Ultimately, to succeed in the profession and to best serve the needs of students and families, independent educational consultants must commit mind, time, and frequent flier miles. Knowledge is our holy grail, and no holy grail is attained without effort and dedication. As students of colleges, we must yearn to learn and be active and engaged in our quest for the holy grail.

CHAPTER 9

The IEC as Manager

EXPECTATION MANAGERS

Independent educational consultants manage students' and parents' expectations (with varying degrees of success!). Students and parents want to know what they can expect throughout the process. In hospitals if we're not told what's happening and when, we get stressed and angry. Such frenzy is what consultants help to manage. The consultant needs to say, "Here's what is going on out there in the world of college admission. Here is what you can expect." We put the process into context and help families see the big picture. Every time we see a student, he or she should feel better about the process.

Consultants are, in a very real sense, expectation managers. This is particularly relevant for the student applying to the 100 or so most selective schools, but also, interestingly, true for the student with more choice. After all, part of the process involves, for most all students, applying to colleges that are more selective (i.e., reaches).

An important part of expectation management is to be sure students are aware of the role they play in terms of the colleges to which they will be admitted. They need to know that while they can't assure admission to a selective college, they can add more "sure bet" colleges to their list. As we know, college acceptances are the result of developing a good list of colleges with many reach schools and with many safeties. (The college list was fully addressed in Chapter 6.)

Expectation management is particularly relevant insofar as relationships with parents. Some parents need to be reminded that what they are paying for is our best judgment—nothing less, nothing more. More specifically, we as IECs must manage parents' expectations by clarifying that we do not perform the following tasks and do not assume the following roles:

- Guarantee admission to any college
- Write essays for the student
- Complete applications for the student
- Serve as a personal travel agent
- Hold the student's hand
- Strategize ways to get a student into an elite school
- Call colleges (In fact, I seldom call colleges to find out how a student's application is progressing or for any other admission purpose; I call only if I have an addition to the file that I feel will not come from any other source. Why should I call if the goal is match?).

Another role of the expectation manager is to be a good teacher. Share articles. Be sure students and parents know we are on their side. We're not setting admission criteria. We're interpreting. Don't shoot the messenger. Is the cup half full or half empty? For most students, the cup is half full due to lots of college options. Explain to students the system used by *U.S. News* to rank colleges. We need to put things in perspective for our students and their parents. College admission officers have one basic job: get kids to apply. We're typically more concerned about match than they are.

Expectation management also includes being aware of how you are doing as a consultant. In other words, while we manage student and parental expectations vis-à-vis college admission, so too must we be cognizant of how we are doing our work and the expectations we have, or should have, for ourselves as professionals. We need to be mindful of consumer satisfaction: Is our work top quality? Are we completing our tasks on time? Is the cost/value benefit of our work appropriate? Are we flexible? Are we dependable? Do we know how to keep our perspective? Can we manage our own feelings? Can we leave home/family issues at the door? Can we balance home and work?

INFORMATION MANAGERS

Educational consultants are also information managers. We are fact checkers. The information explosion has increased rather than decreased the need for families to seek outside help. A Google search for "college admission help" yields 26 million matches. How does one navigate through such an expanse of information?

Consultants put things in perspective for students and their parents. We sort and interpret information. Colleges are proactive and marketing driven; they recruit aggressively. Consulting helps level the playing field. We educate students about the marketing practices being used on them and disabuse them of the notion that they are truly desired by the institutions that send them mail, email, and/or texts, sometimes nearly every day. We show students how they are initially "demographic fodder" and teach them what to look for in a way that gives them a psychological advantage. Consultants also help parents get beyond marketing messages. We dissect statistics with them so that they can be informed consumers, not just dreamy status shoppers.

As information managers, we help students and parents avoid being caught up in the "noise" of college planning. Noise is what everyone is saying. Noise is where everyone else thinks a student should go to college. Noise is fancy brochures and catchy college websites. Noise is the college tour guide who talks only of the school's countless wonders. Noise is rankings. The higher education culture is dominated by rankings. Consultants use inoculation to help families anticipate and circumnavigate the noise of the college planning process. Fit involves honing in on the right information, not being bamboozled by noise.

Because rankings create so much noise, and because IECs can expect parents to show up with the latest version of *U.S. News and World Report* in hand, I share below the criteria that *U.S. News* typically employs to determine its rankings. I ask you to evaluate the validity of this system before I offer commentary.

The *U.S. News* ranking system rests on two pillars. The formula uses quantitative measures that are seen as reliable indicators of academic quality, and based on *U.S. News'* researched view of what matters in education. Once schools have been divided by category, *U.S. News* gathers data from each college on a dozen or so indicators of academic excellence. Each factor is assigned a weight that reflects *U.S. News'* judgment about how much that measure matters. Then, the colleges and universities in each category are ranked against their peers, based on a composite weighted score.

The following variables are typically weighed:
Graduation and retention rates (this frequently represents 20-25% of the total): This measure has two components. The one that is given most weight is the six-year graduation rate. First-year retention rate is the other factor. The graduation rate indicates the average proportion of a graduating class earning a degree in six years or less. Retention indicates the average proportion of students who return to the campus each year.

Undergraduate academic reputation (this frequently represents 20-25% of the total): The *U.S. News* ranking formula gives weight to the opinions of those deemed to be in a position to judge a school's undergraduate academic excellence. The academic peer assessment survey allows top academics—presidents, provosts and deans of admissions—to account for intangibles at peer institutions, such as faculty dedication to teaching.

Faculty resources (this is usually around 20% of the total): Research shows that the more satisfied students are about their contact with professors, the more they will learn and the more likely they are to graduate. *U.S. News* uses five factors to assess a school's commitment to instruction.
   1. Class size
   2. Faculty salary
   3. Proportion of professors with the highest degree in their fields
   4. Student-faculty ratio
   5. Proportion of faculty who are full-time

Student selectivity (this is often about 10%): A school's academic atmosphere is determined in part by students' abilities and ambitions. This measure has three components:
   1. Admissions test scores for all enrollees who took the reading and writing and math portions of the SAT and the composite ACT score

2. Proportion of enrolled first-year students at national universities and national liberal arts colleges who graduated in the top 10 percent of their high school classes or the proportion of enrolled first-year students at regional universities and regional colleges who graduated in the top quarter of their classes
3. Acceptance rate, or the ratio of students admitted to applicants

Financial resources (about 10%): Generous per-student spending indicates that a college can offer a wide variety of programs and services. *U.S. News* measures financial resources by using the average spending per student on instruction, research, student services, and related educational expenditures. Spending on sports, dorms, and hospitals doesn't count toward this indicator.

Graduation rate performance (typically less than 10%): This indicator of added value shows the effect of the college's programs and policies on the graduation rate of students after controlling for spending and student characteristics, such as test scores and the proportion receiving Pell Grants.

Alumni giving rate (about 5%): This reflects the average percentage of living alumni with bachelor's degrees who give to their school during a designated period.

To arrive at a school's rank, *U.S. News* first calculates the weighted sum of its standardized scores. The final scores are rescaled so that the top school in each category receives a value of 100, and the other schools' weighted scores are calculated as a proportion of that top score. Final scores are rounded to the nearest whole number and ranked in descending order.

There you have *U.S. News*' secret sauce.

Now, I share my commentary.

I used to dismiss rankings with a quick comment that *U.S. News* doesn't know Buffy. That, however, was not enough. For the IEC, and indeed for anyone concerned about rationality in the college admission process, the rankings represent a one-dimensional approach to a multidimensional issue. The notion of ranking colleges is anathema to the concepts of fit and match. Consider the following criticisms.

- As a society, we have chosen what to rank and what not to rank. We rank ironing boards, restaurants, cars, etc. But we don't rank churches. Why not? Well, there is not a well-defined set of criteria. Religious institutions are complex; they have different missions, purposes, and foci. How can we compare a Catholic church with a Protestant one? Is one church better than another because it has more money? Is the wealth of the congregants or the wealth of the church a factor in determining its "goodness?" Is it better if a church has a larger congregation? Is it better if the senior clergy is a great sermonizer? What about synagogues? Is one better because the kiddush is catered by a fancy deli? These questions are outrageous, and it's just as outrageous to apply such a thought system to colleges. Are we really expected to buy into a system that feels that all colleges are capable of being put into the same box? Can we use the same criteria to evaluate the University of California, Berkeley with Oberlin College? Since Historically Black Colleges and Universities often are less "rich," are they really of less quality than lots of predominately Caucasian colleges? If faculty pay is higher in New York City, does that make a college in the Big Apple better than a school in Des Moines? Of course not!
- One standard applied to the complexity of colleges and universities is outrageous on many levels. The goals and missions of colleges are vastly different. Even the *U.S. News* categories are entirely too broad. Consider the following three schools which, in a recent ranking, were included in the same category: United States Military Academy, Spelman College, and College of the Atlantic.

The military academy is free and focused on preparing "high-quality commissioned leaders" for the army. Spelman is a Historically Black College that educates women. College of the Atlantic is an "experimental" college that focuses on human ecology. I contend that each of these institutions should be judged on the basis of its unique philosophies and student needs. Considering the same factors (reputation, faculty resources, proportion of professors with the highest degrees, student selectivity, financial resources, etc.) for each school is wholly ineffective in gauging the relative merits of these three schools, and it is equally unfair to all of these institutions.

A very substantial amount (usually close to a quarter) of an institution's ranking comes not from any hard data but from a measure of "reputation," in which *U.S. News* solicits "peer assessments" from college presidents, provosts, and admissions directors, as well as input from high school counselors. *U.S. News* claims that by giving "significant weight to the opinions of those in a position to judge a school's undergraduate academic excellence," the rankings allow for the inclusion of "intangibles" such as "faculty dedication to teaching." Critics say this component turns the rankings into a popularity or beauty contest and that asking college officials to rate the relative merits of other schools about which they know nothing becomes a particularly empty exercise because a school's reputation is driven in large part by—guess who?—the *U.S. News* rankings. Thus, the use of reputation reinforces existing perceptions. In other words, it keeps well known schools at the top. Further, it works against colleges that innovate, colleges that put emphasis on the learning outcomes of their students, and colleges that have a specific focus.

- A major point that I emphasize is that rankings don't take into account measures of the quality of education at each institution, nor is there any consideration of "outcomes." For example, what do students at College X actually learn? Does College X do a great job with learning disabled students? Do students who attend College X get jobs upon graduation? Is faculty salary an indication of passion for teaching? Or, significantly, is this college a happy place?
- *U.S. News* is always tinkering with the metrics they use, so meaningful comparisons from one year to the next are hard to make. Critics also allege that this is as much a marketing move as an attempt to improve the quality of the rankings: changes in the metrics yield slight changes in the rank orders, which induces people to buy the latest rankings to see what's changed.
- Colleges "look better" if they receive a lot of applications, at least in the eyes of *U.S. News*. A ranking of a college increases as it reports more applications. Ranking also increases when a college reports more denials. What often drives colleges to seek more applicants is rankings rather than fit and match.
- The *U.S. News* rankings help to push college costs higher because the formula they use in calculating their rankings rewards schools that spend more money, so colleges and universities do precisely that and, inevitably, they have to raise their tuition to cover costs.
- The metrics used must have a face validity. In other words, if Metropolitan State University, a fine school with a unique mission in Colorado, came out as number one, fewer people would buy the ranking book. But if the "winners" are typically Harvard, Stanford, or Princeton, people will believe that rankings are an adequate measure of quality.
- Because the rankings have a popular audience, they encourage colleges and universities to game the system—i.e., to do what they can to raise their place in the rankings by, for example, spending oodles of money on things that the *U.S. News* formula deems important or by aggressively increasing the size of their applicant pool so that they can turn away a higher percentage of their applicants, thus portraying themselves to be "more selective" and thereby raising their rank. Moreover, I fear that some schools simply provide unreliable data.
- The whole exercise implies a sort of authoritative precision and rigor that impart real meaning to the rankings, but it is simply nonsense to say that, for example, Duke "ranks higher" than Johns Hopkins or that Middlebury should rank 13 spots higher than Wesleyan.

- We live in a culture that is already too obsessed with prestige and cachet. *U.S. News* fosters the notion that if Buffy doesn't get into a top-ranked college, her chance for success in life diminishes. I can't find any concrete evidence for that generalization. Simply put, the rankings exacerbate the status anxiety of prospective students and parents.
- *U.S. News* does, indeed, not know Buffy. Or Brutus. Trying to suggest that certain schools are best, and thus that *every* student would be happy at a top-ranked college is significantly flawed.

As information managers, it is our responsibility not to let noise influence choice.

UNCERTAINTY MANAGERS

College admission, by its very nature, is filled with uncertainty. We're dealing with a process which, even for the student who is not applying to more selective colleges, is filled with unknowns. We don't know who will read a college essay and thus are uncertain about the way to tackle it. Students don't know how their lacrosse abilities line up with those of the team at their favorite college. Buffy doesn't know whether her legacy status will help her get into the University of Virginia.

Further, adolescence itself is a time of uncertainty. The "not knowing" can immobilize students. How your student copes with uncertainty can be, to some extent, determined by how you, as an IEC, handle the various stages of the process and how you yourself cope with the ambiguities involved.

Learning to find comfort in uncertainty is difficult. No one likes to feel helpless. Consultants manage uncertainty through strategies and language geared to help students make good choices. If you are mindful enough to teach your students how to face the unknown in a way that serves them, you will have given your students a life skill that will last many years after they have left your office.

Here are ways of working with uncertainty with our students:

- Take the time to process uncertainty with your student. There is never a convenient time to get sick and miss work, but our bodies force us to stop and take care of ourselves. Uncertainty serves the same purpose; it is a time to stop, redirect attention to what is going on, and form an action plan.
- Think aloud with the student. Say to your student, "Okay, you were deferred from Vanderbilt. That makes me feel confused as I would have guessed that you would have been admitted. The only way I can decrease my anxiety is by moving on to consider your other options. Is there any chance that you can do that with me?" Such an approach serves to verbally acknowledge the uncertainty. Offer understanding such as, "Not knowing how these five schools are going to view your application must be stressful." Then, present ways to cope.
- Keep calm. Stress and calmness cannot occupy the same space at the same time. We cannot buy into the mania that often pervades the admissions process. As consultants, we calm the waters by being calm ourselves. Our offices should be places where college planning occurs in a peaceful and restrained fashion. The hyper, frenzied consultant is not helping with the transition. IEC demeanor is contagious. Hysteria begets hysteria and calm begets calm. This is particularly important in regard to dealing with a very uncertain admissions world.
- Break larger tasks into smaller tasks. Uncertainty is greatest when a student faces the "vast unknown" of college admissions. For example, advise your student not to fret over his or her final college decision when the immediate issue at hand is building the college list. Counsel your student not to focus on the possibility that he or she won't perform well on the ACT or SAT. Instead, focus your student on how he or she can maximize the time spent on test preparation.

- Stay positive. An uncertain student is already feeling anxious and nervous about the college process in general. Providing a point of positivity is amazingly supportive and helpful.
- Repeat important messages. We know, for example, that there are no "perfect" colleges. Emphasizing that fact with your student can reduce tension or stress. An importent message is, "There is more than one right college for you."
- Prepare for multiple outcomes. By ongoing mention of many options and many colleges, the IEC helps deal with the uncertainty of waiting for college results.
- Emphasize the elements of the process that are predictable. We know there are application deadlines and can talk to students about them. We know that the student has to complete applications, and we can lay out a strategy for doing so effectively and creatively. Uncertainty increases when the student doesn't know the next steps. As such, stay several steps ahead of the student and have a plan to get through the process.

In a time of uncertainty, IECs are value exposers and value clarifiers. We deal with logic rather than emotion. We encourage sanity and reason. We provide wisdom, philosophy, and insight. We build mirrors for our students. We need to help Buffy see Buffy.

REFRAMING MANAGERS

The college admission process is also filled with myths and false assumptions.

The IEC tries to reframe perspectives to expose core issues. Reframing is seeing the current situation from a different perspective, which can be helpful in problem-solving, decision-making, and learning. Reframing can help your student constructively move on from a troubling situation to one that is approached in a constructive way.

When working to reframe a situation, consider the following basic guidelines. Keep in mind that, even though the following examples are about another person's comments, you can use the guidelines to shift your own perspectives as well.

Reframing Guidelines
Shift from passive to active
Brutus insists, "I really doubt that I can do anything about my feeling that Dartmouth is the only school for me." You might respond, "What is one small step that you might take to see Dartmouth as just one of a number of super college choices on your list? Would you be open to me telling you about a very different type of college experience: the honors program at the Penn State?"

Shift from past to future
Buffy laments, "I've never been good at test taking." You might respond, "Imagine yourself getting good scores on the next ACT. How would you restructure your study and practice time so that you would be more successful?"

Shift from future to past
Brutus bemoans, "I can't seem to get started on writing my essay." You might respond, "Has there been a time in the past when you had a hard time starting but ultimately you achieved a goal? If so, what did you do back then to be successful? How might you use that approach now?"

Shift from a liability to an asset

Buffy sighs, "I'm such a perfectionist, so I'll never be able to write an outstanding essay." You might respond, "How might being a perfectionist help in writing a great college essay?"

Reframing will prompt Buffy to realize that her anxiety might make her a better writer, that it keeps her on her game, probably guaranteeing that the mistake she is so worried about making will never come to pass. The appropriate response is to embrace her anxiety, not to hate it.

Final Reframing Thoughts

Reframing works best when it has an emotional impact beyond its appeal to the thinking mind. By discovering what's important to your students, you will find out what raises their emotional temperature, and you can utilize what motivates them to help them view things differently.

IECs may have a student or parent who has believed for a long time that there is only a handful of "good" colleges and the rest, by default, are "not-so-good." Changing that attitude can be done, but it requires mini steps, reframing, and redundancy. Coming in and immediately insisting that there are many matches may not be effective. The first step could be to establish the concept of fit and to find the words to suggest that a good match will increase the odds that Buffy will be happy and that, in turn, will lead to better grades and more success in college. In other words, we know where the consulting is going, but we get there gradually, adding perspectives and arguments step by step along the way.

As reframing managers, IECs turn negativity into positivity. We guide students to transcend roadblocks.

CHAPTER 10

Know Thy Students

STUDENTS AND PARENTS: WHO'S WHO AS FAR AS THE IEC IS CONCERNED?

It is important to clarify who's who in regard to the IEC's working relationship with students and parents. The student is the client, and the parent is the customer. The student's needs are central to our work, and everything revolves around their needs. Certainly, parents are important partners in our quest to find Buffy a college where she can thrive academically and be happy. Working with parents is central to our work, and the amount of time we spend with parents is high. But we're here for the student. Our lives as IECs are student-driven.

KNOW YOUR DEMOGRAPHIC

What's our image of adolescents? What words come to mind when we think of adolescents? Awkward? Conflicted? Immature? Mature? Poised? Pressured? Perhaps all of the above. Perhaps none of them. Whatever image we conjure, we have chosen to work with this demographic because we relate to and respect teens. We desire to interact with them as they are growing, learning, and changing.

As consultants, we do what we can to stay tuned in to the world of teenagers. The purpose is not to fit in and/or to be cool; rather, our mission is to understand teen culture. Being in touch with teens' language, mannerisms, and visions enables IECs to pick up cues that help us in our work. Try to read popular news sources, and keep up with social media, television, movies, and music. You don't have to be a trendsetter to know what's trendy.

GENERATION Z (iGen)

Note that though teenage life has remained largely unchanged from what it was in past eras, there are some key differences that are important to be aware of when working with today's teens. As always, teens remain complex and unique. I don't wish to generalize the problems they face and the characteristics they embody. Yet, I feel that it is worthwhile to explore the Generation Z culture because for some of us who grew up long ago, the world is not the same.

Generation Z (sometimes called the Homeland Generation, iGen or iGeneration, or Post-Millennials) is the age group that defines a majority of the teenagers living today. Most demographers define Generation Z as the set of individuals born after 2005 and characterize the group as "Homelanders" because life in the post-9/11 homeland-security state is the only condition they have ever known. As such, these individuals are growing up under tougher circumstances than did the relatively carefree Millennials. The Generation Z age group is a larger cohort when compared to Baby Boomers or Millennials.

Key events in the lives of Generation Z members include the presidency of Barack Obama, the financial meltdown of 2008, and the Great Recession. For many of those born after 2005, an African-American president was the norm and accepted as a natural reflection of their increasingly multicultural worlds. In fact, Generation Z is the most diverse generation yet, and members are born from the largest per capita immigrant group in the 20th century: Generation X.

The financial meltdown and recession of the 21st century impacted the ideals and motivations of Generation Z members. They are often frugal, pragmatic, and anxious about the world. IECs may see these characteristics reflected in students' choices of college majors and employment goals. These young men and women are concerned about academic success as a key to future employment, but they also are increasingly reliant on entrepreneurial, outside-of-the-box thinking that may not factor in post-secondary education at all.

Generation Z has grown up saturated in digital technology. Unlike the hyper-social and unstressed Millennials, Generation Z members are more wary of the potential public damage that social media can have on their reputations, and they often prefer to share their lives either anonymously or privately. These digital natives often cultivate "personal brands" through their public-facing social media while culturing a different, more intimate persona with their close friends. Other effects of the digital age include the propensity for modern teens to be efficient at multi-tasking and to be easily distracted.

The global worries that occupy the minds of many of these teens (partly due to their constant connection to news outlets, social media, and the internet) have also led them to be more aware of world issues, motivated toward social justice, and mindful of the future. Generation Z, as a whole, is more tolerant of others, and many of its members expect shifts in social norms similar to the legalization of gay marriage in the United States in 2015. Teens today express interest in volunteerism, entrepreneurship, and cooperation as techniques to solve world issues.

In all, Generation Z is comprised of globally-minded, slightly stressed, and hard-working individuals who often are not entirely comfortable with the world they live in. Some of them will accept the planet they are given, but many will be motivated by their global awareness to shape our world for the better.

As a final note on Generation Z or iGen, I want to point you to "The Mindset List" (themindsetlist.com). The list was started at Beloit College in Wisconsin and is now affiliated with Marist College in New York. The annual list is made up of items 18-year-olds do and don't remember. The creators state that their goal is to remind their colleagues of which references students in their classes will understand—and which references would be met with blank stares. Given the typical age disparity between an IEC and her/his student, the list is particularly useful. Plus, it is fun to read.

TODAY'S TEENS/TEENS OF YESTERDAY: A BRIEF LOOK AT WHAT HAS CHANGED AND WHAT'S ETERNAL	
Today's Teens	**Yesterday's Teens**
Social media provides a mirror through which teens can readily compare themselves with others. We live in a *selfie society* in which social media users can create mediated identities. Posts are carefully constructed, and photos are perfectly staged to showcase one's best self. Many teens create online personas, which are not necessarily an authentic representation of self. Thus, if a teen is less comfortable with his or her body image, it's hard to get away from it. Those with poor self-images may be particularly amenable to self-criticism as a result of photo-sharing.	How do I stack up against celebrities? Do I have a figure like Madonna? Is Justin Bieber more ripped than I am? Should I get my hair cut like Jennifer Aniston's, or is her look now out of vogue thanks to Angelina Jolie?
Stressed, anxious, depressed, and medicated. Note that the college planning process and the hard core level of admission competitiveness may add to the anxiety that many teens grapple with.	Less documented mental health diagnoses and prescriptions. Perhaps a greater ability to navigate routine setbacks. College competitiveness was less cutthroat.
Peer pressure and competition are exacerbated by social media.	Peer pressure and competition impacted teens on less of a mass-public scale.
Binge drinking (hard liquor) is common on many campuses, and recreational marijuana has been legalized in several states, making it especially accessible.	Less reported binge drinking, beer was the alcohol of choice, and marijuana couldn't be purchased at a glitzy shop with a "Genius Bar."
Any time is screen time: Surfing the web, gaming, social media posting, etc. are part of a daily routine.	Couch potato syndrome: Zoning out in front of the "tube" was a common pastime.

Today's Teens	Yesterday's Teens
Information is available with a simple click. A base level knowledge of just about everything awaits those who search Google.	A trip to the local library or bookstore was necessary to gather information. One may even have known how to use a card catalog. Teens did not truly know everything.
Hookup culture: Many teens today eschew the labels of the traditional relationship for the mobility and freedom of the "hookup." Sometimes exclusive, sometimes not, the hookup allows teens to avoid the emotional commitment that typically accompanies more explicitly labeled relationships. Today's generation may opt for "Netflix and chill"—sexual exploration with emotional detachment.	Let's go steady. Or, let's call ourselves a couple to "legitimize" sexual exploration.
Independence and autonomy: Bring it on!	Independence and autonomy: Bring it on!

TEENAGE DEVELOPMENT

Studies about teens and teenage development reveal that teens go through a process of finding themselves as they seek independence. Below are some of the common themes in studies of the nature of adolescence.
* Improved self-sufficiency
* Improved emotional solidity
* Showing more concern for others
* Inward assessment of experiences
* Development of individuality
* Discomfort with one's body
* Character development
* Influence of peer groups
* Tendency to point out mistakes a parent may commit
* Disagreements with parents concerning independence
* Immature behavior when faced with anxiety

As adolescents look toward the future, studies show they may exhibit:
* Structured working routines show growing maturity in the mental, emotional, and physical levels
* Heightened interest in the future, but main focus still in the present
* Questions and fears concerning personal appeal to the opposite sex and sexual issues generally

Lastly, in terms of general principles and morality, studies find:
* Enhanced capability of structuring aims and objectives
* Fascination with ethical ways of thinking
* Capability of utilizing insight
* Stronger presence of conscience
* Tendency to push the limits and try out vices (sex, alcohol, drugs)
* Desire to choose a model to look up to and to create standards for one's self

Ultimately, over the many years I've worked with teens, I've learned to understand common themes of teenage behavior, but I've learned not to categorize and not to reduce teen behavior to a norm. With teenage behavior being unpredictable, we as adults have to let go of the need to try to make everything logical, rational, and scientific. Teenagers don't often operate that way. The successful IEC understands and empathizes with teens. To flex our knowledge as students of colleges, we must also be students of students.

GETTING TO KNOW BUFFY AND BRUTUS

You open the door and there stands Buffy. She's a high school junior ready to embark on her college search. Yet who is Buffy beyond a client who has come to seek your professional advice?
Is she an aspiring artist? A volleyball star with a commanding spike? A future Yale graduate? The only girl at school without a boyfriend?

Buffy is an individual. She is naïve about many things and knowledgable about many things. She defies categorization. A parent who says, "Buffy is just a typical teenager" leaves me dumfounded. All teens are different. Buffy is not the sum of parental influence or peer pressure; she is neither a product of suburbia nor the epitome of a small town girl. And she is certainly not the incarnation of her GPA or test scores. She is a teenager with her own interests, concerns, worldview, need for autonomy, stress level, learning style, etc. To provide Buffy expert guidance, we need to see Buffy as an individual. (This goes for Brutus, too.)

Getting to know a student and building and maintaining rapport is at the center of consulting success. The fundamental consulting concepts of fit and match begin with knowing our students. Good college advising starts with the student, not with a discussion of colleges. Hence, communication is key. The consultant employs counseling skills to facilitate open discussion and to encourage the student to take the lead. Consultants may need to push shy Brutus so that he will open up and share of himself. As discussed in Chapter 7, be attuned to the student's nonverbal communication. Eventually, when Brutus feels comfortable and becomes communicative, he will assume ownership of his education, guiding the consultant to hone in on his college expectations. The more the consultant learns about the student's values and attitudes, likes and dislikes, and perceptions of self and the world, the more the consultant's recommendations about colleges will ultimately be on target.

Below you will see some of the questions I use in my early interviews with students. When I began consulting, I wrote the questions out on a piece of paper with spaces between each. When the student answered a question, I'd write down his or her response. Other times, I'd intermingle these questions more naturally in the course of a conversation. One way or another, I'd take notes so as to remember qualities about the student. I recommend taking *detailed* notes.

School Questions:
- What do you like/dislike about school/learning?
- Do you work more than/equal to/less than others in your classes?
- Have you worked up to your potential?
- Are your grades an accurate representation of the effort you put into school?
- What has been most challenging for you in high school?
- What motivates you academically?
- What academic strength/weakness has been most helpful/detrimental to you?
- How do you learn best? Can you articulate your learning style?
- What do you guess your teachers say about you?
- Do you advocate for yourself?

- What will you choose to learn when you can learn on your own?
- Is there a book that has had a significant influence on you?
- What classes do you love and hate most in school? Why?
- Describe your favorite teacher. What types of things did you do in his/her class?
- Do you prefer group work or individual work?
- If you had a choice to attend school or not, would you attend? Why or why not?
- Do your test scores reflect how good your teachers are? What do you believe your test scores reflect?
- What are you looking forward to (or dreading) this school year?

Outside of Class Questions:
- What is your favorite activity? Why do you do it? How did you get involved?
- What are your other interests?
- What magazines do you read regularly?
- What TV shows do you try not to miss?
- What websites do you visit regularly?
- What music do you listen to?
- How much time do you spend on Facebook, Instagram, Snapchat, etc. Do you tweet?
- What do you do in your free time?
- Do you collect anything? If so, what and why?
- What are your social strengths/weaknesses?

Personal Questions:
- What words describe you?
- How would your parents describe you?
- What do your parents expect of you?
- How have you made a difference in your high school?
- How have you made a difference in your community?
- Are you a typical student at your school?
- What do you look for in friends?
- Is it important to you to be amongst like-minded people?
- What would you do with a million dollars?
- If you had a free day, what would you do?
- In what way is your room at home a true reflection of you?
- What motivates you?
- Do you have an overarching goal in life?
- Who are some people you admire? Why?
- What makes you angry?
- What have you failed at, and what was your response to failure?
- What are two important decisions you've made since beginning high school?
- What is the one thing people don't understand about you?
- If you had only one word to describe who you are, what would it be?
- What events have shaped your growth and way of thinking?
- If money were no object, what would you want to pursue?
- Can money buy you happiness?
- Where do you see yourself in five years?
- Are you an introvert or an extrovert?
- How would you like to help our world?
- What is most important to you?

- Do you have a strong sense of self?
- What advice would you give younger kids about middle or high school?
- If you had a warning label, what would yours say?
- If you were the ruler of your own country, what would be the first law(s) you would introduce?

College Questions:
- Why do you want to attend college?
- What colleges have you heard about?
- What concerns you the most about going to college?
- What have your parents told you about college?
- What role will your parents play in your college choice?
- Are there significant others (relatives, friends, etc.) you will look to for help in selecting a college?
- If you could make a fortune without going to college, would you still go?
- Do you have the self-discipline to finish an undergraduate degree?
- How do you hope to contribute to your college's community?
- What do you have to offer a college? Why should you be admitted?

And then I typically say:
- Imagine a perfect college for you and tell me about it.

INTERPRETING *COLLEGE MATCH* SELF-SURVEY RESULTS

Another option to help you get to know your students is to have students complete the Self-Survey for the College Bound in *College Match*. When the survey was first published over 20 years ago, it was likely the first attempt to quantify student college-going attributes and to combine those qualities with factors found at colleges and universities. The 80-question self-inventory results in a student "score" for each of the following characteristics:
- School Enthusiasm
- Participant Learner
- Affection for Knowledge
- Basic Academic Skills
- Independence
- Career Orientation
- Social Consciousness
- Self-Understanding
- Academic/Social Balance
- Eagerness for College

If students complete this form and submit it to you prior to your first meeting, you have the advantage of advancing to more specific questions once you meet face-to-face. With the results of the Self-Survey, you can discuss student attitudes about college going, level of interest in the academic as well as the social sides of college life, readiness for college, and a range of other matters.

The "Self-Survey" from *College Match* is included in Appendix C.

To help consultants make the greatest use of the survey, below are pointers on how to interpret the results of the survey. After scoring the Self-Survey, there are some immediate conclusions that can be drawn. The student who is high on independence might be better able to handle the transition to college, for example. But the real value of the Self-Survey is as a conversation starter with students in your office.

Here are a few tips on understanding and using the categories:

School enthusiasm allows discussion of questions such as these: How much of this enthusiasm is for intellectual work, and how much is for the "experience" of college? How hard does the student want to work in college? What is the connection between school enthusiasm and a liking for particular academic subjects? What is the connection between school enthusiasm and being liked and accepted by peers? How does school enthusiasm relate to issues such as location, cost, and sense of community? Does Buffy enjoy some social features of school more than academic features? Or vice versa? Should a gap year be considered?

Our students have not been college students before; as such, we need to help them know about the different ways a college experience can be made more appealing. For many, school enthusiasm doesn't become noticeable until late in high school and in the transition to college.

Participant learner allows discussion of questions of this sort: How does the student perceive the definition of participant learning? How important is participant learning in the student's overall sense of a good fit college? Is the level of interest in being a participant learner generalized, or does it refer to a smaller set of classes or courses (such as the student's major)? Is the student able to visualize large college lecture classes? If not, how can we help with that visualization? How does a student balance an interest in being a participant learner with an interest in being at a large, state school? Or from another perspective, is participating in class more or less important than, say, being at a school with a huge football program?

Note that while the "typical" participant learner is likely to be more fulfilled at a small college, there are many variations. There are smaller classes at larger universities. Exploring ways to make a "big college small" is encouraged. For example, as noted in Chapter 6, honor colleges, house/residential systems, and small colleges within major universities.

Affection for knowledge allows exploration of questions such as: Is affection for knowledge a general trait for the student, or is it specific to particular subjects or one's proposed major? How will this student operationalize his or her affection for knowledge in a complex university environment? Do the student responses to questions in this area refer to a desire for intellectual stimulation, or do they refer to the student's desire for a big name college? Or, is it a combination of the two?

Low scores in this category might be the result of lack of exposure to stimulating academics in high school or earlier.

Independence allows discussion of questions and topics such as these: What are the specific ways that an independent student can find independence on campus? For example, would the ability to choose classes and participate in overall college decision-making make for a better match? Does the student understand what independence means? Is the student unusually dependent on support from mom or dad? If so, what can you do to help the student put this factor into the context of college planning? Does independence extend to mature decision making?

If the student's scores are low, he or she may still be transitioning from dependence to independence. The student may prefer to have choices made for him or her. Some colleges provide more structure, such as freshman seminars and ongoing freshman advising. Those with low scores may need to work on self-discipline and practice assuming responsibility for decisions and consequences. Time management is very important here. A smaller college could provide an environment for gradually building self-confidence and independence.

Social consciousness allows for a discussion of issues such as these: What sort of campus environment is right in terms of political leaning? How attuned is the student to news and politics? Is campus activism a positive in the student's college search? What sort of emphasis on volunteerism is right for Brutus? How interested is the student in sharing favorite causes with friends?

Social consciousness (or social responsibility, social awareness, concern about injustice and problems in society) has had many meanings over the decades. At different points in history, high social consciousness might have been related to being against the war in Vietnam or protesting for equality for women, African Americans, the gay community, and so forth. In more recent years, social consciousness may mean being part of the "resistance" against President Trump. These days, concern about the environment has become a rallying cry for many Generation Z members. Global warming and rights for transgender students are other common concerns.

Low scores here don't mean indifference to the world. Students may not be sensitive to or aware of the numerous opportunities for social responsibility. They may be comfortable with pursuing their own individual goals, or they may have other priorities. They just might not have enough experience to select an issue of importance. Or perhaps their priorities are in other areas.

Self-understanding allows discussion of questions such as these: How will your self-understanding help you succeed in college? Beyond your score in this category, do you feel you have an awareness of your strengths and weaknesses? How are you working to understand yourself better?

If a student doesn't possess great self-understanding, you can help him or her by talking about goals, hobbies, aspirations and other aspects that can define an individual. Students with lower scores in this category might seek better advising programs or a school offering freshman seminars. Low scorers may be just beginning to know themselves. Teenagers' perceptions of themselves are heavily influenced by peers. Perhaps students are overly responsive to the wishes and demands others have for them. They might find it easier to acquire self-understanding and confidence at a smaller, more supportive college than at an enormous university. Note that a low score is not a bad thing. Self-understanding is a skill that many obtain throughout college and is a lifetime in the making.

Academic/social balance allows discussion of topics and questions such as these: What would a balanced life look like for Buffy as a college student? Has Buffy's life in high school been balanced? Does Buffy wish she had more time for academics or social life or family life? How much does she want to "push" herself in college? Would an academic life in college, without much of a social life, be acceptable? Is that better or worse than the reverse? That is, would a social life in college, without a big emphasis on academics, be acceptable or preferable? If "work hard/play hard" sounds right for Buffy's life in college, how does she see that unfolding? That is, does that mean that her weekends are free for socializing?

Remember that balance doesn't mean the student wants a party school. The questions here reflect a student who wants an academic challenge, but also time for clubs, sports, activities, or socializing. The consultant assesses what that balance means through inquiries such as those above.

Basic academic skills allows discussion of questions such as these: How does Buffy translate her academic skills into criteria to use as she selects a college? In other words, what do Buffy's skills in writing, reading, note taking, etc. tell her about herself? Should Buffy pay particular attention to tutoring options or learning resources at her college? How can we help a student deal with distractions? Are Brutus' study and time management skills on par with his peers?

Basic academic skills are the cornerstone of a successful college experience. Yet it is true that rarely are students called upon to really think about these unique skills. You can be helpful in focusing on these traits.

Low scorers shouldn't fear college. They merely need to be have guidance in picking colleges where extra assistance from teachers is readily available and where they can find resources and opportunities to develop their study skills. When choosing classes, they should think carefully about the workload, especially during freshman year. It would help these students to look over the syllabus for each course they sign up for in order to make sure that they understand the specific skills required (how much reading? how much writing? how much does success in class relate to the student's level of participation?).

But there is another way to view lower scores. Such scores may reflect a student who is overly critical of personal skills but fully capable of handling the academic demands of typical freshman courses.

Career orientation allows discussion of the relative importance of these concepts: taking career specific classes; preparing for a specific career; taking a wide range of classes to help decide on a career; taking a wide range of classes in order to be better educated. Does the student view college as a means, in and of itself, of professional or vocational competence? Is it a positive or a negative that a college has many required classes/general education, or core requirements?

The analysis of this category is not always obvious. Being interested in a successful career is a goal for most all students. The IEC sees the distinction between "being prepared to have a successful career" (that goal can be achieved at most colleges) and "preparing directly for my career during my undergraduate days" (that goal means taking specific courses).

There are other nuances here. We know that if students are interested in, say, pre-med, they can major in any subject as long as they complete the courses necessary for admission to medical school (in science and mathematics, primarily). We know that no one major is better than another for admission to law school. On the other hand, there are majors, like engineering, that require direct planning toward that specific degree. The field of business is even more nuanced. Half of those who get jobs in business fields majored in the liberal arts, engineering, or something other than business administration. So the point of discussion with a student is the degree to which taking business classes as an undergraduate will make for a more successful college experience. If students want to take classes in finance, real estate, management, etc., then they should seek a business college or a business major.

One key in working with those who want to major in the performing arts (music, theatre, art, etc.) is to determine how focused the student is. Music majors are equally successful coming out of conservatories as they are coming out of strong music programs in arts and sciences colleges. Of course, there are successful musicians who majored in philosophy.

Remember that a low score in this category is quite common and reflects a student who wants a general, broad-based college education. It does not mean that the student is unmotivated for success in college. A student with a low score is likely open to the wide variety of learning options that college may bring. The low scorer in this category is often fun to work with because he or she is free of the constraints that can come from focusing on a specific career.

Eagerness for college allows discussion of topics such as these: Which aspects of college are you looking forward to the most? Which aspects concern you the most? What adjustments will be necessary for the student to do his or her best in college?

Student enthusiasm, of course, is a great asset in mastering college life.

Low scores can be interpreted in several ways. Eagerness tends to ebb and flow during the high school years. You may have the need to assure your student that some fears about college are perfectly normal. Adjustments are not always easy; neither is change.

RESOURCES TO GET TO KNOW STUDENTS

In Appendix D, you will find the "College Planning Values Assessment," which is designed to help students gain awareness of their desires. Provided in Appendix E, the "Self-Knowledge Questionnaire" is another tool developed to help students recognize their college aptitude which, in turn, grants the IEC knowledge about students' potential for college success. I also direct you to Getting to Know Students at astudentofcolleges.com for lists of materials available to help with the consulting of young people. The resource lists include inventories and instruments intended to help a young person increase his or her college-going self-insight. (The "Self-Survey" from *College Match* is in that category.) You will also see some instruments/websites designed to help with career self-insight. Some IECs routinely use self-insight surveys. Some routinely use career evaluations. At the very least, consultants ought to be familiar with the the many ways information can be both pulled from the student and added to the college planning table in the interest of a thorough and complete consulting process. (Also review Chapter 6 for further discussion of career issues.)

A particular self-insight tool that I like to use is the Developmental Assets framework, published by the Search Institute (search-institute.org). In addition to being a handy instrument for the IEC to get to know a student, the Developmental Assets framework helps the student identify his or her strengths. Going over the "internal assets" with your student can be productive and reassuring. This section includes assets such as school engagement, responsibility, restraint, cultural competence, self-esteem, and so forth. The IEC can use the information gleaned as a conversation starter. There may also be ideas generated that later can be used as essay topics. The Search Institute also has many other useful tools. For example, I sometimes ask students and parents to consider "A Family Relationship Checklist." It encourages reflection about statements such as "We trust each other," "We work together to solve problems and goals," and "We inspire each other to be hopeful for the future."

I believe there is value in our students focusing on their happiness. Attending to happiness has benefits both in terms of overall well-being as well as student attitude about planning for college and being successful once there. I occasionally use questionnaires and other materials to encourage students to think about their happiness.

I like two websites that provide material on happiness. One is "Authentic Happiness" created by Dr. Martin E.P. Seligman (authentichappiness.sas.upenn.edu). Dr. Seligman is a leading researcher in the field of positive psychology. His questionnaires include the following (free by registering on the site): Authentic Happiness Inventory, Optimism Test, and the Grit Survey (a particularly interesting construct for students leaving for college and one developed by Angela Duckworth, author of *Grit*). The other is Dr. Tim Sharp's website: drhappy.com.au. In the resources section of his website, "Dr. Happy" provides several items of interest. I particularly like "The VIA Classification of Character Strengths," which allows students to "tick their strengths" in categories such as kindness, open-mindedness, hope, and humor. The "Guide to Utilizing Your Strengths" asks students to think about strengths such as appreciation of beauty, bravery, and curiosity.

In getting to know our students, we should encourage positivity. Every meeting with the IEC should be a positive one. (Or at least as positive as possible given the topics we are talking to students about!) Part of the planning for an upcoming student meeting is *task*-related. That is, we might need to talk about courses for next year, about colleges to visit during spring break, etc. At the same time as we are thinking about the tasks, we should think about the *experience* we want our student to have during the time we are together. Consider starting the interaction with following up on an interesting, positive tidbit that you learned about the student from a previous time you met. We listen and show that we've heard, we remember, and we are interested.

SPECIAL CATEGORIES OF STUDENTS

Below are several student populations that consultants may serve and should have a general knowledge of. (Note that IECs should have a strong understanding of learning disabilities and that this student population is discussed in length in Chapter 11.)

Athletes

Working with high school athletes presents the consultant with a unique set of variables. Participation in high school athletics is at an all-time high. It has been estimated that over 50% of high school students participate in sports. While landing on a great team at a great university is the goal of many, the truth is that there are more players than there are great schools and great teams. Nonetheless, the search is an important one for many high school students.

Every year, hundreds of thousands of high-school student athletes dream of continuing their sports careers on the collegiate level. For a few (estimated at about 5% of high school graduates), the dream is easily attained. Their superstar status produces the exposure that brings nationally recognized programs calling from across the country, full scholarships in tow. Or they might be financially capable of paying the thousands of dollars that unproven, online recruiting services demand. For the rest, although the opportunities exist, the path to their dream is not so easily achieved. They must wade through a plethora of potential resources, possible scenarios and important decisions, weighing input from parents, coaches and guidance counselors, all while having to maintain their athletic and academic focus.

There are many levels of athletic interest, and the degree to which the IEC needs expertise in guiding athletes varies considerably. There are the heavily recruited high school student athletes, and there are those who are interested in college varsity athletics but equally interested in the academic and social factors. There are also those interested in athletics because it may be a ticket to college without tuition.

There are often many people involved in the transition from high school to college for the athlete. The parent and the high school coach are often central. Parents often have both emotional and financial reasons to see that their daughter/son makes the right choice. The influence of the high school coach varies. Some are "plugged into" their alma mater's athletic network and may, directly or not, guide the student in that direction. Some have a legitimate knowledge base of collegiate coaches; some know only local people. The college coach is clearly another important player. He or she has great influence in the eyes of students. As consultants, we need to be cautious and encourage students to check facts carefully.

Let me switch gears and talk about the consultant's role. While there are consultants who specialize in (or at least are more well versed in) athletic consulting, the comments below are written from the standpoint of the consultant who is *not* an authority.

Families seek me out because I am a student of colleges, and I understand the processes that lead to good decision-making through the college planning months. They do not seek me out for my knowledge of, say, the depth of center fielders at Rice. Indeed, I don't know much (if anything) about what a good golf score might be for Stanford this year or whether Dickinson graduated most of the women's lacrosse team and really needs players. That said, I see my role as understanding how an athlete goes about registering with the National Collegiate Athletic Association (NCAA) and about the general process athletes go through as they present themselves to colleges.

Athletic recruitment and selection are complex and slippery processes. I can't even begin to tell you the times so-and-so coach "promised" Buffy a place on the team and, in the end, no place was offered. Student athletes are only as good as the last prospective player the coach has spoken with. Unfortunately, too many coaches can (sometimes unwittingly) take advantage of the vulnerabilities of young people.

As I explain my services to a prospective client, I point out what I can and can't do in this regard, as broadly outlined above. I hope that students look at lots of factors as they choose a college. If they are strictly focused on the athletic side (and not on a broad range of issues) then they likely will see less value in my involvement.

What about contact with a coach? Does that reduce or eliminate my involvement? If a student has contact with a coach, fine. If the family hired me, they believe that however important athletics is, other factors are also important. Thus, they will tell me about the contact with the coach and we'll go about our business of finding good-fit colleges. I have never, in all these zillion years I've been consulting, ever been in touch with a coach about these matters.

The issue of *influence* insofar as athletes: I use the same approach with athletes that I use with others. To those who say, "I don't have to worry about getting into Penn because my Dad knows someone there," I say something like, "As your advisor, I have to assume, for proper planning, that your odds for Penn are what I think they are if you didn't have this contact." In other words, I go with what I know, not assumptions about what might be. The same for athletes. I tell students my advice is based on what I think most colleges will want to see in such things as seventh semester course selection. Again, that's what I know for sure. If Notre Dame takes you for their football team and is okay with a lighter load, great. But my role, I say, is to give my opinion on course selection for a range of schools. (In other words, I don't have a clue whether this athlete is as good as he says or if he's whistling in the wind but I do know how to advise on course selection.)

I'm clear with my students that I will not know whether they will be desirable to coaches. As suggested above, I work best with the student who wants to view colleges from many angles: admission issues, the fit, the location, the cost, the sports, and so on. If someone is just focused on one variable—sports—I'm not sure I can be of much help. In other words, if the student is sitting at home waiting for emails from coaches and will "jump" at the chance to play at a D1 school just because of the scholarship, I'm not going to bring much to the table by talking about other factors.

The above notwithstanding, putting athletics on the table with other factors in choosing a college can be interesting. Like students with learning or physical disabilities, those with a need for a small college, or whatever, the consultant takes variables and works with them with the goal of finding good college matches.

All college consultants should understand how an athlete goes about registering with NCAA and the general process athletes go through as they present themselves to colleges. Some families do seek college consultants who offer in-depth knowledge of college athletics. For the sports enthusiasts among us, specializing in consulting with student athletes is a viable route toward practice expansion.

For additional information regarding student athletes, please see the National Collegiate Athletic Association at ncaa.org and the National Center of Intercollegiate Athletics at naia.org.

LGBTQ

The lives of America's LGBTQ youth have improved over the past decade. For a wide variety of reasons, there is greater—though by far absolute—acceptance of differences in sexual orientation. But there are still enormous challenges to be met by many LGBTQ teenagers, particularly those growing up in "inhospitable" communities. College may provide LGBTQ teens the opportunity and freedom to become adults in an environment that promotes "choice."

IECs can play a role in helping students in this search, which is why awareness about and sensitivity to the unique constellation of issues that LGBTQ students confront is critical. But getting information about LGBTQ-friendly collegiate environments can sometimes be difficult, and dealing with issues of sexual orientation is foreign territory for some counselors. (Outreach is often advisable and necessary.) Compounding the problem is that while some LGBTQ students are "out," others may not have affirmed their identity or feel unable to discuss their sexual orientation.

Clearly, on one level (transcript, test scores, etc.), the student's sexual orientation is irrelevant to the college admissions process. The twist that IECs need to take into account is that choices need to be fine-tuned with the additional criteria of the character and culture of the schools with regard to gay life and, in addition, the communities/worlds where those schools are located.

Consultants should promote dialogue that addresses factors a lesbian, gay, or bisexual student should consider when exploring potential college options:

- Location: Students may want to select colleges in cities with a large gay/lesbian/bisexual population.
- Extracurricular activities: Delta Lambda Phi is the national gay fraternity. Some chapters are community based—meaning that a student does not have to attend a particular college to join. That is true of chapters in DC, San Francisco, Las Vegas, and Boston (among others). Lambda Delta Lambda is the national lesbian sorority. Fraternities and sororities are not, however, the predominant type of extracurricular involvement for gay students. There are many colleges with gay support groups. Colleges often provide a listing of clubs and organizations in their viewbooks and catalogs.
- General acceptance of a wide diversity of students. Even if the college's support for gay/lesbian/bisexual students is unknown, prospective students should check that a particular college encourages students with a multitude of special interests and perspectives.

- While not always true, colleges with a strong religious basis are more controlled, more traditional, and, thus, less likely to support those with gay/lesbian/bisexual views. On the other hand, colleges run by the Quakers (such as Swarthmore, Earlham, or Haverford) are generally supportive.
- Colleges that are seen as "nontraditional" or "innovative" might provide safe and comfortable environments. There appears to be a relationship between openness in viewing the world of education and looking a new methods of teaching or grading that coincides with a positive view of gay/lesbian/bisexual concerns.

In general, IECs will better serve LGBTQ students by acquiring a knowledge base of resources and affiliations available for this student population. Several are listed below.

- GLSEN, the Gay, Lesbian and Straight Education Network, (glsen.org) works to ensure safe and effective schools for all students and is an excellent resource for both professionals and students. There is a list of over 2,000 chapters in high schools.
- Consortium of Higher Education LGBT Resource Professionals (lgbtcampus.org) is "an organization working towards the liberation of LGBTQ people in higher education." The site includes a listing of LGBTQ centers around the world.

Consultants who are very much in tune to the LGBTQ population may consider marketing themselves as specialists.

Traditionally Underrepresented Populations

The demographic composition of America is changing. The next few generations of college students will not look like the past generation. Most colleges now desire and actively seek a student population that represents the diversity of our country as well as the state in which the college exists. How this plays out, of course, varies greatly from college to college. Colleges differ in their student cultures. Some schools are more open and inviting to African-American students, for example. Some colleges have special programs, unique living spaces, and active multicultural student groups. As such, each consultant has an obligation to be aware of happenings on college campuses especially significant to the African-American or Hispanic student, as well as members of other ethnic/racial groups that have been underrepresented in higher education.

For the white IEC dealing with non-white students, the core work (finding the right match, providing options, sharing how the process works, etc.) may remain unchanged. Many standard counseling strategies and perspectives are in play. Yet, consider for example the special needs of many first-generation college students. Often, these students do not come from homes where college has been discussed or presented as an option, so when these students enter high school, they may not necessarily request courses necessary to be eligible for four-year colleges or universities. The IEC must make sure that students are programmed into college prep courses. First-generation college students may have little knowledge of the college preparation process, and they may lack academic or intellectual confidence in themselves. Thus, the IEC may need to designate extra time to best serve these students.

Unfortunately, there is quite a gap between the needs of non-white students in college planning and the professional, knowledgeable advice available. Awareness of and sensitivity to cultural differences is essential to providing underserved students top-notch college consulting. Understand that many first-generation and underserved students do not have experience in the Western, Eurocentric culture of "sink or swim." Intimidated by the mystique of "going to college," some students give up the entire process when they encounter the first problem that needs solving or after they have made their first planning/process mistake. While I do not advocate handholding, I think our responsibility as counselors is to teach problem-solving and self-reliance so that first-generation and underserved students are better prepared to care for themselves once they get to college. Cultures vary, values vary, and students vary. The more we know about multiple cultures, the more apt we are to help such students and families who seek our guidance. (See resources at astudentofcolleges.com for references in this area.)

Multicultural Students

From the above, let's expand to address multicultural students and the sensitivity that IECs should embrace. Knowing the values of a group of people is important in college planning. Let me provide a specific example. Research often reflects the importance of family in Latino/a cultures. Family might include grandparents, aunts and uncles, cousins, and even close friends. It is common for Latino/a youth to feel a strong sense of obligation in meeting family expectations. A Latino/a student may be reluctant to consider colleges far from home because of strong familial bonds. Welcoming input from extended family is one way that IECs demonstrate cultural awareness. We strive to understand what drives students, and we appreciate cultural values and traditions. As another example, within some Asian cultures, there is a tradition of a strong family hierarchy in which parental authority is revered and personal choice is a lesser consideration. The culturally sensitive IEC is aware of such perspectives and provides appropriate guidance that is respectful to students' upbringing.

Sometimes we will work with students or parents who hold beliefs that contradict our own. In non-professional settings, we may respond to a differing worldview by defending our views or by distancing ourselves from those who do not share our mindsets. Those approaches don't work well for IECs. What this means is not that we need to change our own core values; rather, it means that our core values are not part of the conversation. Our role is to help students meet their needs, and we can do that even if we disagree with some of our students' priorities. To work constructively with diverse clients, IECs should recognize any previously held ideas that they have established about a population based on ethnicity, nationality, race, etc. Culturally skilled counselors acknowledge preconceived notions and do not let biases interfere with their mission to serve others.

A point well worth emphasizing here is that in our work with multicultural students, we should be sensitive and cautious about generalizations and stereotypes. For example, a common stereotype is that Asians are high achievers. Even if the generalization is true on some level, it does not take into account other aspects of a student's personality or attitudes and doesn't allow for the huge variations between specific Asian cultures. We need to acknowledge that each student is a unique individual with a multitude of facets, dispositions, and ideals.

We do not need to have infinite knowledge of all cultures and all peoples. Rather, our goal should be awareness and willingness to learn. For IECs who wish to seek training in multicultural awareness and sensitivity, the American Counseling Association (counseling.org) has published a series of articles on developing multicultural competencies in several areas.

Community College Students

National norms are changing. The trend is increasing for a wider range of students to enter community college directly out of high school. Many students and families feel that a year or two in community college not only saves money but also provides an excellent transition into the world of higher education. As such, the educational consultant has an opportunity to learn more about how two-year schools have changed over the last decade or so. This, from a front-page article in *New York Times* a few years ago, "Long derided as repositories for underachievers, as trade schools devoid of academic rigor, community colleges are recasting themselves as wise first choices for the serious student looking to sidestep crushing debt."

The author, Greg Winter, goes on to say, "More than 168 community colleges now have honors programs intended to catapult their students into the nation's best four-year universities." These students need help, and we can assist them.

Transfer Students

Many students transfer from one college to another. There are consultants who specialize in these students. Many of the same approaches apply to transfer students. The consultant gets to know a student, discusses what he or she is looking for in a college, and presents options. Transferring has its own set of consultant principles, and these principles contribute to deciding whether you can help. Sometimes, a call to transfer is a call for perfection. Sometimes a call to transfer is a call to "find a major," and we each determine whether that is something we can or want to do. Sometimes it is a call for increased prestige. Or, it may be a community college student wanting to move on, or a person whose needs in a college have changed since high school. The consultant determines how he or she wants to operate with these students and has a contract that is explicit about results.

Older Students/Nontraditional Students

There is an increasing need for educational consultants to assist older students in going back to school. Consultants must recognize that more and more students beyond the traditional college age are electing to start (or return to) college. Reasons for this decision range from career change or advancement, divorce, kids, new priorities that come with age, or just a desire to get a college education. Consultants should be aware that it is easy for a student to feel "marginalized" if the college does not have many older (sometimes called "nontraditional") students.

FINAL THOUGHTS

We're students of colleges, but we are also students of students. Indeed, the only way to be a successful student of colleges is to know your students well. Our knowledge of colleges needs a target: it needs a fix on the student for whom we are seeking appropriate college options. This chapter, through discussion of demographics, Generation Z, teen development, and special categories of students, is meant to help with that fix. It has provided ways of thinking about Buffy, a person with unique values, attitudes, and beliefs; a person with unique ways to learn and to interact with others; and a person with unique drives and motivations. Only by knowing Buffy well will our college recommendations maximize the chance that she will be successful and happy in college.

CHAPTER 11

Learning Disabilities Consulting

LEARNING DISABILITIES: WHAT IECs NEED TO KNOW

It's been estimated that 25% of students who work IECs have a learning disability. As such, it is imperative that college consultants are well-versed in learning disabilities. Certainly, there are IECs who specialize in serving the needs of students with learning disabilities; however, as a sizable percentage of our clients fall into the LD population, I strongly believe that all IECs have an obligation to familiarize themselves with learning disabilities, associated disorders, and legislation that affects the LD student body.

First, let's solidify some basics. A learning difference or disability disrupts the learning of people with average or high intelligence due to an irregular profile of cognitive abilities. They may excel in some areas of academia and do poorly in others. In fact, achievement in some areas may fall well below what might be expected for people of their intelligence. Learning disabilities may be accompanied by other challenges, often arising as a result of the learning disability, or as a separate psychological problem. It is not uncommon for children and adults with learning disabilities to have trouble with memory-related tasks or to suffer from attention deficit disorders, anxiety, depression, and other socio-emotional disturbances. Acting out, reclusive, or aggressive behavior can be associated with a learning disability or with the frustration that accompanies learning and social difficulties.

Learning disabilities may be at the heart of or central to sub-par academic performance. On the other hand, learning disabilities can meld into other issues. Or the source of poor performance might be unrelated to learning disabilities. Thus, it is important for the consultant to explore these issues and interrelationships with care and thoroughness.

Learning disabilities are not the same as physical disabilities, sensory disabilities, or psychological disabilities. Pervasive developmental disorder (of which autism is a form) or developmental disability are other categories of maladaptation and not classified as part of learning disability programs in college. (Included in this chapter, however, is a discussion of Asperger's Syndrome.)

The following is a description of common learning disabilities and associated disorders that may impact academic, social, and emotional success. IECs should be familiar with the nature of specific learning disabilities and related challenges. Note that the discussion below is not comprehensive; rather, it is intended to give an overview.

As a prefatory note, it's important to distinguish language-based learning disabilities (LBLD) from nonverbal learning disabilities (NLD). Simply put, LBLD affect one's understanding and use of oral and written language. The degree to which LBLD can present challenges and the particular manifestation(s) of LBLD differ widely. NLD, conversely, do not impair spoken and written language but present other learning challenges.

Dyslexia

Dyslexia is a specific language-based learning disability (LBLD) characterized by challenges with reading accuracy and/or fluency, decoding, and spelling. Neurological in origin, dyslexia results from a deficit in the phonological component of language. Other cognitive abilities are not impaired. Dyslexia may hinder reading comprehension, vocabulary, and background knowledge. Dyslexics usually have difficulty learning the sounds of graphemes, blending sounds into a word, or segmenting words into their separate sounds.

Students with dyslexia may particularly struggle in college with the following demands:
- Volume and complexity of reading
- Complexity of essay assignments
- Note taking and comprehension of lecture material
- Research expectations (gathering, organizing, analyzing, synthesizing)
- Mandatory deadlines/multiple simultaneous due dates

It's best not to assume that parents and students are fully aware of the challenge of the college demands noted above. Let students voice what they know of expectations. Right any misconceptions. Note that the purpose here is not to dash dreams but to realistically ready students for college academics. All students need to know what colleges expect and how the academic rigor may be significantly more intense than what they encountered in high school. IECs should encourage dyslexic students to take advantage of services and accommodations offered at college. In particular, books on tape, text-to-speech software, readers, scribes, notetakers, extended time for tests, and study skills courses may make a world of difference for dyslexic students.

Dysgraphia

Dysgraphia is a specific LBLD that impairs handwriting and fine motor skills. Dysgraphia often manifests in illegible handwriting, inconsistent and/or awkward spacing between words and/or mechanics, poor spatial planning, poor spelling, and difficulty composing written work. Those with dysgraphia often have difficulty thinking and writing simultaneously. Dysgraphia affects a student's ability to take notes and follow the course of lectures. Extended time on written exams and use of a computer are typical accommodations. Some colleges (and standardized test administrators) can supply test forms that require an X rather than a bubble.

Dyscalculia

Dyscalculia is another LBLD that impacts one's ability to understand numbers and math. Students with dyscalculia often have difficulty sequencing, understanding and solving word problems, recognizing mathematical patterns, and applying mathematical operations. Dyscalculia is relatively rare compared to dyslexia. Some colleges allow substitutions (not waivers) for math graduation requirements, depending, of course, on major. Students may need to petition to receive a course substitution.

Nonverbal Learning Disabilities

Nonverbal learning disability (NLD) is a disorder often characterized by a significant discrepancy between higher verbal skills and weaker motor, visual-spatial, and social skills. It is often referred to as a "right hemisphere learning disability." Visual-motor and visual-spatial impairments are relatively rare and not well understood. Learners may have difficulties in spatial awareness, recognition and organization or visual patterns, and coordinating visual information with motor processes. Learners with NLD are usually good readers and are adept at verbal expression and verbal reasoning. The auditory (as opposed to verbal) and visual aspects of communication are difficult for these learners to process. They may have difficulty following instructions that have multiple steps and find transitioning challenging. They often miss subtle social cues such as changes in tone during spoken communication and changes in body language. These learners often have difficulty with the "turn taking" aspects of communication and with shifts in topic or subject matter. They are often perceived as rude or socially inept. Some learners with NLD benefit from specific instruction in social pragmatics.

ADHD

ADHD is a disorder characterized by inattention/distractibility, hyperactivity, and impulsivity. Note that not all of the above characteristics present in individuals. Diagnosis requires clear evidence that the symptoms which do present interfere with or reduce the quality of academic, social, or occupational functioning. It's important to be aware that ADHD may hinder one's ability to regulate emotions such as frustration and anger; thus, ADHD may impact students socially. ADHD is not considered a learning disability; however, students diagnosed with ADHD are eligible to receive special education services under the Individuals with Disabilities Education Act (IDEA). Affecting approximately 11 percent of children aged four to 17, ADHD is a common developmental disorder and often coexists with specific learning disabilities, particularly dyslexia (an estimated 30 percent of dyslexics have coexisting ADHD). Comorbidity intensifies learning challenges. ADHD is a chronic disorder; approximately 75 percent of children diagnosed with ADHD continue to have symptoms into adulthood.

ADHD is often treated with stimulant medication. If a family has disclosed that the student takes medication to control ADHD, the IEC should affirm that the student plans to continue such medication at college and advise the family to plan in advance how the student will access prescription medication. The student may need to see a physician on campus or fill prescriptions off campus, both of which require pre-planning to ensure that no lapse occurs. Students should be cautioned not to suddenly discontinue medication as doing so may result in physical and psychological distress, not to mention the potential academic challenge of being unable to regulate focus and behavior.

Students with ADHD benefit from keen self-awareness of how the disorder impacts them academically, socially, and emotionally. They should understand their capacity to manage stress and change and should build a toolbox of coping mechanisms, including determination and perseverance.

Executive Function

Executive function refers to cognitive management systems. Deficits impact organization, planning, strategizing, and processing. Executive function deficits also affect cognitive flexibility and regulation of emotions. Additionally, low executive function impairs one's ability to pay attention to and retrieve details and to manage time and productivity. Executive function deficit is not a learning disability, but it often presents in the learning profiles of those diagnosed with specific learning disabilities or ADHD. Executive function deficits can adversely affect a student's ability to stay on top of assignments (especially long-term assignments), prioritize, organize course and study material, study and prepare efficiently and effectively, recognize what constitutes essential course knowledge, and activate and retrieve information from memory.

The area of the brain that governs executive function, the prefrontal cortex, is the last area of the human brain to develop, sometimes taking until over the age of 25. (Note that boys' brains typically develop later than girls' brains.) Students with executive function deficits will benefit from strategic organizational, time management, and study coaching. Tips on how the IEC can make the college planning process easier for students with executive function challenges are noted later in this chapter.

Asperger's Syndrome

While Asperger's Syndrome (AS) is not viewed as a learning disability, some symptoms are related. In fact, some of the accommodations helpful to the AS student are similar to those available to students with learning disabilities. As such, it is discussed here.

Asperger's is an autism spectrum disorder (ASD). Thus, it is "on the spectrum," which typically refers to a specific set of behavioral and developmental problems and a group of complex disorders of brain development. A diagnosis of ASD means that a student's communication, social, and interactive skills are affected in some way. Where one falls on this spectrum differs according to behavioral patterns. Even though wildly exaggerated and stereotyped, Sheldon Cooper of *The Big Bang Theory* is clearly somewhere on the spectrum!

Classic autism, or autistic disorder, is the most severe of the autism spectrum disorders. On the other side of the spectrum is Asperger's. AS is considered the mildest of the autism spectrum disorders. It is a high-functioning form of ASD. AS students are smart, some might be intellectually gifted, and most possess high cognitive ability.

Like most labels in behavioral and health sciences, there are a variety of symptoms and clues that may be present in a student with Asperger's. AS students often have issues centered around the process of human communication. They may have trouble interacting productively with others and may fail to pick up the intent behind another person's actions, words, or behaviors. They may struggle with the meaning of humor, sarcasm, or puns. They may be literal with words. Speech patterns may include lack of inflection, a rhythmic nature, excessive formality, loudness, or high-pitch. Additionally, AS students may struggle to express themselves, keep up with conversations, and speak with the right volume and emphasis. They may have trouble making eye contact and/or starting conversations. Keeping emotions in check may be difficult for AS students and can impact their ability to function productively in a team.

It is not uncommon for these students to have an obsessive interest in certain topics. They may engage in repetitive behaviors, routines, and movements. They may lack organization and problem solving ability. They may become disoriented with changes to daily living.

Support for those with Asperger's is available on most college campuses. A few schools have specific programs for students on the spectrum. AS students often benefit from college disability services. Help might include staff and/or tools to assist students with issues such as executive functioning, social competence, academic skills, self-care, self-advocacy and career preparation. There are often services available through the health center, counseling center, and/or learning disability center that can help.

LEARNING STYLES

Learning style refers to a sensory modality (or combination of modalities) that one identifies as being his or her preferred pathway to intake, process, comprehend, and retain knowledge. The main sensory pathways include visual, auditory, and kinesthetic/tactile. A student may identify himself or herself as a particular "kind" of learner (i.e. Brutus proclaims he is a kinesthetic/tactile learner who prefers hands-on activities and experiential learning over reading or lecture). Brutus may have attended a small school where instructors differentiate their teaching approach to accommodate individual learning styles. Neurological studies show that dyslexics best acquire and retain language skills through a multi-sensory approach that activates several sensory pathways simultaneously: visual, auditory, kinesthetic/tactile (VAKT). The IEC should encourage dyslexic students to request and review syllabi prior to enrolling in courses and to choose (whenever possible) courses that are presented using a multi-sensory approach. If, however, only straight lecture style courses are offered, the student should supplement his or her learning with multi-sensory study techniques that incorporate VAKT. Ultimately, most professors are not obliged to accommodate learning styles, and students—dyslexic or not—will be expected to grasp the material however presented. Thus, it is best to be sure that students and parents are aware of this reality and that students consider the nature of the learning environment prior to enrollment.

THE CONSULTANT'S ROLE IN IDENTIFYING POTENTIAL LEARNING DISABILITIES

IECs should also be familiar with signs of a potential learning disability. Should an IEC suspect that a student may have an undiagnosed learning disability that is hindering academic achievement, the IEC should encourage parents to seek a professional evaluation from a licensed diagnostician. The following are signals that may point to a learning disability or related disorder.

- Problems adjusting to new settings
- Poor memory skills
- Problems with open-ended questions on tests
- Avoids reading and writing assignments
- Difficulty processing information
- Difficulty with receptive and/or expressive language
- Difficulty summarizing
- Spelling problems
- Poor reading accuracy/fluency
- Poor grasp of abstract concepts
- Illegible or poor handwriting (print or cursive)
- Pays too little or too much attention to details
- Works slowly or rushes through work

POSTSECONDARY EDUCATION LAW: INFORMING PARENTS AND STUDENTS

If a family discloses to an IEC that the student has a documented learning disability and has received services, accommodations, and/or modifications under an Individualized Education Program (IEP) or a 504 Plan, it is important that the IEC makes sure that parents and the student are aware that neither the IDEA of 2004 nor the Americans with Disabilities Act (ADA) apply to postsecondary education. As such, the IEC should make clear the following realities of higher education law so that families can make informed decisions about college enrollment.

- Colleges and universities are not legally bound to accommodate students' IEPs. IDEA does not cover colleges; essentially, IEPs expire upon high school graduation.
- Postsecondary schools are also not obliged to provide services in accordance with students' high school 504 Plans. High schools fall under ADA Section 504 Subpart D; however, colleges fall under ADA Subpart E, meaning that 504 Plans expire as well.
- Colleges may consider a student application as deficient for admission if the student's transcript reveals curriculum modifications (particularly a foreign language waiver). This potential conundrum is one that the IEC should address with families during the college planning process. (Note that special education coordinators discuss the benefits and drawbacks of modifications with parents and students). Modifications change *what* a student learns, meaning that material that is required learning in the general curriculum is altered or waived to fit a student's learning profile. To be granted modifications, a student must be on an IEP or a 504 Plan. The IEC should understand that modifications are not the same as accommodations. Accommodations relate to *how* a student learns, not *what* a student learns.
- Colleges do not offer curriculum modifications. Some colleges allow course *substitutions* (as prior noted), but colleges do not *waive* graduation requirements.
- LD students are not guaranteed the *same* accommodations in college that they received in high school.

The points noted above should be addressed prior to building the college list. The IEC should encourage any student who has received services, accommodations, and/or modifications in high school to share and discuss the nature of his or her disability and the level of compensation skills acquired in high school so that the IEC can help determine the college environment that will best fit the needs of the student. That is to say, if Brutus received a high level of support during high school, he may need to develop independent learning skills or find a college program that offers the requisite support.

POSTSECONDARY EDUCATION AND LD STATISTICS

- Nearly 100% of high school students with LD receive accommodations or support; less than 20% of students with LD do so in college.
- Students with LBLD enroll in four-year colleges at the same rate as the general student population.
- The rate of LBLD students who attend two-year or community colleges is double that of the general student population.
- The percentage of LBLD students who attend vocational schools is higher than that of the general student population.
- The percentage of LBLD students who complete college is lower than that of the general student population.

LD AND ADMISSION

Below are a few helpful bits of information regarding LD students and college admission.
- Section 504 of the Rehabilitation Act of 1973 declares denying admission solely based on disability illegal.

- Prior to admission, colleges and universities cannot make inquiries regarding disability.
- Students do not have to identify as LD on college admission applications to register for services once they enroll.
- Standardized test scores are not flagged; there are no indicators from College Board or ACT that a student was awarded accommodations during testing.

THOUGHTS REGARDING DISCLOSURE OF LD

Students' feelings about their disability are as varied as the types or extent of disabilities themselves. Some students readily discuss their issues and they know that, if they do, their success in school increases, sometimes dramatically. Other students do not want the LD "label." Students can face skepticism as to whether they are using special classroom accommodations as a crutch—or worse—to gain admission to a selective college. Unlike other disabilities that are more "obvious" such as blindness or a physical handicap, those that involve learning are typically "invisible." According to experts in this area, there is an extra burden of proof associated with those with LD.

I believe that students should report their disabilities when they apply to college. After all, at its core, college searching is about finding a great match. It's about student success in college. The more information the college has about applicants (and the more information applicants have about the college), the higher the likelihood of a successful academic and social experience.

Colleges want to help students. The only way that they can do that is through the student sharing information. Student disclosure also shows self-advocacy, motivation, and an understanding of the disability. Moreover, disclosing a learning disability when applying for admission might give colleges a better understanding of what high school grades or test scores mean in the context of the student's learning profile. For example, modifications made at the high school level (such as sign language in lieu of a foreign language) will be clear to those reviewing the application. Such modifications will not be viewed as deficiencies. Furthermore, there are even colleges that give scholarships for students with learning disabilities.

Many students and parents look at a learning disability as a barrier in getting a higher education. While it can be tough to talk about disabilities and their effect on students, we must understand that being clear and open about disabilities offers students the chance to succeed.

LD AND BEST FIT

From a consulting standpoint, many issues are involved, and consulting strategies vary with each student on the basis of the disability, recognition of the disability, college aspirations, and parental feelings. Whatever approaches the consultant uses, students are always more than a diagnosis, no matter how significant or viable that diagnosis might be. In other words, regardless of the LD needs, the student still needs to fit in, and so the general tone of campus life is as important here (perhaps more important) as it is with any student. Similarly, location, size, etc. continue to be valid variables. LD issues, as important as they may be, still need to be seen in the context of an entire continuum of factors that will be involved in being successful in college.

Often, the best procedure to follow for all students with disabilities and/or disorders is to put the person first and disability/disorder second. This means that we must recognize kids with special needs have the same interests, desires, opportunities, et cetera as their non-disabled peers. College X may be the "best college" for students who are blind—but does that mean it is the best for your student? College Y may be the "best college" for kids who have mobility disabilities, but, again, does that mean it is the best for every kid with that type of disability? Gallaudet may be the "best" for students who are deaf, and Landmark may be the "best" for students with learning disabilities—but "best" for every kid with those disabilities?

This area is not without a certain hype of its own. Glossy brochures for learning resource centers abound. LD is a specialized area, and the consultant needs to understand not only what is needed for the student, but also how colleges differ in their delivery of services. Sometimes we ought to look for a school that has a specific LD or ADHD program.

Sometimes our hunt is for an undergraduate environment that is right—where teaching is appropriate, availability of resources is high, and where the level of general support is high (even if the college is not listed somewhere as having a "good LD program").

It is typically best to select colleges with the usual criteria in mind: size, location, major, cost, SAT/ACT/GPA profile, etc. Students should be advised to contact the appropriate learning center on each campus. Students should meet with or have a conversation with the disability coordinator to discuss their specific needs and concerns to see if the college provides the services or accommodations they require. Students should meet with or speak directly with the coordinator in an attempt to determine the attitude of the coordinator and the prevailing attitude on campus toward students with special needs. Some larger universities assign different disability specialists according to the disability. One person on the disability staff may work with students who are blind and another with students who are deaf or hard of hearing. This may be something to look for when exploring larger institutions. Students must learn to be their own advocate, to ask questions, and to get the answers they need.

ACCOMMODATIONS AND SUPPORT SERVICES

There is a wide spectrum of learning disabilities support at the college level. Colleges and universities are doing more than ever to accommodate students with learning style differences. Separate college planning guidebooks (such as the *K&W Guide*) are devoted to the variety and scope of these accommodations. Websites by IEC colleagues Jill Burstein (College Supports for Learning Disabilities: collegesupports.com) and Judy Bass (College Web LD: collegewebld.com) are excellent LD resources available for a fee.

Under law, colleges must provide certain services to accommodate students with a documented disability that limits their learning. This is done to "level the playing field" with non-learning disabled students.

Colleges are resource rich. They are able to help dyslexic students process text more easily or provide stress management tools. Colleges can make recording or other devices available for students with specific learning disabilities. Students with auditory or visual processing issues might be aided by a disability services office or by resident directors trained to support such students. To receive resources, students must register with disability services.

Below are three tiers of accommodations and services available to students with documented learning disabilities.

Basic Accommodations
Available at most all college (other than those that reject federal funds and are private and religious), basic accommodations generally include extended time for tests, a reduced-distraction site for tests, use of a

calculator or spellcheck device during exams (unless the exams measure calculations or spelling), priority classroom seating, permission to record lectures (with professors' approval), books on tape, and the use of a notetaker. Notetakers may not be readily available at all schools, so students should check in advance to find out if notetakers are paid workers or if they are student volunteers. Basic accommodations are free of charge.

Moderate Services

Enhanced services often include workshops on executive function skills, writing and math labs, access to an academic coach or learning specialist, and access to assistive technology. Such services are generally free of charge. Tutoring services may be available, often at an extra charge.

Comprehensive

Comprehensive programs often require separate admission procedures and additional fees, which may be substantial. Such programs generally include mandatory meetings, support strategy coaching, one-on-one or small group tutoring and workshops, and regular academic monitoring. Workshops may include metacognitive strategies, test-taking strategies, writing skills, and time management. Specialists often advocate for students, and coordinators assist students with securing accommodations. Comprehensive programs generally offer resource rooms with assistive technology. Students who received substantial support at the secondary level may benefit from having the structure of a comprehensive program to ease the transition from high school to college. Often, comprehensive programs decrease support as the students advance to upperclassmen.

Note that there are two dedicated LD colleges in the US: Landmark College in Putney, Vermont and Beacon College in Leesburg, Florida.

SAT/ACT TESTING: CRITERIA AND ACCOMMODATIONS

- College Board (administrators of PSAT, SAT, SAT Subject Tests, and AP exams) and ACT require a current (SAT: within five years; ACT: within three years), official evaluation that documents disability. The diagnosis must be clearly stated, and the diagnostician must have proper credentials. Documentation must present educational, developmental, and medical history, supporting the diagnosis. The functional limitation of the disability must be described, and the recommendations for accommodations must be justified. Generally, the student's school submits accommodation requests to College Board and ACT.
- Students who were diagnosed in high school may face more scrutiny than those diagnosed in middle or elementary school because testing agencies worry that students may apply for special accommodations that they do not truly need.
- Generally, to be granted special testing accommodations, students must provide documentation that they use their requested accommodations at school on a regular basis.
- Testing agencies are prohibited from notifying admissions offices of students' disability testing accommodations.
- Submit documentation early (recommendation of two to three months) to College Board and/or ACT because testing agencies may ask for additional documentation and may initially reject a request.
- Typical accommodations include extended test time (50% or 100%), breaks, private or semi-private testing rooms, four-function calculators, and use of computers. Some students may be eligible for readers.
- Please be aware that College Board and ACT often change their criteria for LD accommodations. Be sure to stay on top of any such changes so as to keep students accurately informed.

APPLYING FOR COLLEGE ACCOMMODATIONS

It is essential that students present a strong case to document their learning disabilities.
- Documentation must be provided by a licensed diagnostician with appropriate training and experience.
- Provide current (generally within three years) psycho-educational and neuropsychological (if claiming ADHD as a barrier to learning) testing.
- Provide a clear diagnostic statement that includes the diagnostic procedure, the functional impact of the disability, and a description of the prognosis. Any anticipated or cyclical changes in the functional impact of the disability should be noted.
- Check with each individual college to determine the acceptable version of psycho-educational testing. Many colleges require the Wechsler Adult Intelligence Scale, Fourth Edition (WAIS-IV) rather than the Wechsler Intelligence Scale for Children, Fourth Edition (WISC-IV). The WAIS-IV can be administered at age 16.
- Provide a comprehensive evaluation of aptitude, achievement, and information processing.
- Achievement must measure reading, mathematics, and written language in both timed and untimed conditions.
- Terminology matters. "Learning differences," "learning difficulties," and "learning styles" are not protected by law; they do not meet the criteria for a diagnosis of a "learning disability." Proper terminology and diagnosis are required to be eligible for accommodations.
- The evaluation should address all previous support systems, services, accommodations, assistive technologies, and auxiliary aids the student has received and the efficacy of all. The evaluation should contain college level recommendations regarding continuation of support along with rationale. Students should request any and all accommodations previously used, regardless of the likelihood of using all.

REGISTERING FOR LD SERVICES

College students must register with the school's office of disability services to receive accommodations. The IEC should encourage students to be proactive and register for services (with admission materials or during freshman orientation) before a potential crisis occurs. Disability services will provide the student with a letter of accommodation (LOA) detailing the accommodations granted by the college. Students must then self-identify with faculty and provide a copy of the LOA. This step should be completed at the start of each term to provide faculty timely notice. Students need not disclose the nature of their disability but must assume responsibility to update faculty of any changes in the LOA. The IEC should inform families that colleges are not required to expunge any poor grades from students' official transcripts; therefore, students should register for accommodations early and make use of them regularly. I can't stress enough the importance of Buffy starting her collegiate experience on solid academic footing with all the support that she needs to achieve to her potential.

TIPS FOR THE IEC: EXECUTIVE FUNCTION

As noted above, students with LD often have difficulty with executive functioning. To help students stay organized, consider the following strategies:
- Start required testing and the college search early.
- Create spreadsheets or file folders with information about each prospective school.
- Use graphic organizers when brainstorming factors important in a college.
- Create to-do lists and check sheets to note all tasks and deadlines.

- Use organizational calendars to note appointments and deadlines. Have students input alerts into their mobile devices.
- Create specific questions for students to ask during college visits. Record answers on spreadsheets or files.

PREPARING FOR COLLEGE: ESSENTIAL SKILLS TO DEVELOP

While most IECs are not learning specialists, they can and should discuss with LD students and families the skills that students should develop in order to be successful in college. Critical to Buffy's success is her ease in discussing her disability and learning profile. Buffy should be able to well articulate her learning needs. If a student is on an IEP, the student's transition coordinator is responsible for developing this skill. Regardless, the IEC can engage the student in such a discussion, coach the student to further elaborate, and practice a dialogue. It can prove quite helpful for the IEC to assume the role of a college official or a professor and to guide Buffy to communicate her needs effectively and confidently.

Many IECs work directly with students to help them develop a number of skills. The IEC can supply handouts and/or refer students to resources. Moreover, in our meetings with students, we can explicitly or implicitly target and teach many of the skills noted. For example, IECs can direct students to set specific and realistic goals to plot timelines for composing college essays or researching colleges. As we help students build essential college and life skills, we should point out students' growth and provide positive reinforcement when they demonstrate competency. Make direct connections as to how the skills Buffy and Brutus are solidifying will benefit them in college: "The strategies that you used to manage your time and knock out the priorities on your task list last week worked well! Using the same organizational system of breaking big assignments into manageable chunks and color-coding priority tasks will help you stay on top of long-term projects and papers." Below are skills that the IEC should discuss with LD students and families:

- Self-advocacy
- Self-determination
- Self-discipline
- Executive function
- Test-taking strategies
- Time management
- Organization
- Stress management
- Goal-setting
- Proactivity

FEDERAL EDUCATION RIGHTS TO PRIVACY ACT (FERPA)

FERPA prevents college faculty and staff from discussing a student's educational information with anyone other than the student. Students at the college level are considered adults and are expected to self-advocate. IECs should encourage students to self-advocate. Students who have had a significant degree of support at the secondary level may need concerted effort to develop self-advocating skills. IEP transition coordinators help in this respect. IECs may need to counsel parents who are concerned about not having access to discuss their student's information with college professionals. There is an option for students to sign a FERPA waiver, allowing college faculty and staff to engage in conversation with parents. Ultimately, the family must make this decision, but IECs may wish to point out that the option exists.

QUESTIONS TO ASK WHEN EVALUATING POTENTIAL COLLEGES FOR STUDENT'S WITH LEARNING DISABILITIES

- How long does it generally take LD students to complete required courses and to graduate?
- Are LD students allowed to take a lighter load and still be considered full-time students?
- What is the retention rate of LD students?
- What percentage of the student population uses LD services?
- What is the ratio of LD students to learning specialists on campus?

- What are the qualifications of individuals offering LD support?
- Who counsels LD students?
- Is tutoring available in all subjects?
- Are tutors specifically trained to understand and provide for the needs of LD students?
- What specific services does the LD program offer?
- Does the college offer courses in study or writing skills?
- What services are fee-based, and what is the cost?
- What assistive technologies are available to LD students and at what cost?
- How well does faculty accept and work with LD students?
- Are there peer support groups on campus?

FINAL THOUGHTS

Due to its prevalence, IECs have an obligation to stay ahead of the curve in terms of knowledge about learning disabilities. I encourage all consultants, even those who are not LD specialists, to be familiar with the terminology, diagnoses, procedures, and various levels of LD support available.

While some students need very specialized programs to be successful, many students with learning differences can and are successful at a wide range of colleges. Recognize your limitations and refer to specialists as appropriate.

IECs have led the way in terms of books, websites, and other resources for students with learning disabilities. Over the past decade, the number of IECs whose practice is specialized in the LD area has grown geometrically. IECA has a specific designation for those trained in the LD area.

Finally, while there are some, it is a rare student whose sole college planning variable is the level of LD support. Students with learning differences need also to consider many factors in making their choice of suitable colleges: size, location, student culture, and so on. The more all of the factors are juggled, the better the ultimate choice.

(See astudentofcolleges.com for additional resources on learning disabilities.)

CHAPTER 12

Parents as Partners
(Buffy and Brutus, Sr.)

MEET THE PARENTS

A good rapport with the parents of your students is a high priority for independent college counselors. This is not only because they are paying your bill. For one thing, parents have information you need. For another, they have a great emotional and financial investment in the process. Parents are primary decision makers; they want what is best for their children. Remember, they may have picked the school district or decided to send their child to boarding school to have better college choices. A knowledgeable consultant sees parents as helpers. I include parents in more meetings than I did five years ago. Parents can offer insight into their child's character, including their firsthand perspective regarding the child's commitment to college planning and potential to succeed in college. The consultant sees moms and dads as people who can help focus the college search, help define their child's successes and struggles, and make it easier for the consultant to be on target in selecting a list of appropriate colleges.

Like their kids, parents vary in their college planning priorities. Some parents, perhaps those who have not gone to college or who were raised in a country outside of the U.S., may not understand the system, the process, or colleges. Other parents are high achievers themselves and worry that their daughter/son may not, because of increased selectivity, be admissible to colleges they dreamed for their kids. Consultants must understand the factors that are important to parents in choosing a college and what their college-going values and priorities are.

Remember, every family that walks through your door has a different set of agendas, hopes and, in many cases, misperceptions. Unlike kids, parents bring a lifetime of experiences to your office. They bring their own experience in college, perceptions of which colleges will "pave the way to success in life," and also stereotypes and biases. Parents can be as easily influenced by their peers as their student might be. (There is a lot of "clone behavior" on the part of parents. If Julia's daughter went to Grinnell, we should look there, too.) They also bring fears, anxieties, and love to the process. Some parents exchange "theories" about which there is no evidence to support. For example, "Northwestern loves essays about divorce," or "The only way to get into Brown is through Early Decision," or "Princeton is looking for kids from here this year." The wise consultant understands the contradictory messages that parents may be receiving from friends and associates and works to plan a college consulting "curriculum" for parents at the same time that he or she is working with their child.

Your consulting "curriculum" for parents includes helping them learn about college admission in the 21st century, how colleges and the process have changed, and how you can help them find four wonderful years for their child. Remember, hostile parents might just be uninformed. Many parents don't know how difficult it is to get into brand name colleges (or even state schools). And they don't know how egalitarian the process has become. In the 50's and 60's, if you went to the right school (public or private) and/or had the right pedigree, so to speak, you had a decent chance of getting into a competitive college. For oodles of reasons, those days are history. We bring value to the table for parents. As later discussed in Chapter 13, IECs give parents clarity in an admission world that is often cloudy.

I welcome and involve parents in the consulting process, but I harness parents' energy. I give them specific "assignments." For example, I ask parents to check on certain college facts. Parents can research a particular college on a student's apply list, scope out the ease of changing majors, determine the level of the college in terms of athletic competition, find specific admissions procedures for learning disabled students, gather information on internship possibilities in political science, or whatever applies to their student. I also get parents on board with application deadlines. It's a win-win scenario when parents help keep students on track.

Moreover, as consultants, we can help show how important it is for students and parents to work together through the college planning months. I like to tell parents how students can be helpful: Students can tell you their thoughts about potential colleges and leaving home. I like to tell students how parents can be helpful: Parents are a good source of information on developing your activity list, brainstorming essay ideas, typing or proofing your applications, and explaining their level of concern about financial aid matters. I also emphasize that students and parents should discuss the college list together and that both parties should have an understanding of the composition of the colleges on the apply list.

Note that most IECs meet more often with parents early in the process particularly to discuss qualities important in finding a college (including the important cost considerations) and to discuss specific characteristics of individual colleges. Later on, when working on applications and essays, the consultant may meet only with the student.

PARENTAL INPUT

From the get-go, it is wise for the consultant to acknowledge the importance of the parents' priorities and concerns regarding the college planning process and to tap into the parents' perspectives regarding their child's degree of readiness for college. To help garner such information, I ask parents to respond to an intake questionnaire. Below are examples of such questionnaires. (For the sake of space, room for responses has been omitted.)

Sample Questionnaire I
Is Your Student Ready for College?
1. Does he/she possess self-discipline and is he/she able to put work before play?
2. How are your student's time management skills? Can he/she independently and realistically budget his/her time?
3. Is he/she willing to seek help when encountering academic difficulty?
4. Does he/she seem self-reliant? Responsible?
5. Is he/she taking on the responsibilities of applying to schools, or does he/she need to be pushed? Is his/her interest in college options self-initiated? Do you think he/she will fill out his/her own college applications?
6. Does he/she meet academic responsibilities at more than a bare minimum level and without constant prodding and supervision by adults?
7. Is he/she curious about him/herself, other cultures, academics, etc.?
8. Is he/she independent? For instance, has he/she traveled from home (without family), visited another country or explored a different culture?
9. Does he/she go outside of his/her comfort level to serve others, and does he/she have a desire to make this world a better place?
10. Is he/she engaged in the life of his/her school, or does he/she attend classes then go home?
11. Does he/she know how to do the laundry and some basic cooking?

Sample Questionnaire II
TO PARENTS: You play a critical role in the process of college planning. And I affirm the importance of your perceptions, insights, and experiences as they relate to your student and his/her education. Your responses to the following questions will help me gain a more complete picture of your student. Won't you please take a moment to respond to this questionnaire? Feel free to leave any question blank or to add additional thoughts. Please return it to me at your earliest convenience. Thank you.
1. As you think about your son/daughter planning for college, what concerns do you have?
2. What words would you use to describe your son/daughter?
3. Briefly comment on your son's/daughter's readiness for college (writing, speaking and reading skills, for example).
4. What do you see as your son's/daughter's attitude toward going to college?
5. What are your expectations of your son/daughter in the college planning process?
6. What qualities or factors do you consider to be important in identifying a college for your son/daughter? For example, do you have thoughts on location? Academic competition? Religious orientation? Size? Academic offerings? Prestige or name recognition? Cost?
7. List colleges you have considered for your son/daughter, if any.
8. What role would you like to play in the college planning process?
9. What do you want most out of the time we spend together?
10. Do you have any other thoughts/comments that may be useful?

Sample Questionnaire III

1. Tell me about your son/daughter:
2. What are your goals for your son/daughter?
3. Do you see your son/daughter pursuing any specific career? If yes, explain.
4. What do you see as your child's academic strengths?
5. What do you see as your child's personal strengths?
6. What do you see as your child's academic weaknesses?
7. What do you see as your child's personal weaknesses?
8. What are your child's extracurricular activities (in and out of school, including hobbies)?
9. How has your child spent the summers since the ninth grade?
10. What jobs has your child held?
11. What three words first come to mind to describe your child?
12. What colleges are you most interested in at present for your son or daughter?
13. Please list your educational background, including all degrees, schools where earned, and year earned:
14. Names, ages, and colleges (if applicable) of other children:
15. What are the limitations to the expenditures you will be willing to make for your child's education?
16. Will you be applying for financial aid?
17. Did both parents participate in the completion of this form?
18. Do you have any questions for me at this time?

PARENTAL FEEDBACK

Keep in mind that parents are your customers. Gathering feedback from customers (and addressing concerns) is essential in running a successful business. At the end of service, I regularly present parents with a form that allows them to express their level of satisfaction with my work. Below are two sample forms.

Client Satisfaction Survey Sample I

I enjoyed working with you very much this past year, and I'm excited about your child's new life at college. Each year I ask the families I work with to fill out this questionnaire—ANONYMOUSLY—and mail it back in the envelope provided. The information is very important to me in helping me meet the needs of clients. Please circle the type/level of service provided and include any comments below. Thank you for your time.

1. Providing factual information about the financial aid process:
   ❑ unsatisfactory ❑ satisfactory ❑ more than satisfactory
   comment:

2. Providing and explaining affordability:
   ❑ unsatisfactory ❑ satisfactory ❑ more than satisfactory
   comment:

3. Providing factual information about the application process:
   ❑ unsatisfactory ❑ satisfactory ❑ more than satisfactory
   comment:

4. Providing strategies to strengthen the student's application:
   ❑ unsatisfactory ❑ satisfactory ❑ more than satisfactory
   comment:

5. Providing assistance with application and essays:
   ❑ unsatisfactory ❑ satisfactory ❑ more than satisfactory
   comment:

6. Providing help with meeting deadlines for testing, applications, and other paperwork:
   ❑ unsatisfactory ❑ satisfactory ❑ more than satisfactory
   comment:

7. Negotiating, when necessary, between views of parent and student:
   ❑ unsatisfactory ❑ satisfactory ❑ more than satisfactory
   comment:

8. Assessing and understanding student's academic and social needs:
   ❑ unsatisfactory ❑ satisfactory ❑ more than satisfactory
   comment:

9. Availability; accessibility:
   ❑ unsatisfactory ❑ satisfactory ❑ more than satisfactory
   comment:

10. Guidance in making a final college match that's affordable and meets student's other requirements:
    ❑ unsatisfactory ❑ satisfactory ❑ more than satisfactory
    comment:

11. Would you refer my services to others? Why or why not?

12. Comments about other topics I haven't included here:

Client Satisfaction Survey Sample II

1. Has your experience been a positive one? Please explain.
2. What services have been the most helpful?
3. What services have been the least helpful?
4. How do you feel the college search process worked for you? Do you have any thoughts on how this process could have been better for you?
5. Is there anything you would like to see different in terms of services offered?
6. Did your student feel "in charge" of the process throughout the time we worked together?
7. How would you change this process if you could?
8. Did your experience meet your expectations? If not, please explain as much as you can.
9. Do you feel that the fee for services was lower than, right on, or higher than you think is fair for what you received?
10. Would you be willing to be a reference for future clients?
11. Were you able to reach me when you needed to? Was I prompt is carrying out the various stages of your work?
12. Briefly summarize your experience with College Consulting Services, Inc. Please give as much feedback as possible to improve my services in the future.

PARENTAL STYLES

While organizing by parental "style" is stereotypic and misses the unique qualities of each parent with whom you work, the following is intended to orient consultants to the ways parents approach the college admission process:

Absentees

Some parents are under-involved. They will sit on the sidelines and need to be encouraged to become more active and need to be reminded that they, too, are an integral part of the process. These parents may benefit from reading books on college admissions and may need guidance as to what role they should play. Parents need to tell you how important certain issues, like cost, will be in the final decision about where the child will go to college.

Control Freaks

Control freaks have specific ideas about how the college process ought to proceed, but they want you to articulate their ideas. They wait to suggest a college idea you may have "forgotten." These parents need to be reminded that you are a partner, an advisor, and a consultant. You are not hired to implement a strategy already established by the parent. In fact, sometimes for these parents, turn their question around at them: "Why did you hire me?" In other words, the parents who are moving ahead with their agenda needs to be reminded that, in fact, you did not coerce their involvement with you. Given their voluntary involvement, your role (and theirs) may need to be clarified.

Helicopters

These are parents who enlist a team of people (educational consultants included) to assist with a variety of special needs and interests for their child. Helicopter parents sometimes act like ventriloquists; they finish sentences started by the student. In "When Drugs Mask Our Society's Failings" (*The Age*, 2004), Tanveer Ahmed refers to a parenting style called "hyper-parenting" in which parents are intensely involved in managing, scheduling, and enriching all aspects of their children's lives. Hiring you is just the next step in a series of strategies that included lining up tutors, seeking psychological and psychiatric evaluations, talking to teachers, coordinating weekend and summer activities, and so on. Clearly, over-involvement will hinder the student's leadership role through the college admission months and diminish the chances of a successful college experience. The child is no longer 12 years old. We're now talking about the student leaving home and becoming independent. The college planning months should provide opportunities for that growth. These parents are often micro-managers.

Capulets and Montagues

These parents are looking for you to be the *middle-man* between them and their child. Some parents are "on separate pages" when it comes to college planning. Some are divorced and (overtly or covertly) dealing with unresolved marital issues. But remember, if there is a conflict, express your feelings to all of the parties involved. "We've got a problem," the wise consultant says. "Let's find some ways to approach this." The problem should not shift to the consultant.

Go-getters

Go-getters have a pretty good idea of what you can do for and with the family, but they just can't resist spending hours of time on the college planning process. Since these parents are going to be so involved, it is your task as the consultant to help them be efficient in their time utilization. In other words, you will want to direct parental thinking and action into productive and constructive parts of the college search.

Movers and Shakers

The Movers and Shakers know so-and-so who will help get Buffy admitted to the school of her choosing. The appropriate strategy here is to underscore your concern for the right match. I often say to families that I have to go about my advising with the assumption that there are no contacts. If Penn is a reach for a particular student, I will not move it to another category on the basis of the parent proclamation, "I know the president of the university." Sometimes, these parents need a friendly reminder that you've been hired for advice and connections are unrelated to the goals of your work.

Designer Jeans

These parents are looking for name over fit. It is inconceivable to them that their child may not be accepted to Harvard or Yale, or even the best local school. They are not interested in hearing about a school that is less known. They may feel that life is about going to the right schools; indeed, they may have moved into a new neighborhood so that Brutus would attend the more prestigious school. With this type of parent (or family, as the student is often in agreement with his or her parents), I sometimes say, "You know, the more focus there is on the name-brand colleges, the more potential tears and stress there will be over the next year. Yes, the unknown is stressful, but let's program for success. We will look at reaches as well as backups, but let's concentrate on where Brutus can really be happy." Here is some language when working with parents who seem to put a high value on prestige. To get into the best graduate schools, with the biggest names, a student's undergraduate experience has to be stellar. A school that is too hard for him could be setting him up for disappointment for graduate school admissions. In a school that is a right match, he can earn high grades, make valuable relationships with teachers, and maybe co-author an article or work on cutting-edge research. He can take the hardest curriculum and gain leadership positions in his extra-curricular interests. He can graduate with a rich college experience and a competitive transcript—just what graduate schools are looking for.

Elitists

Related to the Designer Jeans are the Elitists. They believe that they and theirs are entitled. Rules do not apply to them. They believe that they are special and deserve special treatment. They may have difficulty accepting that their child may not be admitted to the university of his choice just because they are who they are.

Fat Cats

These are the parents who think that "money talks." These parents believe that the way to get one's way is to mail a check. These parents need to be reminded that Harvard, for example, could fill its entire freshman class with such students if it wanted to. These days, many variables are considered, and there is seldom a linear relationship between one student (or parent) quality and an acceptance letter. It's also important to continue to remind parents that you control what you control. In other words, say something like, "You know, Mr. Fat Cat, I can't consider your contacts in my assessment of good match colleges. You hired me to offer advice in those areas in which I am knowledgeable."

Enablers

The Enabler is related to the notion of codependency. Codependency is an unconscious addiction to another person's abnormal behavior. Codependent parents do everything possible to hide facts about the student or to rationalize them away. They may hide (again, often unconsciously) the student's lack of social skills and/or the student's idiosyncrasies, believing that their child is the "all-American type." Codependent parents may deny their own needs and desires and focus completely on the student and his/her image. Sometimes codependent family members become enablers through denying that problems exist. Enablers "clean up" after the student, ever mindful of tarnishing the image of the student that they have projected. Such parents allow the student to blame teachers, declare perfection, or what have you. A former student shared with me the story of a junior who was very bright but had not performed consistently in school. He and his mom were sure that his grades would increase as a junior because the previous year's problems were teacher-related, school-related, life-related . . . everything but student-related. It took this consultant a few meetings to realize that the well-meaning mom had been snow-jobbed by this very charming student. She went to bat for him at school, work, etc. and never held him accountable for his behavior and performance. She regularly made all kinds of (convincing) excuses for him. She was, quite probably, hoping that the consultant would assume the role of the "villain." For this family, the consultant had to be businesslike and clear about outcomes and consequences: "That's great that you expect to bring that D up to an A. If you do so, these are some options to consider. If you don't, these are the options we're looking at."

Joined-at-the-Hips

With a family that is enmeshed, the boundaries between parent and child are blurred. Similar to the Enablers, these parents have difficulty separating themselves from their child and often parent to please, sometimes impeding their child's growth. It can be difficult to intervene in this family dynamic, but the consultant needs to try to establish boundaries—at least in regard to college planning. Meet the student alone as often as possible and don't allow too much "we" talking: "We are applying to Wooster," "We think it is best to go to an Eastern school," and so on. Sometimes in dealing with parents who are joined-at-the-hips with their child, I remember an adage that such parents should consider as Buffy and Brutus leave for college: "If you can't leave me, I haven't been a good parent."

Shape-Shifters

There is so often a disconnect between what parents say in the presence of their students, and what they say on the phone or through email. These parents (or one of them) claim at your group meeting to be utterly supportive, to just want to see their child happy. Later you get a message from that same parent saying, "I can't believe my daughter has any Cs. We didn't raise her this way. It's totally unacceptable." With these kinds of folks, I typically speak to them about the mixed messages they are sending and how confusing it is for their son or daughter. Sometimes they don't even realize they're talking in such contradictory ways until they are politely confronted with it, or they report that they "just can't help it."

Train Wrecks

These families are disengaged and lack emotional involvement. Parents and children fail to communicate with each other. Disapproval and judgments can run rampant in these families. This style is like that of the Absentees, but perhaps a bit more pathological. We're not therapists, but we can understand the behaviors here and try to work toward finding the best match for the student in any way possible. Getting the student together with the parent may be helpful here to encourage exchange and interaction.

Awfulizers

The "awfulizing" parents are tough to deal with and require skill in patience in keeping things optimistic. To these parents, everything in college planning is awful—Brutus won't get into any college, his essay is junk, the schools he's chosen are pathetic, the system is rigged in favor of some other group of students, and so forth. (They can use a dose of positivity from Dr. Happy!)

*****

While the labels for parents are entertainingly familiar, they also remind me that it's dangerous to pigeonhole people, put parents down, and attribute a student's problems to parental shortcomings.

INTERACTIVE STRATEGIES FOR WORKING WITH PARENTS

Communication with parents is key to consultant success. The ability to interact with parents competently, reliably, and persuasively is a skill. You wouldn't be in this field without counseling skills and intuitive abilities. Most of your interactions with parents will require the skills you have learned/developed over the years. Below are strategies to help IECs interact well with parents.

Recognize parents' power. Power is not used here in the negative sense. Parents are more involved presently than in years prior. Use their power to your advantage, or risk having that power used against you.

Reconstruct the playing field. Focus on the broad picture and on the student. A parent may ask, "Is it okay for Becky to take the SAT three times in her junior year?" It's wise to reframe the question: "What are Becky's priorities for the remainder of the junior year?" "What grades does James need to get into Dartmouth?" can be reframed as, "What can we do during this year to help James become an interesting and curious person?"

Use the "I'm confused" strategy. Think out loud. For example, you might say something like, "Let me understand. I'm confused: You said that Brutus works best in smaller classes and with personal attention, and yet you are feeling that State U is the best choice?" Here's another example: "Now, let me see if I have this straight. You seem to be saying that prestige is very important and yet you don't want Buffy at a highly competitive college. Help me connect the dots."

Fight the consultant's instinct to keep everyone happy. Note that negativity and disharmony exist, and fight the consultant instinct to make everybody happy. People who become educational consultants are caring and compassionate. And that's terrific! But sometimes we have to recognize that the price of keeping everyone happy is either too high in terms of mental fatigue or in terms of keeping an eye on the ball—or else it's not possible. We want everyone to be happy, and we mostly succeed at that. But some families don't have such harmony—and there will be those who are merely negative. Be okay with some dissatisfaction if you have done your best and tried to work through issues.

Use time to your advantage. Stall when appropriate. Waiting gives parents time to calm down and discuss their concerns. An instantaneous response is not necessary. I learned the "time delay" technique as Dean of Students at the University of Denver. (To give you the context, Teddy Roosevelt was president.) Because I was so busy, there were times when I simply could not call a student back within 24 hours or so. I began seeing a pattern: When I called in a day or two, many "crises" were averted. Either the problem had been resolved on its own, or it was seen as much less troublesome. I still use the technique. Oh, sure, there are students or parents who really do have something that is a crisis; however, let's face it, we're not brain surgeons. Yes, we want to be responsive, helpful and empathetic, but giving our clients or customers time to reflect and do some problem-solving on their own can be cathartic and efficient.

Be self-assured. A bit of conceit is okay in the pursuit of getting the job done. Do not be egotistical, but tell parents that you have visited colleges and that you understand the process of applying. "I have visited colleges and it's my career…" Good consultants are knowledgeable and up to date. Emphasize your experience and competence. Use phrasing such as, "My experience indicates…"

State your limits early. I highly recommend that you state your limits prior to signing a contract. As emphasized throughout this book, under-promise and over-deliver. I overstate my inability to find the ideal school; perfection is not the goal. We have plenty to offer, but we don't have perfect solutions to every issue. Set limits with time. Be a professional. Don't be used.

Control what you can, and recognize and share what's outside of your control. What is it you can control? Lots of things. Even most. You can control your own rationality, your own good judgment, and your own focus on what is best for the student. You control your knowledge of colleges and your awareness of the process. What you can't control is admissions decisions or mixed messages parents receive from others. Share your knowledge and enlighten parents.

Keep the student front and center. Hold meetings in your office with parents and student in attendance. Student needs to take leadership of the process. Some parents intentionally or unintentionally leave the student out of the equation on matters where the opinion of the student is vital. Some parents may want to handle matters directly with you. They may regularly speak for their student. They may say, "WE are applying to Wooster and Beloit." Redirect these parents to allow the student to take ownership of the process. I've found that students are often ready to disagree with their parents. But whether they agree or disagree, their input is vital. So while we want parental input—in fact, we must have it—it's the student whom we want to take the role of leader.

Wooster

Recognize and appreciate cultural differences. Author, retired educator, and blogger at College Counseling Culture (collegeculture.net) Will Dix states, "[In college counseling]…so many cultural ideas intersect: race, class, aspiration, status, and the American dream." In *Counseling the Culturally Different*, Sue and Sue state, "A culturally skilled counselor…is one who actively attempts to understand the worldview of the client."

ESTABLISHING BOUNDARIES

It's important that the IEC take time to consider the distance required from parents for maximum professional success. Below are some of the boundaries that I establish as well as some tips for cementing them into practice.

- I tread very lightly with parents who are unsure about whether I can be helpful. I make the case for my involvement with passion, but if a family is not sure, I move into "underselling" mode. That is, an unproductive relationship may result if I have to practically coerce a family to work with me. The same is true if I see too many red flags at my initial, free consultation. Some red flags that I watch out for include: Buffy doesn't seem able/willing to assume responsibility; one or both parents are completely unrealistic about the current admission scene; the student and/or parents feel (on any level) that I'm going to help Buffy get into a selective college; anyone involved in the college planning process is unwilling to buy into the basic philosophical and ethical underpinnings of my practice.

- Some parents want a paid nudge. While it is true that many counselors involved in working with adolescents do some nagging, this is not the "stuff" of which a profession is made. Yes, I admit to being a nag on occasion—but only in the context of providing information about colleges and the admission process. Educational consultants, it seems to me, must be more than hand holders. (By the way, there are adolescents who need "life coaches" to help them get organized, and I'm not opposed to someone helping students meet deadlines, learn study skills, and so forth.) If someone wants a career as a confidant/organizer/nudge/friend/cajoler to adolescents, fine. I understand, at least on one level, the need for that role. In fact, one could likely make a decent living doing just that. But I'm not convinced of the primacy of that role as a best practice for the field of consulting over the next decade.

- Setting priorities is an important task for the consultant, particularly when it involves parents. Despite parental perception, rarely is there an emergency. No one's life hangs in the balance. I'm very careful about choosing the right communication method to use. For example, if a parent writes or calls with an issue that is filled with subtlety ("Can you give me a couple of backup college names?"), I respond that we should schedule a meeting. I say that it's not fair to Buffy to explore colleges without her input. Further, I argue, the art of discussing issues around a table is important to good college planning. Another technique I use with parents who are constantly calling/writing is to confront such overstepping head on. For example, I'll call Mrs. Bigshot and say something like, "You've called frequently this week, and there are clearly several issues on your mind. I want to help you through them. Given my schedule, and assuring that I make the time to consider all the implications of decisions on Buffy's college happiness, let's schedule more routine meetings. That way, we can sit around and explore lots of issues—and the interrelationships between them. To get started, how does Wednesday at 4:15 look?"

- As far as parents calling at night and treating the consultant as if he or she is always "on call": grrrr! It's wrong. When I feel I am being "abused," I call a meeting to share my concern. Often, it is either panic (in the parents' minds), or else they haven't accepted either me or my role as a consultant. One thing I find is that my demeanor and my approach to my clients must say *I'm a professional, and I'm worthy of being treated like one.* Beyond being clear in terms of limits at the start of the engagement, we must present ourselves as people with knowledge, experience, and skills that have value. That doesn't mean being pompous; rather, it means being assertive enough to be treated fairly.

PRINCIPLES FOR WORKING WITH DIFFICULT PARENTS

The following pointers are provided to aid your thinking of general communicative strategies (some will work with students, too!) and to offer additional tools for your repertoire. Note that there is no such thing as the collective "parent." There are individual parents, and all of them have diverse concerns and specific values they'd like to impart to their kids. While some micromanage, others are invisible. While many are a pleasure to work with, some are taxing. To avoid and/or nip contention, consider the following tips.

When you must air concerns:
- Begin potentially charged conversations by sharing something positive about the child.
- Be sure to communicate your concerns early.
- Don't accuse or judge; just state how you feel about the situation.
- Don't generalize.
- State the problem clearly.
- Address only the specific issue.
- Keep the discussion focused on the needs of the child.
- Keep a record of all communication and contact you have made with parents.
- Note all conversations in writing.

When parents have grievances:
- Listen carefully and attentively.
- Allow parents to vent their anger and frustration.
- Avoid being defensive.
- When speaking to difficult parents, do not sit behind your desk; rather, move your chair close to and in front of the parents. This lets the parents know that you are comfortable and confident.
- Be selectively silent, denying difficult parents attention and power.
- Before you react or suggest a solution, it is important that you understand the problems or issues, especially from the parents' point of view.
- Don't be stampeded into an immediate response or quick resolution to the problem just to end the conference.
- Take notes.
- Always document what's going on—both in and out of formal meetings.

FINAL THOUGHTS

I want to end with a few words about making parents happy. The goal of our work is not, in fact, to make everyone happy. Of course, we work hard to discuss issues with everyone and to use our skills in negotiation, consensus building, and communication to increase the likelihood that parents and students will have a positive experience with us. But I find that those of us in helping, service professions can be overly sensitive to the slightest hint of dissatisfaction. That fixation can be disabling. We strive to find compromise and consider varying perspectives. But at some point, we need to let go of the feeling that any negativity means a lack of success. We provide our best judgments. Sometimes I need to remind myself that the fight itself (or the discussion or the sharing of opposing views) is worth having. Not everyone will like every suggestion I make. I'm hired to give opinions that are in Buffy's best interests. Buffy herself may disagree with some of them. At the end of the day, my level of satisfaction does not rest with others. It rests squarely with me. If I feel I have been considerate, fair, open with my thinking process, and caring, then it's been a good day.

CHAPTER 13

Higher Education and Admission Landscape

SURVEYING THE COLLEGIATE LANDSCAPE

The landscape of higher education has never been more scenic. The range, breadth, and depth of colleges in the US is amazing. By all accounts, the US has the most developed system of higher education in the world. Think about it: thousands of colleges serve millions of students. The state university system has grown wildly in the last 50 years, and the private university system offers a multitude of options.

The American system of higher education is unique in many ways. In Germany, France, and the United Kingdom, college entrance is based almost entirely on external national academic exams at the end of high school. Extracurricular activities, sports, and community service do not factor in to college admissions. Moreover, in Great Britain, students apply to study a given subject. This is more than just declaring a major—practically all of the three or four years of study required to earn a bachelor's degree are devoted to the main subject. Most universities teach through a combination of large lectures, private study, and smaller seminars, and there is often more emphasis on final exams than on coursework or term grades. The "Oxbridge" system differs as it uses a tutorial system wherein one or two students meet bi-weekly with a tutor (i.e. a professor) to read and discuss an essay on a given topic (resulting often from assigned readings). The professor neither quizzes nor grades the students; rather, he or she provides verbal feedback. After two years, students sit a marathon of written exams and do so again at the end of the entire four years.

Here, let's survey the collegiate landscape and address the mission and purpose of each type of school within the American higher educational system.

Two-year Colleges

Two-year institutions, typically referred to as community colleges, award the associate degree—associate of arts (AA) or associate of science (AS)—following successful completion of a two-year, full-time program. There are two basic types of programs at community and junior colleges. Some programs are strictly academic and designed to prepare students to transfer to four-year institutions with bachelor's degree programs. Others are more practical or applied and provide career training in specific areas. This second type of school does not usually prepare students for transfer to a four-year institution though some of the credits earned may be accepted by a four-year institution. Rather, the latter offers technical programs that prepare students for immediate entry into the job market. Although some are private, most community and junior colleges are publicly supported by the state and local communities.

Nowadays many two-year schools have clearly stated agreements with four-year schools to accept students who take a prescribed curriculum and maintain a specified grade point average. This system, spawned by higher education policies in states like California, has spread nationwide. In addition to honors programs for top students, many two-year schools have added or increased the numbers of students in residence halls. This is an area of major growth on the higher education landscape, and the IEC will want to be a leader in increasing visits to two-year schools.

Helping students understand the value of community college is important. What often hurts us as IECs is the message that some parents communicate to their children. Generation X parents may believe that community college is a step down from a four-year institution and may dismiss the great strides these colleges have made in recent decades. This tends to be less true in states like California which has a higher education structure that encourages the value of the two-year school.

Four-year Colleges and Universities

The college or university awards the bachelor's degree. The bachelor of arts (BA) or bachelor of science (BS) degrees are the most common, but a variety of bachelor's degrees by other names are also granted. Bachelor's degrees are typically awarded following successful completion of a four-year, full-time program. Programs in some fields of study or at some institutions can be longer than four years, and students often take longer than four years to complete their degrees.

The differences between a college and university can be subtle. A college, in the traditional sense, is smaller than a university and often focuses on the liberal arts and sciences. A university normally includes three types of schools: undergraduate colleges, various categories of professional schools, and a graduate school. Large universities are routinely divided into colleges—liberal arts, business, engineering, architecture, law, and so forth. Generally, a university offers more majors and research facilities. Class size often reflects institutional size, and some classes may taught by graduate students. There are both public and private colleges and universities in the United States, and some have an affiliation with a religious denomination.

Public Institutions

The state university or state college is supported financially by public funds. As such, these colleges offer tuition rates well below that of most private colleges and universities. Tuition is higher for out-of-state students. State institutions usually give special consideration to in-state students. Admission requirements for out-of-state applicants can be highly selective. This is especially true for the state university systems in Virginia, Texas, North Carolina, Michigan, California, and Florida.

Private Institutions

Private schools generally have higher costs because they do not receive the same primary funding from the state and federal government. Private colleges rely on tuition, fees, endowments, and other private sources. Private colleges are usually smaller than public colleges and can offer more personalized attention (and some believe, more prestige).

Trade and Vocational Schools

Trade schools provide students with a set of specific skills and knowledge related to a particular job or career field. Trade school might be right for the student interested in fields such as aircraft or automotive mechanic, brick mason, broadcast technician/sound engineer, carpenter, commercial diver, construction equipment operator, construction manager, crane operator, diagnostic medical sonographer, diesel mechanic, electrician, industrial machinery mechanic, medical records technician, paralegal, pile-driver operator, plumber, respiratory therapist, web developer, welder, and wind turbine technician.

Students typically earn a certificate, vocational diploma, or associate's degree from trade and vocational schools. The goal is most often an immediate job (or at least immediate demand). Many of these jobs are in high demand, particularly in health and construction trades, with expected growth to continue. Furthermore, because more young people have been choosing college over trades, the shortage of skilled workers is growing. Current workers in skilled trades are older and will soon be retiring. Young workers are needed to fill their shoes.

The length of time needed to complete these programs varies. It doesn't hurt that students pursuing these schools likely will not have to deal with huge college debt. The average trade school degree costs much less than a traditional four-year degree.

One downside is that students often don't receive a general education, which means that their skills are very focused. Another is that many of these programs are terminal; that is, they end with the student earning the skill necessary for success in a specific field. As such, most credits from these programs will not transfer.

These days IECs ought to be knowledgeable about trade and vocational schools and ought to welcome students who are interested in these options to our practices. For many decades, students interested in being tradesmen and tradeswomen have not generally sought the advice of a consultant. Indeed, there is a general belief that "college planning" includes two and four-year college options and thus not traditional trade schools. It's time for that perception to change.

One of the hurdles for us to try to overcome is parent perception of these schools. Parents need to be educated that there are many bright young men and women who ought to at least consider a vocational school. Further, there are good jobs available and good money to be made!

Other Distinctions and Categories

3-2 Engineering: These programs give the student an experience of studying at both a liberal arts and sciences college and one that is more career focused. Students study at a liberal arts college for three years and then at an engineering college (at another institution) for two years. At the end of five years, the student receives a bachelor of arts from the liberal arts school and a bachelor of science in a selected engineering field from the engineering school. Most liberal arts and sciences colleges (without engineering programs, which includes most of them) offer some form of 3/2 arrangement with schools such as Cal Tech, Columbia University, and Washington University. Besides 3/2 programs in engineering, some colleges offer arrangements such as 4+1 or 3+4 that combines arts and sciences with fields such as business, teaching, medicine, and law.

American Indian-Serving Colleges: American Indian Higher Education Consortium (aihec.org) represents 34 colleges in the United States and one Canadian institution. Montana alone has seven tribal colleges.

Foreign Colleges and Universities: Increasingly, students are considering options outside of the United States. Canada, in particular, is recruiting heavily in the United States. Exchange rates in recent years have made attending school in Canada attractive to American families. In addition, American colleges overseas are more plentiful than ever. (See resources at astudentofcolleges.com.)

For-profit Colleges: Often referred to as proprietary schools, they are privately owned and run for a profit. They are "educational businesses" that offer services and courses similar to those at other institutions. Perhaps the best example is the University of Phoenix.

Hispanic-Serving Colleges: There are an increasing number of colleges that have a quarter or more Hispanic students. The Hispanic Association of Colleges and Universities (hacu.net) represents more than 450 colleges and universities.

Historically Black Colleges: These schools found their origins in the time when African American students were systematically denied access to most other colleges and universities, but they are still an important part of the higher education landscape. These schools offer students a unique opportunity to experience an educational community that is particularly supportive of racial identity and is goal oriented.

Honors Colleges: An honors college is typically found at a larger public institution and offers students an advanced curriculum. An honors college is different from an honors program. An honors program provides an enriched selection of classes while a true honors college offers more challenging curriculum. Some students accepted to honors colleges are also given scholarships. An example of an honors college is the Clark Honors College at the University of Oregon. It has its own facilities (library, classrooms, computer lab, faculty offices, and so forth), and students are required to complete a thesis.

Liberal Arts Colleges: These can be public or private, but most are private. They offer a broad base of courses in the humanities, social sciences, and sciences. Most focus mainly on undergraduate students. Classes tend to be small, and personal attention is available. These colleges are designed to give students a broad cultural foundation in the arts and sciences, and they offer a four-year program leading to a number of degrees. Much of the first two years of study is in required *core curriculum* courses, and the last two years are in a major concentration.

Military Academies: To prepare for a career of national service, the following are options: United States Military Academy, United States Naval Academy, United States Air Force Academy, United States Coast Guard Academy, and United States Merchant Marine Academy.

Music and Art Schools and Conservatories: These schools generally require the submission of a portfolio or other demonstration of student talent. Competitive art schools may offer a variety of general education classes, but they are primarily designed to develop the artistic talents of their students. Conservatories of music typically require auditions.

Online Education: The availability of online courses and degrees has never been greater. Some colleges that offer online degrees are for-profit but, increasingly, mainstream colleges are providing coursework available through one's computer. In fact, it is not uncommon for students, particularly at large, state schools to take some of their regular coursework online.

Religiously Affiliated Colleges: Some private colleges are religiously affiliated. The affiliation may be historic only, or it may affect day-to-day student life. Most religiously affiliated colleges are Christian (Roman Catholic and Protestant), and there are a small number of Jewish and Islamic institutions. (See resources at astudentofcolleges.com for reference lists in this area.)

Technological Institutions: These are degree-granting colleges that offer intensive training in engineering and applied sciences. Undergraduate study may sometimes run five years in cooperation with liberal arts colleges on the 3-2 plan.

Women's Colleges: Although almost all colleges in the U.S. are coeducational, there are a few single-sex schools, primarily women's colleges. Women's colleges began largely because of the inequities in education. It was felt that women were not called upon in class and that expectations were lower for women than for men. In other words, professors expected men to do better. It seems to me that there are two primary advantages to women's colleges. One is that the women's colleges truly work to enable students to be successful in either finding a job or vocation after graduation or in gaining admission to graduate school. I think the feeling of empowerment women's colleges provide is remarkable. The second advantage relates to the first. Graduates of women's colleges seem confident and especially able to withstand the bumps and bruises of life. Though I'm not certain how graduates develop such tenacity, I've sure noticed it.

THE COLLEGE ADMISSIONS TERRAIN: HOW TO HELP FAMILIES DECIPHER A CONVOLUTED ROADMAP

College admission in the 21st century is more convoluted than it needs to be. It seems as if the wheel needs to be reinvented with each passing admission season. On the face, the process is relatively simple: Spell out the admission criteria and admit those who meet the requirements. If only it were so simple! We have great universities, and we have great students. The process of getting them together, however, is often tangled in a mess of interests: politics, social reform, media, and finances, to name a few. The stakes have gotten higher. More money is involved. Colleges are multimillion—even billion-dollar enterprises. One-upmanship has become the rule instead of the exception. Colleges fight for students like bees for honey. Sadly, it is sometimes the students who get caught in the crosshairs. Admissions decisions are not necessarily rational, and IECs walk many families through the labyrinth of the system.

We can start here: There are more kids applying to college today than ever before in history. Additionally, there are constantly increasing numbers of talented and outstanding applicants—world class athletes, rock stars, winners of amazing awards and distinctions in forensics, journalism, fine arts, leadership, and so on. There are kids who have written and published short stories, poems, and scholarly articles and who have played at Carnegie Hall, and so on. There are over 35,000 high schools in the US; thus, there are 35,000 students ranked at the top of their classes. Competition is fierce.

Admission is lopsided. Most colleges (over three quarters) admit four out of five students who apply. Elite colleges (which include no more than 5% of all colleges), however, admit a sliver of those who apply. It is essential for IECs to educate families about the selective admissions process because it is more convoluted than the non-selective admissions process.

Admission philosophies have changed. Selection of students at elite colleges is now based largely on social engineering. Years ago, it was about wealth, social standing, and family tradition. For example, if Brutus went to Exeter, the chances were good that he would get into Harvard or one of the Ivies. After WWII a shift in college admission occurred. Students were admitted on merit alone—the smartest got in (those with the highest test scores, the highest grades, etc.). Following the Civil Rights movement and the Bakke Supreme Court case, college admission philosophies shifted again toward increased diversity. (Further discussion of changes in admissions is presented later in this chapter.)

At the moment, who gets in at the most selective colleges is the result of many carefully made decisions. First, the college decides how much money to spend recruiting students. Even colleges accepting a small percentage of applicants spend hundreds of thousands of dollars (some considerably more) extending their reach through mailings, presence on Facebook and Twitter, and so on. Second, colleges decide the size of their freshman class. Finally, colleges decide on the student characteristics of successful applicants. The most important factors influencing admission decisions today are quality of courses taken in high school, grades, teacher recommendations, test scores, intellectual curiosity, activities, and submitted written materials. Yet so much of elite college admission is about having a balanced class. The process of balancing involves geography, gender, legacy status, racial diversity, athletic accomplishment, and a myriad of other factors. Those characteristics, by the way, can change from one year to the next. Well-rounded students may be desired one year and more pointed students (high school scientists, for example) the next.

It's interesting to talk to admission officials at the drool schools. They will tell you that they long for a "representative" class. Even though many of the schools in the Ivy League athletic conference get 20, 30, even 40,000 applications a year, deans and directors will tell you how much they want more students from, say, Nebraska, or more Native American students, or more students with thus-and-so distinguishing feature. A dichotomy exists: while students and parents try to pry kids into a narrow range of colleges, these same colleges are not satisfied with the applicants they receive and feel the need to recruit like crazy to find those more suitable to their needs. Selective schools reject thousands of amazingly qualified students even though the accepted student and the rejected one can have the same profile. Admission is unpredictable.

Let's use a football stadium to describe selective college admission. Imagine that this football stadium is big, holding 100,000 students. The seats in the stadium belong to admitted students. Let's reserve seats for the top one or two students from each high school. As stated above, there are some 35,000 high schools, so at this point, most seats are taken. Then let's reserve 10,000 or so seats on the basis of incredible singular distinctions (accomplishments on a national or even international basis in sports, speech and debate, juggling, 4-H, drama, and on and on) as well as geographic and ethnic diversity. Finally, lets hold thousands of seats for athletes, legacies, and other special categories. Is there room for Buffy amid all of this? Maybe. Maybe not. She might be able to grab a seat, but so much will depend on the day of the game. Will everyone show up? Will Buffy's credentials put her in one of the seats, or will she be relegated to the lines waiting to get in? As impressive as she is, Buffy might end up not even close to the stadium. This is the sort of logic we need to employ to help our students and their parents understand selective college admission. What first looks like a lot of seats becomes fewer and fewer as the hordes come marching in.

Families, by and large, have little idea how difficult admission has become. They tend not to know, or refuse to believe, the numbers of students applying to colleges today and the numbers of truly amazing applicants. Furthermore, some students and some parents believe that if Brown and Dartmouth are reaches, then certainly Northwestern and Tufts are "reachable." That's not necessarily true. In fact, Northwestern (and Tufts and Boston College and Williams and Southern Cal) are taking the same students (on the basis of academic and extracurricular accomplishments) that Brown and Dartmouth were taking 15 or 20 years ago.

Ultimately, are more selective colleges "better"? Do not confuse admission selectivity with academic rigor. Plus, don't confuse selectivity with quality. While there is a correlation, all are different variables for the IEC. For example, the University of Chicago admits a much higher percentage of students than, say, Dartmouth, and yet is, according to all my research and evidence, more rigorous academically. Of course, academically gifted students attend both institutions, but students at Chicago tend to be more scholarly and more intellectually focused. Similarly, UCLA is typically more selective (particularly for an out-of-state student) as compared to Lafayette, but many (including me) would argue that the intellectually curious student is more likely to be happy at Lafayette. This (and the discussion above) is by no means to suggest that we should discourage students from applying to selective colleges. As IECs, we should encourage well qualified students to apply to selective schools. We simply need to educate families about the nature of admissions today. Such discussions help smooth bumps in the consulting process.

A Look Back at Selective Admissions

Let's take a quick U-turn and return to a bit of history. Below, I share some excerpts from an interesting essay, "The Birth of a New Institution" by Geoffrey Kabaservice. This piece was published in the *Yale Alumni Magazine* in December, 1999. Kabaservice discusses how an historic shift in the admission philosophy at Yale changed the course of selective admissions.

A framework: "During the 1930s, while president James Conant of Harvard was envisioning an educational structure that linked success to testable merit, Yale's admissions policies still emphasized inherited privilege, tending toward the creation of an elite social caste."

The status quo: Whitney Griswold was Yale's president in 1950. According to Kabaservice, "Some idea of how Griswold's anti-modernizing stance translated to the level of undergraduate admissions may be imagined by considering the wall of obstacles and biases raised against an applicant from an excellent, competitive public high school such as New York's Bronx High School of Science in the early 1950's: The student came from a public high school, which Griswold considered unworthy; he scored highly on aptitude tests, which Griswold discounted; he had a specialized education, which Griswold thought disqualified him for the liberal arts; he focused on science or technology, which Yale considered unsavory; he was almost certainly from a non-wealthy family, which handicapped him in that era before need-blind admissions; and he had no Yale alumni connection or feeder-school tradition to boost his candidacy."

A new spin: Yale's admissions policy began changing in the 1960s; by the 1980s, admission based on diversity and "social engineering" was the norm. When Kingman Brewster was president of Yale, he hired Inslee ("Inky") Clark as dean of admission. Clark brought new perspectives to the admission office. He increased the size of the admission staff and initiated a recruitment policy centered on "talent searching."

His first class, in 1970, was markedly different than in the past. Suddenly, a majority of students came from public high schools, Yale met the financial need of students, and students came from more states. Kabaservice notes, "The faculty was astonished and delighted by the leap in academic ability. Scientists were particularly gratified. The chairman of the chemistry department was moved to write Brewster that "[a]ll of our staff who have had any contact with this year's freshmen agree that someone has done a spectacular job of recruiting. We are accustomed to meeting excellent students in introductory courses but never in such numbers." Partly due to Brewster's preferences, the class also contained an unprecedented number of artists, musicians, and actors. A student symphony orchestra was founded during this period, and its first conductor recalled that during the Brewster years, "music grew and flowered in a way that makes campus life today almost unrecognizable to anyone who attended the college before 1968."

The correlation to selective admissions today: What happened at Yale was, in large part, the same scenario playing out at other very selective colleges. When privilege, wealth, and preparatory school were the keys to admission, there was not much need for a college consultant! But when talent searching began, when students from public high schools were sought, when financial aid began to differentiate one college from another, when orchestras and singing groups and athletes were sought, so too did the need for students of colleges. That need continued to expand as college admissions deans put their own stamp on their admissions operations. Some schools gave more weight to geography of applicants, others wanted more athletes, some relished the "preppy" image of the 1960s, and some longed for more individualism. In later years, the availability of merit aid and of meeting demonstrated need, made colleges more and more distinct and unique.

THE INNER WORKINGS OF ADMISSIONS OFFICES

IECs should also explain to families how colleges organize their admission efforts. Below is a broad outline.
- Large state universities tend to have clerks and "paper handlers" (or, more accurately these days, online application handlers) who read applications and, often, make the decision. Many of these schools have published course requirements and an index that combines GPA, rank, and test scores.
- Some universities (like many University of California schools) train people in the community to read certain parts of the application.
- Some large publics (and privates) have one procedure for the students who clearly are acceptable or not acceptable and another for those who are somewhere in the middle.
- Some colleges have a point system for evaluation (for example, there may be three parts to the evaluation—academics, extracurricular, and "personal"). Others use one overall numerical evaluation (1 for "we must admit" to 5 for "doesn't seem attractive"). The process of evaluation is really quite subjective. Often, the more selective the institution, the more subjective the rating.
- Several categories of students get more of a review: legacies, athletes, members of sought-after demographic groups, et cetera.
- Public colleges and universities typically view in-state and out-of-state students quite differently.
- Small, selective liberal arts colleges may bring most applications to a full committee. (Those that don't go to the committee are applications that are clearly either acceptable or deniable.)
- One common way for selective colleges to organize their admission office is around "regional representatives." A particular representative handles applicants from certain states. He or she reviews folders from his or her territory and "scores" them. That person's evaluation then goes to the next level above (perhaps the director) who either concurs or brings the folders to a committee. Some colleges have two readers and then, if questionable, the application goes to the committee or to the director or dean).
- Some of these committees (by the way) are just admission officers. But at some colleges, committees include faculty members and/or administrators.

Admission is orderly in its own way, and often colleges are content that what they are doing makes some logical sense. But, the fact is that no "ultimate guide" to evaluation exists. Evaluative approaches differ from college to college and admission officer to admission officer. That's why the IEC's job is to keep an eye on choices—plural—as opposed to choice—singular.

THOUGHTS REGARDING DEMONSTRATED INTEREST

There is quite a brouhaha in regard to the idea of demonstrated interest. Demonstrated interest is a variable that admission officers consider in the acceptance process. Colleges want to be sure that they are accepting students who will actually attend as opposed to those who merely check off a college's name on a generic application. Sure, that makes sense from an admission standpoint, especially because rankings are impacted by the number of accepted students who attend.

Here's the brouhaha that's the talk of the IEC town: Are there truly reliable measures of interest? Isn't it pretty easy to fake interest? Moreover, to the extent that demonstrated interest typically includes a campus visit, doesn't this give an advantage to the student who can afford the trip? I say much of the fracas is hype. Seeing as IECs can't control the variables that admission offices consider, how do we best advise our students regarding this slippery issue?

My thoughts: Good consulting means to tell students to demonstrate interest. Here's how students can do so without breaking the bank for a visit:
- Get on the mailing list of colleges that interest them.
- Write colleges and inquire about special freshman programs and faculty research interests.
- Attend the meeting if a college representative visits a high school.
- Visit the college's booth at local college fairs.
- Follow colleges on social media, doing so with authenticity and moderation. (While a college wants a student who is interested and knows about the school, a college is not interested in the student who is trying too hard to stand out.)
- Thoughtfully answer supplementary essays that ask for reasons why the school is of interest.

In other words, students should not email a college for no reason and should not send roses to the director of admission! Let's try to keep demonstrated interest in perspective, perhaps at simmer rather than full boil.

IECs AND ADMISSION OFFICERS: RELATIONSHIPS AND ROLES

Our profession relies directly on a congenial, open relationship with college admission officers. After all, admission offices strive to bring to campus students who fit their collegiate environment. A student attending the right college brings life and energy to both the classroom and to campus; thus, our work as students of colleges resonates with admission officers. Admission officers provide us with valuable information about their institution: new programs, initiatives, institutional goals, and policy. Seeing a college from the perspective of an admission officer is invaluable in keeping current.

Some colleges have an admission official designated to work with IECs. The invitation of IECs to college-sponsored tours has increased at least tenfold in the last decade. Hundreds of colleges send representatives to attend professional IEC meetings, and new IECs are typically overwhelmed by the amount of mail and email they receive from colleges.

But with this increased trust comes increased responsibility. Most of our contact with admission officials focuses on our need to better understand the college: to gain general information about campus life, resources, and academic opportunities. If I can't find an answer to a question on the college's website, or if my IEC colleagues are not able to help me, I wouldn't hesitate to reach out to an admission official. I recognize, however, that admission officers are busy people, and I want to use their time efficiently.

While I enjoy good relationships with college admission officers (and I've spent a good deal of time cultivating those interpersonal relationships), I am also aware of the ethical limits of my professional relationship.

I am normally a "silent partner" with the college in terms of student admission. But I am very much a "noisy partner" in respect to understanding the priorities and values of the college and recommending students who will thrive at that institution.

Unless explicitly asked, IECs should not call a college to jawbone for admission. That is unethical. There is no need, and that is not our role. We should avoid even the appearance of applying influence on an admission decision. Telling an admission officer the reason that Brutus changed schools in the 11th grade might be valuable and worthy of sharing, especially if I felt that the change affected Brutus' performance. And, particularly, if I felt that the school counselor did not know (or if no counselor existed), then, with permission, I might write or call.

If I were working with a very fragile student and believed that her or his fragility should be communicated, I likely wouldn't hesitate to contact the admission office; however, I believe it is best to err on the side of caution in these matters. Call or write if trust has been built. Call or write if you have something relevant to share. When you do contact admission officials, remember that you are representing the entire IEC community.

Be particularly cautious in interacting with very selective colleges (those who admit, say, fewer than 20% of those who apply). At these schools, the pressures on admission officers are particularly high. Everyone who knows Buffy wants her to be admitted. In such a climate, we want to avoid the perception that a contact is for the purpose of influencing an admission decision. One has more freedom when it comes to working with less selective colleges or colleges where the admission office is reaching out, encouraging our involvement. I'm certainly responsive to an admission officer who asks for my help or who asks me to contact him or her with information about candidates I am working with. But even with these colleges, I believe it is especially critical to be mindful of ethics.

IECs are hired to provide choices, not to provide admission to any school. That is not only true because of the way we are paid, but it is also because of the essence of our profession. It is contrary to our roles as advisor, guider, and teacher. We are not lobbyists for our students. As students of colleges, our obligation is to the choice process generally, and not admission to one institution specifically. We visit colleges to learn about them, not to hobnob with admission directors in hopes of getting someone admitted.

I sometimes hear colleagues talk about "advocating" for a student in the admission process. If "advocating" implies pressure to get someone in, then it is inappropriate. If "advocating" means knowing that College A is a better fit (even in terms of admission) than College B, then it is appropriate. If "advocating" means knowing that College X is looking for red-haired girls from South Dakota, that's perfectly appropriate. Also appropriate is my telling the student that College Y is eager for more female scientists.

Admission officers are getting used to our role. As such, our relationship with admission officials over the next decade will solidify our rightful place at the table. That rightful place is to direct our students to good choice colleges. After all, doing a good job at this will mean the college gains a happy student, one who is more apt to stay until graduation.

(See astudentodcolleges.com for admission resources.)

CHAPTER 14

Money Talk

The astute consultant knows the process, knows the forms, and knows the jargon of financial aid. He or she is also aware of the types of aid available and has a working knowledge of the operation of different types of grant, scholarship, work study, and loan programs. Through research, the consultant is also insightful about the ways different colleges deliver their financial support to students. Though this is not the place for a primer on financial aid, there are overarching principles and practices important to the IEC, and they are covered in this chapter.

What I feel is most valuable to independent educational consultants is to point out how we can best educate our clients in regard to college costs and to emphasize the scope of our practice in regard to financial aid consulting. We have an obligation to help families navigate the financial aid process, yet we should not presume to manage a family's finances.

TO APPLY OR NOT TO APPLY: THAT IS THE QUESTION

The IEC informs parents that, indeed, there is always a risk that applying for aid may have an influence on their student's admissibility and that there are only a handful of colleges that are truly need blind. The greater risk, however, is that a student ventures off to college without the financial stability to focus on his or her studies and be successful. Financial stress can certainly lead to a negative college experience and academic underachievement. Moreover, it's a recipe for disappointment if a student is admitted to a school but is unable to attend due to finances. An even worse case scenario would be to attend and incur a financial burden that adversely affects the student's and the family's style of living for years to come. The bottom line is that if a family needs financial aid to cover college costs, the IEC should recommend applying for it.

NAVIGATING THE FINANCIAL AID PROCESS

It is virtually impossible to tell a family whether they will qualify for aid. The formula is complex and depends on a number of factors. However, the IEC can advise parents that by using an Expected Family Contribution (EFC) Worksheet (available on most of the major financial aid sites such as finaid.org), they can roughly determine the amount they will be expected to contribute to their student's education. Inform parents that the EFC is based on family size, total income, assets, and number of children in college. The amount of the parents' contribution is subtracted from the college costs to determine "need." For example, explain that a family earning $150,000 with a child attending an in-state public university may not qualify for aid, yet a family earning $250,000 with two children attending private colleges likely will. Be sure to explain that the cost of attendance varies from school to school, but the federal EFC does not change based on the school Buffy attends.

Be aware, however, and inform parents that different colleges may calculate their EFC very differently from the federal EFC, particularly if a college requires the Profile. At certain colleges, the Profile is used to determine the amount of nonfederal aid to be awarded to a student. There are about 200 colleges that require that the CSS Profile be completed in addition to the FAFSA. Those colleges use the CSS Profile to assess the student's eligibility for the college's own institutional aid dollars. Typically, it is selective colleges that require the CSS Profile including the Ivies, the University of Michigan at Ann Arbor, William & Mary, Georgia Institute of Technology and the University of North Carolina at Chapel Hill. There is also a group of 23 colleges that make up what is known as the 568 Presidents' Group, which was formed by the presidents of those institutions for the purposes of assessing students' ability to pay for college using a "consensus" methodology. The 568 Presidents' Group schools also require the CSS Profile to be completed, but they treat students' assets and parents' home equity differently (more favorable to families) than the institutional methodology does.

Aid policies specific to individual colleges can cause the calculated EFC to differ by thousands of dollars. The best estimate of possible financial aid can be obtained by using the net price calculator on the website for a particular college, especially for those colleges requiring the Profile. The net price is the difference between the total cost of attendance—tuition and room and board, if applicable—and gift aid (grants and scholarships). This is the amount families will have to pay from savings, income, and loans to cover college costs.

Advise parents that financial aid planning should proceed along with college choice planning. Generally, parents should plan to complete the FAFSA or the CSS Profile soon after October 1st for need-based financial aid (the federal term for aid offered to a family based upon family income/assets). Any college or university that awards federal student aid must require that students complete the FAFSA to determine eligibility for federal aid (it works for most state aid, too). Most colleges and universities nationwide use the FAFSA as their sole application for need-based financial aid, so students applying for aid at those colleges only need to complete the FAFSA.

Students and families are able to file the FAFSA using tax information from up to two years ago.

FAFSA4caster, https://studentaid.ed.gov/sa/fafsa/estimate, helps a potential applicant determine estimated federal student aid eligibility.

EDUCATING COST-CONSCIOUS CONSUMERS

Independent educational consultants work in a cost-conscious atmosphere. For most families, the cost of higher education is a significant part of college planning. The IEC educates cost-conscious families how to find the best fit college at the best price. Step one is to encourage students and parents to work together as they explore college options. The IEC explains to parents that, however awkward, they should make clear to Buffy the extent to which they are able to contribute to her college education. If, for example, enrollment hinges upon scholarship offers, or if Buffy is reluctant to accrue student debt, the IEC points families to colleges that offer high quality education without a high ticket price. As students of colleges, IECs can debunk the myth that the more expensive the college, the better the education and the better Buffy's chances to score a lucrative job after graduation. Colleges want you to believe that if it costs more, it's better and worth the investment. While education at the schools that cost $60K+ is no doubt good, it's also true that families should look for colleges that are "just as good" that cost less. We play a critical role in the shopping process by introducing (or further informing) families about their options. Discussions about college costs offer opportune moments for the IEC to bring to the table quality colleges that are affordable. (Please refer back to our discussion of cost and value in Chapter 6.)

IECs can point cost-conscious families to programs such as the Western Undergraduate Exchange (wiche.edu), which grants students in western states a reduced tuition level at many two-year and four-year colleges. Many (but typically not all) undergraduate majors are available to students at participating colleges and universities, but students may need to meet certain grade average requirements to qualify for the tuition discount. Similar programs are available in other parts of the US, such as the Midwest Student Exchange Program (msep.mhec.org) and the Academic Common Market, sreb.org/academic-common-market, for students from many southern states. As such programs make it financially feasible for families with moderate incomes to consider out-of-state tuition, IECs make sure that families know of and explore cost-saving opportunities.

Additionally, as part of orchestrating the joint effort between students and parents to research cost-appropriate colleges, the IEC educates families about merit aid, which includes scholarships, grants, and discounts that are not based on demonstrated financial need but instead are awarded to students on the basis of their accomplishments, skills, or demographic. Students are assigned the task of finding colleges where they may be eligible for merit aid. The IEC aids in this process by suggesting that students broaden their college search to consider lesser-known schools, colleges in locations that are outside the zone of preference, or small schools that are likely to have plenty of merit aid available. Students then contact the financial aid office of the schools that interest them and inquire whether the college offers merit scholarships, how and when to apply for that merit money, and whether a separate application is required.

The IEC also educates cost-conscious families about scholarships. While students should be encouraged to apply for any scholarships for which they are both eligible and realistic candidates, it is important to keep several factors front and center.
- First, the competition for scholarship money can be stiff, especially for larger awards. Even scholarships of $500 or less attract numerous applicants. Every dollar the student can secure will help defray costs, but consider how many awards of this amount (or less) will need to be cobbled together to cover just one semester of college expenses.
- Second, many scholarships are awarded for only a single year of college. The student may be limited to receiving only one scholarship or may need to reapply every year.

- Third, many scholarships come with stipulations such as maintaining a minimum GPA, serving in the military, or entering a specific field of study. In some cases, if the requirement is not met, the student may forfeit the scholarship or may even be held liable for funds already spent.
- Fourth, unless the student already has the scholarship in hand, never count on scholarship awards to make up any shortfall in college fees.
- Lastly, families should check with the financial aid offices at the colleges on the student's list. Outside scholarships may reduce the amount of grant aid offered by a college.

Though financial aid decisions and scholarship awards are out of families' control, the IEC should also discuss the following approaches that families can utilize to reduce college fees.
- One of the most effective ways for a young person to reduce college costs is to enroll at an in-state public college.
- Living at home during college, especially if the student attends an in-state public college, can save thousands of dollars.
- Families can save thousands of dollars if a student starts at a community college and then transfers to a four-year school. Many states have strong articulation agreements under which students who graduate from a state's community college with an associate's degree are guaranteed admission to one of the state's four-year public colleges.
- Another way to cut college costs is to reduce the amount of time needed to complete a degree. High school students can earn college credit through participation in programs such as International Baccalaureate (IB), Advanced Placement (AP), College-Level Examination Program (CLEP), and Proficiency Examination Program (PEP) tests. Students may also have the opportunity to take dual enrollment classes either at their own high school or on a college campus. Students who enter college with sufficient college credits may be able to graduate in three years. This option may work well for the young person who is highly motivated and eager to begin a career or pursue an advanced degree. Some colleges offer programs that streamline requirements, which may allow a student to save a year's tuition. Examples include programs that combine a bachelor's degree with a master's degree in business or those that accelerate preparation for medical school by cutting one year from undergraduate studies.
- Students can significantly lower their college costs by being good managers of their money and their time. Keeping track of how money is spent can help a student plug the holes in the budget where cash is going to frivolous or unnecessary expenses.
- Students can earn money for college by working part time during the school year and full time during the summer. Even if a student doesn't qualify for Federal Work-Study, there are usually plenty of part-time jobs on or near college campuses. Studies have shown that rather than take away from the student's scholastic work, working ten to twelve hours a week during the semester can actually help improve student grades.
- Some colleges provide free or greatly reduced room and board to students who work as head residents or resident assistants in campus residence halls. Some schools pay students in leadership positions in student activities, such as president of the student body or editor of the student newspaper.
- Students who have demonstrated the ability to handle their course load and budget their time effectively should consider taking an extra class each semester and classes during the summer semester in order to graduate more quickly. Some colleges do not charge extra tuition for taking a heavier academic load and/or charge lower tuition during the summer semester. Another strategy for saving on tuition involves taking classes during the summer at a local community college, where costs are less.
- If possible, students should try to avoid changing academic majors or transferring from one college to another. Both courses of action may increase the time required to complete a bachelor's degree.
- Once enrolled in college, students need not give up on scholarships. An online search of scholarships yields numerous awards available to currently enrolled students. Some colleges and universities

award scholarships within specific majors as the student advances. Students should check with their individual colleges and departments for details.

- Parents should take advantage of tuition prepayment discounts if available. Colleges may offer up to a 10% discount for early payment. If prepayment is not an option, be sure and pay college fees on time because late payments may incur substantial penalties.
- Consider tuition installment plans as a less expensive alternative to student loans. Tuition installment plans allow families to pay the college bills in monthly or semi-annually installments over the academic year. Tuition installment plans do not charge interest but may charge a modest sign-up fee.

STICK TO THE SCOPE

IECs make it clear that it is beyond the scope of our job descriptions to tell families whether they should shuffle their resources in some way or get a second mortgage. Unless we have the requisite knowledge, we don't advise on such things as insurance planning, investment planning, income tax planning, retirement planning, fiduciary responsibilities, and financial plan development. If families desire professional assistance to meet their financial goals and objectives, I refer them to a college financial planner. I also frequently direct parents to financial aid officers. They can be very helpful in providing information about their institution and about the process in general.

Of course, there is a lot about the financial aid process that we should be aware of. Even though my work as a college administrator included financial aid, I have had to continually update my financial aid and college cost database. I do so by attending sessions at conferences, participating in webinars on the topic, keeping up with the financial aid literature, and talking to IECs with a specialization in the area.

The bottom line is that as IECs, we need to be aware of financial aid issues and understand the financial aid process enough to engage knowledgeably with students and parents. It is best, however, to leave money management to pros in that industry.

THINK THROUGH DEBT: TIPS FOR THE IEC TO PROVIDE TO FAMILIES

Education debt is usually considered "good" debt because it is an investment in a child's future. However, each family must determine how much education debt is acceptable. Families must make this decision, not the IEC. Again, stick to the scope of our practice.

Below are tips that the IEC can recommend to families:
- Research extensively before applying for a loan.
- Federal student loans are cheaper, more available, and have better repayment terms than private student loans. In addition, federal student loans are eligible for income-based repayment and public service loan forgiveness, whereas private student loans are not.
- Private student loans offer unlimited loan amounts, but they have higher interest rates and more restrictive repayment terms than other options.
- It may be common sense, but it is important to emphasize that families should only borrow as much as their student needs. Higher education is best viewed as an investment much like a house, car, or share of stock. Its worth depends on the skills and motivation of the primary user: the son or daughter. Good advice is to finance one's education, not one's lifestyle. In other words, advise families to borrow for tuition and modest living, not for a private residence hall room.
- Remind parents not to overlook the possibility that their student may need additional loans to complete his or her degree or to attend graduate school.

- Another smart piece of advice to impart to families is to try to keep student loan debt in sync with the student's earning potential after graduation. Some young professionals in lower-paying fields find themselves having to postpone buying homes or starting families because they are still paying off their student loans. The Bureau of Labor Statistics offers a helpful salary estimator at bls.gov/bls/blswage.htm.
- Make it clear to families that both they and their child may have loans to repay. Parents' ability to repay and the student's ability to repay are likely to differ significantly. While the student's ability to repay a loan may be affected by the profession he or she chooses, age may be a factor in the parents' ability to repay. Parents should not sacrifice a retirement nest egg to finance education costs (and thus risk becoming a burden to their child).
- Advise families not to treat loan limits as targets. They can and should borrow less than the amount allowed under the annual and aggregate loan limits. Many financial aid experts believe that total student loan debt at graduation should be less than the parents' annual salaries.
- Instruct families to determine what the expected monthly payments will be once the loan is in repayment. Typically, the loan payment schedule will be calculated automatically and attached to the loan when it is granted.
- Encourage a reality check. Advise families to consider whether they would still make the investment at twice the price, because realistically, that's what it will cost. Every dollar spent in student loan money may cost the family about two dollars when they repay the debt.

A good educational planner might offer some general financial aid advice along these lines:
- Students should receive help finding colleges where they might be eligible for merit scholarships. To do that, students sometimes have to broaden their college search. (We know, for example, that more merit dollars are available at small private schools.)
- The consultant helps the family understand the need-based financial aid process (you can acquire this knowledge by attending professional meetings and seminars offered by the College Board and others) and by helping the family interpret government financial aid methodology. Families often find that the most challenging part of the process is collecting all of the necessary financial documentation. Advise them to allow sufficient time for this.

Here is some additional advice I give to parents:
- If in doubt at all, apply for aid. Many don't apply because they think they won't qualify.
- Colleges pay financial aid officers to be helpful; therefore, parents and students who have financial aid questions or concerns should contact financial aid officers directly.
- Don't assume expensive private colleges are out of the question as some may offer significant aid. For example, in a recent year, Harvard University reported that the average range of family income of students receiving financial aid was $65,000 to $150,000. The families in this range contributed less than 10% of their own income toward meeting the cost of tuition.
- Don't wait too long to file the Free Application for Federal Student Aid form with the US Department of Education.
- Don't believe there are magical ways to find thousands of dollars through scholarships. Hard work and careful attention to college search options is key.
- Don't pay for private scholarship help; rather, sign up for free services such as fastweb.com, finaid.com, or salliemae.com. Check out other useful sites such as collegeboard.com, scholarships.com, fafsa.ed.gov, and collegedata.com.
- Don't shell out a fortune for a tutor who will help Brutus write a knockout essay for a scholarship application if Brutus is a long shot candidate and if the scholarship does not dwarf the tutoring bill.
- Don't be duped by the "unclaimed aid" myth. It is not true that millions of dollars in scholarship money lie unclaimed and therefore Brutus should forego sleep to stake his claim on these funds. In

reality, scholarship money that goes unclaimed is often earmarked for ultra-specific student categories and thus not available to 90% of students. Let Brutus sleep.

- Don't be too quick to dismiss the economic value of the undergraduate years. (That is, it's not true that where you get an undergraduate degree doesn't matter as much as where you get a graduate degree.)
- Don't be too quick to dismiss the advantages of borrowing money and/or an on-campus job.
- Be aware that both the FAFSA and the PROFILE tax student assets at a much higher rate than they tax parent assets, so it may be beneficial to move money from a student account to a parent account before filing. The amount in bank accounts to be considered is the amount in the account on the filing date.

THOUGHTS REGARDING THE WORTH OF HIGHER EDUCATION

Because money talks in our society, we are often asked to be part of a discussion on the monetary worth of higher education. It is not uncommon for families to question the value of a higher education. I find this perception particularly common if parents buy into the argument that higher education exists primarily for career preparation. Buffy's folks may wonder why they should pay $70,000 for a liberal arts and sciences education for her when she is undecided on a career. Their concern is heightened if Buffy wants to major in English.

While we are not necessarily spokespeople for the higher education industry, we have an obligation to provide arguments in favor of college attendance. Of course, not all students are college bound, and many live productive, successful, and fulfilling lives without a college education. But most families seek our services because the student is college bound. As discussed throughout this book, I believe that the undergraduate years are especially significant in terms of student growth and development. During undergraduate years, Buffy will grow as a person and solidify her values. Being exposed to a range of ideas and people is inherently valuable. And over the past decade, even dyed-in-the-wool liberal arts colleges have made room for career counseling, career fairs, internships, and other ways to make the educational experience both intellectually rich and economically advantageous. Thus, I share these thoughts with parents who ponder the worth of higher education.

I'm also mindful of the great bulk of literature that shows students reaping significant fiscal benefits from an undergraduate education. The National Association of Student Financial Aid Administrators has compiled research on the value of higher education. It can be found on their website (nasfaa.org) under the "Research" link.

FINAL THOUGHTS

Indeed, the college money scene provides mixed signals. On one hand, colleges are using more of their funds for financial aid. Colleges are giving more of their income to financing students. At some schools, less than 30% of students pay the full price (often called the "sticker price"). On the other hand, many colleges are not keeping up with consumer need, and financial aid is hard to come by. Middle income families will continue to face an uphill battle in their ability to afford higher education. Generally, however, merit-based aid is increasingly available. Many state universities are providing merit-based aid (in the form of scholarships) for students with high test scores and top grades. Finally, there is room to negotiate price, and there is financial aid discounting, leveraging, and preferential packaging. Perhaps with a swift kick in America's fiscal policy, higher education will become more easily accessible for all. In the meantime, IECs can point families toward college options that both fit their budgets and fit Buffy's needs.

(See resources at astudentofcolleges.com for a list of financial aid resources.)

CHAPTER 15

Essentials of College Planning

PREPARING FOR COLLEGE ADMISSION

College planning includes all the ways that students build skills and knowledge that will lead to success in college. It is the responsibility of the consultant to help students understand how their choices, especially in terms of academics and extracurricular activities, impact their future college options. We help them know how they can prepare (in terms of courses, tests, and so forth) for the transition between high school and college.

ESSENTIALS OF COLLEGE PLANNING

I talk to students about the "essentials of college planning." These elements are the core of preparation for college. As the anchors of college planning, these factors should be addressed as early as freshman year. The essentials include: course selection, grades, recommendations, testing, non-academic time, and individualized factors.

I. Course Selection

We help students decide on the (often) difficult task of balancing at least three factors: course level difficulty, grades/GPA, and "having a rich, healthy life." The latter includes skills and knowledge that allow students to mature, think about themselves and the world, and develop character, values, and both interpersonal and decision-making skills.

On the surface, the answer to a student's question whether to take AP English is straightforward. The student should take the course that's the natural academic progression and provides the most opportunity to learn. But the answer to such a question may be much more complex. The IEC needs to take the following into account: how hard the student wishes to work, the student's priority on academics over social life, the student's desire for an A in the course, and the student's college aspirations. It's important for the IEC to know the student well and to help the student to self-reflect so as to answer such questions honestly for him/herself.

There are students who feel that if they don't take the hardest classes offered at their high school, they won't have college options (or that, given that they want to go to Prestige U, they have to take all AP classes their senior year). Sometimes, in these situations, and when I sense that the proposed academic program might be too demanding, I ask the student to consider the distinction between 1) what's best for college admission, and 2) what's best for him or her. I feel that kids should be kids and that high school is not just about getting into college.

That said, what do colleges want? It is hard to be precise since there are so many differences in how colleges look at course selection. For the most selective colleges, students should go well beyond the requirements for graduation.

Generally, here are the high school subjects and the years often required for college consideration. Requirements for admission vary greatly from college to college and changes can occur frequently.

English: 4 years
A strong background includes language and literature.

Mathematics: 3-4 years
A strong math background is especially important for students who plan to enter technical fields, the natural sciences, health sciences, or quantitative social sciences (such as economics or psychology.) In addition, most colleges of business look carefully at the math background of applicants.

Science: 3-4 years (with as much lab science as possible)
For future science or engineering majors, four years of science including one year each of biological science, chemistry, and physics is typical.

Social Studies: 3 years
Breadth is important here. Beyond traditional history and government classes, schools offer courses in economics, psychology, sociology, and anthropology.

World (or 'Foreign' or 'Second') Language: 2-4 years of one language
Some colleges count American Indian languages and American Sign Language as well.

Electives: Students should take the opportunity to explore interests through classes in areas such as accounting, computer science, electronics, graphic design, journalism/communication, media/film studies, photography, public speaking, theology (some schools, notably Catholic or Christian, may require several semesters), social networking/new media, visual and performing arts (many colleges require some coursework in visual and/or performing arts such as drawing, sculpture, painting, photography, choir, drama, band, orchestra, dance, and film), vocational education (such as woodworking, metalworking, automobile repair), and web design.

Academic Rigor

Most high schools offer honors or advanced classes. In today's competitive world of college admission, more and more school districts (to some extent the result of parental and societal demands to get more students into "good" colleges) have added academic rigor to their curriculum. Some districts have specialized magnet schools.

AP or IB courses are usually taken during the third or fourth years of high school, either as a replacement for a required course (e.g., taking AP English as a replacement for a standard junior or senior English course), a continuation of a subject (e.g., taking AP Biology in senior year even though one already took biology in freshman year), or a completely new field of study (e.g., AP Economics or AP Psychology).

The use of AP or IB exam results varies from college to college. Some institutions use examinations for placement purposes: students are exempted from introductory coursework but may not receive credit towards a concentration, degree, or core requirement. Institutions vary in the selection of examinations they accept and the scores they require to grant credit or placement, with more elite institutions tending to accept fewer examinations and requiring higher scoring.

College Admission Requirements Example

To illustrate requirements for college admission, here are the course requirements for the University of California. Students applying for admission must complete 11 of the 15 A-G courses by the end of their junior year. Note that the fulfillment of these classes is not a guarantee of admission. Some of the UC schools take only a fraction of those who meet these minimum requirements (and admission is even more competitive for students from out of state). Here are the A-G subject requirements:

History/social science (A)—Two years, including one year of world history, cultures and historical geography and one year of US history, or one-half year of US history and one-half year of American government or civics.

English (B)—Four years of college preparatory English that integrates reading of classic and modern literature, frequent and regular writing, and practice listening and speaking.

Mathematics (C)—Three years of college-preparatory mathematics that includes or integrates the topics covered in elementary and advanced algebra and two-and three-dimensional geometry.

Laboratory science (D)—Two years of laboratory science providing fundamental knowledge in at least two of the three disciplines of biology, chemistry and physics.

Language other than English (E)—Two years of the same language other than English or equivalent to the second level of high school instruction.

Visual and performing arts (F)—One year chosen from dance, music, theater or the visual arts.

College-preparatory elective (G)—One year chosen from the "a-f" courses beyond those used to satisfy the requirements above, or courses that have been approved solely in the elective area.

II. Grades

Ah, grades. The ultimate tests of intelligence. The ultimate tests of motivation. Hmm. Are they? It's certainly debatable. What we do know for sure is that high school grades, coupled with level of rigor, are the most important admission factors. Remember the importance of asking a student these questions about his or her upcoming year course selections: Is the level of classes the highest level you can handle comfortably? Will the classes allow you to get the grades you expect of yourself? Will this schedule allow you to be a well-rounded person, a person with interests and activities that will enable you to productive student, friend, and citizen?

Juggling these variables with students is one of our tasks. It is not always easy. The super competitive student might want to do everything possible to get the "A"— even if it means forgoing sleep and facing intense anxiety. This student is under the misperception that "perfection" is what it takes to get in. Other students may feel that a B average is not good enough for any college.

So how does the IEC deal with grades? What is important is the dialogue. Yes, Brutus should work hard. After all, his full-time job is being a student. I want Brutus to realize that higher grades yield greater choice. I want him to recognize the power of his grades and to work to his potential.

But our role remains the same for an A student as well as a B student. In both cases, we are identifying good fit colleges. Unlike parents, we are not necessarily judging what getting a B in a class means; our eyes are on the match.

Parenthetically, sometimes the B student is more interesting for the IEC. It is said that most any teacher can teach an A student because these students are motivated and will pick up the material regardless of the competence of the instructor. But the B student needs great teachers in college. He or she can be reached or "turned on" by one professor.

I find that talking to students and parents about grades early in the process is productive. I like to know how the parents deal with Brutus' grades and the expectations that are part of the family dynamic. Such knowledge helps me understand what the student is feeling as the consulting process unfolds.

III. Teacher and Counselor Recommendations

Students should carefully consider the teachers whom they ask for recommendations. Students in the early years of high school should know how important teacher recommendations are and think about the importance of establishing collegial relationships with their instructors. In the sophomore and junior years, the student should target specific teachers whom they will approach as application times nears. Students should meet with teachers to talk about the recommendation and be ready to discuss things such as: Why am I interested in going to college? What do I want to learn about in college? How will I contribute to a college campus? What would I like the teacher to say about me as a student? As a person? Some teachers request a résumé so that they have a full list of the student's achievements handy while they compose the recommendation. Some IECs help students put a résumé together.

Most colleges require a report from the high school counselor. Students should be told of this part of the admission process so that in case they have not established a connection with the counselor, they know that it's beneficial to do so. Certainly, at most high schools, counselors are attentive and engaged and know their students well. However, at some high schools, particularly those that are large and urban, counselors may not know students well. In all scenarios, the IEC should encourage Brutus to meet with his counselor and to supply the counselor with information that may be helpful in writing his recommendation. Brutus might even want to send an email to his counselor stating why he wants to attend college and his plans for the future. Perhaps Brutus will share his attitudes, values, or beliefs with the counselor. Counselor recommendations are an important part of the process, but colleges understand that it's Brutus' teachers who likely know him best.

IV. Standardized Testing

Many things have changed since the first students took the SAT in 1926! The SAT has been "recentered" and "recalibrated," and the ACT is increasingly popular. The two are different tests with meaningful overlaps.

The SAT was revised in recent years. The College Board reports that the latest version of the test is designed to better "align with high school curricula," to measure "what you need to succeed in college," and to return to the 1600 scoring (800 points possible on the two sections: evidence-based reading and writing and mathematics. In the multiple choice sections, the new format has four answer choices rather than five for every question, more time is available to finish the test, and there is not a penalty for choosing the wrong answer. Sentence completions involving obscure vocabulary words are no longer part of the test; rather, questions that ask students to figure out the meaning of a word are based on context now and utilize words that "students will probably encounter in college or in the workplace long after test day." Additionally, the grammar/mechanics questions are now very much like the ACT questions in that students essentially edit an essay, choosing the best option to revise (if necessary) faulty grammar, mechanics, style, logic, and organization.

Like the ACT, there is an optional essay section. The essay now requires students to analyze and "explain how an author builds an argument to persuade an audience." The essay question is the same for every test; however, the documents students examine change for each test. The ACT recently revamped its essay section, essentially in alignment with the SAT's changes.

The ACT is comprised of four sections: English, math, reading, and science. It may be important to note to students who fear science that the science section does not focus on particular course knowledge but rather involves reading and interpreting data, charts, and graphs. Students who have not taken high level science courses need not avoid the ACT.

ACT scores range from 1 to 36. The composite score is the average of the four sections. There is no penalty for incorrect answers; they are treated as omitted questions. Most colleges want students tested on an essay, so students should take the ACT with Writing.

Since colleges do not look at the SAT differently from the ACT, I suggest comparing PSAT and pre-ACT scores to determine which test to prep for and/or take. Which percentiles are higher? Which test does the student feel more comfortable with?

Students should take a few timed, practice ACT and SAT tests on paper and then take each test on an official test date before senior year. If the student performs significantly better on one test and wants to improve his/her score, focus practice on that test.

There are several helpful online diagnostic tools to help students determine which test is better suited for them. The IEC should point students to such resources. (See Business and Office Tools for testing resources).

Students have a choice of which test and which test date to report to colleges. IECs should be familiar with "superscoring," the process by which colleges use the best parts of tests taken on different dates. In other words, superscoring on the SAT means that the college will take the highest individual evidence-based reading and writing, math, and essay scores from all test sittings. On the ACT, it means that the highest score of each section (English, math, reading, and science) will be taken and averaged to make a new superscore. Not all colleges superscore, so students need to check policies at colleges of interest.

I don't find that colleges are concerned about the number of times students take the tests, but I caution students that retaking endlessly in a quest for perfection is seldom the right approach. Research shows that the most significant improvement usually comes after the second attempt at the official test. Taking the test three times or more shows no significant additional improvement. So, I advise students that if they are happy with their score after the second try, relax and move on to other college admission tasks.

Please see Chapter 16 for information on test optional and test flexible school policies.

SAT Subject Tests
SAT Subject Tests are one-hour multiple-choice tests that focus on very specific subject areas. Less than 5% of colleges require these tests. If required at all, colleges require one or two.

There are tests in English (literature); history (United States and world); mathematics (two levels offered); science (biology—ecological and molecular, chemistry, physics); and languages (nine of which are available).

Although most students take SAT Subject Tests in their junior year, there are some tests that students should take as soon as possible after finishing a class. This is true when there is no expectation of continuing coursework in a subject within which the student is proficient. Some students take (or retake) Subject Tests in their senior year.

The SAT provides reliable information about the Subject Tests and good practice tests.

The following is a common testing timetable for a student from a high school with fairly high college aspirations:
- Grade 10: Pre-ACT and the PSAT
- Grade 11: PSAT again in the fall; either SAT or ACT in winter or spring; and perhaps one or two SAT Subject Tests in June
- Grade 12: SAT or ACT if not already taken; repeat either test to potentially improve scores (if desired); and also perhaps one or two SAT Subject Tests

Test Preparation
Test prep will not teach students the fundamental skills and knowledge that they should have acquired during high school. It can help refresh knowledge. Test prep may help students become more comfortable with the tests. Extensive test prep is not likely to dramatically boost their scores, and it may distract students from other priorities such as grades and extracurriculars.

But test preparation has become the standard, and students are advised to consider their test prep options. Beyond learning the strategies for taking the tests and/or learning about specific content areas (geometry, grammar, etc.), there are additional ways to improve one's score. For example, students can learn to relax through meditation or yoga. They can practice tension-release exercises or dealing with noise and distraction.

There are a variety of test preparatory resources available. Students can choose an extended (typically six-week) test prep class, a private tutor, study books, flashcards, computer programs, or some combination of these approaches. I like to emphasize to students that use of time *during* the test itself is an important element in test-taking; thus, regardless of the preparation method used, practicing while someone else is watching the clock makes good sense.

Helping students identify test preparation strategies is a part of the repertoire of most IECs. Some IECs provide test preparation assistance themselves (or under the umbrella of their practice). If not, consider creating an informative newsletter or detailed handout for your students that addresses test prep options. General advice about testing might convey the knowledge that colleges now leave it up to students to determine whether to take the ACT or the SAT. The newsletter or handout might list test-taking strategies, test preparation books and websites, test prep classes at the student's high school or within the local community, commercial test prep classes (both free and for-a-fee online test prep options), and personal coaches and tutors.

I recommend keeping a *record* of students' score changes in accordance with their specific test prep regimen. In other words, if I got wind that Brutus had worked with Clara Nett, a local tutor, and that she was in tune with ways to put air into his practice rhythm, I would note his test performance after his course of study with her. The same goes if Buffy's scores were piping hot or merely lukewarm after working with Mike Rowave. Such analysis helps me refer students to the best test prep options. (I guard against making referrals to those whom I like; rather, I refer to coaches and tutors who are especially good at their work.)

V. Non-Academic Time

We should encourage students to contract or expand their activity lists as appropriate. It's important for IECs to promote dialogue about high school activities. Is the student using his or her time wisely? Are there activities the student should be encouraged to pursue? Is time available? Given other priorities (like grades), should some activities be dropped? Should activities be added?

Students should do something productive with their time and understand that how well they manage time is an indicator of success in college. I share with students that colleges seek depth and commitment in activities as opposed to a mere listing of clubs about which the student has little interest. Colleges look at in-school and out-of-school activities in a similar way. Working during the school year looks great for a student whose college attendance depends on work-study. I also talk to students about their summer activities. I encourage each student to stay—or become—an interesting person. Students should keep an ongoing list of activities and honors beginning in the ninth grade.

VI. Essentials Determined by Individual Need

The final "essential" includes any factor(s) important to an individual student. While cost is important for most all college shoppers, there are students for whom cost is so significant that it should be considered at most student meetings. These students and their families may need to begin to identify potential college funding options in the early years of high school.

The same can be said for learning disabilities. While there are many students whom we see with various LD issues, there are those whose college choice is completely related to learning resources. Athletics might also be a driving factor, or for visual or performance artists, compilation of a portfolio or preparation for auditions might be central to the process. There are students who come to IECs to focus on college essays, thus establishing help with applications is essential. Also, while career planning (or at least exposing the student to the world of careers) is likely to come up through the process of advising, it may be a central focus for some students. Finally, there are families, perhaps first-generation students or non-U.S. citizens, who may need help understanding the system of higher education.

FINAL THOUGHTS

I call items such as course selection, grades, and extracurriculars "essentials" because they are the center of effective consulting. Advising students in these areas not only may help them find great college matches but may also help them be better educated and more insightful communicators! It is rare that a meeting with a student doesn't include discussion of one or more of these areas discussed in this chapter.

CHAPTER 16

The Art of the Application

ADVISING ON APPLICATIONS

In the typical comprehensive package, a good deal of time is spent helping the student work through college applications and written materials. While the first section of the Common Application requires nothing more than filling out basic facts, the second and third sections—activities and the personal statement, respectively—require a good deal of writing. Consultants typically focus on the last two sections and on supplemental material for individual colleges.

Even though I use the Common Application as the example of generic applications, others are the Universal College Application (universalcollegeapp.com), the Common Black College Application (eduinconline.com), and the application for the Coalition for Access, Affordability, and Success (coalitionforcollegeaccess.org).

ACTIVITY LIST

Admissions officials are interested in seeing how students use their time, and we can help students present an accurate and interesting picture of their extracurricular lives. Students need to convey a lot of information in a relatively small space. As they are limited to only 150 characters per entry, we help them make the most of every word.

Students often need direction in terms of what to include in the spaces on the Common Application (and/ or the other generic applications) as well as how to organize a longer résumé (if one is used). Some students don't understand that, in the college admission world, the word "activities" is defined broadly. It includes sports, jobs, internships, community service, clubs, choir, student government, fine arts performances, et cetera. It also includes summer activities, volunteer work, political activism, and unstructured activities like cooking, robotics, family responsibilities, collecting vinyl records, tinkering with computers, or participation in religious or non-secular youth groups.

The IEC can be helpful by brainstorming activities with the student. As with essays (discussed in the following section), spending time on the activity list is important. I've seen students spend weeks and weeks on personal statements and essays and little time with their activities list. That's a mistake.

When crafting the language of their lists, students should be guided to vary their vocabulary, use active verbs, and avoid vague phrasing. They should also emphasize tangible, measurable impact. For example, Whom did your activity help? How many people? How much money did you raise? So instead of jotting, "Raised money for children in Afghanistan," a student might write, "Raised $4,000 to provide daily breakfast for students attending the Kunduz Primary School in Afghanistan." Instead of noting, "I was an intern at a veterinary clinic doing different things," the student might write, "Organized diagnosis notes, sterilized tools for surgeries, assisted with X-ray analysis." Moreover, as with a traditional résumé, guide students to use present tense verbs to denote activities that are currently on their plates and past tense verbs to denote activities they no longer partake in.

Students should also do their best to inject some personality into their descriptions. Admissions officers know what lacrosse is, so why not describe the activity with a sense of humor or mention how the camaraderie or sportsmanship aspects of the game are the most rewarding?

Here are some examples of activity list entries:

Sports Editor of The *Surveyor*, School Newspaper
Responsible for brainstorming, supervising, and revising articles by student writers.

Swahili-to-English Letter Translator
Translated letters sent by supporters to impoverished children in African countries.

Math Tutor at Chambers Elementary School
Using concrete, physical puzzles and quizzes to simplify concepts, taught basic math skills to third-graders.

Here are a few general activity list guidelines:
- It's not about the number of activities listed. It is better to show significant involvement, leadership, and personal growth in fewer activities than it is to write superficially about a slew of activities.
- Admission officers are looking both for well-rounded students as well as "more pointed" students. Thus, an activity list can be equally impressive with two or three significant activities as it is with ten.
- Be sure that the students spend time thinking about the order in which activities are listed. They are giving admission offices a window into their time priorities.

- Students should not exaggerate their involvements (either in terms of contribution or time commitment); on the other hand, they should not be modest.
- Of great importance is that the description written for each activity makes sense on its own. Readers of the Common Application will not be able to call and ask for clarification. If the description is not clear, students may lose the credit they deserve. For example, saying, "I work for the *Surveyor*," would leave admission officers wondering what the *Surveyor* is and what the scope of the work encompassed. (The *Surveyor*, by the way, is the name of my high school newspaper. I was sports editor!)
- As far as leadership, it is important to describe how the student's actions affected other people. How many people were led? What gains were accomplished?
- In terms of weeks per year and hours per week, these should be the student's best guess.

Because space on the Common Application is limited, I often encourage students to submit a more comprehensive activity list directly to each school to which they are applying. I often tell students: "Don't think your accomplishments speak for themselves. You've got to share what they mean."

ORIENTING STUDENTS TO THE QUALITIES OF A STRONG PERSONAL STATEMENT

College essays (also called personal statements) allow a college to become acquainted with the applicant as a person and student apart from courses, grades, test scores, and other objective data. They also demonstrate a student's ability to think and organize thoughts. The consultant's initial role in regard to advising students about the personal statement is to orient students to the purpose of the essay, which, ultimately, is to reveal character. How does a writer accomplish such a task? Through relaying a personal experience that led to growth, learning, or an insightful new perspective about oneself or the world.

In my mind, the topic itself is less important than the revelation. Is it better that Buffy write about her injury during the first few minutes of her championship field hockey game or her interest in Japanese animation? The answer lies in which topic better allows Buffy to illustrate her character. Students should be encouraged not to describe an event; rather, the goal is to describe *how* the event shaped or influenced their character or worldview. Consultants educate students about the qualities of strong college essays: They reflect feelings, perspectives, attitudes, and values; they present the student as insightful, curious, contemplative, vulnerable, or modest. Essentially, college essays should depict the student as human, not superhuman. IECs advise students against using an egotistical tone. Nothing turns admission people off more than applicants who see themselves as the center of the universe! The personal statement should engage the reader and give him or her a more personal sense of who the student is and how well the student can articulate in writing.

Consultants also emphasize that the most time-consuming part of the college application is writing the personal statement (and any supplemental essays, which are addressed below). Students should spend time crafting their essays, polishing (to the best of their ability) everything from content to syntax to diction. Typically, several drafts are necessary before the essay reflects the student's best effort. Encourage students to make use of creative writing techniques they have learned in English classes and to ask their English teachers for feedback.

ASSISTING STUDENTS WITH THE COLLEGE ESSAY

Consultants assist as students move through the writing process. As discussed throughout the book, however, we don't write essays for students, and we should not be too heavily involved in editing. It is essential to be clear about expectations and services early in the relationship so that families understand your role. Each consultant makes a decision as to the extent to which he or she offers help on essays. What difference does it really make if you're heavily involved? After all, if you don't help, the parent or the school counselor will. Yes, that might happen. But we have lessons to teach our students and one of them—a basic one—has to do with academic honesty and integrity. Importantly, it's the student's voice that should be heard.

That said, I encourage you to brainstorm with students, to help students see how the scope of their experiences may, in fact, present potential topics. I like to have an "essay brainstorming" session to unearth some potential topics and develop an outline for the topics that seem to work best. "What would you want a college to know about you?" is a question I often ask as I begin to work with a student on his or her essay. I might then probe more deeply by asking students to describe a couple of memorable days in their lives and why they were memorable. Or I ask them to tell me about their aspirations, beliefs, and values.

I then go over the essay prompts from the Common Application (again, other applications noted above may be substituted for the Common Application) and have students compose rough drafts on two or three of the choices. (Even sophomores and juniors can benefit from writing drafts to these prompts.) Sometimes the prompt that a student is initially drawn to may not spark an engaging draft, but the second or third choice may present an avenue toward crafting a quality piece.

One of the big problems of essay work often occurs if students think that the essay will "make or break" their application, and thus they feel that they have to write a masterpiece. Such pressure leads many students to freak out and freeze. As advisors, our role is to counsel students away from self-defeating pressure and to help them think through strategies that will allow for more essay productivity.

To get students going, I give them the following tips:
- Don't stress over writing the perfect essay. Don't stress over figuring out what the college wants to hear.
- Don't fixate on writing what you think colleges want to hear.
- There are no *good* or *bad* topics. There are, however, essays that are better than others.
- Consider your values and your philosophies.
- Ask: "What would everyone else say if they were writing about your topic?" Then discard all of that and write YOUR story about the topic.
- Don't think: What have I done? Rather, think: How have I grown?
- Think "me" not "we."
- Uncertainty about things is good.
- Showing vulnerability is good.
- Because you've done something wonderful doesn't mean you will (or should) write a wonderful essay about it.
- Don't try to find big words. Try to sound human and, most importantly, try to sound like you!

Additionally, there are a lot of books on essay writing that consultants can peruse and refer to students. Some tell how to "do" an essay and some provide examples. I have not found, generally, that these books are either used very much or, quite honestly, offer that much for most students. The "example" books (*College Essays That Work, College Essays That Made a Difference* and that sort of thing) are okay, but such texts often intimidate students by making them think that their views are mundane as they compare their ideas with those of an essay from the book. Another popular author in this category is Sarah McGinty, an IEC from Boston. *On Writing the College Application Essay* by Harry Bauld is a classic in this genre. Ethan Sawyer, a former student of mine has unique and worthy perspectives about essay writing. His website and webinars are illuminating. There are a variety of free essay materials available on Sawyer's website (collegeessayguy.com).

The best strategy I've found is for students to write, write, write. Even AP English students need to set aside large chunks of time to work on essays. The more drafts, the better. I encourage consultants to ask students to write early drafts of essays—and to keep writing. I agree with author Robert Graves who said, "There is not such thing as good writing, only good rewriting."

What do I do if I've pushed and prodded Buffy to further develop her essay but the well is dry? When I feel the student lacks additional insight or creative juice, it's time to get a final draft and move on. I would never rewrite to the point where the essay is essentially mine. Contrary to what some parents think, there are no perfect essays in the same way as there are no perfect colleges. My work with Buffy has to reflect my best judgment about how far to push, how many rewrites to encourage, and how many major changes to make. I'm not going to turn Buffy into Maya Angelou. Rather, my job is to know Buffy, teach her as much as I can about the essay process and what colleges look for, and help her edit her written pieces.

In closing, I offer the following (ancient) wisdoms:
- When starting work on essays, remind students who they are writing for. College admission offices vary in how they operate, but studies show that most essays are read by "junior" members of the admission staff. That means most readers are in their 20s or 30s, and most are paid modestly. These admission officials are also fairly diverse. Most are in admissions because they regard it as a way to connect with young people. Most are optimistic and are looking for reasons to admit. These factors should be considered as students determine the story they want to tell. Avoid essays that can be interpreted as "affluent student goes on trip and discovers how lucky she is." That is a trap IECs need to be aware of, particularly in dealing with more affluent clients. An essay about hot air ballooning over Tibet would have to be amazingly compelling to work.
- Essay work starts with students reflecting, exploring, and vocalizing. Encourage students to think about the *stories* that make up good essays: insight into time utilization; analysis of what makes them think; perceptions about family, friends, animals, and objects of desire; perspectives about life, living, and the world; and so on. Sitting with teens in the sophomore or junior years to generate ideas can be time well spent. With ideas outlined, it is normally fairly easy to craft or mold essays.
- Students should think about/plan for/work on personal statements and essays throughout high school. They should be advised that if they have the option to write something about themselves (about an experience, for example) in an English class, the final draft may be worth saving for future use. They should also keep copies of paragraphs that they write about themselves when applying for a summer job, an internship, etc.
- Recognize (and tell students) that everyone who reads their essay is likely to have a different perspective. There is no objective criteria for assessing an essay. I often recommend that students choose one primary essay advisor. I tell students that I will review from the perspective of an independent educational consultant. The fact that I'm not the English teacher, or the parent, or the uncle who went to Princeton, etc. makes my perspective unique.
- In lieu of providing sample essays, save snippets from student essays and share them with your students. If I read a great introductory sentence, I might save it. If there are sentences that show particular insight or vulnerability, I save those as well. These brief passages have proven helpful to some of my students.
- Use the rapport that you've built with your students as an asset. Recognize how far you can push for improvement. Sense when to joke about an unfinished essay. Know when to prod or cajole inconspicuously. Rapport goes a long way.

SUPPLEMENTS: LET THE WRITING CONTINUE!

Many colleges have supplements to the application (be it the Common Application, Universal Application, Common Black College Application, or the Coalition for Access, Affordability, and Success) for two reasons: (1) to determine how much the applicant knows about and wants to go to the school; and (2) to ask specific questions of the applicant that the general application prompts do not cover. Many schools include the following question in their supplements: "Why us?" They want to know why the applicant has chosen to apply to their particular school. Schools use this question as one way to determine an applicant's *demonstrated interest* and to assess the student's enthusiasm for the school. Schools also use supplements to gauge a student's *fit* with the general tenor and vibe of the school. Some schools have a unique personality and want to make sure that students can find a solid place within that community.

With a few notable exceptions, the more selective a college, the more likely that the supplement will be challenging to complete. Supplementary essays often focus more on the individual and attempt to probe into a student's thinking. Supplements vary by college and often need to be written separately for each school; however, students can certainly *recycle* appropriate text and incorporate sentences or sometimes paragraphs into another piece.

Examples of Supplemental Questions
- "Why do you want to attend our school"? Related questions: "Why are you a 'good match' for our university?" "What is it that you like the best about our university?" "How will you contribute to our university?
- "In this essay, please reflect on something you would like us to know about you that we might not learn from the rest of your application, or on something about which you would like to say more."
- "Share with us a few of your favorite books, poems, authors, films, plays, pieces of music, musicians, performers, paintings, artists, blogs, magazines, or newspapers. Feel free to touch on one, some, or all of the categories listed, or add a category of your own."
- "Why are you drawn to studying the major you have selected? Please discuss how your interests and related experiences have influenced your choice."
- "What matters to you, and why?"

Students should be specific and detailed in their responses, especially when prompted to discuss their interest in a particular school. IECs can guide students to refer back to research and/or visit notes and reflections. If certain programs, research options, distinguished professors, etc. greatly intrigue Brutus, he should be sure to share his enthusiasm and show that he truly knows the school and can contribute to the student body. Admission officers can sniff out generic responses in the same way that human resource professionals have a nose for cover letters that don't speak to the nature of the position or company.

COLLEGE INTERVIEWS

College interviews may play a role in admissions but not to the degree that parents (and/or students) often stress about them. For some very selective colleges, interviews are a required part of the admission process. Some colleges do not offer interviews, and as far as the bulk of colleges are concerned, interviews are optional. But like other admission criteria, the IEC assumes that an interview is important.

An interview is often a way to sell the school to the student. Interviews promote college visits, which are a big draw to colleges that feel that seeing the campus will have a positive impact on the student. It is helpful for the student to see the interview as a place to get questions answered and to understand the particular college better.

Like essay writing, interviews can be over-coached, and preparation can be excessive. The IEC can help the student think about interview dynamics and might stage a "mock interview" with the student, asking questions that are commonly included in interviews. At the least, such an encounter can increase student confidence. Talking to a student about his or her reasons for wanting to attend a particular college can be helpful. I also encourage students to think about one or two facts about themselves they would like to convey, if possible, in the interview. In other words, what one or two qualities, attitudes, or values does the student want to share? Generally, it's best to share that which the college might not otherwise know about the student. Perhaps it's an interest in medieval history; perhaps it's taking a special interest in visiting grandmother in an assisted living facility; perhaps it's the need to walk in the park thinking about career goals.

The interview is essentially a conversation, and students who have good eye contact and present themselves as teenagers (not as robots who will say anything to "get in") are likely to have a good interview. My experience is that even students who are shy or are not natural conversationalists can have a winning interview if they focus and speak! Those who interview at colleges don't necessarily look for smooth and polished. Most are content with maturity and growing.

ADVISING STUDENTS WHEN TO SUBMIT AND COMMIT

Another component of advising on application completion involves helping students decide which track to take as far as application options.

Most colleges admit students on a "rolling" basis, meaning that applications are reviewed and acted upon as they arrive in the admission office.

While application due dates vary considerably by college, selective colleges often require applications to be submitted on or about January 1 of the student's senior year. Colleges make a decision on these applications on or before April 1. Students then have until May 1 to commit to attending their college of choice.

A small percentage of colleges (often those that are more selective) offer students the option of applying early.

Early Decision (ED) is an application option that allows students to apply earlier than is typical (often November 1 or November 15) and receive an admission decision by December 15. The ED application contains a contract that binds the student to attend if admitted. Students agree to enroll in the college if admitted and are offered a financial aid package that will meet his or her needs.

This earlier timeline is an advantage as ED applicants know where they stand early in the senior year. While other students may receive admission decisions in March and April, the ED candidate has known for many months where he or she is going to college.

Should students apply ED? It's a decision that involves serious thought between consultant, the student, and the parents. If College X is Buffy's clear and definite first choice, and she (and her parents) are ready to make the commitment, then going ED may be wise. To have a clear and definite first choice, the student should have visited and conducted a good deal of research to validate the college as the best match. A student doesn't want to slam the door of his or her college search before he or she truly explores many options.

Financial aid is another factor in deciding whether ED is a viable option. If a student is admitted ED, he or she does not have the opportunity to compare financial aid offers from more than one university. Thus, if financial aid (or cost in general) is a factor in choosing a college, it may not be advantageous to apply ED. Each institution has its own way of determining how much a family can reasonably pay for college, and the outcome of that process is only revealed after the student is offered admission. When admitted ED, students only get that one offer of financial aid.

Some students consider using ED as a "strategy" for getting in. I caution against this approach for several reasons. One is that it's the ultimate match that matters the most, and rushing into a decision for the sake of admission may not allow the student the time to consider all of his or her choices. Further, students and parents can misread the statistics and overestimate the student's chances of getting in early. For example, at College Y, the percentage of students who get in via ED is, say, 30%. The percentage of students who get in via regular decision is, say, 20%. This doesn't necessarily mean it is easier to get into College Y via ED. Why? Because the students who are part of each of these pools (the "early pool" and the "regular pool") are different. That is, often the best students often apply early, and so a larger percentage of those students are admitted—not because they applied ED, but because they are especially outstanding students.

On its website, Emory University offers good advice about ED:

"We also recommend against applying ED for students who are only considering the binding commitment for *tactical* reasons. Students focused on just "getting in" and students who view applying ED solely as a strategic move, put simply, shouldn't. Applying to colleges should not be seen as winning a game, and students who over-analyze statistical data about ED are approaching the process from the wrong direction. Selecting an ED admission plan should be about fit, 100% of the time."

All of that said, it should be noted that many colleges are eager to find students who are definitely going to attend. As such, they may give a slight advantage in the admission process to a student who has committed to attending. Colleges want to hit their admission targets, and a "bird in the hand" is often compelling.

Another "early" option is Early Action (EA). Under this plan, a student applies by either November 1 or November 15 and receives an admission decision by December 15. This is considerably earlier than getting an admission decision in March or April. Unlike ED, EA does not bind the student to attend if admitted. Applying EA is typically an easier choice as compared to ED. Students can apply to as many early action schools as they like.

Should a student apply early action? One consideration in answer to that question is the progress of the student's application and personal statements. I've seen students rush to complete their application for EA and, in their haste, send a second-rate application. Students who send essays and personal statements that are still being edited or fine-tuned may end up with their application denied. Further, if Brutus needs to retake the ACT or SAT, or add some SAT Subject Test scores to his portfolio, or needs first quarter grades to show he's doing better academically, probably none of these results will be available to be included in an EA application.

There are other "early" options. One is *Single-Choice Early Action*, an option that doesn't require the student to commit to a particular school, but restricts students from applying to other schools early. Another is *Early Decision, Round 1* and *Early Decision, Round 2*. These follow most of the traditional ED rules, with the difference being the due date. In other words, there are colleges that have an Early Decision, Round 2 option with applications (and inherent commitment) not due until January of the senior year. Finally, some private colleges have a *Restricted Early Action* option. Typically, a restrictive early decision policy allows students to apply to public colleges and universities under their regular decision program, but they agree not to apply to other private colleges or universities under an Early Action, Restrictive Early Action, or Early Decision program.

IECs know that decisions about whether to apply early are complex. Further, instructions from colleges can and often do change from year to year. Students must be guided to read the fine print to be sure they are following both the language and the spirit of the requirements of the college. Knowing the student well, the parents' priorities, and the rules of the admission process allow consultants to discuss the pros and cons of these options (particularly Early Decision) with each student.

TEST SCORES OPTIONAL: DO I DARE SHARE?

In Chapter 15, we discussed standardized testing as an essential of college planning. In regard to application completion, there is another component related to testing that IECs must have a handle on: test optional and test flexible schools. Yes, (Brutus gives an audible sigh and Buffy a yay!) some colleges do not require test scores for admission. Nowadays, hundreds of colleges welcome students to apply without submitting their scores. Schools such as Bates (via their long-term admission dean Bill Hiss) have been test optional for many decades, and others have joined in recent years. Test optional colleges include Bowdoin, Wesleyan, and Smith. Bates has the following answer to the question of whether to submit scores, "Bates has been test optional since 1984, and maintains that testing is not reflective of each applicant's future success at Bates. We firmly believe in our policy and respect each student's choice regarding the submission of test scores."

There are also colleges that are test flexible. This is a variant of test optional. For example, a school may give the student the option of not sending SAT or ACT scores but require one or more Subject Tests or the results of AP scores. Some schools will waive test submission for students who have a minimum GPA or who are applying to a specific program.

Whether Brutus should submit scores has consulting implications. Our responsibility on the admission side of working with Brutus is to advise in a way that will maximize his chances of having as many options as possible. I feel that students should view their scores holistically and—with a realistic appraisal of their courses, grades, activities, teacher recommendations, et cetera—determine whether test score submission is worthwhile. If I feel that Brutus' application is stronger (for whatever reason) without test scores, I advise that test scores should not be submitted. Moreover, my experience is that if a college or university says it is test optional, they mean it! In large measure, these colleges believe (as indicated above) that high school performance (grades) is a better indicator of success in college as compared to test scores. These schools also believe that test anxiety is real and that judging a student on the basis of a few hours in a hot, stinky high school gymnasium is not the way to evaluate a student's college potential.

The go-to resource for IECs who want the lowdown on colleges that do not require test scores for all or some of the students they admit is FairTest (fairtest.org). According to FairTest, there are over 1,000 colleges and universities that have various sorts of test optional policies, "including more than 300 'top-tier' institutions."

FairTest also posts some great "fact sheets" on their website on topics including: "What's wrong with standardized tests?", "Standardized testing and students with disabilities," and "Healthy medical school admissions."

CHAPTER 17

The Finale and the Launch

Students will receive one of the following letters from colleges: an acceptance, a rejection, or a waitlist notification. Deferral letters are another admission "action," and these decision letters are discussed below.

The end of the college planning process involves helping students decide which college they will attend. As a great IEC, your students will have many college acceptances! That is, your work helped your students generate college lists that included schools at all sides of the selectivity scale, thus resulting in students having an array of choices. Remember, however, the Schwartz construct addressed in Chapter 6. Sometimes having a heap of choices is overwhelming. And so, the work of the IEC is not necessarily complete when acceptances roll in.

ACCEPTANCE LETTERS

Receiving acceptance letters is a time for celebration. Thumbs up! High five! Fist bump!

And then we slow down and advise. I believe that students (and their parents) have a great need for our advice at this point in the process. The college planning months can be long and arduous, and Brutus may be tired of the whole process. So when an acceptance letter arrives, he may rush to make a deposit and commit to housing. In some scenarios, that works. In other situations, it is not in a student's best interest to commit immediately.

Further, I find that students (and their parents) can be influenced by things that will not have an effect on Brutus' success or happiness at college. For instance, a student may misconstrue the wording of an acceptance letter, creating a meaning far beyond its intention. Or the PS on the acceptance letter from a college might make Brutus feel that it's the best choice for him (without him realizing that perhaps the admission office of that school writes personal notes on the bottom of *all* acceptance letters).

The final college choice is a major choice. Unlike the choice of which colleges to consider or which colleges to apply to, this choice is a commitment! There are no longer reaches or "low chance of admission" colleges. We're looking at "real" options. For students in love with more than one college, the ultimate choice may be stressful. At this point in the college planning process, we can go back to the basics of the purposes of our consulting by encouraging Buffy to answer these questions: Which of these colleges will push but not shove you? Which is the one where you are most apt to be happy? Which one will allow you the most opportunity to continue current interests and add new ones? Which will give you the most opportunity to learn to be a great communicator? Where will you thrive? Where can you have the greatest chance of being all you are capable of being? Where can you learn to be an active and responsible voter and citizen?

The IEC may also advise to visit or revisit top choices. Yes, this could involve travel, but it could also involve a return to original research. What qualities made College A a great match? Why was it included on the list in the first place? Buffy can go back and read online reviews of the college, read the description of the college in the guidebooks, and/or can call the admission office and request to speak to a student. Buffy might also find it helpful to look at the research interests of faculty members in her subjects of interest.

Another tool that the IEC can employ at this stage is another discussion about trade-offs, as they are critical to so much of the college planning process. College A is an ideal size and has a great major in geology. College B is a bit bigger than ideal, has a geology program that is not as strong as College A's, but it is, overall, a better academic institution. Which to choose? We can help students weigh the options, and we can encourage the student and the parent to use "trade-off language."

We can also hone in and help students and families weigh the financial differences. College X might, with a half scholarship, cost $30,000. College Y, also with a scholarship, costs $35,000. Is Y $5,000 better than X? Is Y a better match?

I suggest talking to students and parents in February and March of the senior year about the importance of considering the final choices very carefully. Talk to them about the fact that making the right choice at the end is as important—indeed more so—than earlier decisions about colleges. Again, the final choice is a commitment! Emphasize the importance of seeking your counsel in making a final decision.

IECs should not be passive during this process. While the decision is in the hands of the student and the family, it is our responsibility to make our preferences known. After all, we likely have visited all or most of Buffy's colleges and we've had many opportunities to get to know her. Our opinions are valued.

Well worth discussing at this critical stage is the role that risk plays in college choice. Recall our discussion regarding risk in Chapter 6. As Buffy makes a decision of which college to attend, it may be in her best interest to explain to her that college should stretch students out of their comfort zones.

Remember that Buffy's need to be stretched may be different from Brutus'. At its core, a collegiate experience is a growing experience. The undergraduate years are a unique time to develop values, attitudes, and philosophies. Pushing beyond one's comfort zone means interacting with a wide range of people, taking classes in new subjects, and being exposed to cultures different from one's own. Critical thinking and intellectual engagement are two important goals. Reinforcing existing attitudes is often not as elevating as being exposed to differences. Yes, there is a place for sameness in college selection, but there is also a place for imbalance and variability. The final college choice is a great time to engage students in a discussion about these issues.

In terms of how long Buffy can mull over her decision, no schools require students to provide a housing deposit before May 1, but with big state schools (where housing may be tight), it's best to secure housing early. As soon as Buffy makes the final decision, she should send a deposit to assure her place in the first year class.

A final note on acceptances is that students need to keep their grades up. Colleges have been known to retract their offer if a student's grades fall significantly. Inform students of this fact. "Senioritis" must not knock Brutus out of the ring. You might keep Brutus on his toes by asking him to send you quarterly grades during the last semester. Encourage extra assistance or tutoring if you feel that might help Brutus keep his grades up. I often liken the final semester of high school to a "practice run" for the student's first year in college. I tell Brutus that he is on his own (now that he's been admitted) and must act responsibly by getting good grades to demonstrate the motivation needed to make for a successful first year of college.

REJECTION LETTERS

Developing a good, comprehensive college list typically means applying to some schools where the odds of admission are low. Hence, dealing with rejection is often part of the admission process. The kind words of the IEC at this point of the process are essential. Students will feel disappointed. They may question their hard work in high school. A denial letter stings and can sadden the IEC as well. After all, we've grown to know and appreciate the student. We have spent considerably more time with the student than the college has spent on his or her application. While it is tempting to suggest that the college that has rejected the student is really not the best fit, this argument can fall on deaf ears. It is also tempting to say that the admission process is sometimes unfair and that good students are often left without an acceptance while others, perceived as less well qualified, have gained admission. Both of these statements, while perhaps truthful, overlook the feeling of dejection that is typically present whenever such a setback hits.

Let's remember that it's practically impossible not to take a letter of rejection personally. Nevertheless, we can help the student deal with the news. Never has admission to college been as difficult as in the last few years. Furthermore, admission is a subjective and sometimes unpredictable process. Admission directors often state that the process is imprecise and seldom reflective of who will be most successful in life.

As discussed in Chapter 13, what drives selective admission decisions today is what the college needs, not what any individual applicant possesses. A college admission office should never dictate a student's worth. We need to help the student rally and move forward quickly.

We also know that reactions to such setbacks distinguish a person with character and grit from one who whines and loses confidence. Brutus' ability to handle a denial with guts says a great deal about him as a person and will help him be a successful college student wherever he decides to attend.

THE WAITLIST

Waitlist decisions can be challenging for both the student and independent educational consultant. When Buffy receives a letter offering a place on the waitlist, it can feel like being stuck in limbo. This is the most complex alternative because it is so tenuous and uncertain, and it is difficult—indeed impossible—to predict the outcome. The number of people accepted off the waitlist varies dramatically from school to school and from year to year. If Buffy is placed on a waiting list, she should "keep calm and carry on." This is an important decision-making time, and Buffy needs to be rational as she determines her next moves.

First, it is imperative that the student evaluate the schools that offered admission and decide which of them he or she wants to attend. It is neither feasible nor appropriate to wait to hear from the waitlist college(s) before deciding. Indeed, most schools don't know if they will have a space until well after May 1. Sometimes students feel a college is "better"—more selective, for example—if it put them on a waitlist instead of admitting them. We can point out the reality of the situation. If a student applies to two equal colleges, one school might accept the student, and the next might wait-list or reject the student. The admission decision has no relevance to the academic excellence of the colleges. Students should visit accepted schools (a second time, if necessary), and decide where to attend. Once the choice is made, advise the family to send in a deposit to secure Buffy's place for the fall. Some waitlisted students are happy to choose from colleges that accepted them and remove their names from the waitlist so that they can move on. On the other hand, if the student and the IEC feel strongly that a waitlist school is a good match, the student should "pursue the waitlist."

Pursuing the waitlist is something you can help with. Think about ways your student can demonstrate his or her continuing interest in the school. Two ideas to consider are sending a letter of continued interest and submitting his or her most current grades (if outstanding). The student should explore these and other options with you. Keep in mind that at most colleges, there is no way to calculate chances of getting off a waitlist. As such, you (and your student) need to be okay with a period of ambiguity. Further, waitlist letters often provide the IEC with the opportunity to explore the totality of the search process. It is a time when students need a boost of confidence. It is a time when it may be good to once again return to the basics with questions such as: What makes a good-fit college? Of all of your choices, where will you be most likely to be happy and successful academically?

This is a good time to share some wisdom with your student. We know that no college is perfect, and while it's tempting to believe that College X or University Y is the only place where Buffy can be happy, the truth (as we know) is that wonderful opportunities await students at many colleges. Our post-waitlist meetings allow the student to ventilate his or her feelings. The IEC can help the student put the outcome into perspective, rebound, and make his or her college years—wherever they may be—meaningful and valuable.

DEFERRAL LETTERS

Deferral letters typically come earlier in the cycle, but they are mentioned here as a type of admission decision students may receive. Students who are deferred are reevaluated later in the admission cycle; in other words, they are told, "We need more time to make a decision." If the student is still interested in the college, I often advise students to let the admissions office know of the specific reasons why the college is a good match. In other words, this is a place in the process where demonstration of interest can be helpful. Some students send additional letters of recommendation, mid-year grade report, or other materials that might strengthen their admission profile. Colleges vary in their openness to receiving additional information, and so you want to be sure your student understands the deferral policy of the college. Discussion with your student around the ways, if any, to respond to a deferral letter often is productive. Not only is the discussion of how to respond to a deferral letter important, but this is often a first glimpse at how a college sees a particular student. That is, it may be time to assess the entirety of the apply list and to make additions or adjustments if necessary.

THE FINAL MEETING

During the final meeting, the IEC addresses issues related to beginning college. This is a time to address Buffy's concerns, help her select first-year courses, and help her understand the core curriculum, and so forth. This meeting can be highly rewarding as the student prepares to embark on a new adventure. You can discuss success in freshman year: "College is a wonderful time in your life. It is filled with new experiences, new ideas and new discoveries. Your success in college is not a function of your high school grades or your SAT scores. It is a function of your determination, motivation, organization, and ability to handle a new situation."

IECs need to realize that there are students who are good at getting their feet into doors (including getting into college), but they are not as good at being successful once they are admitted. So let's not consider the student who gets into Prestige U as being in the driver's seat over the course of life's meandering path. While it's true that there are successful people who graduated from Yale, there are an equal number of productive and effective individuals with degrees from Minnesota or Temple.

You might share with Buffy the following scene from the play *The History Boys*:

> A teacher asks a student who attended Oxford, "What happened at Oxford?"
> The student answers, "It didn't work out."
> "What happened?" inquires the teacher.
> "All the effort went into getting there, and then I had nothing left," sighs the student.

Encourage Buffy to stay on her A game! Applaud her achievements and remind her that her adventure as a college student is a four-year venture. She should end her senior year with a bang, make the most of what may seem to be a short summer, and put her whole heart into a joyful and rewarding college experience.

THE TRANSITION TO COLLEGE

The IEC is central in helping students make the transition between high school and college. One of the most important ways IECs accomplish this goal is by fostering student understanding of who's who and what's what on college campuses.

IECs provide incentive for students to use their college years to develop intellectually, socially, and emotionally. College is a chance to explore and discover, to grow and wonder.

My sense is that most students could do more to maximize their talents during their college years. Some students are resourceful and take advantage of what's offered, but many need a push to engage. Those who need a nudge need to be told that the high price they (or their parents!) are paying for college includes incredible services and personnel. Taking advantage of all the aspects a college has to offer not only makes the student more well-rounded, knowledgeable, and interesting, but it also good money management! Typically, students have access to an abundance of services and amenities for little or no charge beyond tuition and fees. Guide your student to make a list of resources and activities and offices to check out during the first semester.

Below are campus resources that students should know about. Students may not need them right away or may never need some of them, but chances are good that Buffy and Brutus may visit most of these at some point in their college careers. Being familiar with them—where they are located, what they offer, what their policies are—will mean that students are one step ahead.

Be sure that your students are aware of the variation in names of college officials and campus organizations and offices. For example, "Office of Multicultural Affairs" might be "Diversity, Inclusion, and Equity" or "Gender Equity," or "Multicultural Advancement and Student Success" or even "Cultural Understanding." Also, it is important to tell students that just because someone has a fancy title (or even if she or he is a "Dean" or "Director" or "Grand Poobah"), these folks are generally very student-friendly and are employed by the college to help them.

Academic Advising
- Colleges and universities have different models for advising. Most assign students an academic advisor. The advisor may be a faculty member or a professional advisor. Sometimes advisors are assigned by major or department. Most schools have some person, office, or department that oversees the advising system. All students should know where this central office is located.
- Sometimes connected to other academic resources and sometimes separate, the learning center is another important office for students to check out. Some of the very best students use writing or tutoring help in college. Unlike many high schools where students only use tutoring if they are struggling or in danger of failing, writing and tutoring centers on most campuses are filled with the most motivated and high-achieving students. Some learning centers offer a dedicated math lab, a speaking center for oral presentations, computer labs with trained assistants, peer tutors, peer mentors, peer advisors, class review sessions, workshops on time management and effective studying skills, and reading and test-taking skills.
- Broadly, students are well advised to get to know their professors. Professors' office hours are an underutilized resource for getting better grades, college advice, and life tips that might be long-lasting.
- In addition, students should know about teaching assistants (TAs). While they are more common at large universities, even smaller colleges use them. A TA is typically a graduate or postdoctoral student who is responsible for helping the professor teach a course. Some teaching assistants grade papers and exams, some lead discussion sections, and some offer tutorial help. Often, a TA is not as busy as the instructor and may be more receptive to student questions and issues.
- Finally, I think it's important for students to find adult mentors. While these folks may not formally wear the academic-advisor hat, they may be able (and very willing) to help steer a student toward internships, career ideas, study abroad programs, and so forth. I like to encourage all first-year college students to identify a mentor (or at least a trusted adult) by the end of the first semester.

Activities
I've been thinking about the connection between involvement in college activities and overall satisfaction in college for a long time. In fact, as a graduate student and dean at the University of Denver, I conducted a study that found that students who were engaged in campus life were more likely to be happy. They were also less likely to transfer. As such, we ought to encourage participation in student activities as a way for

students to experience personal growth, meet new friends, share common interests with other students, faculty and staff, and have some fun outside the classroom.

Talking to your student about the myriad ways of becoming involved on campus is time well spent. Here is a list of activities, adopted from *College Match*:

- Academic clubs/organizations such as English Society, Business Student Association, Pre-Med Society, Political Science Association, American Society of Civil Engineers, Computer Club, Robotics Club, Astronomy Club, Writing Club
- Admissions office assistance such as giving tours, contacting prospective students, developing admission policies
- Athletics/sports/recreation such as varsity, club and intramural sports, bicycling, outdoor adventurers, sailing, Ultimate Frisbee, climbing club, floor hockey, bowling, Quidditch club
- Debate/forensics/public speaking
- Environmental groups such as Greenpeace, Rain Forest Action group, Climate Action Network, Green Residence Hall
- Fraternity/sorority (Greek organizations) sometimes organized through Panhellenic Council (sororities) and Inter-Fraternity Council (fraternities)
- Government such as residence hall judiciary board, various leadership councils and advisory committees, student senate
- International student organizations/multicultural group such as Arab, Italian American, Vietnamese, Latino Student Organization
- Job (full- or part-time) both on and off campus
- Journalism/communication such as newspaper, yearbook, literary magazines, radio stations, television stations, other campus publications
- Musical activity such as choir, jazz ensemble, marching band, rock band, chamber orchestra
- Religious groups including Sikh Student Association, Jewish Student Union, Fellowship of Christian Athletes
- Reserve Officers' Training Corps (ROTC)
- Social action/political/community service group such as College Democrats or Republicans, Association of South Asian Progressives, Students of Color Coalition, United Students Against Sweatshops, Healthy Bodies, Healthy Minds (substance abuse), Amnesty International, Habitat for Humanity, National Organization for Women
- Special interest groups such as Lesbian, Gay, Bisexual and Transgender (LGBT) Resource Center, commuter students, international students, women students (with programs on issues such as making connections, re-entry programs, gender equity, and violence prevention), veteran students, undocumented students, multicultural center
- Student programing such as planning for speakers, exhibits, or concerts
- Performing arts such as drama, dance, visual arts, improv club, comedy club, reenactment clubs (including Revolutionary War reenactments or Live Action Role-Playing Games, LARPing)

Athletics

- The athletic center helps students access many organized and recreational student opportunities. Most campuses provide gyms, cardiovascular equipment, group exercise classes, and handball/racquetball courts. Athletic opportunities also may include bike or skate shops, hiking or outdoor activities clubs, yoga, bowling, and even cha cha lessons.

Career Services

- A growing number of college career services offices have programs that are specifically aimed at freshmen and sophomore students, not just at seniors. Even on campuses without career services for underclassmen, visiting the career counseling department should be a must-do first-year agenda item. Students can take assessment tests on their skills and interests and read about a huge variety of different careers. Career services personnel can help students learn what's out there in the job market and the steps required to be prepared for professions. Most teenagers are more or less familiar with the road to law or medical careers, but which courses, skills, internships or graduate programs are right for an aspiring sommelier or CIA cartographer?

- Most college career offices also maintain long lists of internships and even paid jobs for both the school year and summers, often with tips from past students who have already held these posts.

- Students can also do practice interviews with professionals who can help build strengths and downplay weaknesses. These professionals also teach networking and resume writing skills. It is unlikely students will ever have so many career resources available again; thus, they should be prodded to make use of them.

Counseling and Psychological Services

- A counseling center is often located in or near the health center. Large universities tend to have many clinics that might be attached to the student center. Many counseling centers have a variety of professionals including social workers, psychologists, and psychiatrists. While some students seek out help for serious problems, others recognize that a counselor can serve as a good sounding board when it comes to the smaller concerns that adjusting to adulthood can spawn (relationships, dating, sexual issues, nutrition, self-image, and so forth).

Disability Support

- The Disability Support Services office provides invaluable resources for students with physical and/or learning disabilities. In regard to physical disabilities, services might include help with living accommodations, assisted technologies, curriculum modifications, peer mentors, adaptive sports, and transportation. For students with documented learning disabilities, this office coordinates exam accommodations, note taking assistance, and early registration. Support services available through this office often include adaptive technologies, accessible media (e-text, media captioning, etc.) advocacy, audio recorded lectures, etc.

Financial Aid

- This office offers the information students need on qualifying for, applying for, and receiving financial aid. As need-based aid (and some merit aid) is offered on a year-to-year basis, students have an obligation to stay in touch with this office.

Health Services/Health Center

- All students need to know where the health center is, center hours, policies for making appointments, services available, and process for emergency help. Most campus health centers do examinations, lab tests, X-rays, and perhaps even more extensive services. Importantly, the health center can refer students to local health care centers or hospitals as necessary.

- Wellness centers are becoming common on college campuses. They tend to focus on *holistic* development and support of students, including the social, emotional, intellectual, physical, financial, and the spiritual dimensions of life.

Housing

- The Office of Residential Life (or University Housing) works to provide a safe, supportive, and inclusive residential community. This office attends to on-campus undergraduate housing, family housing, and off-campus housing. Residential Life deals with items permitted and not permitted in dorms and on-campus, roommate issues, and electric and cable needs.
- The first contact students may have with a "college official" is with a resident assistant (RA). An RA is assigned to a specific residence hall floor or wing and is paid for his or her work. The job of the RA is to assist students with academic, social, spiritual, and personal matters, plan programming and community events in the hall, and manage crisis situations. An RA is typically aware of campus resources and can refer students to specific offices for additional support.

International Center

- The International Center is a great resource for international students as they transition to life in the United States. This office also works with American students as they plan to study, work, or travel abroad.

Library Reference Desk

- Even though we can access lots of information on computers, academic research still requires the services of an expert. College and university libraries have willing assistants whose sole job is to help students find the resources they need for their projects. These reference librarians have made a career of tracking down resources and are excited to help students find what they need.

Orientation Programs

- Students will find "getting to know you" sessions, informational sessions, and advising sessions during "new student" days. During this time, students learn about school policies, general rules, the honor code, etc. Orientation gives students the chance to make friends, get acquainted with roommates, purchase textbooks, and become comfortable with navigating the campus. Talk to students about how to use orientation days to their advantage. If students are unable to take full advantage of orientation, they will need to plan for other ways of learning about the campus.

Registrar

- This office typically handles questions about tuition and fees, transcripts, degree verification, and enrollment/registration. The Cashier's Office and/or Student Billing Services is often housed here.

Religious/Spiritual Life Office/Campus Ministry

- Most colleges have active religious groups and programming. If this is an area in which your student has found meaning before college, continuing involvement in this area may be especially meaningful as he or she is away from home and dealing with establishing a new life at college. Additionally, many campuses now offer mindfulness retreats and programs.

Security/Safety

- In addition to providing the usual jobs associated with police, security offices may offer free seminars about campus safety and techniques for dealing with theft in residence halls.

Student Union

- Students should realize that their peers are perhaps their most important collegiate resource. A peer might one day become a mentor, a colleague, or a boss. Students should befriend as many people as possible. A great place for students to interact with peers is the Student Union. Students stop there on their way to and from classes to grab coffee or a meal, meet up with friends, take a quick study break, read the news, nap, engage with their mobile devices, pretend not to look lost, seek air conditioning or heat, and dodge the most dodgy weather.

Technical Support

- Colleges have computing centers that not only provide technical support but also advise on different software programs. Campuses may have a computer lab offering classes or workshops. Students can also buy computers or software at discounted prices.

FINAL THOUGHTS

We're sometimes admonished not to "shoot the messenger." This cliché seems apt in regard to the IEC when it comes to admission decisions. Comprehensive college planning means that Brutus will likely be accepted at some colleges, rejected at others, and deferred or waitlisted at others. Admitting Brutus is not a decision that the IEC makes. However, the IEC certainly advises Brutus to make a wise and weighed decision. Yes, some students already have a decision in the bag (acceptance from ED, for example), but the thorough IEC knows that his or her work is not complete until the grand finale of Brutus' acceptance decision. The IEC empathizes with families, knowing that deciding on a college brings new hopes, dreams, and fears to both students and parents. We engage with and guide families using specific techniques and language. Our primary work ends when we've launched young Brutus off to college and he's decidedly content, confident, and thriving.

CHAPTER 18

Growing and Evolving

PRACTICE EXPANSION

Ah...expansion! How great it feels to write this chapter! In the early days, most IECs were solo practitioners, marketing efforts were minimal (think of a world without the internet and social media as tools for growth), and venturing outside the bounds of a small practice to service a wide range of students was foreign. Times, however, have changed. Today, many IECs are expanding their practices by adding associates or staff, marketing strategically, and reaching beyond their local community to serve a broader population.

This chapter explores three primary ways of practice expansion: changing delivery model, adding personnel, and marketing new curriculum areas. Identify your business goals, weigh your options, and expand at a pace that feels reasonable and comfortable.

I. CHANGING YOUR DELIVERY MODEL

Perhaps the simplest route to practice expansion is changing delivery model. Those who offer services on a per-consultation basis may switch to a comprehensive program. Or a common approach to increase revenue (which may also increase job satisfaction) is to trim the number of hours included in a comprehensive program, thereby freeing time to take on additional students. For example, I might tell clients that my comprehensive plan includes up to 18 one-on-one meetings. Yet if my end-of-year analysis suggests that I could be just as effective meeting fewer times—perhaps 12 meetings—I may have time to add more comprehensive students to my practice.

Another potential option is to add students virtually. In most practices, the time involved in working with e-students is less than working face-to-face. You might build clients from other states, or add international clients. Due to the time differences, working with international clients may afford more hours during the day that are available for domestic consulting. When it is midday in New York, it is late afternoon in London and evening in Abu Dhabi.

Adding group sessions to your delivery model offers yet another route to practice expansion. In addition to having clients who pay on a comprehensive basis, you might have four to six group sessions for students not already in your program. You could hold a group session at a library, church, or community center and address topics such as "Writing Tips from the Experts," "How to Build Your College List," or "What Ninth-Graders Need to Know About College Planning."

Boot camps are a popular group meeting method. Generally designed to cover one topic or related topics over an extended period of time, boot camps often attract new clients who seek a very specific scope of service. Topics that the IEC can offer are limitless and include college planning, test preparation, and essays. You might design a two-day boot camp geared for students who are entering their senior year. It could cover building a college list or essay and application completion. The variations can reflect your top area of expertise. You might create a boot camp for parents only, emphasizing how to help students transition from high school to college. Design your curriculum, establish a set fee for all participants, market your offerings, and set up camp. Boot camps can be held in your office or at another central location, and unlike traditional seasonal camps, boot camps can be held throughout the year, and mosquito repellent is unnecessary!

IECs can also expand their practices by conducting college planning programs at local businesses. For example, Hornet Foods or Bumblebee Financial Planning, Inc. might hire you to conduct lunch hour or evening programs for their employees/clients.

Some IECs have also found that working as a college counselor at a local high school (public, charter, or independent) can be beneficial from several levels (salary, networking, etc.). In the same way, positions might be available at a local nonprofit or community-based program aimed at high school students.

There are many permutations possible in respect to changing delivery approaches. Pepper business savvy with creativity, and be aware that even minimal restructuring can result in practice growth.

II. ADDING PERSONS TO YOUR PRACTICE

Many independent educational consultants work alone; however, consultants joining forces seems to be on the rise. Adding another person into one's practice may provide a number of advantages: the ability to see more students, the chance to divide the labor, and/or the ability to expand your consulting curriculum. This option is popular among consultants who cannot take on new clients and have to refer prospective families elsewhere. It is also popular among those who merely want to add variety and new directions to their practice.

There are several ways to add personnel. You can formally merge your practice with the practice of a colleague. If you and the colleague each have well-established practices and are doing the same work, it makes sense to form a partnership so that both of you are clear on solitary and joint expectations. In such a partnership, you may want to ascribe yourself the title of "president" or "principal" or "founder" to establish your position.

Another option is to hire a consultant who works for you. A common way to do this is to provide your employee with a place to practice (under the auspices of your well-known name) and to take a percentage of the income the employee brings to your practice. Beyond hiring a person to work in your office, you might consider adding associates who work remotely.

You might hire a *generalist* (someone whose responsibilities are similar to your own) or a *specialist*. If a specialist, the person might be hired to perform duties in one or more of these areas: essay writing, test preparation, financial aid, and/or career counseling. The specialist may work with students with learning disabilities or may counsel at-risk teens. Taking on an associate who does different work is somewhat easier than teaming up with someone who does the same work as you do because you each bring special skills to the table.

Tips for Expansion
Over the years, I've discussed expansion with many of my colleagues. Below are some of the notions that were generally agreed upon.
- Never take on an associate, even if that person is a good friend, without a signed agreement between you and the associate. Failing to do this is the surest way to ruin a friendship or to set up a professional relationship that's doomed to failure.
- Professional liability insurance only covers an associate if he or she is a W-2 employee. If you pay your associate as a 1099 independent contractor, which is the usual manner in fee-splitting situations, that person needs to get his or her own liability insurance. It is a good idea to insist on this step because your associate will be using your business umbrella, and you could be held liable for his or her actions.
- A non-compete clause in your agreement may sound like a good idea, but realistically these are rarely enforced. To enforce one, you would have to spend money suing your former colleague. (This has the potential of reflecting badly on both of you in the community.) Then again, you might be able to preserve a non-compete clause on moral and ethical grounds.

Clearly delineate each of your responsibilities and how both the workload and fees will be assigned and/ or divided. If you get first option for all clients, say so clearly in the agreement. If you will be training this person, don't be too generous in the initial fee arrangement. You have valuable information and have taken a long time to develop your process. Make clear when training begins, what it entails, and when it will end.
- Decide on a company name unique from your individual or company name that implies a more limited service that clearly describes what you will jointly do.
- Impress upon your associate the need to maintain confidentiality of information that he or she garners during tenure with you. It is wise to discuss this fully rather than assume that the individual truly understands what this means. We deal with children and their families; they have a right to the expectation of privacy when they share their lives with us.

- If you are taking an associate to open or staff a second or third office, you are at a minimum entitled to a percentage of the proceeds billed by that office for at least some period of time. In some cases, you may want to pay all bills associated with the additional office—utilities, lease, and equipment—and take a smaller percentage of the remaining surplus. Be sure to clearly define that percentage, for how long will you take it and, most importantly, construct a mechanism by which you can verify billable services.
- Hiring new personnel takes time. As such, it is important to consider your time availability and your desire to be a mentor.
- Make sure that new personnel are philosophically in line with your ideals, and know that this takes a good amount of communication. Making a mistake by taking on the wrong person can have devastating effects.

Finally, there are federal and state guidelines to be followed in the area of adding personnel. It is essential that you comply with both federal and state guidelines in determining whether your associate falls under the classification of independent contractor or employee. According to the Internal Revenue Service's website: "The general rule is that an individual is an independent contractor if the payer has the right to control or direct only the result of the work and not what will be done and how it will be done." The definition continues: "You are not an independent contractor if you perform services that can be controlled by an employer (what will be done and how it will be done). This applies even if you are given freedom of action. What matters is that the employer has the legal right to control the details of how the services are performed." Further explanation notes: "If an employer-employee relationship exists (regardless of what the relationship is called), you are not an independent contractor." To assist in determining a worker's legal status (and thereby all applicable tax liabilities), the IRS and individual states provide "tests" to differentiate between independent contractors and employees. Note that noncompliance may result in substantial penalties on the part of the employer. Thus, be sure to structure working relationships in accordance with applicable laws, which are always subject to change.

Agreements/Contracts

Just as you carefully construct your client agreements, the agreement with an associate must be equally clear. I have seen both elaborate and very simple agreements, some constructed in legal terms and others written in conversational format. Each has its value, and it is up to you what you use. I suggest that no matter what you use, have an attorney or trusted advisor review it before presenting it to your associate for signature.

The following sample agreements offer varying degrees of formality. Formal or informal, a signed agreement is a legally binding document.

Agreement 1
EMPLOYMENT AGREEMENT

THIS AGREEMENT, entered into on this ___ day of _____, between Brutus' College Consulting (hereinafter called "BCC") and Shanda Lear (hereinafter called "Associate").

WITNESSETH

In consideration of the mutual covenants and agreements contained herein, the parties agree as follows:

1. ENGAGEMENT: BCC hereby engages the Associate as an independent educational consultant upon the terms and conditions hereinafter set forth:

2. TERM: The engagement of the Associate hereunder shall commence as of the date hereof and shall be for no specific term. Associate shall be engaged on an at-will basis. Upon termination of this Agreement, Associate shall be entitled to receive all compensation earned by him/her through the date of the final day of active engagement.

3. COMPENSATION & DUTIES: During the term hereof, Associate will be paid XXXX dollars per hour during the training period. The training period ends when BCC determines that Associate is capable of handling clients on his/her own. Upon completion of the training period, Associate will receive XX% of the client fee for the first 10 clients worked with and XX% of the client fee for each client thereafter. Associate will perform the duties and responsibilities as directed to her by BCC.

4. ANTI-PIRATING PROVISIONS: The Associate recognizes and agrees that BCC is engaged in a highly competitive business and that during his/her engagement (s)he will have access to BCC's confidential information and client base. The Associate agrees that upon termination of this Agreement (s)he will return all confidential information, and will not, for a period of one (1) year, disclose or use any of BCC's confidential information for the benefit of him/herself or any other person or entity. Associate further agrees that upon his/her termination, (s)he will not, for a period of one (1) year, directly or indirectly solicit any of BCC's customers or potential customers regarding services relating to or similar to those provided by BCC.

IN TESTIMONY WHEREOF, the parties have executed this Agreement on the day and year first above written

YOUR COMPANY NAME: ASSOCIATE:
By: By:
SIGNATURE: ASSOCIATE'S SIGNATURE:
TITLE: ASSOCIATE'S TITLE:

Agreement 2

This agreement is between Mary Super Consultant (hereinafter named the Director) of Mary's Consulting Company (hereinafter named MCC, Company) and Joanne Newbie (hereinafter named the Associate).

A. Overview of collaboration:
1. The Associate shall hold the title of Assistant Director during her training period which shall be deemed to have ended in six months.
2. The Associate shall hold the title of Associate Director once membership in one association is attained and six months have passed.
3. The Associate may not work with clients outside either the MCC umbrella or the scope of this agreement.
4. Pro bono work is encouraged, and the Associate must bring each case to the attention of the Director.

B. Splitting of fees:
1. The Associate will receive XX% of the fees paid by clients in which the Director had a marketing, selling, or closing role. Clients who call the office or respond via the MCC website without expressing a preference will be considered to fall in this category since they come by virtue of the reputation the Director has developed in the community.
2. The Associate will receive XX% of the fees paid by clients she acquired on her own. This starts immediately. [NOTE: This is an incentive for the Associate to beat the bushes to get clients. Obviously, the percentage to the Associate in this category is higher than the percentage in Item 1. I have heard of 60/40, 70/30 and even 50/50 splits depending on the generosity of the primary consultant. Be cautious! Remember that you are still paying all the operating bills!].
3. All invoices and payments will be made through MCC, and the Director will compensate the Associate immediately upon receiving payment. In cases where time payments are made, the distribution will occur as a proportion of each payment.
4. The Director and the Associate will discuss the terms of any client agreement for anything other than a full service package, and the fees will be split as specified in Items 1 and 2 above.
5. If the Associate organizes a community education program or seminar where participants pay fees, she will receive XX% of the profits and the Director will receive XX%.

C. Promotion and marketing:
1. MCC will provide the Associate with social media access, business cards, stationary, folders, promotional ideas, and other office and marketing supplies as needed and appropriate.
2. The Director will market MCC throughout the local area. The Associate may participate in these networking activities and presentations as she wishes.
3. The Associate may arrange marketing seminars on her own with the Director's approval so that the Company message is consistent and the materials used are valid.
4. The Director will review any materials sent out under the MCC name. Materials which the Associate develops and uses during her tenure with MCC become the property of MCC.

D. Record keeping:
1. The Associate will provide contact and academic information for addition to MCC's database.
2. The Director will keep track of payments through this database.
3. The Associate will keep the Director informed of her schedule to ensure sufficient client coverage is available at all times.
4. The Associate will maintain confidentiality of all client records and of the client list itself.
5. The Associate will maintain confidentiality of all business matters of the Company.

E. College search and admissions processing materials:
1. All MCC consultants will use the same process and materials including online and social media communications. Changes to the process and materials can be discussed with the Director at any time. Newly developed materials and forms become the property of MCC.
2. MCC will provide the Associate with the materials she needs for each client.

F. Evaluation:
1. The Director will be responsible for distributing evaluations/surveys to clients in the spring of the student's senior year. She will share these evaluations with the Associate.
2. The Director will advise the Associate of her progress as a consultant and the likelihood of a continued collaboration via a quarterly meeting.

G. Associate's responsibilities include, but are not limited to:
1. Enrollment with a provider of professional liability insurance within three months of beginning the association with the Director.
2. Beginning the process for membership in the Independent Educational Consultants Association (IECA) and/or the Higher Education Consultants Association (HECA) immediately on signing this agreement.
3. Join the National Association for College Admission Counseling (NACAC) within two years of association with the Director.
4. Attend the IECA Summer Training Institute and/or the HECA new member orientation within two years.
5. Take courses or work toward earning a certificate through the University of California, Irvine Independent Educational Consultant Program beginning immediately.
6. Attend at least one professional conference in the first year of association. This may be HECA, IECA, or NACAC.
7. Develop a schedule of college visits within two years of the signing of this agreement. The goal is 25 visits per year. The Director will provide a list of consortia tours for the Associate to consider.
8. Costs for items 1 through 7 above are the Associate's to absorb.

H. Director's responsibilities include, but are not limited to:
1. Maintenance of a website to promote the firm.
2. Ongoing advertising efforts (written and electronic) which include listing the Associate.
3. Maintenance of office space, secretarial services as necessary, and needed office supplies.
4. Sharing all financial information that may affect the Associate.
5. Providing business cards, office supplies, social media access, and office equipment necessary to accomplish the tasks involved in serving clients.
6. Planning seminars and/or writing blogs to develop the client base.
7. Maintenance of client database via the XYZ Management System. This includes financial, academic, and biographical information as required to both serve the client and divide the fees.
8. Assuring billing on a regular basis.
9. Providing regular feedback to the Associate to assist in her development as a consultant.

Agreed to on this _____ day of _____, year _____.

COMPANY NAME: ASSOCIATE:
By: By:
YOUR SIGNATURE: ASSOCIATE'S SIGNATURE:
TITLE: TITLE:

Agreement 3

EMPLOYMENT, CONFIDENTIALITY, NON-COMPETITION AND NON-SOLICITATION AGREEMENT

I, _____, in consideration of my continued employment at will with Buffy College Preparatory Corporation ("BUFFY COLLEGE PREP" or "BCP"), and the salary or other compensation to be paid for my services during my employment with BCP, agree as follows:

1. Duties.
   A. Requirements of Position: My position title with BCP is College Counselor. As such, my job duties for college counseling include: using BCP's philosophy for creating college lists, communicating with parents, and being a private facilitator for the student and family as they go through the college search and application process. I understand that reasonable customer service is a priority for students and their families; as such, I will give my contact information to clients.
   B. Duty of Loyalty: During my employment with BCP, I will devote my best efforts and full loyalty to my employment with BCP, and I will hold no other employment or engage in any other business that would interfere with my ability to fully perform my job responsibilities at BCP.

2. Confidential Information.
   A. Definition of BCP's Information: As used herein, "Confidential Information" includes, but is not limited to: (a) current and former client and student lists; (b) prospective client and student lists; (c) curriculum; (d) training materials; (e) test preparation materials; (f) counseling materials; (g) the identities, contact information, buying habits or practices of any of the Company's customers; (h) the Company's advertising and marketing strategies, methods, research and related data; (i) the names of any of the Company's vendors or suppliers; (j) the cost, type and quantity of materials and/or supplies ordered by the Company; (k) the prices at which the Company obtains or has obtained or sells or has sold its products or services; (l) the Company's costs, methods and objectives; (m) any technical information owned or created by the Company or licensed from another entity; (n) any inventions, techniques or proprietary methods; (o) any "trade secrets" as such term is defined in the Uniform Trade Secrets Act and applicable common law or any other Confidential Information of, about, or concerning the business of the Company; and/or (p) such other Confidential Information or data of any kind, nature, or description as may be designated as "Confidential" from time to time by the Company. Notwithstanding the foregoing, I understand that the definition of "Confidential Information" does not include employee terms and conditions of employment and that I have a right under the law to discuss my terms and conditions of employment with others.
   B. Non-Disclosure of Confidential Information: I acknowledge and agree that, during my employment with BCP, I have been and will be privy to confidential nformation, which has or will be developed by BCP at substantial investment of time, effort and money and that such Confidential Information would be useable by me to compete against BCP, to the commercial detriment of BCP. I agree that I will not divulge, disclose or communicate in any manner whatsoever, either directly or indirectly, any Confidential Information (as defined herein) to any person or entity outside BCP, nor will I use Confidential Information in any way except as required in the course of my duties for BCP or as authorized in writing by BCP. I agree and acknowledge that this non-disclosure obligation continues, without limitation, throughout my employment with BCP and after the cessation of my employment with BCP.

3. Access to and Return of BCP's Property.
   A. BUFFY COLLEGE PREP Property: I acknowledge and agree that the following is BCP's sole and exclusive property: (i) all documents, files, records, telephone records, recordings, texts, accounts,

notebooks, computer hardware, software and files, electronic mail, or other storage media and any copies thereof, containing, referring to or constituting BCP's Confidential Information, as defined in Section 2(a) of this Agreement, (ii) all documents, files, records, telephone records, recordings, accounts, notebooks, computer hardware, software files, electronic mail, or other storage media and any copies thereof, whether or not containing, referring to or constituting BCP's Confidential Information, which are obtained or created at BCP's expense, using BCP's property or equipment, or during my BCP work hours; and (iii) all equipment, computers, tablets, smartphones, supplies, vehicles, furniture, file cabinets, lockers, product samples, books, training materials, periodicals and other materials provided to me by BCP, in the course of my employment with BCP, or at BCP's expense.

B. Access to BCP Property: I acknowledge and agree that BCP shall have full right of access to all BCP property as defined in Section 3(a) of this Agreement, that I have no privacy rights with respect to any such property, and that I will turn over to BCP any such property immediately upon request.

C. Return of BUFFY COLLEGE PREP Property: I agree that upon the termination of my employment with BCP, I will immediately return BCP any and all BCP property in my possession or under my control.

4. No Solicitation of Customers, Employees and Sources of Supply.

A. Customers: During the period of my employment with BCP and for a period of two (2) years after the cessation of my employment with BCP, I will not, in any manner whatsoever, directly or indirectly, on my own behalf or on behalf of or in association with any other person or entity, except for the benefit of BCP, (a) solicit, procure, accept, refer, place, service or encourage the business of any customer of BCP with whom I had knowledge, contact or dealings during my employment, (b) encourage any customer to discontinue doing business with BCP, (c) reveal the names and addresses of any such customers to anyone without the customer's express, written permission, (d) provide information relating to these customers to anyone else or conspire with others to enable them to solicit or obtain said customers or to do what I am prohibited from doing myself, or (e) interfere in any manner with BCP's relationship(s) with its customers. The term "customer" includes the family members of students, including, but not limited to, siblings, step-siblings, and cousins.

B. Employees and Sources of Supply: During the period of my employment with BCP and for a period of one (1) year after the cessation of my employment with BCP, I will not, in any manner whatsoever, directly or indirectly, on my own behalf or on behalf of or in association with any other person or entity, solicit or attempt to hire or attempt to induce, encourage or entice (1) any employees of BCP to terminate their employment with BCP or (2) any vendor, supplier, or licensor to discontinue dealing with BCP or to in any way affect the employees' or suppliers' contractual or economic relationship with BCP. After the cessation of my employment with BCP, I also will not disparage BCP to current BCP employees.

5. Non-Competition.

A. Purpose: I understand that the purpose of this provision is to acknowledge certain of my responsibilities relating to the protection of Confidential Information, trade secrets and protection of the business of BCP from improper use and/or unfair competition for a limited period. I acknowledge and agree that I have Confidential Information belonging to BCP and an in-depth knowledge of its operations and business relationships with suppliers and customers to which I would not have had access but for my association with the Company and which would be damaging to BCP if disclosed or used in any capacity other than my employment for BCP. I further acknowledge and agree that my services to BCP, described herein, are critical and unique and have been cultivated through extensive experience provided by BCP and after considerable resources expended by BCP.

B. Restrictions: During the period of my employment with BCP and for a period of two (2) years after the cessation of my employment with BCP for any reason, I agree that I will not, in any manner whatsoever, directly or indirectly, own or have any ownership interest in any business which is engaged, directly or indirectly, in the business of helping student with their college search, or college essays within a 20-mile radius of where I performed services for BCP during my employment provided.

6. Obligation to Inform BCP.

A. I agree to inform BCP, upon the acceptance of employment subsequent to employment with BCP, of the identity of new employer, the nature of such employer's business, and the new position, duties, and responsibilities.

7. Obligation to Inform Succeeding Employers.

A. Until the expiration of two (2) years following the termination of employment with BCP for any reason whatsoever, I agree to inform each subsequent employer, prior to accepting employment, of the existence of this Agreement and to provide such employer with a copy of this Agreement.

8. Miscellaneous.

A. Enforcement: I acknowledge that the provisions in this Agreement are reasonable and necessary for the protection of BCP's business, that my breach of any provision in this Agreement will result in irreparable injury to BCP's business, and that BCP's remedy at law for damages in the event of such breach will be inadequate. Accordingly, I agree that, in addition to any other remedies to which BCP shall be entitled to seek and obtain both preliminary and permanent injunctions to prevent and/or halt a breach or threatened breach of any covenant contained in this Agreement. I further agree that should I breach this agreement and/or dispute or challenge the enforceability of any provisions of this Agreement, the restrictive periods set forth in Section 5, above, shall be tolled until such time as my breach has ended or until my challenge or dispute has been resolved. If BCP is awarded an injunction or any other remedy in connection with the enforcement of such provisions, _____ agrees to pay all costs and expenses (including Attorney's fees) reasonably incurred by BCP in such enforcement effort.

B. Effect of Agreement: This Agreement supersedes all previous written or oral agreements with respect to the subject matter hereof. I acknowledge that this agreement does not create a contract of employment for any particular term, and shall not be deemed to alter the at-will nature of my employment with BCP. I further acknowledge and understand that either BCP or I can terminate my employment at any time, for any reason or no reason at all, with or without notice. I further acknowledge that no verbal or written statements of any kind by any person may contradict or alter the terms of this agreement or my at-will status, unless contained in a separate written agreement and signed by a BCP partner. Any waiver of any terms or conditions hereof or thereof shall not be construed as a continuing waiver but shall only apply to the particular transaction involved.

C. Severability: If any provision or part of a provision of this Agreement is found to be in violation of law or otherwise unenforceable in any respect, the remaining provisions or part of a provision shall remain unaffected and the Agreement shall be reformed and construed to the maximum extent possible as if such a provision or part of a provision held to be in violation of law or otherwise unenforceable had never been contained herein.

D. Applicable Law: The parties hereto consent to the personal jurisdiction and venue of the courts, (state or federal) located in the State of Mississippi. This Agreement shall be governed by, and construed in accordance with, the laws of the State of Mississippi as though made and to be fully performed in said State.

E. Successors and Assigns: This Agreement shall be binding upon my heirs, executors, administrators and assigns and shall be enforceable by BCP and its successors and assigns.

Employee: Date:
Signature:

Witness: Date:
Signature:
Witness Printed Name:
Witness Address: Witness Telephone & Email:

III. BECOMING A SPECIALIST

The options for specialization have expanded exponentially in recent years. There are still consultants who are generalists, but more and more are deciding to add a specialization. The specialization can either replace a standard curriculum or, more commonly, a specialization is added on top of existing tasks. While there is overlap, the following are two broad categories of expansion: one-step specialization and those that involve two or more steps.

"One-Step" Specialization

IECs can use their existing curriculum but add targeted groups on the basis of learning about a new group of students. In prior chapters, we discussed some of the populations that can be added to a practice: athletes, LGBTQ, first-generation, international students, LD, students considering community colleges, and students interested in attending trade schools.

"Two-Step Plus" Specialization

Two-Step Plus involves changing your curriculum in order to expand and could include any of the specializations mentioned in the "one-step" category. For example, if you are already well versed in community colleges, it would fit in the category above. If, however, you need a learning plan, adding community colleges would fall under this two-step category. The learning plan would include research, visits to some two-year schools, and/or talking to knowledgeable colleagues. The same can be said for working with athletes. Being a consultant with general knowledge about NCAA rules and other basics is one type of specialization. Being informed about the intricacies of consulting with figure skaters or fencers would likely require more than one step.

Below are many areas of "two-step plus" specialization.
- Countless families find the financial aid process difficult to navigate. An IEC can become a specialist in financial aid matters by adding credentials, taking courses, and attending relevant conference sessions. Your professional association might have an affordability committee which would present learning opportunities.
- Specializing in career planning is on the rise. Please refer back to Chapter 8 for educational opportunities designed to prepare for this niche. See resources at astudentofcolleges.com for more sources of information on these topics. Also see Chapter 6 for a discussion of students' need for such services.
- Specializing in consulting performing or visual arts students may be especially appealing to IECs who love the arts and want to guide new generations of talent. The IEC who wants this specialization is advised to develop a learning plan that might include perusing the many books and websites devoted

to these areas, becoming familiar with portfolio preparation and tryout procedures, and talking to folks in the field (such as teachers or counselors at performing arts high schools and colleges).

- Consulting graduate students is another growing specialty. While there are similarities, the graduate student admission process is different from undergraduate admission. There are IECs who are graduate generalists and those who are graduate specific. In the latter category are those who specialize in a particular area of graduate school: for example, law schools, medical schools, and/or MBA programs.
- Specializing in consulting parents about boarding schools may interest some IECs. Recall that IECA started with boarding school consultants. Like in the college sphere, the learning curve in this area leans heavily on personal visits to schools. This specialization may intrigue IECs who wish to work with younger kids.
- Therapeutic consulting is a specialty that requires considerable training because of legal risks and emotional responsibility. This specialization involves working with students who need a residential treatment center, wilderness therapy, a psychological or behavioral hospital, or other types of individualized remediation. IECA (iecaonline.com), the National Association of Therapeutic Schools and Programs (natsap.org), and Therapeutic Consulting Association (therapeuticconsulting.org) have information on training requirements in this area.
- International travel lovers may wish to specialize in consulting international students. Such consulting has several sub-specialties. An IEC might visit colleges in Europe and build a specialization as a knowledgeable person to go to for those looking to attend college there. Another option is for the IEC to seek students from countries outside the US. The learning curve includes being familiar with US admission policies for international students and becoming proficient in the ways that colleges vary in their inclusiveness of students from different parts of the world.
- Finally, consultants can add a specialization in gap year programs. There are students who, for a variety of reasons, want to explore areas of interest before beginning college. Specialists in this area have in-depth knowledge about specific programs domestically and perhaps internationally. Once Brutus decides to study German or build yurts in the backcountry of an African village, the IEC can match programs to his desires. Before leaving the gap year discussion, I want to address a couple of IEC issues involved in advising students on gap year options. To begin, the IEC needs to deal with the misperception that if a student strays from the straight and narrow academic path, he or she won't ever go to college. Even worse, some parents believe that if Buffy takes a gap year, she may be undermining her potential for life success. Contrary to that notion, my years of practice convince me of the value of a year off for many students. A gap year might even help with eventual college admission. Many colleges see a productive gap year as evidence of a student's motivation and variety of interests. Colleges typically ask for an account of how this time was used. The gap year specialist can help Brutus make excellent use of his time.

FINAL THOUGHTS

Each of us makes a choice about growth within our own practice, and the word "evolve" means something different to each of us. You may be comfortable staying small and serving the same client base throughout your career. That's okay. If you are serving those students well and deriving satisfaction from your work, so be it. But even serving the same clientele is not without growth potential. Each of us can learn new consulting techniques or learn about new programs at colleges. And we should! The most successful practitioners—no matter how small or how large the practice—continually self-reflect and commit to self-improvement.

Alternatively, you may want to move in new directions. You may feel that bigger is better or at least that different is better. You may feel a need for intellectual stimulation or to meet the needs of additional (or more varied) students. Indeed, there is room to grow in this field. There are colleagues who can help and mentor you if you want to change directions or alter your current delivery model. My hope is that you keep pushing yourself and thinking about ways to make more of an impact on the lives of young people. To do so, it's helpful to regularly evaluate yourself as an IEC, and periodically review Appendix B where you will find "Assessment of My Practice." This instrument can be used again and again to help you grow and evolve—or merely just re-evaluate.

CHAPTER 19

A Principled Practice

I think it is fair to say that the future of the profession of independent educational consulting depends on the ethics of its practitioners. Those entering the field now are coming in at a time when there are ethical standards in place. NACAC, IECA, HECA, and the American Institute of Certified Educational Planners have all developed codes of conduct that can serve as models for current professionals. (Please see Appendix A.)

Societies have always had rules, regulations, expectations, and values that have guided their history. The same is true of professions. Hippocrates said, to paraphrase, "do no harm." When I think of ethical guidelines for consulting, the following admonitions come to mind. I consider them best practices. The guidelines below recap many of the principles discussed throughout the book. Compiled as a whole, these standards offer a framework for how to operate a principled practice.

1. It's best practice to under-promise and over-deliver.
2. It's best practice not to take advantage of the vulnerability of students or parents going through an often stressful life change. Making decisions about where to attend college and how to pay for it are

major life decisions. Like the wedding or the new baby business, unscrupulous consultants can take advantage of family defenselessness by overstating the importance of their work and/or charging too much. I am chagrined and dismayed when I hear reports of consultants who charge extraordinarily high fees, who over-promise, and who use family vulnerability or college-going anxiety for self-gain.

3. It's best practice to establish with clients realistic expectations of the benefits and results of our services with clients.

4. It's best practice to recognize that consultants are paid for advice, counsel, and good judgment and to make that emphasis known to clients. Independent educational consultants should not advertise that they guarantee admission or have contacts that will lead to admission. Part of this is to clearly articulate the breadth but also the limits of your service. Families pay for reasoned and knowledgeable advice. They don't pay us to write essays for their students or to complete students' applications. They don't pay us to "fix" students' weaknesses. We help students discover qualities about themselves that they can share with college admission officers. Thus, families don't pay us to market an applicant or to strategize ways to get Buffy into Yale. We don't "package" students (in the sense that we don't work to fit students into a structure that differs from their strengths and weaknesses). Parents also don't pay us to be their travel agent or hired nag.

5. It's best practice not only to learn as much as you can and to keep contact with colleagues, but also to be active in a professional association. It's best practice to care about doing your best in representing your profession.

6. It's best practice to keep current: attend conferences, read current publications in the field, join and participate in organizations relevant to your area(s) of practice; continually visit colleges. Independent college counselors strive for professional excellence and should put a high priority on continuing education and professional development.

7. It's best practice to avoid conflicts of interest (or the appearance of), and that the consultant discloses to clients any circumstances that might influence judgment or objectivity. It's best practice not to accept fees or remuneration from colleges for the placement of a student/client. It's best practice to disclose any ties with a college.

8. It's best practice to represent colleges fairly, honestly, and without bias. One should be completely objective in recommending colleges. Where one went to college or his or her liking or disliking of admission procedures or admission officers at individual colleges should have no bearing on the consultant's recommendations.

9. It's best practice not to regard college admission as a game to be played or a prize to be won.

10. It's best practice to empower students. When the consultant does the work for a student, the consultant creates an unhealthy co-dependency. Yet, I agree with those who say that sometimes hand holding is required. I find that to be particularly true of first-generation college students and others who are less savvy about admission. What I try to avoid is hand holding when it means discouraging student growth. Each of us needs to judge the level of involvement we have with our students and make the determination if or when to step back. Sometimes in an effort to get things done, it is easier to "just do it" for the student. Such efforts, even if well intentioned, are not professionally sound.

11. It's best practice to recognize special gifts in every student. Getting into Wooster is just as important as getting into Princeton and can have the same, or greater, educational value.

12. It's best practice to discuss fees openly and frankly with families at the beginning of the relationship.

13. As possible, it's best practice to give of your knowledge and experience to those who may not have the ability to access your services. The possibilities are endless but include volunteering at college fairs or other community programs aimed at college planning, seeing pro bono clients, and writing articles for neighborhood papers. It's best practice to be involved with community-based organizations.

14. It's best practice to work cooperatively with local high school counselors. Consultants should encourage families to seek out their high school counselor and take advantage of what the school

offers in terms of programs, resources, etc. Sometimes school counselors know that a consultant is working with one of their students; most of the time they do not. Consultants who put down high school counselors do nothing to help the profession.

15. It's best practice to interact with admission officers as colleagues with the same goal: to find a good match for each student. Beyond the most selective institutions, most colleges encourage dialogue with consultants. Yet, even at these colleges, the bulk of dialogue pertains to "fit" issues rather than "admission" issues. We are, from an admission standpoint, mostly silent partners in the process. Consultants don't get clients into college; rather, we provide a perspective about colleges based on travel to colleges and a keen understanding of the process. It's best practice not to call colleges to find out how a student's application is progressing or for any other admission purpose. If a mom or dad says, "Oh, I know Buffy will get into Washington U. because I know the President," or "Buffy will surely get in since I've given money each year since I graduated," it's best practice to tell the parent that your estimate of admission chances is not affected by anything except things you know: the student's credentials and your sense of what the college is seeking in candidates. Consultants don't control admission decisions; consultants control their own knowledge of the student and how much they know about the admission competitiveness of that school. IECs who call admission offices for inside information are promoting the old image of the consultant as jawboning for admission.

16. It's best practice not to discriminate on the basis of sex, race, color, religion, sexual orientation, nationality, or ethnic origin.

17. It's best practice to protect student privacy and to share confidential information only if the family gives explicit permission.

18. It's best practice to be totally forthright in our advertising claims.

19. It's best practice to provide a positive voice in the dialogue of the transition between high school and college.

20. It's best practice to only accept clients for whom you have the requisite experience and competence to serve; otherwise, refer to a colleague who can better serve the client. It's best practice to know how to say, "I don't know."

21. It's best practice to meet the student at least once face-to-face. Ours is an interpersonal profession; it works as a result of the give and take of conversation. It works because face-to-face encounters allow for maximum visibility of communication channels such as voice pace and intonation, timing, facial expression, posture, personal appearance, and gestures. Further, rapport builds as people sit in the same room and share an interactional space. That said, FaceTime, Skype, Zoom, and so forth have allowed IECs to connect electronically. That change broadens the number of students we can help. The benefits and disadvantages of e-consulting were discussed in Chapter 5.

22. It's best practice to be sure every student has your educationally sound choices.

23. It's best practice to encourage students and parents to follow directions given by colleges: If a college explicitly forbids a student from applying to more than one college in an early decision plan, the IEC ought to direct the student accordingly. This is also true about tuition deposits, original essay preparation, and so forth.

24. It's best practice not to fudge it when you do not have an answer. Sure, fudging a little is a temptation that can be hard to resist. Even after years of doing this work, I am occasionally tempted to respond with an answer I'm not so sure about. I wish I knew why that is. Maybe it's because I want to be seen as the "authority" or the "expert." Maybe it's because families are paying me for advice, and I feel the need to sound knowledgeable. But I remind myself to resist the temptation. My current and future clients and fellow IECs deserve no less of me.

25. It's best practice (in all practices) to do no harm.

As stated, the best practices listed here are not exhaustive; rather, they are representative of the sorts of operating standards upon which an ethical practice is based.

Remember that consultants rely heavily on word of mouth. If we operate ethically and families are pleased, they will send others our way. Any IEC who promises Ivy admission is simply not going to last long. Ultimately, the failure rate will catch up, and the client base will evaporate. Such people can hang on for a while, even many years, but they will eventually fade from the scene. There are many examples of such failure over the last decade.

Unfortunately, as in many fields, the unethical and the unscrupulous can get the most ink. Almost a decade ago, newspapers published articles about consultants charging $30,000 and hobnobbing with admission deans at country clubs in order to get their students admitted. My feeling, and certainly my hope, is that excesses will be less and less tolerated and that families will see IECs for what they are: students of colleges and the transition process, guiders, advisors, and matchmakers.

As noted throughout the book, I would stop seeing a family if there is a significant disconnect between my own ethical base and theirs. I don't control what families do outside my office, but I do control my advice and my condemnation when the student or the family even appears to be contemplating an ethical lapse. Often, just telling the family about the potential of a problem is enough. Parents who think "everyone" sends in multiple deposits, for example, are told that is not the case. (Further, that "everyone" does it doesn't matter. What matters is my advice that it's not the right thing to do.)

We are teachers and advice givers. We expose unethical parental and student behavior and comment on it. We're not clergy, but we have an obligation to be crystal clear about our expectations of appropriate student and family behavior.

We all have a responsibility to uphold the integrity of our profession. A couple of years ago a consultant from Denver asked me if I viewed her as a threat. If she practices ethically, she's no threat to me. Prospective clients will explore, and she'll get some families, and I'll get others. What will hurt me is if a consultant is unethical, or if a consultant promises more than he or she can deliver; such a consultant hurts our growing reputation.

The public perception of the field is very much based on what any *one* consultant does and says. If you are entering the field, there is a heavy burden on you to do your best: Run an ethical practice, set your limits, and do what you think is right. Remember, you provide the guidance and advice that will frame your students' and parents' perceptions of college planning and the college experience. Your work ethic reflects on the profession as a whole.

CHAPTER 20

The Joys of Consulting

Here we are at the final chapter—the farewell. It's my hope that both novice and established IECs fare well and that this chapter and the book as a whole provide a sense of possibility, direction, and joy. I've put my heart, mind, and soul into this profession and have been rewarded in countless ways. I hope that you put your all into independent educational consulting, too. In this chapter, I share with you my goals for the profession. As independent educational consulting is a field with a strong future, we should unite and aspire toward the goal of providing students and families with top-notch knowledge, service, and guidance. I also leave you with success strategies, a ten-pronged blueprint to help you get the most out of your decision to work as an IEC. And once again, I emphasize the importance of providing wisdom to our students, and I share some wisdom toward the end of the chapter. Remember that we do not just educate students about colleges; rather, we help young people to grow up and begin understanding the responsibilities that come with making decisions. We work with Buffy and Brutus as they begin the task of determining the qualities that might make them successful professionals, honorable individuals, and engaged citizens. As we teach our students about colleges and the admission process, we also teach responsibility, priority-setting, organization, and patience. Through help with essay writing, we teach our students to be self-reflective and vulnerable; we teach Buffy and Brutus that being real with admission officers is better than being pretentious. We help students see who they are and how others who don't know them well (like admission officers) may view them. While we work to assure a lot of acceptances, we recognize that college planning may mean a rejection or two. Working hard yet being rebuffed is a lesson best learned at a young age.

Finally, it seems appropriate to end the chapter with the joys of being an independent educational consultant. I share ten joys, but please know that I could easily increase that number tenfold.

GOALS FOR THE FUTURE OF THE PROFESSION

In case the preceding chapters have left you with the notion that the profession of independent educational consulting is fully developed, this is my chance to state—perhaps for the last time—that we are in our infancy. We are still at work developing a body of knowledge that will serve our long-term needs. While membership has increased, the professional associations have work to do to assure the public that those who are members are people of integrity, people who know counseling as well as they know consulting, and people who genuinely care about students who are taking off on an important journey. The associations also need to be certain that conference sessions target core philosophies and go beyond current fads and fancies. We've come a long way, but we still need a set of agreed upon values. After all, when IECs talk about educational options, their responses to basic questions tell the story of who we are as professionals and individuals—and, ultimately, affect the success of the entire profession.

I wrote about ten goals for the IEC in the early 2000's. They were disseminated widely, and I used them in giving the closing address at the IECA Summer Training Institute for many years. They are revised for this book, but only slightly. I feel they still reflect the challenges we face in the next few decades. I hope that you take them to heart and recognize their role in making you a better IEC. Independent educational consultants who embrace these goals will do wonders to improve the lot of all of us in the field and those who will follow us.

1. To learn. Being knowledgeable is our lifeblood. The profession of educational consulting is based on facts, yet it is also based on inferences drawn from experience with different colleges, different schools, and with different kids. That experience base is the reason someone comes to see us. As true as that is today, it will increase in importance over the next decade. We need knowledge of the admission process, and we need knowledge of colleges. We owe it to our students to know what we're talking about. We need to be able to converse with students and parents about the feel/atmosphere/environment/culture of different institutions. The enemy of this profession is not competition from one another. The enemy of this profession is incompetence and simple answers. Don't worry if you don't know everything. Worry if you think you do know everything.

2. To network. Consulting can be solitary. Many of us practice by ourselves. Even IECs who work under the same umbrella can be set in different locations. But we need to affiliate. After all, we may make false assumptions about certain colleges, schools, or about the process itself. We need to share our assumptions so that realities are unearthed and so that we can continuously move from assumption to reality. We need to take every opportunity to share perspectives with colleagues. Most significantly, we each need to ask questions of colleagues. It is not "cool" to know everything. It is not "cool" to think that once you've been in this profession for five or ten years, you are somehow less of an expert if you ask for a colleague's opinion about a college or about a tough counseling situation. It's "cool" to be inquiring, and it's "cool" to share ignorance as well as knowledge. That's how we grow.

3. To join. While joining is related to networking, I feel that it is important enough to separate. Every independent educational consultant should belong to IECA, HECA, NACAC, and/or other appropriate associations. Moreover, each consultant should move toward being a Certified Educational Planner. It seems so simple to me: If we want respect as professionals, we need to be part of congregations of professionals who work for the betterment of the field. Associations provide a forum for discussion. They offer the chance to grow and share ideas. They are spokespeople for the profession. Most of all, they offer a chance to interact with like-minded individuals on a quest to fulfill students' dreams.

4. To cooperate. Independent educational consultants are a part of a group that includes, at its core, school-based counselors and school and college admission personnel. It's important that we recognize the inter-relationships that are necessary in those relationships. For example, we should acknowledge and refer to school counselors as colleagues and partners; we should encourage students to connect and work with school counselors; we should take part in local ACAC activities and ask counselors to join us in proposing a mutually agreed upon topic to a regional, state, or national ACAC. Cooperation may not always mean interaction, but it means trusting each other and being positive about the roles we each have in the process. Maligning others does not help the field of independent educational consulting. What helps the field is if we each recognize our roles and do the best job for our students.

Our need to cooperate extends to others as well. We need to cooperate with those who might touch our sphere of involvement—psychologists, career counselors, financial aid specialists, and so on. The field of independent educational consulting is a small one. Our size grows as we share with our peers and become part of the larger educational community. I would also like to see more cooperation between IECA and HECA. A unified front would create a much louder voice in the educational world and would also effect more resources toward public understanding of the role of the IEC. At a minimum, it is my hope that task forces with members of both organizations will join hands on salient industry issues. Such a move will surely have a positive impact on the growth of the profession.

5. To adhere to ethical principles. Being ethical is central to our profession. If we want to fudge a little who will know? If we want to suggest that we can do more than we can do, who will know? If we want to criticize our colleague down the road for no reason, who will know? If we act in an unprofessional way on a college tour or talklist, who will know? Who will know? Each of us. We need to have the internal drive and motivation to do what is right. The ethics of the profession have changed over the past 20 years, and ethics will continue to change. When I first entered the field, it was common for consultants to call admission offices, not necessarily for the purpose of schmoozing for admission, but to talk to an admission representative about things like application status. The consultant transmitted information to the family, suggesting that he or she was connected or even central to the process. Now, consultants are most often silent partners, working to help a student in the development of a list, but not suggesting influence. It isn't important if I know a college admission director, but it is important that I know the college. We each have an obligation to uphold the new standards. On one hand, no one is watching. On another, the educational community is watching. Carefully.

6. To develop a thick skin. The field of educational consulting has made huge strides in the last decade in terms of others' perception of our need and understanding of our purpose. Old images are hard to change, and there is still lack of clarity. Some high school counselors continue to feel that families should not pay for outside help. Even though we have seen a surge of support in recent years, some college admission folks still need help understanding our roles as information providers and good fit experts. No longer are we "advocates" in the admission sense of that word, nor are we in business to "grease the wheel" so that our students have a better chance of gaining admission somewhere. We share our knowledge about colleges so that students have more choices. Our students know what's out there. We do not create more anxiety about the admission process; indeed, we are frequently the calmest adult voice in the process. Finally, some members of the media just love to lump us in a category with test prep providers, paid essay writers, and costly financial aid search companies. That will change. I'm confident of that. But, in the meantime, we need to grow thicker skin. Be willing to share the changes in the profession with those who are skeptical. Speak up for the profession. We won't be liked by all (what profession is?), but we will be stronger by not hiding from our successes. Families by the scores are benefiting from our work. Let the skeptics know.

7. To be financially successful. Look at the history of educational consulting. In the early days, most if not all those who entered the field did so for humanitarian reasons. Bless them. They wanted to help kids. They were husbands (but more often wives of breadwinners) and were doing something they enjoyed. But philanthropy doesn't make a profession. Professionals, by definition, have income-sustaining careers. That doesn't mean someone needs to get rich or that the first priority has to be making money. What it means is making money is one goal of the consultant. It means that we accept the fact that we're doing good work for our kids and that good work is compensated. Any lingering guilt associated with paid consulting should end. How many students do we need to help before we can say, once and for all, that we're okay (thanks, Stuart Smalley) and that our fees are worth it? Tens of thousands are enough. We're worth it.

8. To reach a wide range of students. This may be our most important goal. Good college counseling is essential at all levels. College counseling is not an upper income need; it is an upper, middle, and lower income need. It is a public and a private school need. I believe that each of us has a responsibility to seek students and parents who would not typically come into our offices. For some, that means adding more students from other income levels. Or it could mean seeking students from groups such as homeschool, transgender, community college, first-generation. You get the idea. The truth is that there is a world of need out there. We cannot be complacent.

Over the life of the profession, there have been accusations that IECs only serve the wealthy or that we "give another advantage to already advantaged students." These accusations have historical validity. In the early 80's, most students seen by IECs were living in affluence on the East Coast. Jill M. Smith, in her 2014 dissertation from Brandeis, talks about, "the *admission industrial complex* of commercial enterprises designed to help students strategize about admissions and give them information about colleges." She calls IECs and test preparation coaches part of the "shadow education . . . that exists outside of schools and largely benefit economically advantaged students." I believe time has shown that IECs largely work with middle income families and indeed that some have committed their practices to lower income families, first-generation students, or others who are not advantaged. But images—particularly for a profession as small and as young as ours—are not displaced easily. We have work to do.

To move up to the next level, our practices need to more accurately reflect the population as a whole. As a profession, we must be aware that enormous numbers of students nationwide don't know that they are "college material" and do not seek help. We need to broaden our scopes in terms of socioeconomics, race, religion, sexual orientation, gender, age, and range of academic achievement. Some of us become comfortable in our own cocoon and don't think as much as we should about all the students who may not fit into our existing box but for whom our expertise may be especially meaningful. This not only means seeing some students on a pro bono basis, but it also means expanding our marketing plans and establishing a new baseline for service. It means learning the language of breadth in developing a clientele and considering innovative ways to use technology to deliver services.

I sometimes hear veteran consultants happily proclaiming that they are "full" (that is, they have reached the limit on the number of students they can handle in any one admission cycle). We should all rethink what being "full" means in our practices. Does it mean that we are trying to find those who, for whatever reason, may not have us on their radar screen? It should. Does it mean offering a range of service options in order to be affordable to a range of families? It should. Connecting with nonprofits, making special efforts to expand our social media presence, and networking with those who may know of someone who can use our advice are all strategies to consider. We should also consider giving talks, designing webinars, or posting free materials and links to resources on our websites. Simply put, let's share our knowledge.

9. To enjoy being an educational consultant. Oh, yes, I know that there are lots of great careers, but this one is special. Being in a helping profession is special enough, but the contentment grows exponentially if we add helping students grow and thrive and be all they are capable of being. Then add the fact that, unlike some helpers, students (at least most of them) want to see you. Then throw in the fact that these are kids who are (again, in large part) amazing to work with. They are open to suggestions, they are bright-eyed, and they are ready to learn and eager to laugh. But there is more. Colleges are fascinating places to visit and to learn about. They are often steeped in tradition yet dynamic. And look around at the people who choose education as a career. By and large, they are kind, caring, and have values that are solid and respectable. Finally, the field of consulting is growing; new credibility comes with each passing day. The fun of seeing a young person grow and knowing you've played a part in that growth is remarkable.

10. To recognize our responsibility. With the fun of the profession come the responsibilities. Listed above are some of them: to keep learning, act ethically, cooperate, reach out, suggest that there are many fine match schools for every student, be honest with clients, meet only as many times as necessary to get the job done without creating dependency, and recognize our own need for help.

We also have a responsibility to fill this profession with knowledgeable, ethical people. Established IECs should work to identify great new IECs. Let's reach out by actively soliciting mentees, teaching classes, and being open about what we find to be the best strategies for IEC success. We cannot leave it to chance that the field will grow; we have to make it grow. In addition to adding principled people, I'd like to see many skin colors and backgrounds in our ranks. Our profession should look more like the population as a whole. Diversity in the field will, by definition, increase the reach of the profession.

In addition, our most coveted responsibility is to each student we see. Remember that people are not hiring a service or a process; they're hiring an individual. They are hiring you. They are hiring your wisdom, insight, and sound perspective. Ours is a profession based on trust, and we must be trustworthy. Our word has to mean something. We have an obligation to see the best in our clients. Students (and parents) are learning, and we are teaching. That relationship requires the best we have to offer. It requires that we take our work seriously and give all we are capable of giving. Our students and our profession deserve no less.

Independent educational consulting is a career whose time has come. It has grown up. More and more people are entering the field with exceptional credentials. The goals are clearer, and the standards are more established. We will sustain that growth if each of us works, first and foremost, for our kids. We need to give each of them the time and the expertise they need to make an informed choice. Our kids are number one. But our growth is sustained, in addition, if each of us works, at least a little, for our profession. We each have an obligation to make this field all it is capable of being.

SUCCESS STRATEGIES

1. Be a Value Added

IECs are paid as a value added. If you can't articulate what that value is, families shouldn't hire you. Engage every family in discussion of value added.

When are you NOT a value added? Here are a few examples:
- When Buffy's parents feel there are only one or two colleges where she can be happy and are not open to exploring others.
- When Buffy clearly doesn't perceive that your work together can be successful.
- When Buffy has issues beyond your competency (for example, she needs physical or emotional accommodations in college that are well beyond the scope of your knowledge).
- When Buffy's parents are hiring you exclusively to "get Buffy in."

2. State Your Limits

State your limits and make expectations clear before beginning to work with families. I make it crystal clear that I do not in any way get students into selective colleges. Exaggerate weaknesses. I overstate my inability to find the ideal school and tell families that success is not guaranteed. As you know, I like to under-promise and over-deliver.

Make it clear to parents that you are on their side. You do not set admission standards, and parents should not kill (or maim) the messenger. Explain to parents that you understand their frustration and that one of the most stressful parts of your job is dealing with incredible students who may not be admitted to particular schools. State your feelings directly and openly.

Set limits to your time. Even an emergency room physician is not on call 24/7.

Remember that sometimes issues that come up are best dealt with by a professional in mental health. You might need to say something like, "The issues you raise are important. I have found that parents like you (during this period) often need to talk to a counselor." (I like the term counselor better than therapist or psychiatrist.)

3. Pick Your Battle

Sometimes you will need to move slowly and methodically through a student case. Choose your battles carefully. Act in the best interest of the student even if an overzealous parent wishes to run the show. Let it go if Buffy's mother insists that Buffy applies to 16 colleges; put on your battle gear if only one of the 16 is a backup school.

4. Concentrate on the Student Experience (the 51%)

Forty-nine percent of our work involves processes and routines. But to be successful, you need to be a 51er! Fifty-one percent of our work involves interpersonal dealings with students, parents, and colleagues in the world of education. Success hinges upon positive consumer experience. We must be empathetic, understanding, rational, and able to anticipate needs. A glitzy website or well "liked" Facebook page are not the secrets to success; engaging with students in a meaningful way and helping them discover who they are and what they want both in and from a college experience is a strategy for success.

Another aspect of being a 51er is to keep the fun in college planning. Attitudes are contagious—particularly around families. Our society is producing the most anxious, stressed out, sleep deprived, over-tested, over-judged generation ever. We've got to lower the volume. College planning is important, but so is mental health. Put things in perspective. Has anyone died because of being waitlisted at Washington University? What is this going to mean in 20 years?

5. Step Outside of Yourself

If the IEC constantly brings up his or her history and perspective about his or her right or wrong decisions in regard to college choices, students will quickly bore. Honestly, Brutus likely doesn't care how much I valued the camaraderie of my fraternity brothers because he has already expressed a disdain for Greek life. Buffy will quickly tire of my tales about attending a small liberal arts college as she longs for lecture halls where professors step up to a podium and speak into a microphone.

Where the IEC went to college, his or her liking or disliking of admission procedures at individual colleges, etc. should have no bearing on his or her recommendations. Successful consultants step outside of their worlds; they check their egos at the door.

Of course, there is a time and a place for sharing personal stories. There are times when one's experiences can aid a student in thinking about a problem or an issue. The point here is simply that the focus should be on student needs.

6. Make Self-Evaluation a Constant

Do not become complacent. Reflect on your strengths and weaknesses. Question your approach, your reasoning, and your follow through. Ask yourself: What else can I learn? How better can I handle difficult circumstances?

7. Consciously Add Humor to Your Routine

Hone in on your humor and embrace it. I'm no Jim Gaffigan, but perhaps a bit Rodney Dangerfield. If students start to drift, I hit them with a pop quiz.

When I started consulting, which of the following were true?:
  A. Methuselah was a baby.
  B. I researched colleges by the light of the moon (while my dog howled at it), as electricity had yet to be discovered.
  C. Michelangelo was an apprentice artist.
  D. I visited colleges by the common mode of transportation of the day: horse and buggy.
  E. Students arrived in my office wearing waistcoats and hunting frocks and carrying bayonets, a canteen, and a knapsack with items such as salted beef and a gill of dry beans, as they had spent most of the day fighting in the Revolutionary War.

I occasionally award a bonus point to students who have a wry F to offer.

8. Connect

Connect with colleagues, and join local, state, and national organizations and associations. Share information, experiences, questions, and wisdom. Enjoy a virtual cup of coffee with colleagues across the country and a refill with local colleagues. Attend conferences and come prepared with questions. Network. Do not let the I in IEC stand for isolated.

9. Put The Puzzle Together

Every new client is a new puzzle. The key to the puzzle is not written here or anywhere. There is no standard protocol. It's always a new task to figure out how to use your best judgment in helping a student through the college admission process.

When I saw my 50th student, I questioned what would work best for that student; even now, as I meet with my 3,000th (or whatever the number seen by someone who has been doing this work since before dogs were domesticated), I still question the best approach to serve that student.

Don't think that you can put the puzzle together simply because puzzle-solving is a logical process. Chemistry counts. Who you are is what counts. In other words, you may have an abundance of knowledge, or have a perfect IEC "system" or "curriculum," but unless the student trusts you and you build rapport, the best consulting techniques have a limited chance of being successful.

It is a privileged perch, that of the IEC. One gets to witness a lot. The privileged perch, however, can be difficult. For college planning success, motivation counts more than a student's grades and test scores. The student who makes a commitment to work with the IEC is the student who will have the most—and the best—college options. Always let Buffy know that she has a hand in the puzzle.

10. Have a Plan B

Be nimble, adaptable, and fluid. Lean on your strengths. Be broad-minded. Be able to see the big picture. You may need to broaden (or narrow) your business model and beat the bushes for new clients. Be prepared to brave the business waves. Bounce back. Keep acquiring new knowledge. Remember the importance of ongoing self-evaluation.

WISDOMS

Try to spend at least a few minutes at every meeting with a student to provide adult, mature, inspired wisdom. The wisdom can be deep, but it doesn't have to be. It can be a simple reminder that having many career choices is a blessing, not a conundrum. It can be wisdom relating to how to make the college years successful. It can be something you have learned about time management that you feel a student should try.

We can't get lost in the weeds. We can't be fixated on setting and meeting deadlines. We're not only here to correct a glitch with the Common Application.

Be wise and inspire your students.

I offer the following list of wisdoms—some profound and some simple—that you can share with students (or ponder yourselves).
- There is a forest of tall and mighty colleges beyond the trees.
- Today's choices (succumbing to "senioritis" versus battling the virus) affect tomorrow's outlook.
- Saying "I do" to a college before dating others may lead to being stranded at the altar or filing for divorce.
- "Undeclared" in regard to a major is better designated as "multi-interested." That's no euphemism!
- An essay that is written hastily may be dismissed hastily.
- Few things in life are perfect, other than my lasagna.
- Character is who you are, not who you create for the purpose of wooing admissions officers.
- High school is best not viewed as a once-in-a-lifetime audition for college to which you must devote every waking moment polishing your lines.

- College is not simply a steppingstone to graduate school or a career; it's a path to self-discovery—a four-year growth experience.
- Fit and match trump a big name.
- While college rejections scream headline news, acceptances can easily fill every other column.
- Do not put all of your energy into getting accepted to college only to find yourself too pooped out to succeed once you get there.

JOYS

Our work is based on such exciting things: potential, choice, hopes and dreams, a place for everyone.

But there are so many more joys. Let me end with a few others:

1. The joy of working with teenagers. Each is so unique. Thank you, Buffy. Thank you, Brutus.
2. The joy of being in business for yourself: setting your own hours, being flexible, and determining the boundaries of your practices.
3. The joy of being good at something. It feels good to be an expert in a specific area.
4. The joy of continuing to learn. We are forever students of colleges.
5. The joy of traveling to and learning about colleges. After all, each is unique and culturally interesting.
6. The joy of witnessing change.
7. The joy of working with colleagues through a support network.
8. The joy of solving puzzles. What is the best fit? What is match? What can I say that will give the student confidence and move the student forward?
9. The joy of being a provider of options.
10. The joy of laughing with students, parents, and colleagues. We laugh a lot, and that keeps us centered.

Embrace the joys!

Help me

Help me find a path
where I can succeed,
where I can make good friends,
where I can have fun,
where I can make a good living,
where I can be happy,
where I can find some way
to be recognized for something good,
where people will care about me,
where I will be accepted for who I am,
where people will look more forward
than backward and give me a chance,
where I can have an exciting adventure.
Help me, help me, they say.
Help me to be all I can be.
Help me find some of life's precious moments.

APPENDIX A

Professional Standards and Codes of Conduct

Higher Education Consultants Association
Standards and Ethics

Preface:

A statement of Standards and Ethics is not meant to address, nor can it be expected to address, all questions or concerns that might arise in the conduct of working with students, families, high schools, colleges and universities and other professionals as an education consultant. Rather, a Statement of Standards and Ethics provides a framework guide.

It is expected that members of the Higher Education Consultants Association will uphold the following Statement of Standards and Ethics as they conduct their practice.

HIGHER EDUCATION CONSULTANTS ASSOCIATION STANDARDS AND ETHICS

HECA Mission Statement:

The mission of the Higher Education Consultants Association is to support independent education consultants as they work with students and parents during the transition into higher education by providing professional development, advancing ethical standards of conduct and promoting equity and access to higher education for all students.

Core Values of the Higher Education Consultants Association

The Higher Education Consultants Association's Standards and Ethics Statement for our members is based on four core values:

Sound Advice:

HECA members discuss appropriate educational options with students and families and make referrals to other members/organizations when indicated.

Integrity:

HECA members clearly communicate what services they offer and do not guarantee admissions or financial aid results. HECA members act in the best interest of the student.

Respect:

HECA members respect the student/school relationship. They strive to work as a team with other independent consultants, high school counselors and related professionals. They respect students' work and encourage student ownership of the application process.

Confidentiality:

HECA members respect the confidential nature of their relationships with students, families and related professionals. In light of our stated mission and guided by our core values of sound advice, integrity, respect and confidentiality, the HECA Board of Directors has approved a Statement of Standards of Ethics for HECA members. A statement of Standards and Ethics is not meant to address, nor can it be expected to address, all questions or concerns that might arise in the conduct of working with students, families, high schools, colleges and universities, and other professionals as an education consultant. Rather, a Statement of Standards and Ethics provides a framework, or a guide.

As a professional community, we members of the Higher Education Consultants Association will hold ourselves and each other accountable for upholding the HECA Statement of Standards and Ethics as we conduct our practices. HECA members pledge to act in accordance with the following Principles and Standards:
1. Standards for Working with Students and Families
2. Standards with Respect to Relations with High Schools and Colleges
3. Standard with Respect to Relations with Vendors
4. Standards for the Education Consulting Profession
5. Code of Conduct for Individual Consultants

I. HECA Standards for Working with Students and Families
HECA members:
- Serve the interests of students and families by providing accurate, unbiased information about the college planning and decision-making processes.
- Respect issues of confidentiality and students' rights to privacy throughout the process. Confidential information is shared with others only with the written consent of the student and/or family.
- Respect the values and expectations of students and families while presenting professional advice that is sound, honest, and candid.
- Respect the college planning and decision-making processes as learning opportunities for the student and family. In this spirit, the HECA member counsels and advises in the college research process, provides guidance, direction and review, but does not complete or submit a college application on behalf of a student.
- Provide information to students and families that is:
    - Accurate and timely, and is based on research, college visits, participation in professional organizations and attendance at national and regional educational conferences and meetings.
    - Based on evaluation of the student's academic record, standardized tests, interests, activities, future plans, and family circumstances.
- Counsel and encourage students and parents to approach the college application and admission process ethically and honestly.
- Advise students and families of the importance to take responsibility for understanding the policies, requirements, and timeliness in meeting deadlines for each college to which they apply.

II. HECA Standards with Respect to Relations with High Schools and Colleges
HECA members:
- Respect the procedures and requirements of the student's high school and prospective colleges. Seek to complement the work of high school counselors and to work cooperatively and collaboratively.
- Neither solicit nor accept remuneration, gifts, services, or rewards from any institution, agency or organization for the placement or recruitment of students. To do so is considered outside the realm of ethical behavior. This policy is not intended to apply to gifts of nominal value, nor to fly-ins or campus visits which are considered a beneficial part of the consultant's education.

III. HECA Standards with Respect to Relations with Vendors

HECA members:

- May not receive commissions of any amount. However, HECA encourages vendors to offer discounts and/or scholarships to clients of HECA members.
- Vendor-sponsored counselor meetings are acceptable for professional development of HECA members.

IV. Standards for the Education Consultant Profession

HECA members shall:

- Acknowledge one's own limits in terms of knowledge, experience, and expertise and make referrals, as appropriate.
- Accurately, and with integrity, represent and promote their services in writing, including statements of fees and payments.
- Agree that promise or guarantee of college and/or university placement is beyond the scope of an education consultant and may not be communicated or inferred from written or verbal statements made by a HECA member.
- Avoid conflict of interest or the perception thereof. It is incumbent on the HECA member to acknowledge the source and scope of such conflict. The client is thus given the opportunity to proceed or end the relationship.
- HECA members adhere to and uphold the standards and ethics of the National Association for College Admission Counseling (NACAC) Statement of Principles of Good Practice with particular attention to the Mandatory Practices and Best Practices sections.

V. Code of Conduct for Individual Consultants

HECA members shall:

- Act professionally, responsibly, and ethically in all relationships with students, families, high schools, college admission personnel, and colleagues.
- Recognize the importance of confidentiality in performing their work.
- Act with integrity, respect, courtesy and thoughtfulness in all transactions.

Recognizing there are specific issues that are common to education consultants in the conduct of their practice, the following Statements serve to guide HECA members in interpreting and applying the HECA Statement of Standards and Ethics:

In the conduct of their practice, HECA members shall:*

- Represent and promote their services with accuracy and honesty.
- Not accept any reward, service, or remuneration from any college, university, agency, or organization for placement, referral, or recruitment of students. This does not apply to gifts of nominal value that in no way obligate the recipient.
- Comply with all laws and regulations regarding students' rights to privacy with particular attention to regulations in the Family Educational Rights and Privacy Act, FERPA.
- Respect all student information (including transcript, test scores, financial resources, institutional preferences) as confidential.
- Secure permission from the student and/or family before revealing any information about students or their admission process, including but not limited to decisions and/or scholarship and financial aid awards.
- Not make any written or verbal guarantee of college admission or placement, or guarantees of financial aid or scholarship awards.
- Not make disparaging statements about postsecondary institutions.

- Not make unethical or unprofessional requests of, nor make disparaging statements about, school-based counselors, college admissions representatives, or other independent education consultants.
- Not advocate to colleges or universities on behalf of students, unless expressly invited to do so by the college.
- With written student and/or family permission, a HECA member may confer with high school counselors, college representatives and related professionals on matters related to college admissions and financial aid.
- Counsel students to meet all application requirements and deadlines.
- Counsel students to respect the college planning and application policies and requirements of his/her high school.
- Caution and advise students to use internet resources with maturity and discretion.
- Be encouraged to actively engage in pro bono work and to volunteer in education-related professional and community organizations.

Further, in their work with students HECA members strive to:*
- Approach and conduct the college planning and application process in an ethical, conscientious, and responsible manner.
- Introduce a range of post-secondary opportunities and programs to students and their families while recognizing decisions are made by the student and/or family. Encourage students and families to conduct thorough research of the academic and co-curricular programs, selection process, and other distinguishing features, of colleges and universities.
- Assist students to develop a list of colleges that are a "good-fit" - a list that is balanced, realistic, and reasonable in number.
- Provide information about scholarships and the financial aid application process.
- Encourage students to utilize the resources of their high school, the high school counselors, and advisors.
- Provide advice that is consistent with the policies and procedures set forth by the student's high school regarding enrollment in rigorous or higher level courses.
- Advise students on the types and uses of standardized admission tests and not suggest special educational testing for the sole purpose of securing extended testing time.
- Advise students to be the sole author of their application and essays and counsel against inappropriate assistance from others - however well meaning. HECA members may provide general guidance, direction and review of the application, as needed, to minimize unintentional errors and omissions.
- Assist students in approaching the college admission and decision-making process in an organized manner.
- Advise students to report changes in the academic record or personal conduct once an application is submitted.
- Advise students to notify colleges in a timely manner of their intent to withdraw an application, accept or decline offers of admission and to deposit at only one school.
- Advise students who choose to defer admission that they should follow all conditions as outlined by the deferring college.

* Incorporating the Mandatory and Best Practices of the NACAC Statement of Principles of Good Practice

[Statement approved by the Higher Education Consultants Association (HECA) Board of Directors, June 2016]

Independent Educational Consultants Association
Principles of Good Practice

All IECA members are required to pledge adherence to these Principles when admitted to membership and annually with membership renewal.

INTRODUCTION

These Principles are designed to promote and maintain the highest standards of professional service and personal conduct among all IECA members (hereafter referred to as "members").

While it is understood that ethical issues are not always clear-cut, these Principles are meant to provide guidance and to be adhered to in a manner consistent with good ethical judgment and avoidance of even the appearance of impropriety.

All members are required to pledge adherence to these Principles when admitted to membership and annually with membership renewal.

I. COMPETENCE

A. Members practice within the boundaries of their competence, which derives from relevant education, training, acquired knowledge and professional experience. They are straightforward about what they are—and are not— competent to do. In cases with elements outside their competence, they either consult with or refer clients to appropriate colleagues.

B. Members continually update their knowledge of educational options, both in breadth and in depth, through such activities as site visits, attendance at professional conferences, continuing education and professional reading.

C. Members know and understand the philosophies, values, missions, goals, approaches and methods of the schools, universities, programs and therapeutic institutions (hereafter inclusively referred to as "Schools/Programs") they recommend.

D. Members are familiar with and adhere to state and federal laws relevant to their practices.

E. Members are familiar with and strive to meet the expectations on competencies set forth in the Standards of Excellence for IECA Member Consultants, found on the IECA website at: www.iecaonline.com/members. html#reference

II. MULTIPLE RELATIONSHIPS AND POTENTIAL CONFLICTS OF INTEREST

A. Multiple relationships exist when a member has a relationship with a School/Program that may create or appear to create a conflict of interest. Such relationships include, but are not limited to, owning or serving as a consultant to or board member or employee of a School/Program.

    i. Members are expected to avoid multiple relationships that could reasonably and foreseeably give rise to actual or perceived conflicts of interest, interfere with the ability of the independent educational consultant (IEC) to provide objective service, embarrass the student or family, or compromise the confidence or trust basic to the client- consultant relationship.

B. When such a multiple relationship exists, the member must disclose in writing the existence, extent and nature of that relationship. This disclosure should include a consent form for clients to sign, indicating that they have been informed of this additional role and agree to proceed with the services.

C. When a member provides services to a client in his/her capacity as a member of another licensed profession or professional organization, he/she acts in accordance with the ethical code of that profession or organization and within its guidelines regarding multiple relationships.

D. Members shall avoid not only conflicts of interest but also the appearance of conflicts by being forthcoming with clients, colleagues and Schools/Programs.

III. RELATIONSHIPS WITH STUDENTS AND FAMILIES_

A. Members treat students and their families with respect and decency, with sensitivity to their special strengths, values and needs.

    i. Members are aware of and sensitive to cultural, individual and role differences, and do not discriminate or condone discrimination based on age, race, gender, sexual orientation, language, religion, ethnicity, disability, national origin or socioeconomic status.

    ii. Members shall not write application essays or any portion of an essay for students. Their role is to serve as advisors, to question, coach and encourage students to fully and honestly express the best that is within them.

B. A member's primary obligation is to assess, make recommendations for, and represent each student accurately and fairly based upon a professional evaluation of the circumstances, requirements of the case, and needs of the student.

    i. The member has additional obligations to the student's parents/ guardians, who are also his/her clients and involved in the placement process.

C. During the placement process, with appropriate consent, members may communicate with other professionals, including School/Program admissions officers, other consultants and therapists, in addition to the student's parents/guardians.

    i. Members maintain confidentiality of records, notes and client information and disclose confidential information only with written consent and on a need-to-know basis.

    ii. Members provide substantially consistent information to the student, family members and all other professionals involved in the placement.

D. Members are clear and forthright about the nature and scope of their services.

    i. Members disclose fees and financial arrangements in writing before services begin.

    ii. Members neither guarantee placement nor outcomes.

    iii. Members inform clients of their confidentiality policies.

E. Members retain their principles in all social media (Twitter, Facebook, Listservs, etc.) interactions and do not include identifyable personal client references there or in public presentations.

IV. RELATIONSHIPS WITH COLLEGES/PROGRAMS/SCHOOLS

A. Members neither solicit nor accept compensation from Schools/Programs for placing or attempting to place students with them. They scrupulously avoid behavior that might be construed as soliciting or accepting compensation.

    i. Compensation includes, but is not limited to, any form of payment, in money or in kind, and any sort of favor or special treatment to reward or encourage placements, even from Schools/Programs where finder's fees are commonly considered appropriate. Expressly forbidden are quid pro quo relationships involving referral of clients tied with referrals back to members and relationships that promise the exclusive or more favorable use of a particular School/Program. Gifts received from a school or program totaling less than $75 in a calendar year shall not be considered compensation.

    ii. Expenditures by Schools/Programs to educate IECs regarding particular Schools/Programs are not considered compensation, as long as they are customary, ordinary, and reasonable. Travel, lodging and meals associated with visiting a School/Program or a working lunch when a School/Program representative visits an IEC are customary, ordinary, and reasonable expenditures.

B. Members must avoid words or actions that might give the appearance of applying influence regarding admissions process, decisions or other interactions.

C. Members must abide by the standards set forth in the Code of Conduct for IECA members on College, Program and School Tours.

    i. Members accept invitations only from Colleges/Programs/Schools within the scope of their practice or evolving practice, and only when the visit would customarily be needed to assess them. Members may request invitations but not demand them.

    ii. Visits are a cost of doing business for consultants. Members must not imply, demand or otherwise solicit reimbursement for these expenses.

    iii. When reimbursement is offered without solicitation, members do not request the use of specific airlines, special sights, lodging accommodations or upgrades (beyond what is necessary for a disability); or reimbursement for anyone other than oneself, or for expenses not agreed to in advance.

V. RELATIONSHIPS WITH OTHER INDEPENDENT EDUCATIONAL CONSULTANTS

A. Our organization and members subscribe to and practice ethical, honest, and respectful behavior in all actions with our client families, the public, and other IECs. We are responsible for the integrity of our own actions and the actions of our associates and employees.

B. Members accept payment only for work performed. They do not receive commissions or other payments for enrollment in or referrals to programs or vendors; nor do they accept remuneration for referring clients to other consultants or other related professionals, unless such relationships involve ongoing coordination, responsibility and oversight for delivery of services. This policy should not be interpreted as interfering with formal, ongoing business relationships a consultant may have with partners, associates, or employees in which a portion of fees paid support company overhead or remuneration agreements.

C. Ordinarily members do not pay one another for serving as resources, although a member may make financial arrangements with colleagues on a one-time or ongoing basis to assist with placements involving aspects outside his/her competence or practice preference or, when in the judgment of the member, another member will produce a superior result.

VI. ADVERTISING AND OTHER PUBLIC STATEMENTS

A. Members will not make disparaging public remarks about any school, college, program, or other IEC, either verbally or in their print or electronic communications.

B. In dealings with the public, including paid or unpaid advertising, members represent themselves honestly, avoiding misrepresentation of what they say or refrain from saying. They claim special competencies only if such competencies are demonstrable. Members do not contribute to heightening anxiety surrounding admission.

C. Members are familiar with and strictly adhere to the IECA Logo Usage Guidelines, found on the IECA website at: www.iecaonline.com/bene ts_logo.html

© Independent Educational Consultants Association June 2014

The National Association for College Admission
Statement of Principles of Good Practice

The National Association for College Admission Counseling (NACAC) has several policies in place to "guide the work of the organization and to maintain high standards of integrity and practice among its members to better serve students." The Statement of Principles of Good Practice (SPGP) includes several policy documents. Below is the Introduction, Preamble, and Core Values of the SPGP: NACAC's Code of Ethics and Professional Practices.

INTRODUCTION

This document reflects NACAC's long-standing commitment to principled conduct among professionals who support students in the college transition process from secondary school to postsecondary education and in the transfer process between postsecondary institutions.

All NACAC members agree to abide by the Statement of Principles of Good Practice (SPGP): NACAC's Code of Ethics and Professional Practices. Since membership in NACAC and its state and regional affiliates is institutional, organizational, and individual, members must adhere to the Code of Ethics and Professional Practices and take responsibility for their institution's actions, including the actions of departments and offices that are not under the member's purview, as well as agents, consulting firms, vendors, and others who act on behalf of their institution.

Even with our best efforts, this document cannot anticipate every new admission or recruitment process or strategy that may be enacted. We hope, however, that professionals will always honor the spirit and intent of this document. As the college admission landscape continues to change, adjustments to the language, procedures, or behaviors advanced in this document will be considered.

The SPGP: NACAC's Code of Ethics and Professional Practices is divided into four sections:
- Sections I and II articulate the ethics and practice of our profession.
- Section III is a glossary that focuses on definitions and stipulations that are important for understanding this document. We urge readers to pay particular attention to the definitions for colleges, candidates for admission, counselors, deadlines and time zones, laws and regulations, deposits, secondary schools, student-athletes, and transfer students.
- Section IV outlines NACAC's Education, Monitoring, and Compliance procedures. It shows readers how to file a complaint and how NACAC follows up on complaints. It also specifies the consequences of noncompliance.

PREAMBLE

Postsecondary education has the power to transform an individual's life by providing a path to personal fulfillment, a meaningful career, and the realization of dreams. Its power can lead our society to a future that includes engaged citizens and a more prosperous 21st century.

College admission and counseling professionals help students make thoughtful choices about their futures. Our work is guided by principles of honesty, integrity, transparency, equity, fairness, and respect for students and fellow professionals. These values guide us in our service to students and families, our institutions, society, and each other.

Promoting ethical admission practices has been the cornerstone of the National Association for College Admission Counseling (NACAC) since our founding in 1937. The Statement of Principles of Good Practice, which with publication of this document, is renamed SPGP: NACAC's Code of Ethics and Professional Practices, protects the interests of both students and institutions by upholding a college admission process free from coercion and discrimination. The SPGP: NACAC's Code of Ethics and Professional Practices serves as the basis of our profession and an affirmation of what we stand for.

Our profession strives to ensure that the students we serve and all of our colleagues are valued and supported. We thrive by embracing and engaging our unique identities, experiences, and perspectives, and we are committed to increasing the enrollment and success of historically underrepresented populations. We are dedicated to promoting college access and addressing systemic inequities to ensure that college campuses reflect our society's many cultures, stimulate the exchange of ideas, value differences, and prepare our students to become global citizens and leaders.

The SPGP: NACAC's Code of Ethics and Professional Practices is the conscience of our profession. It guides our actions in the face of current and emerging pressures. It empowers us to build trust and find common ground while we work to ensure that every student's dignity, worth, and potential are realized in the transition to postsecondary education.

Core Values

Education

> We believe in and are committed to educating students, their families, the public, fellow education professionals, and ourselves about the transition to and within postsecondary education.

Fairness and Equity

> We believe our members have a responsibility to treat one another and students in a fundamentally fair and equitable manner. Our institutional and individual members strive to eliminate from the education system bias based on race, ethnicity, creed, sex, gender identity, sexual orientation, socioeconomic status, age, political affiliation, national origin, or disability. We view this as fundamental to our responsibility as educators.

Professionalism

> We believe that ethical behavior is the foundation of the counseling, admission, and enrollment management profession. We are responsible for the integrity of our actions and, insofar as we can affect them, the actions of our member institutions, organizations, and individuals.

Civility

> We believe members should conduct dialogue with respect and openness to differences, listening to various perspectives from a place of support and understanding. Members should strive to disagree without being disrespectful, abusive, or demeaning.

Collaboration

> We believe the effectiveness of our profession—college counseling, admission, and enrollment management—is enhanced when we work together to advocate for students and their best interests.

Trust

> We believe our profession is based upon trust, mutual respect, and honesty with one another and with students.

Social Responsibility

> We believe we have a duty to serve students responsibly by safeguarding their rights and their access to and within postsecondary education.

[Statement approved by the 2017 NACAC Assembly, 2017]

APPENDIX B

Assessment of My Practice

The field of Independent Educational Consulting requires a wide range of aptitudes, perceptions, interests, skills and sensitivities. The purpose of this assessment is to provide a self-evaluation of 59 areas important to success as a consultant.

Please assess your strengths and weaknesses using the following scale and also include any comments below each item. There is also space at the end for overall comments.

1—Major Weakness
2—Weakness
3—Neutral (it is neither a strength or a weakness)
4—Strength
5—Major Strength
6—Not Applicable

Consulting

	1. Building and maintaining rapport with students
Comments:	

	2. Building and maintaining rapport with parents
Comments:	

	3. Being a process-oriented consultant (managing the process)
Comments:	

	4. Being a knowledge-focused consultant (providing information about colleges)
Comments:	

	5. Being involved with professional associations
Comments:	

6. Networking/staying connected to others in the field
Comments:

7. Telephone skills (comprehensive yet efficient)
Comments:

8. One-on-one skills
Comments:

9. Written communication skills
Comments:

10. Managing information (able to remember and keep track of student issues, college choices, etc.; keeping up on my reading and research into colleges and students)
Comments:

11. Managing expectations (able to help families/students be realistic about admission chances, "selling" less competitive choices to families, etc.)
Comments:

12. Keeping up on my visits to campuses
Comments:

13. Keeping up with youth culture/trends in teenage life
Comments:

14. Negotiating (helping students/families resolve issues as they arise, being assertive with parents about fees, etc.)
Comments:

	15. Guiding the student as opposed to "doing the work" for the student
	Comments:

	16. General problem solving (thinking through and exploring issues with students and familiar.
	Comments:

	17. Managing change (ability to adapt to new ideas, new demands from students/families, new admission directions, etc.)
	Comments:

	18. Diagnostic skills, psychological assessment, and therapeutic skills as appropriate to my work
	Comments:

	19. Monitoring professional codes of ethical conduct
	Comments:

	20. Expanding/learning/being creative
	Comments:

	21. Able to self-regulate, make adjustments as needed to my counseling strategies and my learning opportunities
	Comments:

	22. Enjoying my work
	Comments:

	23. Balancing personal and professional time
	Comments:

24. Staying motivated and excited about my work
Comments:

25. Able to say no, to not be used or taken advantage of, and to set limits on time and availability
Comments:

26. Able to take criticism without defensiveness—both by clients but also other professionals
Comments:

Business/Professional

27. Balance of energy exerted for output produced
Comments:

28. Size of practice (the number of students I see, am I twiddling my thumbs?, am I overloaded?)
Comments:

29. Success as a professional through technology (e-mail, traditional media, social media, etc.)
Comments:

30. Depth/variety of practice
Comments:

31. Scheduling skills (determining hours, being aware of appointment duration)
Comments:

32. Organizational skills and office management (keeping track of workflow, setting priorities, etc.)
Comments:

	33. Annual income/money management
Comments:	

	34. Accounting/finance savvy
Comments:	

	35. Maintaining records for professional memberships, certification or licensure
Comments:	

	36. Planning/setting priorities and goals/adhering to a business plan
Comments:	

	37. Being aware of my strengths and weaknesses as a professional and making ongoing adjustments
Comments:	

	38. Keeping up with legal issues affecting my practice
Comments:	

	39. Marketing skills (ability to get the word out/articulation of the benefits of the services I provide)
Comments:	

	40. Clear understanding and communication to families of the limits of my practice
Comments:	

	41. Office problem solving (thinking through new strategies to be more effective in running my office and overcoming issues as they arise)
Comments:	

	42. Ability to work long hours, if necessary, as well as handling several things at once
Comments:	

Personal Resources/Lifestyle:

	43. Motivation to complete projects/tasks
Comments:	

	44. Promoting my business successfully
Comments:	

	45. Efficiently managing my time (I devote time appropriately to needs)
Comments:	

	46. Easily adapting to the constant changes of clients, admission, or the industry
Comments:	

	47. Ability to relieve or control stress in a healthy manner
Comments:	

	48. Creating a "safety net" in the event my business fails
Comments:	

	49. Network of family members/friends who appreciate my work and support me in my goals
Comments:	

	50. Current level of comfort with my knowledge and training
Comments:	

51. Having a plan for additional knowledge and training
Comments:

52. Innovation to improve my process or practice as a whole
Comments:

53. Risk taking or management of uncertainty and discomfort
Comments:

54. Personal discipline and willpower to see my goals through
Comments:

55. Found balance between income and happiness
Comments:

56. Willingness to change when things are not going my way
Comments:

57. Insightful in terms of understanding the needs of my clients and able to satisfy those needs effectively.
Comments:

58. Failure is something that I can, and do, use to improve myself and my practice
Comments:

59. I can attract new clients or "seal the deal" with those who inquire about my practice
Comments:

OVERALL COMMENTS

Questions to ponder: What strengths do you have? Can you employ them more? What about weaknesses? How can you overcome them? What obstacles to your success have you encountered? How do you measure your successes? What will you change to improve your practice? What can you start today? This month? This year? How can I be happier and more successful as an IEC?

_____

_____

_____

_____

_____

_____

_____

_____

_____

_____

_____

_____

_____

_____

_____

_____

_____

_____

_____

_____

_____

_____

_____

College Match Self-Survey

Self-Survey for the College-Bound

Respond carefully to these questions about your educational attitudes, goals, and perspectives. Be truthful and genuine as you answer each question. Keep in mind, there are no "correct" responses. For each item, check the appropriate answer category—"strongly agree," "agree," "somewhat disagree," or "disagree." Even if you are unsure of an answer or your response falls between two categories, answer every question but check only one answer per question.

Item	Strongly Agree	Agree	Somewhat Disagree	Disagree
1. There are several social issues or causes that I care about deeply.				
2. I often participate in class discussions.				
3. I enjoy reading.				
4. I feel I know myself pretty well.				
5. I'm excited for my college years to begin.				
6. There are at least three things I can do better than others around me and at least three things others can do better.				
7. If I don't understand something in class, I typically feel comfortable asking my teacher a question.				
8. School is fun.				
9. I normally am enthused about the classes I am taking.				
10. I can identify at least one school subject or topic about which I am truly passionate.				
11. I believe one of the most important reasons to go to college is to get a job.				
12. I want to organize myself so I have time for both homework and for out-of-class activities.				
13. I love learning for the sake of learning.				
14. If I want to do something on a Saturday afternoon, I usually don't need my friends to do it with me.				
15. I am satisfied with my listening skills in my classes.				
16. I can truly say I enjoy school.				
17. I will enjoy college a lot more if I can see how my classes apply to real life.				
18. I am interested in and feel comfortable talking about current events.				

Item	Strongly Agree	Agree	Somewhat Disagree	Disagree
19. Going to college means growing, learning, changing. In other words, it is not just *the thing to do*.				
20. I enjoy learning things on my own (and not just for a class).				
21. I enjoy hearing and discussing other students' ideas in class.				
22. I see college more as a time for preparing for a career than for discovering my academic interests.				
23. A college with a blend of studying and socializing is important to me (even if I'd need to sacrifice my grades a little bit to enjoy college).				
24. Even if my friends weren't there, I would still like school.				
25. My friends and I enjoy discussing concepts and new ideas.				
26. My parents don't have to remind me to study or do my homework.				
27. My English teachers commend me on the quality of my papers and written assignments.				
28. Making others happy is one of my primary goals.				
29. Most of the time, I feel others understand me.				
30. On most homework assignments, I do everything that needs to be done.				
31. I am comfortable making some decisions without my parents' input.				
32. I want to commit at least part of my life to bettering society.				
33. Unless I have decided on a career, it will be hard to choose a college.				
34. On most days, I look forward to going to school.				
35. Assuming there was a campus speaker on an interesting topic I knew little about, I'd likely attend.				
36. I am the sort of person who is comfortable going outside of my comfort zone.				
37. There is more to college than going to class and doing homework.				
38. I'm usually good at prioritizing my time to get my studying done.				
39. I usually find class discussions stimulating and interesting.				
40. Learning about many different academic subjects—history, English, math, and so on—is interesting to me.				
41. I usually initiate my own social activities.				
42. I tend to lose interest if class material isn't relevant to the real world.				
43. By late summer, I'm eager to go back to school.				
44. The college philosophy "work hard/play hard" appeals to me.				

Item	Strongly Agree	Agree	Somewhat Disagree	Disagree
45. I see many benefits in going to college.				
46. I seek out ways to demonstrate my concern for political, national, and/or international issues.				
47. I seldom get "tongue-tied" when trying to express myself.				
48. Taking lots of different subjects in college (English, math, history, etc.) is not as appealing to me as focusing on those subjects I like.				
49. I usually go beyond class requirements, not because I have to, but because I am interested in the class.				
50. I like colleges that emphasize pre-professional programs (pre-med, pre-law, pre-business, etc.).				
51. I want to go to college as much as my parents want me to go.				
52. It is easy for me to identify my favorite class in school.				
53. When I know the answer to a question in class, I usually raise my hand.				
54. I do not feel pushed into going to college.				
55. I am not afraid to take a position with which others will disagree.				
56. One of my top goals is to develop a philosophy of life.				
57. One of the prime reasons to go to college is to meet people who will be influential in helping me get a job later in life.				
58. I like a challenge, but I don't want to be academically overwhelmed in college.				
59. I can explain why I want to go to college.				
60. I like teachers who encourage me to think about how academic subjects interrelate.				
61. I am ready to begin thinking about my future and planning for college.				
62. In college, it will be important that I have time to spend with my friends.				
63. Learning by discussion is more fun than learning by listening to a teacher lecture.				
64. I keep up with news, politics, and international affairs via the newspaper, internet, radio, or podcasts.				
65. It is not that important for me to look and act like my friends.				
66. When I walk into class, I feel prepared and ready to share what I know.				
67. Thinking about one of my weaknesses doesn't make me feel uncomfortable.				
68. The thought of going to college doesn't scare me.				
69. I'm pretty good at making decisions.				

Item	Strongly Agree	Agree	Somewhat Disagree	Disagree
70. Writing essays and papers is relatively easy for me.				
71. Building good relationships with teachers is important to me.				
72. I am willing to study hard in college, but I also want time to be involved in activities.				
73. As far as intelligence, I want the other kids at my college to be similar to me.				
74. I can easily identify the special qualities my friends like about me.				
75. If asked, I could easily list two or three words that describe me.				
76. My note-taking skills are good.				
77. I believe I know how to motivate myself to be successful in school.				
78. I am comfortable with my reading speed and comprehension.				
79. I seldom get homesick when I'm away from home for a few days.				
80. I enjoy volunteering my time to help people in need.				

Self-Survey Scoring

Scoring your answers is easy if you follow these steps:

1. Go back to the first page of your Self-Survey.
   Above the words "Strongly Agree" write a 9.
   Above the words "Agree" write a 6.
   Above the words "Somewhat Disagree" write a 3.
   Above the words "Disagree" write a 0.

2. Each of the questions you answered corresponds to one of eight overall categories relating to you as a person or as a potential college student. In the categories listed below, the numbers refer to each numbered survey statement.

   For each statement, you will refer back to the survey to see which column you checked.

   Depending on your response—"Strongly Agree," "Agree," "Somewhat Disagree," or "Disagree"—you enter one number—9, 6, 3, or 0, respectively. For example, starting with the category "School Enthusiasm," let's say you disagree with the statement "School is fun." That is statement number 8. You would enter a "0" on the first line next to the number "8."

   Go through and fill in all of the blanks for each of the eight categories.

3. Total your score in each category.

School Enthusiasm	Participant Learner	Affection for Knowledge	Basic Academic Skills
8 _____	2 _____	10 _____	3 _____
9 _____	7 _____	13 _____	15 _____
16 _____	21 _____	20 _____	27 _____
24 _____	39 _____	25 _____	38 _____
30 _____	53 _____	35 _____	47 _____
34 _____	63 _____	40 _____	70 _____
43 _____	66 _____	49 _____	76 _____
52 _____	71 _____	60 _____	78 _____
Total _____	Total _____	Total _____	Total _____

Independence	Career Orientation	Social Consciousness	Self-Understanding
14 _____	11 _____	1 _____	4 _____
26 _____	17 _____	18 _____	6 _____
31 _____	22 _____	28 _____	29 _____
36 _____	33 _____	32 _____	67 _____
41 _____	42 _____	46 _____	69 _____
55 _____	48 _____	56 _____	74 _____
65 _____	50 _____	64 _____	75 _____
79 _____	57 _____	80 _____	77 _____
Total _____	Total _____	Total _____	Total _____

Academic/Social Balance	Eagerness for College
12 _____	5 _____
23 _____	19 _____
37 _____	45 _____
44 _____	51 _____
58 _____	54 _____
62 _____	59 _____
72 _____	61 _____
73 _____	68 _____
Total _____	Total _____

What Do the Categories Mean?

School Enthusiasm

If you scored in the mid 30's or higher, you probably feel comfortable with the tasks and central qualities of school. In general, you like attending classes and have positive feelings about the academic nature of school.

If your score is lower here, there are several possible interpretations. You may enjoy some of the social features of school more than the actual classes, teachers, and classroom information. You many not have found school to be a successful academic experience, and your struggle with school may affect your attitude toward it. Your school attitude may impact your feelings about planning for college, your willingness to enter a challenging college environment, the level of competitiveness you prefer, as well as your motivation to stay in school. Do you have the motivation to be successful in college? You may not have enjoyed high school because particular characteristics of your school may not have been right for you. If that is the case, you have a chance to choose the college that provides the kind of environment that suits you. Your analysis of the factors that matter to you in a college (*Chapter 3*) will be particularly important in finding a college you can be excited about attending. You also may want consider these questions: Is the time right to enter college? Would you benefit from a year of travel, work, or some other activity before entering college?

Participant Learner

If your score in this category is in the mid 30's or higher, you likely want to take an active, rather than passive, approach to learning. You are not comfortable merely taking notes and regurgitating the teacher's lectures—you want to get involved! You normally do the homework your teachers assign, not because you have to, but because it helps you learn. Likely, you participate in class discussion, enjoy it, and learn from your peers. You read the textbooks and may read additional material on a topic that interests you. Because learning and understanding are so important to you, you are assertive in asking questions of teachers and fellow students. You likely will be most comfortable at colleges where professors are readily available and lecture classes are not huge. In addition, you will want opportunities for discussions and seminars as part of your college experience. High scorers should consider smaller colleges.

If you scored in the lower 30's and below, you have several factors to consider. You may be interested in and committed to learning but prefer to learn quietly and deliberately rather than participate verbally in class. Course lectures, reading, and out-of-class assignments are normally sufficient for you to learn the material. For you, class size probably will not be as significant a factor. Lower scores here suggest that you may not mind being in a large class, and a bigger university would meet your needs.

Affection for Knowledge

If you scored in the 40's or higher here, the life of the mind is exciting to you. You may read widely on a variety of topics, and you enjoy learning for the sake of learning, not because you may get a good grade. You enjoy talking about ideas and philosophies and trading perspectives with others. Students with high scores here should seek academic challenges and colleges that will stimulate their minds. Keep in mind, however, that "big name" colleges are not the only ones that provide intellectual stimulation and that there are dozens of colleges outside the Ivy League Athletic Conference that are intellectually challenging. For some students, nontraditional colleges that do not stress grades may be worth considering because they can offer freedom to follow your curiosity wherever it takes you, without worrying about a GPA.

Lower scores suggest that you are less comfortable with intellectual ideas and concepts. Perhaps you haven't yet have been exposed to compelling topics, issues, or ideas that excite you. You may not have had experiences that gave you a love of learning. You will want to be cautious about applying to a college that expects you to start your first semester with a serious academic focus. You may want to use college as a place to try classes or subjects with which you are unfamiliar; you might be pleasantly surprised by how fascinating a new subject can be. On the other hand, if you have a few specific areas that interest you, you might prefer a college where the classes are more directly related or applicable to these areas.

Basic Academic Skills

If you scored in the 40's or higher, you are likely to have the skills particularly valuable to success in college—writing, reading, note-taking, and prioritizing. You may find college a bit less demanding than you expected, thanks to the strength of your academic skills. There are several considerations for the student with a lower score in this category. You may want to search out colleges where some extra assistance from teachers is readily available and where you can find resources and opportunities to develop your study skills. When choosing classes, think carefully about the workload involved—reading requirements, term papers, and other assignments—especially during freshman year. However, lower scores in this category also may reflect a student who is overly critical of personal study skills but fully capable of handling the academic demands of typical freshmen courses.

Independence

The questions in this category focused on your willingness to make your own plans, follow your instincts, and act independently of others. Are you ready to make the decisions college students face every day—choosing classes, setting your own schedule, negotiating with roommates, determining your own social "do's and don'ts"? Students who score in the 40's or higher will likely be comfortable with such freedom. Having already shown that you take charge of your life, you are less apt to act irresponsibly while away from home and less in need of others' approval before making important decisions. In addition, given your self-sufficiency, you may not need the "excitement" of a college in a large city because even at an isolated college locale you will be able to generate activities and create a social network.

If your scores were lower, you may still be transitioning from dependence to independence. Rather than be overwhelmed by choices your freshman year, you may want some decisions made for you. Some colleges provide more structure, such as a core curriculum or series of required classes, and offer a range of planned activities and events to attend. You may also need to work on self-discipline and practice assuming responsibility for your decisions and their consequences. A smaller college could provide the perfect environment for gradually building your self-confidence and independence.

Career Orientation

A score of 40 or higher in this category indicates that you view college as a means to an end, a way to achieve other lifetime goals and attain a position of professional or vocational competence. Because you see college as a vehicle for vocational preparation, you may want to explore professionally related majors and seek colleges where you'll able to keep "on track" toward meeting the demands of your chosen career. As you consider colleges, review the general educational requirements that students must fulfill. Too many required humanities courses, for example, may be less appealing to you than the freedom to concentrate on subjects of interest early on.

A lower score in this category is quite common and reflects a student who wants a general, broad-based college education. You are likely very open to the wide variety of learning experiences that college may bring. For you, college may be a time for academic experimentation, a place where you can test a variety of ideas and career paths. You may want to explore traditional liberal art colleges with many options in the humanities, social sciences, and sciences. Whether it's liberal arts or something else, you are on track to discover your likes and dislikes in college.

Social Consciousness

Scores in the high 30's and above suggest you care about the world and may not be satisfied with the status quo. Your concern about the state of the world may influence your life and lead you to seek outlets for your compassion and empathy. Colleges that might appeal to you include those with political action committees, volunteer opportunities, or other activities geared to reaching out beyond the bounds of campus. Some colleges place an explicit value on recognizing one's responsibility to the world.

Lower scores here could have several connotations. You may not be sensitive to or aware of the numerous opportunities for social responsibility. You may be comfortable pursuing your individual goals, or you may have other priorities. A low score doesn't mean you don't have a social conscience! It may merely reflect that, at present, the drive to help others is less strong than other motivators in your life.

Self-Understanding

A score in the high 30's and above suggests that you are in touch with your own good and bad qualities and are accepting of yourself. You are fairly comfortable with who you are and don't let others direct your thoughts and behaviors. This self-awareness will aid you in adjusting to college and in making decisions once you enroll. You will be less prone to modulating your behavior to impress others. You are comfortable with your abilities and personality and such comfort will enable you to make mature decisions in college. If your score was lower here, you may be just beginning to know yourself. Teenagers' perceptions of themselves are usually heavily influenced by peers. Is it possible that you are overly responsive to the wishes and demands others have for you? Your focus on pleasing others may override your personal wants and needs. You might find it easier to acquire self-understanding and confidence at a smaller, more-supportive college than at an enormous university. Look at schools where you'll be a big fish in a small pond. Lower scores are not necessarily bad! Self-understanding is a skill that is a lifetime in the making.

Academic/Social Balance

If you scored in the high 30's and above, both academics and extracurricular experiences are priorities for you. You will want to choose a college where you can have a balanced life, where you can pursue your studies, participate in sports or other activities, and still have some time for yourself. Colleges known for a "work hard/play hard" philosophy may appeal to you, but consider your college choices carefully—being certain you are not getting in "over your head." You will want to choose a college where you are academically similar to the majority of students, where you are as likely as anyone else to understand the material in your classes, where you are able to spend about the same amount of time studying and still have a life outside of the classroom. In researching colleges, look carefully at the characteristics of students who enroll. What were their grade point averages? Test scores? Did they take courses in high school fairly similar to the ones you have chosen?

There are several ways to interpret a lower score in this category. Perhaps you are focused more on academics and want college to be all about learning. Or maybe you value your social life more than your studies and want college to be all about having fun. If academics are your highest or even your only priority, you may be comfortable at a college that is academically intense. If social experiences matter most, you will want to consider colleges where you will have time to get involved in campus activities and time for your friends.

Eagerness for College

Scores in the high 30's or above signal that you anticipate college in a favorable way and are looking forward to the collegiate experience. Adjustment will likely be easy because your enthusiasm will be a great asset in learning to master college life. Although you may have some concerns about college, your attitude is generally positive. Because you played a primary role in deciding to attend college, you likely have specific goals to make the most of your college years.

Lower scores can be interpreted in several ways. Just because you scored low here doesn't mean that you are not "college material" or are dreading the college experience. Eagerness for college tends to ebb and flow during the high school years. But a lower score is worth thinking about. Are you motivated to attend college? You will want to give special consideration to the ways you can make college a satisfying and productive experience. Some fears about college—such as leaving home and being independent—are perfectly normal. If your score was lower in this category, involving yourself in the planning and decision-making processes will help you feel more in control and less like you are being pushed into college. But think carefully about, and seek assistance with, the timing and the nature of your college years.

Interpreting Your Self-Survey Scores

The survey you just completed and the interpretation that follows in the next worksheet are intended to encourage you to think about yourself as a college student. By looking at your scores and seeing what they mean within each category, you should glean insight about yourself—your attitudes, strengths and weaknesses, aspirations, and fears. This information will be essential to your college planning process.

There is no definitive answer to what a specific score in a category means for you. In the preceding sections describing each category, you saw words like "scores in the mid 30's or higher suggest . . ." and "lower scores suggest . . ." This lack of specificity is purposeful because these scores can be evaluated in many ways. It is up to you to read the descriptions and to determine what, if any, meaning a particular score has for you. Your score in one category might give you insight into something important, and your score in another category might be less meaningful.

Finding meaning in high scores is a bit easier than doing so for lower scores, but remember, there is no hard-and-fast interpretation of a lower score. In the category "School Enthusiasm," for example, the first paragraph interprets scores "in the mid 30's or above." The next paragraph is an analysis of the meaning of "lower scores," i.e., a score from 0 to the mid 30's.

Keep in mind that your score—whether higher or lower—is on a continuum. Thus, your interpretation of what your score means in this area will vary if your score was a single digit or in the teens versus the high 20's or low 30's. In other words, the description associated with a low score might be more true of you if your score was a 6 as compared with a 29.

Finally, don't get hung up on the numerical aspects of the interpretation of your scores. The goal here is to provide information that can serve as a springboard in your quest to find colleges that are a good match for you. "High" and "low" numbers are less significant than using the information here to come up with match colleges that correspond with your attributes and beliefs.

APPENDIX D

College Planning Values Assessment

Name: _____

Students have different reasons for going to college. Eleven reasons or values are found to be most important to students as they think about college. Knowing about your values is the important first step in identifying the colleges where you will fit in and be happy.

To complete the assessment, read through the list of 11 values —A through K. RANK each of them from #1 (the most important to you) to #11 (the least important to you) on the basis of your answer to the following question:

What do you want college to do for you?

Each student will rank them differently; hence, there are no "right" answers. Whereas several, or even most, of these values may be significant for you in one way or another, the goal is to decide which three are the most important.

When you are finished ranking them, go back and CIRCLE the THREE most important ones .

_____A. To provide me with a place to learn and study.

_____B. To provide me with opportunities to interact with teachers in and outside of the classroom.

_____C. To provide me with lots of fun experiences.

_____D. To prepare me to make a lot of money.

_____E. To provide me with recognition for accomplishments.

_____F. To get politically involved and/or to use much of my college years to help those who are disadvantaged.

_____G. To prepare me for a career.

_____H. To enable me to be more independent.

_____I. To provide opportunities for me to grow religiously or spiritually.

_____J. To provide me with a variety of new experiences.

_____K. To let me receive a degree from a prestigious school.

What do your college planning values say about you?

If *A* is among the top three priorities on your list, you will want to explore the academic character of the colleges you are considering. Although all colleges are, by definition, intellectual centers, some put more priority on challenging students and pushing them to their limits. Reading about the academic features of the colleges you are considering will be important. Your high ranking of this value says that you will be able to take advantage of intellectual opportunities at college. You may want to select a college where your SAT or

ACT scores are similar to or slightly above the ranges of other admitted students—at those colleges you will be able to shine academically. You may desire to take an active part in classroom discussions and will want a college where the student faculty ratio is low.

If **B** is among your top three priorities, you feel challenged and stimulated by academics and classroom learning. You will want to find a college where your mind will be stretched. You will want to choose a college where you can explore a range of new academic subjects. A liberal arts and sciences college may give you an enriching breadth of academic offerings. You will want to look for a college where academic clubs are popular and where you have a good chance of knowing professors and sharing ideas with them. Access to faculty is important to you and you will want to look at the student faculty ratio in colleges you consider. Also note the ratio of undergraduate students to graduate students. Primarily undergraduate institutions will be the colleges that may best be able to meet your needs, because you will be the focus of teachers' attention. Teachers at such colleges place their priority on teaching and are not distracted by the needs of graduate students or by pressure to balance teaching and student time with research and writing.

If **C** is circled, you derive satisfaction from social opportunities. You will want a college where the academic demands will not diminish your ability to socialize. You likely will want a good balance between the social and academic sides of campus life. You will want to explore the percentage of students who get involved in intramural sports, clubs, or fraternities and sororities. Look at your college choices on the basis of school spirit and sporting events offered. Consider popular campus events—see if they sound exciting to you. Also look at the percentage of students who stay on campus over the weekend. You will also want a college where it is easy to make friends. Both small and larger colleges would be appropriate for you. Although a larger college would expose you to more students and a larger quantity of potential friends, studies show that students at smaller colleges become more involved in activities and build deep friendships more quickly. Look for supportiveness and camaraderie in the student body.

If **D** is circled, you will want to consider earning potential, advancement opportunities, and the future market for the careers you consider. You will want to consider this value in your career planning. Remember, however, that there is no sure road to riches! You not only must pick a career direction carefully, but must choose a college where the potential for academic success—good grades—is high. The name of a particular college is less important than good grades or contributions to campus life when securing a good job or being admitted to graduate school. Even if you find that a particular career has tremendous earning potential, those earnings may come to only those who are most successful in the profession. Look at average salaries, but also consider your interests, values, and personality before making your final career choice. Be sure to take advantage of hands-on learning opportunities. Perhaps, for example, there are internships that meet your needs. Also, finding good, career-focused summer jobs can be helpful.

If **E** is high on your list, you take pleasure in being known for your success in an area of interest. For instance, you might feel good about being recognized or known in school as a good student, a top athlete, or a leader in a club. No doubt this type of recognition contributes to your confidence. You might look for colleges where you will be able to acquire or continue to receive this recognition. Often, recognition is easier to achieve at smaller colleges where you would not be competing against large numbers of students hoping to achieve the same recognition. You will also want to choose colleges where it is easy to get involved and where the activities offered are appealing to you. You may want to consider the benefits of being a "big fish in a small pond."

If *F* is important, that value will no doubt guide your vocational or avocational pursuits. You may find yourself choosing a career in which this value can be fulfilled, or you may seek opportunities on a college campus where you can be of service to others. You will want to choose a college where community service is valued. Consider the activities available and note whether community service -related involvements are among them. Colleges vary a great deal in terms of political awareness. At some colleges, students are attuned to national and international events, often express feelings about current issues and policies, and, in general, show interest in political things. Students at other colleges show no interest in these matters and find other ways to interact with peers.

If *G* is circled, you may know what career you want to pursue or you may be concerned but uncertain about your career decision. If you have tentatively selected a career, you will want to choose a college where you can take courses leading to the attainment of a degree in your chosen field. Explore whether a college you are considering offers the course work you desire. You will want to make a note of the most popular majors and the strongest majors as they are listed. If you don't yet know what career would suit you, remember that, for most careers, a broad, solid liberal arts foundation is considered good preparation. You will want to look at opportunities for internships and take advantage of the career planning and placement office at your chosen college. Finding a career that will be fulfilling is one of the most important choices you will make in your life. Your selection of a college will be your first step toward achieving your career goal.

If *H* is circled, personal autonomy is important to you. College is, in general, a time for independence, and students are often anxious to make their own decisions without parental involvement. If you feel you can handle lots of independence, you will want to look for colleges where there is some freedom in choosing courses and where students are given responsibility for their own lives. Colleges vary in terms of these factors. Note which courses must be fulfilled by all students. Be certain that you will not be stifled by too many rules and regulations. You may also want to look for colleges where the personal development of students receives high priority. A priority on independence also suggests that you will be comfortable being away from home and on your own.

If *I* is one of your top three choices, you will want to look first at the religious life of each of your college options. There are two ways to consider religious life on college campuses. First, the question of how religion affects the day-to-day life of the college. For example, are biblical references made in class? Are religious convocations mandatory? Second, the question of whether there is a religious heritage at the college. Many hundreds of colleges have historical relationships with a religious denomination, but this tie does not effect the rules or the general life of the students. (For example, the college may have a certain number of religion classes required to graduate, but these classes are typically broad-based and not doctrinal.) You may want a college that has a relationship with your particular religious group. Or you may desire a large number of students who belong to the same denomination as you do. As you explore colleges, you will also want to see if the college has a commitment to the values and ideals held by you or your family.

If *J* is appealing, you like newness and will likely be stimulated by new experiences and new activities. You are in for a treat at most colleges. New experiences are the "stuff" of which college is made. You may see college -going as an adventure and will want to pick colleges where you can meet your need for stimulation and excitement. Because you value newness, you should not hesitate to attend college in a different part of the country, or to experience an environment or a climate that is quite different from your high school. You will also want to look for evidence of diversity in the student body.

If *K* is appealing, be cautious. Students who are overly concerned about this value might find college planning traumatic and even painful, because of the admission selectivity of "name brand" colleges. Even though it is perfectly acceptable for students to be attuned to the overall excellence of a college, academic quality and prestige are not the same thing. Some colleges are well-known because of, say, a fine football team or because of academic excellence in a subject like psychology or physics. Although it is appropriate to look for a strong faculty and a highly regarded college, you want a college that will give you the greatest chance of academic success. It is success in college, not just academic reputation or prestige, that will lead to admission into graduate school or a broad selection of jobs.

Now that you've read about your top three values, answer the following question: *In your own words, what do your top three values say about what you are looking for in a college?* You should write down your response to this question and share it (along with the names of your three highest values) with your counselor, consultant, parent, or others that are helping you find a college that's good for you.

APPENDIX E

Self-Knowledge Questionnaire

Name: _____

The following seven items—A through G—will help you in thinking about yourself as a college student and the ease with which you will likely proceed through the college selection process. Read each statement and determine whether it is true or not true of you. After each question, you will see numbers ranging from 1 to 5. Circle 1 if the statement is very true of you. Circle 5 if the statement is not true of you. Use 2, 3, or 4 to reflect varying levels of preference. Be realistic and honest.

A. My academic abilities for college (such as reading, writing, and note taking) are good.

Very true of me	1	2	3	4	5	Not true of me

Academic abilities such as reading speed and comprehension, writing, note taking, calculating, speaking, and listening are important for college students. You will be called upon to use such skills in your college classes. If you are confident about your academic skills, you can approach picking a college with the ease of knowing that you will be able to master the academic rigors of college life. If you circled 3, 4, or 5, you will want to work on these skills in your remaining time in high school. You will want to choose colleges where you can work to strengthen these skills. Some colleges provide a learning skills center in which you are able to get help if you are having difficulty writing a paper or understanding the content of a class. If you are less than confident, you might look to colleges where you will not be intimidated by the skills of the other students.

B. My study skills and time management are good.

Very true of me	1	2	3	4	5	Not true of me

Study skills and time management are two of the most important qualities for an efficient and productive college student. Successful college students are average or above in organizing themselves for studying, scheduling, using study time productively, and differentiating important content of a lecture or a book from supplementary information. In addition, they complete assignments on time and don't get flustered if they have several papers due or a couple of tests on the same day. If you circled 3, 4, or 5, it is important to work on improving these skills during your remaining high school days. You might consider the following:

- Seek help from your parents, a teacher, a counselor, or a learning specialist in becoming more organized.
- Try keeping a calendar. Anticipate each step necessary in preparing for every test and every paper.
- Be responsible for your own appointments.
- Check to see if a study skills course is offered at a local community college or university, or consider reading a book on study skills.

C. I am motivated to succeed in college.

Very true of me	1	2	3	4	5	Not true of me

Motivation is definitely the most important skill you bring to college. Those students who want to succeed do succeed! Studies show that it is motivation, not your SAT scores, that determines academic success in college. Motivation means knowing not only that you want to go to college, but that you also want to be a student. Some students want to go to college for the fun aspects but forget that college is primarily an academic experience. So if you circled 1 or 2, great! You're off to a good start. If you circled 3, 4, or 5, it may be an appropriate time to consider your wants and needs in a college. What sort of college would help motivate you? Would a college with a balance between academics and social life be appealing? Would you be more motivated if you were near a large and interesting city? Would nice weather be a distraction rather than an energizer? Is a trade or technical school best for you? Have you considered taking some time off between high school and college? Considering such questions is important, and the time to do that exploration is now.

D. I am a good decision-maker.

Very true of me	1	2	3	4	5	Not true of me

Decisions, decisions, decisions. The college selection process is full of decisions! What colleges will I initially consider? To which colleges will I apply for admission? What college will I eventually attend? You will be facing these decisions in the upcoming months. If you circled 1 or 2, you are on your way. If you circled 3, 4, or 5, think about an important decision you made recently. Why didn't it go well? If you can analyze your decision-making weakness in that situation, it may help to avoid any potential pitfalls in your college decision-making. The following suggestions will help you improve your ability to make the right college choice:

- Clearly articulate what you're looking for in a college. Write down those features that will make a college right for you.
- Involve lots of people and resources in your search for a college. Your parents, counselors, and friends can help you.
- List and compare pros and cons of alternative colleges. Every college has both.
- Evaluate each college on the basis of the criteria you set for yourself. Remember, you're looking for a college where you will get in and fit in.

E. I'm a good information gatherer; for example, I am usually able to find books, websites, and so on to help me compose a research paper.

Very true of me	1	2	3	4	5	Not true of me

Finding a college requires you to be a good researcher. There is so much information about colleges to sort through and analyze. If you feel you can do good research, you're on your way. If you circled 3, 4, or 5, the following ideas may be helpful:

- Use a college guidebook to find colleges that are consistent with what you want. Remember that your primary concern is where you will fit in. Use your college-going values and your responses in this questionnaire to guide your thinking about colleges that will match you.
- Work closely with your college counselor, and seek impressions from students and others with reliable and up-to-date information about colleges of interest. You will make a better decision with credible and extensive input.
- Look for differences in features that are important to you. Is ease of making friends important to you? What about balance between academics and social life? Do you want teachers to know you?

F. I feel I adapt to new situations easily.

Very true of me	1	2	3	4	5	Not true of me

Everyone goes through changes in life. Some move through transition periods with great ease; others find them more difficult. You may have experienced the changes that come after a change of schools (even from middle school to high school), the illness or death of a relative, or the divorce of your parents. If you circled 1 or 2, you are not likely to be intimidated by a college in another part of the country or a college very different from your high school. If you circled 3, 4, or 5, you may want to carefully look at colleges that are a bit closer to home or colleges where the same values, perceptions, and attitudes as were true in your high school exist. Almost everyone has fear and apprehension about leaving for college. But if that fear is significant, you will want to choose a college where you will feel comfortable. Visits to college campuses may be particularly significant in feeling good about potential choices.

G. It is easy for me to meet people and establish friendships.

Very true of me	1	2	3	4	5	Not true of me

Identifying and nurturing friendships is an important skill for college adjustment. If you circled 3, 4, or 5, you will want to look carefully at colleges where there are few cliques, where there is an atmosphere of sharing, and where students report that it is relatively easy to integrate into the campus environment. Your choice of a college is a quest for a good social fit. Your thorough review of college information and visits to college campuses will be helpful in assuring your ability to fit in and be comfortable.

You should share your responses to this questionnaire with your counselor, consultant, parent, or others who are helping you find a college that is good for you.

ABOUT THE AUTHOR

Dr. Steven R. Antonoff

"I live in Denver, Colorado—the place where I grew up and the place that I love. I live in the same house my parents built in the early 1950's. After having dogs most of my life, I now share my home with two British Shorthair cats, Gus and Wilbur, whom I hope to enroll in Katz Academy as they are in dire need of education. I confess that I am somewhat of a workaholic and am intent on developing new hobbies and interests for my decrepitude. That's particularly difficult because of my long list of deficiencies. For example, I'm a lousy athlete, a hopeless artist and musician, and I have no idea how to play poker. That said, I appreciate a wide range of music, I'm a great fan of Broadway theater (and have a prized collection of theater posters), and I try to bike and hike as often as possible. I particularly like travel, and my trips to visit colleges are often planned so that I have at least a few hours to explore on my own. Finally, I love New York City and try to get there as often as I can."

Steven R. Antonoff

For over 35 years, Steven R. Antonoff has built his knowledge of colleges and universities. As an independent educational consultant, Dr. Antonoff has worked with more than 3,500 students and has visited (and revisited) hundreds of colleges. He has also played a key role in shaping the profession of independent educational consulting, developing certification standards, and creating and teaching a curriculum for the field.

Dr. Antonoff is the author of two popular and long-standing college planning books: *College Match: A Blueprint for Choosing the Best School for You and The College Finder: Choosing the School That's Right for You.* The thirteenth edition of *College Match* was released in 2017, celebrating 25 years in publication. College Finder, now in its fourth edition, was published by Wintergreen Orchard House. Since 1993, *College Finder* has been a go-to source for helping students and college counselors build college lists. *Barron's Profiles of American Colleges* has included Dr. Antonoff's article, "Know Yourself," for almost 20 years.

A popular speaker and webinar presenter, Dr. Antonoff has covered a wide range of topics. Session titles include: "The Best Resources for the Independent Educational Consultant," "Ranking the Academic Quality of Colleges," "Parents and College Planning," "Solving the College Admission Puzzle," "College Shopping: Getting in and Fitting in," "The World Is Flat and Only Ivy League Colleges Are Good: Myth, Reality and Wisdom in College Planning," "College Admission—Separating Fact from Fiction," "Lifelong Learning Opportunities," "The High-Maintenance Parent," "A Career in Independent Educational Consulting," and "College Planning: De-stressing or Distressing?".

Dr. Antonoff is a member of the Higher Education Consultants Association and has been a frequent conference speaker. He consults with the International Baccalaureate Latino Association at a Denver high school. He has also served on the by-laws revision task force for the National Association for College Admission Counseling.

Dr. Antonoff is an instructor and member of the advisory board for the certificate program in independent educational consulting through the University of California, Irvine (UCI). He previously taught educational consulting courses through the University of California, Los Angeles (UCLA) college counseling program. His former students are independent educational consultants and college counselors, practicing both nationally and abroad. Dr. Antonoff also chaired the first five-year evaluation of the UCI certificate program.

Dr. Antonoff is the founding chair of the commission on credentialing of the American Institute for Certified Educational Planners (AICEP). The commission grants the CEP designation to those who demonstrate advanced consulting skills and pass a board-certified assessment.

Instrumental in the founding of the Independent Educational Consulting Association (IECA) Summer Training Institute, Dr. Antonoff has served on the faculty for nearly two decades. He is past chair of the board of trustees of the IECA Foundation, the charitable arm of the professional consulting association. Previous positions in IECA include president, board of directors; nominating committee chair; long-range planning committee; and strategic planning committee. In addition, Dr. Antonoff chaired the search committee to hire the association's chief executive.

Dr. Antonoff was the first recipient of the IECA Professional Achievement Award, created to recognize the member who has contributed the most to developing the profession of independent educational consulting. Presented annually, the award is now known as the Steven R. Antonoff Award for Professional Achievement.

Before becoming an independent educational consultant, Dr. Antonoff spent 11 years in college administration, serving as dean of admissions and financial aid, executive director of admissions and student affairs, and dean of students at the University of Denver. He earned an undergraduate degree in psychology from Colorado State University, as well as a master's degree in education and a PhD in human communication studies from the University of Denver.

By Dr. Steven R. Antonoff

The College Finder: Choosing the School That's Right for You! Wintergreen Orchard House

College Match, A Blueprint for Choosing the Best School for You is available from many major national sales outlets and www.EDUconsultingMedia.com

Write to info@EDUconsultingMedia.com to inquire about bulk discounts and signed copies.

ACKNOWLEDGEMENTS

My IEC colleagues have provided knowledge, inspiration, and camaraderie. I thank them for their role in crystalizing the practice principles described in this book.

Thanks to the Independent Educational Consultants Association for giving me the opportunity to train participants at the Summer Training Institute for over 20 years. Some content here was originally created for the Institute. More broadly, my insights into the needs of professionals have come, in part, as a result of my participation in the governance and the trainings sponsored or coordinated by IECA. Additionally, IECA has given me the chance to present materials at conference sessions over the years. Some of the material in this book originated from these conference sessions. Revisiting and revitalizing such material has been a labor of love.

Over the years, I have benefitted from watching a new association gain traction. HECA involvement has been helpful in my seeing the camaraderie that exists between and among IECs. Watching HECA develop over the years has been professionally rewarding.

Roz Wais earns my thanks as editor of this book. In a series of "dumps" over a 22-month period, Roz received thousands of pages including my speeches, my presentations, my teaching and training materials, and more. Impressively, she put these divergent pieces together, creating content that is cohesive and coherent. Roz captured my voice, highlighted my humor, and weaved broad concepts together with clarity and with heart. Her contributions to the chapter on learning disabilities and the sections on essay writing exemplify her expertise in these areas and her dedication to serving college-bound students.

Erika Gritters of I/O Designs in Denver takes credit for the design elements throughout. She took our simple Word documents and turned them into professional, printed pages. I thank Erika for her continued work on my publications.

As the content of this book is dense, I brought aboard an illustrator to break up pages a little bit. Milan Glosic's images appear throughout the book. Milan, who lives in Kucevo, Serbia, couldn't have been more open to suggestions. His illustrations exemplify his vision and his talent.

My student team here at Antonoff Associates helped me with research, fact-checking, and compiling resources for the book's accompanying website. Thanks to Georgia Grace Armatas, Jimena Cristerna, Robert Schwartz, and Patrick Curtin. I want to express individual thanks to Andrew Schwartz. Andrew provided meaningful help with the business chapter. In addition, his suggestions in the final editing of the manuscript were substantive.

Also helpful were Gus and Wilbur, my British shorthair cats who reminded me of the importance of getting away from my manuscript every once in a while, sitting on the floor, and playing. No doubt due to my influence in finding good fit schools, they both will be enrolling at Katz Academy next year. They may change their minds, but so far they plan to major in napping.

Finally, thanks to Buffy and Brutus. Over many decades, several books, and countless presentations, Buffy has been the name I've given to a generic high school student. Buffy has always been there for me whenever I felt the need for more than "a student." She's been in high school a long time (more than 30 years, to be precise), but, to her credit, she never bores of college planning and always realizes that a "perfect college" does not exist. Brutus, new to the Antonoff team with this book, is also due thanks. He's a good college planning role model in that he spends a lot of time thinking about himself and thinking about colleges. Brutus is eager to find a college where he'll be pushed but not shoved, where he'll discover more about himself, others, and the world; and where he'll be happy. While some have speculated, his relationship to Buffy remains a closely guarded secret.

INDEX